FRIENDS TALKING
IN THE NIGHT

FRIENDS
TALKING
in the
NIGHT

Sixty Years of Writing
for *The New Yorker*
by

Philip Hamburger

ALFRED A. KNOPF

NEW YORK

1999

THIS IS A BORZOI BOOK
PUBLISHED BY ALFRED A. KNOPF, INC.

All of the essays in this book were originally published
in *The New Yorker*.

Knopf, Borzoi Books, and the colophon are
registered trademarks of Random House, Inc.

ISBN 0-679-43883-1
LC 98-75736

Manufactured in the United States of America
First Edition

To the memory of Harold Ross

There is a joy in the pursuit of anything.

—Robert Henri, *The Art Spirit*

Author's Note

All the stories in this book first appeared in *The New Yorker*. They are loosely arranged under *New Yorker* headings: Talk of the Town, Profiles, and so on. Here and there, some have been excerpted. In a sense, this is an autobiography—my writing life over a long, often funny, turbulent, and endlessly fascinating period. I went to work for *The New Yorker* in 1939. I have wandered all over its pages and have also wandered all over the map—from the vibrant sidewalks of New York to the melancholy pampas of Argentina, from a conversation with Dwight Eisenhower in Gettysburg, Pennsylvania, to Hitler's aerie in Berchtesgaden. And always with complete editorial freedom to go where I wished and write as I pleased.

Acknowledgments

I cannot possibly express my gratitude to all the wonderful people I have worked with over the years. For the preparation of this book special thanks to Pamela McCarthy, Jacob Lewis, Erin Overbey, Christopher Shay, Peter Canby, and Tina Brown at *The New Yorker*; to Judith Jones at Knopf; to Peter Matson; to Edith Iglauer Daly; to Bobbie Bristol (without Bobbie Bristol there would be no book); and to Anna Walling Hamburger—the sea and the sky.

Contents

TALK

In many ways, Talk of the Town was the heart and soul of *The New Yorker*. Notes & Comment took up the first page and represented the editorial stand of the magazine. Then followed the Talk stories themselves (people, places, up, down, all around), each one a complete entity written with great care and deep respect for the English language. I have never quite recovered from the experience of joining the staff and having my Talk pieces edited by Harold Ross himself, on Friday evenings in his office, line by line. I think it was Mr. Ross's way of sizing up his new young nonfiction staff people. He made it clear that, above all, he was looking for *content* laced with humor. And there was a certain grandeur to the anonymity of Talk, the sense of being part of a prideful institution. Mr. Ross also established the policy that any Talk story, although unsigned in the magazine, could be reprinted in a book with full credit to the writer.

Bettmann Archive

One of the many local enterprises for which we must thank Herr Hitler is the Bettmann Archive. The Archive is a collection of some fifteen thousand photographs of old manuscripts, works of art, mechanical devices, historical characters, household objects, and whatnot, intended to tell graphically the story of man and his work through the ages. It was started ten years ago by Dr. Otto Ludwig Bettmann, then head of the Rare Book Department of the Berlin State Art Library. He went about the libraries and museums of Europe with a Leica, gathering material on the history of reading. This proved so interesting that he branched out, building up a file of several thousand pictures on many subjects before 1935, when he lost his position and had to leave the country. Casting about for a livelihood in the United States, he decided to exploit his Archive commercially. Now he has a chromium-furnished office on West Forty-fourth Street, and four office assistants—another refugee and three Americans. He is consulted principally by school authorities, publishers, magazine editors, and advertising agencies. The pictures are enlarged to five-by-seven-inch glossy prints, and sell for from five to ten dollars, depending on their rarity and the size of the order.

Dr. Bettmann can dip into his Archive and come up with a pretty complete photographic history of almost anything that might pop into your head—Beautiful Women, Corsets, Headaches, Love, Pain, Plumbing, Rain, Shaving, Sugar, Traffic, Umbrellas, or Vegetables. His file on Trailers goes back to 300 A.D. When Dr. Bettmann and his colleagues run across an old and interesting picture, they try to figure out some angle that would give it commercial value, and are usually successful. Recently, for example, they came across an old print of some medieval schemer who had worked out a system of communication whereby people with megaphones relayed messages from hilltop to hilltop; this they sold to a broadcasting company as a picture of the first network. Lately Dr. Bettmann has been busy working up a history of Fur, which was put away in Jaeckel's cornerstone; it will hardly matter, in the cornerstone, whether the record is comprehensive or accurate, but Dr. Bettmann's Teutonic conscience kept goading him to perfection. The fastest-moving item at the moment is Umbrellas; he thinks Chamberlain is responsible for that.

Dr. Bettmann, a spare fellow of forty or so, is happy as a lark in the United States. He has married an American girl, and they live out in Jackson Heights. He keeps up his academic contacts by lecturing occasionally at Columbia or the Brooklyn Institute. He's endlessly pleased by the ease with which you can consult a book in an American library, or get an interview with an American executive. "In Germany, it's all letters and formality," he told us. Another pleasant novelty is the way our scholars keep up with political and social problems. Dr. Bettmann knows moments of despondency, his colleagues told us, usually when business has slacked off. Then he sits in his office, muttering, "What can we do? What can we do?" Then, likely as not, somebody will call up for a pictorial history of Happiness, and he's a new man.

Mr. Shakespeare

We hadn't been to a séance for some time, so we accepted an invitation to one at Dr. Edward Lester Thorne's United Spiritualist Church the other evening, the more readily because it was announced that William Shakespeare was to attend. Dr. Thorne, who turned out to be a stout, earnest medium, had promised to produce Shakespeare in spirit and knee breeches, hoping thus to collect the money which the Universal Council for Psychic Research offers to the first medium who can produce anything in the ghost line that can't be duplicated by natural means. Joseph Dunninger, the illusionist, is head of this organization and he was present, along with the press and a number of friends of Dr. Thorne, of both sexes. The church is a room on the second floor of a building at 257 Columbus Avenue, over a drugstore, and there all assembled before a black-curtained cabinet. Dr. Thorne began by telling the gathering that Shakespeare had already visited him on four occasions, that he had popped in first without warning and said casually, "I am William Shakespeare." The room was filled with a heavy, sweet perfume. "That's Bacon," said a man from the *Sun*. Along with others, we inspected the inside of the cabinet and found no sign of Shakespeare's spirit, or anything else. Poking around behind it, we came upon a pulpit, which, we gathered, was for use on more solemn occasions, and in it we saw such natural phenomena as a can of Alka-Seltzer, a bugle under a glass bell, and a sign reading, "Doctor Out. Will Return at Six." Everyone sat down facing the cabinet and Dr. Thorne went into it, closed the curtains, took off all his clothes, and threw them out. Dunninger thereupon went in, carrying a black robe, to inspect him. He came out a moment later. "The gentleman is quite nude," he said with dignity.

While Dr. Thorne was going into a trance, a group of his friends in the back of the room struck up some hymns. These included "Abide with Me," "There's a Land Fairer Than Day," and "Where He Leads, I Will Follow." The room was dark except for several dim blue lights, the largest of which flickered over a portrait of Dr. Thorne with a halo. Presently eager little moans were heard from the cabinet, followed by a high, girlish voice. "Hello," it said. "Hello," called back one of Dr. Thorne's friends. "That's his spirit control, Sunbeam," explained a lady next to us. "My momma's here, my poppa's here," squeaked Sunbeam, "and Mr. Shakespeare is right beside me." At this point your correspondent was hit in the face by a rose which sailed out of the cabinet. We put it in our buttonhole. "I will count to three," continued Sunbeam, "and the cameramen will take pictures of ectoplasm." Sunbeam counted to three, and what appeared to be a face towel waved across the opening. The cameramen didn't get organized quickly enough and missed the picture. The ectoplasm obligingly returned and waved again. There was a slight pause, more moaning, and finally a deep bass voice. "Thou hast asked for me and here I am," it said. "I am Mr. William Shakespeare." Shakespeare went on to say that he and Bacon were one and the same person. "I want you to get that clear," he told us, and he seemed to mean it. Suddenly a thin, white face, with a white goatee, appeared at the opening, staying long enough to have its picture taken. Mr. Dunninger seemed unimpressed. "Come out, Shakespeare," said Dunninger. "Come in, Dunninger," said Shakespeare. Along with Dunninger and a Mr. O'Neill of the *Herald Tribune*, we went into the cabinet. No Bard. No Sunbeam. Only Dr. Thorne in a black robe and a cold sweat. "Give me air!" cried Dr. Thorne, coming out of a trance that seemed genuine to us. He staggered from the cabinet and drank a Coca-Cola.

Dunninger said that he had seen a face but that he wasn't a bit mystified. "I can produce an elephant from that cabinet," he announced, "or three girls and Julius Caesar." No one disputed him. Dr. Thorne looked disappointed when Dunninger told him that he wouldn't get the money. One of the women in the back said that Shakespeare had red eyes and looked tired. "Excuse me," said Dr. Thorne suddenly, rushing across the room, "but you are stepping on my drawers."

Refugee Reading

Literate, intelligent refugees from the Nazi-dominated countries gravitate frequently to the Public Library when they come to live here, and most of them talk over their problems with Miss Jennie M. Flexner, an alert and kindly lady who has served as Readers' Adviser there ever since the position was inaugurated, eleven years ago. Miss Flexner and her staff are at the service of any reader who wants a bibliography of special reading drawn up for him. In the case of the refugees, of course, the demand is always for books that will help the new citizen to understand the United States—its language, customs, history, and geography. Foreigners are more geography-conscious than native Americans, for some reason. In outlining courses of reading for refugees, Miss Flexner tries to slip in literary antidotes for what she has discovered are the three great misconceptions about this nation: (1) that gangsters lurk on every hand, making it dangerous to venture out after dark, (2) that political graft is rampant in every department of the government, and (3) that one must never discuss politics where there is any danger of being overheard.

The refugee newspaper is the *Times*, with no close second. They read it patiently, from beginning to end, using a dictionary if necessary. "The Epic of America" and "Only Yesterday" are about tied for the non-fiction honors. Other popular non-fiction titles are "Middletown in Transition," "John Brown's Body," and "The Autobiography of Lincoln Steffens." Willa Cather is the most popular novelist. There is a steady demand, among refugees, for "Alice Adams," "Ruggles of Red Gap," "Laughing Boy," "So Big," "Hugh Wynne," and "The Scarlet

Letter." People just beginning to explore our literature are tactfully steered away from fantasy, social caricature, and proletarian indignation, on the theory that it would needlessly confuse or depress them. There was hell to pay one time when a refugee got hold of Robert Nathan's "One More Spring," which you may remember as a super-delicate fantasy about the Central Park Hooverville. He brought it back and asked for a detective story in German instead. "What's going on in your parks?" he asked Miss Flexner.

Europeans are fascinated by the American Indian, and take out all sorts of books on the subject, both fact and fiction. (James Fenimore Cooper is, or was until *der Führer* purified the libraries, a great favorite in Germany.) Some of the refugees can't get used to the idea of an impartial, unpropagandized library. One German lady, discovering on the shelves a copy of Streicher's *Der Stürmer*, ran out of the room with tears streaming down her cheeks; one of the attendants caught up with her, and convinced her that the Public Library hadn't gone Nazi. It turns out that the American novelists who have been most popular abroad are Lewis, Dos Passos, Dreiser, Hemingway, Upton Sinclair, and Joseph Hergesheimer. Miss Flexner is not convinced that this is all for the best. Whenever it is suggested to a refugee that he might find greater opportunities outside of New York, he is likely to turn pale and murmur, "Must I go to Main Street? Must I live in Gopher Prairie?" The Library people try to explain that "Main Street" is the result of a tantrum which Sinclair Lewis got over years ago, but it's uphill work.

Tunneller

What we want to be when we grow up is a tunneller in Macy's. To explain what a tunneller does, we first have to describe Macy's conveyor system, by which packages are sent from the wrapping rooms on each floor to the loading platform in the basement, where they are put into the delivery trucks. The conveyors are spiral metal chutes, about three feet high and two and a half wide. They go round and round and down; or, in other words, they're like spiral staircases, only they're chutes. That clear? There are twenty-four of them, in groups of three, throughout the store. Many times a day, but especially around Christmas, the basement-bound parcels get jammed in the chutes. Macy's employs six men as tunnellers, to dive into the chutes, slide down to the place where the jam has occurred, and start the packages moving. The senior tunneller, a stocky Irishman named Mike Reynolds, has been at it for twenty years.

Expounding the technique of his peculiar job, Reynolds told us first that the only equipment he carries is a flashlight. He wears overalls and waxes the seat of them. The architects who installed the chutes expected that trouble-shooters would be lowered into them by ropes, but this didn't work out; the winding of the chutes created too much friction. It was Reynolds who developed the proper technique. He climbs in, feet first, braces one shoulder against one side of the tunnel and his feet against the other, and, *zip*, he's out of sight. By pressing harder with his feet, he can slow down, or come to a complete halt. Reynolds used to work in his bare feet, but switched to rubber-soled shoes several years ago, after sliding into a rather messy can of spilled Maltose.

The surface of the chutes is waxed, and most of the pileups result from packages coming to a dead stop on surfaces where the wax has worn thin. During the Christmas rush, the trouble is usually caused by parcels carelessly tossed in by temporary helpers. These weeks, Reynolds makes about two hundred descents a day. He has the job of breaking in new tunnellers, who are invariably terrified. Reynolds gets in first, and the two of them slide down together, Reynolds showing the fledgling how to handle himself, and remarking occasionally, "See? Nothing to be afraid of." Most of the chutes have an opening on every floor, but several drop five flights without a break, and one levels out at a point over the executive offices. There is no interruption of normal activity when Reynolds goes into a chute; the packages continue to slide down along with him. He allows small packages to pass him, and supports big ones with his shoulder until he can clear the way. Then he climbs out at the next exit. Once he was severely conked by a chair rushing down behind him, but he can remember no other disasters. The other day, one of Reynolds' colleagues was tussling with a large, unruly package, trying to get it unstuck, when another piece of merchandise, equally immense, swept down and pinned him against the first package. No word having been heard from this man for an alarming interval, Reynolds went to the rescue, travelling along on a tide of Christmas gifts. "I was up to me ears," he told us. The man was rescued O.K., you'll be glad to learn.

Reynolds' big moment comes at the end of the banquet which some of the employees hold once a year, just after Christmas, in the restaurant on the eighth floor. When it's time to go home, Reynolds bids his friends good night and dives into a chute. It's always an effective exit.

Emergency Messengers

We were one of the handful of journalists who attended the Army's pigeon demonstration at Rockefeller Center last week. We got to Rockefeller Plaza just in time to dart off by subway to Kew Gardens with a private and two pigeons. Six other privates, each bearing one or two pigeons in wicker baskets, headed at about the same moment for other outlying parts of the city, where they planned to release the birds. The rôle of the pigeons was to rush back to Rockefeller Plaza, thus demonstrating that in the wartime event of every other means of communication being destroyed in New York City, the birds could carry on. The pigeons we accompanied were Nos. 1054 and 1064, and their custodian was Private Felix Orbanoza, of the Signal Corps. Pursuant to orders, we all took an F express (Parsons Boulevard) at 11:10 A.M. While we were roaring to Queens, Orbanoza shouted to us that all the pigeons involved hailed from Fort Monmouth, New Jersey, and that, to the number of fourteen, they had been living in a trailer in Rockefeller Plaza for a week, establishing home ties. They had previously taken short excursions through the canyons of midtown, and once had visited Harlem. Except for two of them who were eaten by a pair of hawks that hang out behind Saks on Madison Avenue, they had all made successful preliminary journeys.

Throughout the subway ride, Nos. 1054 and 1064 maintained a calm, indifferent air. Private Orbanoza told us that a pigeon man must become intimately acquainted with his charges and practically live with them. He himself does his reading in his pigeons' loft, allowing them to look over his shoulder. We arrived at Kew Gardens at 11:34 and Private Orbanoza ducked into a drugstore to phone his sergeant back at Radio City. He ducked out again, hurried across the street to a vacant lot, and turned the pigeons loose. They swooped into the air, heading first north, then west, then east, and flew away.

We tore back to Radio City to see if a man could beat a pigeon by subway, arriving there at 12:06 and learning that No. 1064 had got in three minutes earlier and finished his lunch. That made his time twenty-four minutes. There was considerable talk of Mac, an old service bird, who had already returned from Washington Heights, and a blue-checked hen who had made it from Hudson Terminal in fourteen minutes. A brigadier general, a major, and several other commissioned officers sat around a table in the Plaza waiting for the birds to check in. They did so with such regularity that it was decided to add interest to the proceedings by taking Mac to the top of the R.C.A. Building for a nose dive. Mac was liberated, and to cries of "There's Mac!" dived like a Stuka, levelled off over the British Empire Building, and landed beside the brigadier general. Mac thereupon cooed for his lunch, reminding a man from the Rockefeller Center staff that the commissioned officers and reporters had been invited to lunch in the Rainbow Room. No. 1054 hadn't come in when we left, but soon after we sat down it was announced that all the pigeons had returned. Squab was served for lunch, which we assumed was just a coincidence.

Basenjis

We paid no attention whatever to the 3,870 barking dogs at the Morris and Essex Kennel Club Show in Madison, New Jersey, the other Saturday, our sole and limited objective being the four Basenjis, the barkless dogs from the Belgian Congo. We pushed determinedly through howling ranks of schipperkes, schnauzers, papillons, Pekes, and pugs, and finally found the Basenjis in a far corner of one of the tents, quietly watching a fat poodle being sprayed with an atomizer. The Basenjis had satiny brown coats and the build of fox terriers; their faces bore the wrinkled, worried expression of investment counsellors. They were in charge of John Lang, a sallow, barkless keeper who had brought them to New Jersey from the Aurora, Ontario, kennels of their owner, Dr. A. R. B. Richmond, who imported them from England a year ago. They are one generation removed from the Congo. Lang pointed out to us Koodoo and Kwillo (males) and Kiteve and Kikuku (bitches). "In the kennel, Kiteve is called Stella and Kikuku is known as Fatty," Lang told us, and at the sound of their names the bitches uttered a strange, singing chortle. "They're oodling," said Lang. We asked him about the nature of the oodle. "You know—oodle," he explained. "Like Swiss oodlers."

Lang told us that Basenjis are highly prized as hunters in the Belgian Congo and the natives consider two of them fair exchange for a wife any day. A pair of them can pull down a gazelle or jackal. They scent their quarry as far as eighty yards away. While hunting, they wear wooden bells around their necks, so the natives can follow them through the tall elephant grass. They were palace favorites at the courts of ancient

Egypt, as evidenced by rock engravings of Basenjis seated at the feet of Pharaohs (circa 2300–4000 B.C.) which have been preserved, or were preserved, in the Egyptology Department of the British Museum. The breed fell into obscurity for a good many centuries, but in 1895 a pair were shown in London. These died of distemper, and no Basenjis appeared again in England until 1932, when several were imported from the Sudan. By 1937, a Basenji fad was under way in England, and the English Kennel Club officially classified them as a sporting breed. Three generations have now been bred in England, and four months ago, in Ontario, Kiteve and Kikuku gave birth to five and four pups, respectively. The only Basenji resident in the United States at present belongs to Byron H. and Olga H. Rogers of Poundridge, who have him kennelled on the outskirts of Boston. Male Basenjis are firm creatures and rule the house; a bitch, for example, wouldn't dream of eating until the male has finished. Basenjis are affectionate, especially with children, and generally remain quiet, except during the mating season, when they engage in continuous oodling.

Lang had no idea whether their throat structure differed from that of other dogs, so we dropped a line to Dr. Richmond in Canada on this point. He promptly replied that he didn't know, either, why the dogs are barkless but suspected that their vocal cords have atrophied from generations of silent hunting. He said that Basenjis delight in tracking down reed rats, vicious, long-toothed creatures weighing about twelve pounds, and that one essential of a reed-rat hunt is absolute silence. Dr. Richmond also said that he intends to take the matter up with someone at the University of Toronto, hoping to get some light on the subject.

Finance

Last week we felt dizzily like a party to some of Wall Street's deeper complexities when we called in at the offices of Merrill Lynch, E. A. Pierce & Cassatt the afternoon that firm amalgamated with Fenner & Beane to form the largest brokerage-and-investment house in the United States—Merrill Lynch, Pierce, Fenner & Beane (please don't ask us what happened to Cassatt), ninety-three offices in ninety-one cities and membership in twenty-eight security and commodity exchanges. This merger was the culmination of a series of earlier ones, beginning in April, 1940, when Merrill Lynch consolidated with E. A. Pierce & Co. and Cassatt & Co., forming Merrill Lynch, E. A. Pierce & Cassatt, which last May absorbed Fuller, Rodney & Co., Banks, Huntley & Co., and three offices of Sutro Bros. & Co. The idea of people having to make out checks to Merrill Lynch, E. A. Pierce & Cassatt, Fuller, Rodney, Banks, Huntley, and three offices of Sutro Bros. & Co. was apparently too much for all concerned, so several of the names disappeared, like Cassatt. We never did find out what happened to Cassatt.

We finally found Mr. Robert Magowan, one of the new firm's sixty-seven partners, an old Merrill Lynch, etc., man who kindly took us in hand and explained that if a considerable amount of confusion seemed to exist, it was mostly because of the job of legally transferring customers' securities to the new firm. Under Stock Exchange regulations, some partner or other had to sign personally all of the stock certificates around the consolidated place, and there were three hundred thousand certificates. "Damn nonsense," said Magowan. Most of the signing had been done over the weekend preceding our visit, twenty-one partners having been rounded up on verandas and in locker rooms and put to work. A number of them heroically sat and affixed their signatures for twenty-one hours. Some of the men working in the defense industries should have seen them. "Allen Pierce and Alph Beane were down," said Magowan, referring to members of the High Command. He added that Merrill was away from these parts on vacation and that Fenner was in New Orleans. Lynch is dead. The high-voltage penmen knocked off for lunches and to refill their pens occasionally, and some of them listened with one ear to a Dodgers broadcast.

We expressed our regret at not having seen the partners at work and Magowan took us into one of the rooms on the chance that some of them might still be in action. "Any partners here today, Joe?" Magowan asked a clerk. "Yep, two," said the clerk, pointing out a pair of earnest, elderly gentlemen wearing straw hats and doggedly signing away at a book-keeper's desk in a corner. They glanced up briefly at Magowan. "Sorry, but you can't sign these," one of them said. "O.K.," said Magowan. "Fenner & Beane people," he whispered. Naturally, not all of the partners know each other yet, and sooner or later the largest brokerage house in the country is going to do something to prevent their brushing by each other in the halls without nodding: a series of cocktail parties during the winter, or something. Five hundred rubber stamps with the new firm name were on order at the time of our visit and are to be distributed to big customers for convenience in check-writing. As for the telephone operators, they have been instructed for the time being to greet all callers with the full, pulsating name, "Merrill Lynch, Pierce, Fenner & Beane."

Notes on Freedom

For our money, the most impressive moment in the I Am an American Day ceremonies in Central Park a couple of Sundays ago was a brief speech by Learned Hand, senior judge of the United States Circuit Court of Appeals for the Second Circuit (New York, Connecticut, and Vermont). Next day not a newspaper in town quoted his remarks, so we went down to the United States Courthouse on Foley Square to get a copy from the Judge himself. He is a rugged, stocky man of seventy-two, with bushy eyebrows. During our call he evidenced a tendency to prowl around his chambers, which are approximately half the size of the Grand Central waiting room. "Three or four people have called me about the speech," he said. "I'm glad they liked it." He handed us a typescript and we will quote some excerpts, with the wish that we had space for more: "Liberty lies in the hearts of men and women; when it dies there, no constitution, no law, no court can save it; no constitution, no law, no court can even do much to help it. . . . The spirit of liberty is the spirit which is not too sure that it is right; the spirit of liberty is the spirit which seeks to understand the minds of other men and women; the spirit of liberty is the spirit which weighs their interests alongside its own without bias; the spirit of liberty remembers that not even a sparrow falls to earth unheeded; the spirit of liberty is the spirit of Him who, near two thousand years ago, taught mankind that lesson it has never learned but has never quite forgotten: that there may be a kingdom where the least shall be heard and considered side by side with the greatest."

Judge Hand told us that all his decisions and speeches are written in longhand, frequently after hours of intense struggle. "For me, writing *anything* is like having a baby," he said. "I take long walks through the park and think and think before putting down a word. I don't deliver a speech to the trees, like Roscoe Conkling, or anything like that. Never dictate. Can't get the hang of it. But I've written countless thousands of words, and the Definitive Hand," he said, pointing to the bookshelves, which lined the room from floor to ceiling, "is along those walls. Mighty dull stuff."

Judge Hand feels that latter-day oratory has taken a turn for the worse. "Too many people have other people write their speeches," he said. "Why, just the other night I was sitting on the dais with the wax-works at some banquet and a fellow rose and made some intelligent introductory remarks. Then he reached into his pocket, pulled out a paper, and said, 'I paid fifty dollars for this speech, so I better deliver it.' *I* ducked out." Judge Hand said that when he was a boy up in Albany, orators were the most envied personages in town. "There wasn't much theatre or music in those days, so the orator satisfied everybody's yearning for drama," he went on. "The orators talked a good deal of fustian—lots of Webster is fustian, for example—but they were creative and did their own writing and nobody much cared what they said." He had little traffic with Fourth of July speeches when he was young, concentrating instead on firecrackers, but his cousin, Judge Augustus Hand, who is also a colleague on the bench, took a more serious attitude toward Independence Day. He used to go out in the fields with his sisters and together they would read aloud the Declaration of Independence.

The maiden name of the Judge's mother was Learned; hence his first name. Few people can resist calling attention to its relevancy in his case. For instance, when President Conant of Harvard presented him with an honorary degree some years ago, the citation read, "A judge worthy of his name, judicial in his temper, profound in his knowledge, a philosopher whose decisions affect a nation." Judge Hand has been on the Circuit Court of Appeals since 1924; for fifteen years before that he was a judge in the Federal District Court, Southern District of New York. Lawyers don't seem to mind much when cases of theirs are lost by reversals on appeal if the reversal is made by Judge Hand, and jurists rank his decisions with those of Holmes and Brandeis. His remarks in Central Park were a simplification of many earlier speeches and a lifetime of thought. "Democracy can be split upon the rock of partisan advantage," he told us. "Believe me, if majorities in legislatures pass bills merely to press their advantage and say, 'Let the courts decide,' liberty will not be preserved in the courts, it will be lost there." Judge Hand moved to the window and looked down on Foley Square. "I believe Holmes felt that way," he said.

Back

Over the years, we have been on hand many times to watch the boys and girls take off from Grand Central for their summer camps, but not until last week had we seen them return. We have now, as the saying goes, seen everything. On the morning in question, the Terminal was a rich pie of delights. We walked through on our way to work and idly stopped to listen to a fifty-piece, all-female brass band, which had placed itself at the east end of the main concourse and was playing "America the Beautiful" in dance time. A cardboard sign identified the musicians as "ALL GI GIRLS SPAM POST 570 MINNESOTA." "Yah-yah-boom-boom, dah-dah-boom-boom, deee-deee-deee-deee-dah-dah—whaaam," blared the band, and the onlookers applauded. Behind us a group of Legionnaires raced past, shooting cap pistols at two nuns, who leaped into the air and fled through the gate of Track 25. "Behind the ropes! Camp train!" shouted a pale-faced guard, and in a twinkling we found ourself pressed, in the company of several hundred other people, against some ropes facing Track 24. "Camp Robinson Crusoe?" asked a man behind us. "Could be Robinson Crusoe," said the guard. "Could be Wa-Qua-Set, Seneca, Pontiac, Happy Acres, Tanglewood, Pocahontas, Ripogenus, Millinocket, or Mt. John Adams. I'm told 'camp train,' so I say 'Camp train.' *Behind the ropes!*" "There he is!" said a lady beside us. "He has his paddle!" We peered through the open gate, and far down the platform we could make out a group of children being formed into some semblance of a line. "And where does he think he will *keep* the paddle?" asked a man beside the lady. "Herbert," she said, "if you are not willing

(20)

to welcome the boy gracefully, go home." "Now they're coming!" someone cried. The line moved toward the gate. As the first boy came through, a man ducked under the rope, picked him up, and kissed him. "I finished it," said the boy. "Finished what?" asked the man. "Finished stuffing the robin!" said the boy. *"Behind the ropes!"* cried the guard. Nobody paid any attention to him. We were pushed through the ropes from behind. "Hold this," said a boy. We took a white box from his hands. "What's in it?" we asked. "Seven frogs," he said. We handed the box back to him. Three boys walked past, carrying, respectively, a Chemcraft set, a small totem pole, and a silver trophy. "The Samuel F. Edelbaum Annual Award for the Boy Who Did Most for Camp," said the winner proudly. "Where is my son's trunk?" an elderly man asked us. "Fell off at New Haven," we said. "Why were *you* on milk squad?" a lady asked a plump, red-faced boy in knee breeches. "Because of the graham crackers," he said. "Midgets and Papooses to the left, Junior Chiefs, Green Arrows, and Squaw Men keep right!" shouted a man wearing pince-nez, through a green megaphone. "Fire Tenders and Senior Moccasins report behind the information booth!" "Why did my son's trunk fall off at New Haven?" the elderly man asked us. "Because it had a Yale lock," we said. "Yah-yah-boom-boom, dah-dah-boom-boom, deee-deee-deee-deee-dah-dah—whaaam," went the band. "I'm the biggest, toughest, noisiest man in Arkansas, and I can lick any kid in the station!" cried a Legionnaire, shaking a finger in a child's face. A small boy staggered through the gate, bowed low under the weight of a knapsack. "Must you wear that?" asked a man who rushed to greet him. The boy glanced up, smiling painfully. "I gained three pounds," he said. "Fire Tenders and Senior Moccasins have responsibilities!" cried the man with the megaphone. *"Behind the ropes!"* said the guard. "We put the horse in Uncle Brick's cabin and left it there all night," mumbled a passing brave. "I've lost my lizard," said another. "We are trying to locate Papoose Brecher!" shouted the man with the megaphone. We figured we would not know the Papoose if we saw him, so we departed.

Winter Walk

Last week, we took a winter walk, finding ourself, almost before we knew it, down in the old part of Manhattan, near the fish market and the cordage houses and the stores that sell nets and twine. An icy wind was blowing, and icicles hung from the rear ends of trucks, and everybody who walked past us was preceded by a small white puff of steam. At the corner of Fulton and Water Streets, we glanced into the window of a fish store at a tumbled mass of enormous lobsters, who, lying on a bed of ice, looked colder than we were. We said hello to a policeman who was standing beside a horse. The horse was also a member of the Department, and was wearing a handsome blue-and-gold blanket. "Greet loves the cold weather," said the policeman, patting Greet. The dock of the Standard Fruit & Steamship Co. was frigid and forbidding—a long, deserted, wind-swept runway. It must have been warm inside the nearby offices of the Domino Sugar Company, however, for through its windows we could see, bending over their desks in a huge room, a couple of dozen clerks working in their shirtsleeves. A man walked past us eating ice cream from a Dixie cup, and a messenger hurried through the streets, right behind him, carrying a cardboard box and seven containers of coffee. We dropped by the offices of the Grace Line and picked up some literature on winter cruises. The far-off warm places beckoned—Bahía, Santos, Cartagena, Montevideo, Tocopilla, Coquimbo. The literature showed llamas and palm trees and swimming pools. We walked around some more in the cold, and dropped into the Cocoa Exchange. Trading had just ended, and the cocoa traders, hats on, were preparing to step out into the cold themselves. "Most of the cocoa comes from the Gold Coast of West Africa," a friendly man told us, "and from Brazil, and from Nigeria. All hot countries. *Very* hot countries." We stepped outside again, and passed another messenger rushing containers of coffee through the streets. We found ourself in front of Fraunces Tavern, and the tavern looked inviting, so we stepped inside for a spot of brandy, then went upstairs to the second floor, to the room where George Washington took leave of his officers on December 4, 1783. "I cannot come to each of you," he said, "but shall feel obliged if each of you will come and take me by the hand." (A picture of the General, in a corner of the handsome old room, showed him on his knees, praying at Valley Forge in the snow.) When Washington left Fraunces Tavern, he went down Whitehall Street and boarded a barge. We walked down Whitehall Street and took the Staten Island Ferry. Last time we took the ferry, the fare was a nickel. It was still a nickel. As we rode across the harbor in the cold, we stood in the bow of the boat and, glazed ourself, studied the ice on the freighters and the barges. Hundreds of commuters stood in the heated cabin, their newspapers pressed to their noses. Miss Liberty looked cold but beautiful. We passed the floating driftwood incinerator that burns up old pilings and driftwood; its fire was going, and burned like a second beacon in the harbor. Then St. George loomed up, a New England town—New Bedford, perhaps, or Nantucket. The vast commuting crowd pressed forward as we docked, and poured off the boat. On the way back, it began to snow, and we watched Manhattan, its lights on by now, move toward us through a silvery swirl of flakes.

Spring Walk

Spring came at last, and we walked—where else?—along Spring Street. It was balmy and clear, and the sky was a thin, Manhattan blue. Two girls were playing potsy, and the gaming area, on the sidewalk, had been marked out with yellow chalk. A springy color, yellow, and full of reminders of birds who have returned because they like the weather here in the spring. We stopped for a while in the playground at the corner of Mulberry and Spring, and watched a lady stir some chicken-noodle soup in a paper cup. She was stirring the cup of soup for a tiny, pink-cheeked lad in a baby carriage. He watched her stir the soup, and he smiled the smile of a boy who knows that he is about to be fed. The air was filled with brown rubber balls being tossed back and forth by boys in their shirtsleeves. There were bright shouts and bright smiles, and the weather seemed to be affecting everybody. "Nice warm day, isn't it?" a lady said to us. "Yes, Ma'am," we said. "Well," she said, "we have it coming to us, we have it coming to us. We've had a long wait this year." She, too, was tending a baby carriage, but she wasn't stirring chicken-noodle soup. Some old men were sitting on the benches in the playground, watching the kids play ball and watching the ladies with the baby carriages. Some of the men had their heads back and were dozing. We felt hungry, and dropped into a light, clean, beautifully table-clothed restaurant called Lombardi's, across the street from the playground. "How do you like the weather?" a waiter asked us. We said we liked it fine, and ordered a homemade antipasto, and some baked clams, and some *mozzarella* cheese, and some grapes. "The grapes come from

---

Spring Walk

South America," said the waiter. "They are seamless grapes—beautiful and very light green." We figured he meant seedless, and when they arrived, we dipped them in a bowl of cool water and admired their light-green color and springy taste. "It's been a long winter," said the waiter as we paid our check. "Everything's all right now. I'll take an hour off at four, and just walk around."

We left the restaurant and just walked around, and passed a spice store and a wine store, and we could smell cinnamon in the air, and vanilla. We passed the Pied Piper Press, and yarn houses, and a place that sold lemon powder, and in the yard of the Spring Street Presbyterian Church we saw a rosebush, with the buds peeping out tentatively. We passed a vegetable cart, and bought two eggplants. Two for a quarter. We could also have bought apples and bananas and tomatoes, but the eggplants were enough to carry. We passed Thurston & Braidich, importers of tonka beans, gum karaya, gum tragacanth, and gum arabic. We went into a wholesale doll store, and the man said he didn't have many dolls—dolls are a Christmas item—but he did have a beautiful doll blanket and a beautiful doll pillow, of deep-pink organza with embroidered ruffles, and pink roses, and stars of blue. He said that an eighty-nine-year-old lady who lives on Thompson Street, around the corner, had made the pillow and blanket. "The pillow has a cretonne center, and the lady's name is Josephine Giuseppa," said the man. We bought the pillow and blanket (one dollar), and soon found ourself, as we inevitably do, down by the water—along the Hudson, and then aboard a huge liner about to set sail. We went up to the boat deck and joined a group of passengers who were standing in the sun drinking Scotch-and-soda. They invited us to join them—it was that kind of day—and somebody made a toast to spring. We didn't ask where they were going, since it made no difference. The idea was to set sail in the sunlight. "Everybody is happy on a day like this," said a lady to us, clinking glasses. "Winter is over," said a man beside her. *"Bon voyage!"* we said to them. "Keep your eyes on spring." Then we walked home, with our topcoat over one arm.

Lonely Day

Election Day, here in the city, is one of the quietest of all days. We voted early. We were up and out of the house and headed for the polls a few minutes before six. Our street was dark and silent, the air was crisp and brilliant, and the day held promise. We don't have far to go to reach the polls—a few steps south, past the barbershop, the hardware shop, and the tailor shop, and a few steps east, downhill (with the river at the foot of the hill). On our way south, we saw the moon, and a faint light in the rear of Mr. Strandbury's store (he delivers papers); his newsstand was still bare. Turning east, we saw the river far below, and streaks of blue and orange in the morning sky. We vote in a luggage shop barely the size of a steamer trunk—a cramped, cluttered establishment, its floor covered with suitcases, handbags, and piles of old belts, its walls inexplicably plastered, from floor to ceiling, with photographs of stars of stage, screen, and television. At one minute to six, we were outside its doors. Two people were ahead of us—a ruddy-faced man, gray at the temples and wearing a trim brown topcoat, and a shambling, preoccupied man, coatless. "I vote at the crack of dawn because I like to vote at the crack of dawn," volunteered the ruddy-faced man. "Besides, I work in Brooklyn, and I've got a ride ahead of me." The coatless man had something on his mind. "Somebody has to lose," he said, half to himself. We peered through the window of the store. It was ablaze with light. Precinct workers bustled around a long table, clearing away paper cups and cartons of coffee and opening long, narrow registration books. We spied Jackie Gleason on the wall, smiling, and Bing Crosby beside him. Crosby looked serious. "We Can't Please Everybody But We Try," said a sign in the window. "Deposit Required on All Repair Work." A young policeman was hovering over the voting machine. He unlocked something on one side and tested the green curtain, and the door to the luggage shop was opened. It was precisely six o'clock.

Voting was swift and silent. The ruddy-faced man was a man of decision—in and out and off to Brooklyn. The coatless man took a moment longer, but merely a moment. Then he, too, was off, still preoccupied, still pondering. Our turn came next. For us, voting is a moment of controlled breathlessness. We promise ourself each time to be calm, collected, master of the machine and of ourself, and yet when the curtain closes and we are alone, we pull down the levers with passionate haste. In a moment, we were again outside the booth, having voted. A line had formed behind us, bursting the confines of the luggage shop and spreading out to the street. Nobody said anything.

Day had reached the city with the swiftness of our vote. The sun was over the river's edge now, and the orange-and-blue streaks were becoming a deep and satisfying blue. We walked around for quite a while. It seems to us now that we must have walked around most of the day, as preoccupied as the man who had preceded us into the booth. Fruit stores were the first to open, displaying their seasonal riches—the purple grapes, the shiny red apples. The fruit stands seemed to hold promise. Next, the flower stores opened, and we saw row upon row of mellow, rust-colored pompons. The streets were still silent, and the traffic was light. People were coming out of the apartment houses now, silent and determined, aloof and subdued, acting very much alone even when they were walking with others. We looked in on many schoolhouses, with long lines edging toward the green curtains and the levers and the moment of doing what one thinks is right, and it seemed to us that this was also, perhaps, one of the most private of all days, each man an impressive island unto himself and yet each man a part of the whole. We went down to the office and tried working, but it was no go. The silence of the city, the thought of all those lines edging forward, was too much with us, and we started to wander again. A minor errand (made work, really) took us down to Astor Place, and we passed Cooper Union, shut tight, its Great Hall closed. We stopped to read a plaque commemorating the appearance there of Lincoln, not yet nominated, in 1860. He had come East in a new, ill-fitting broadcloth suit to plead, with eloquence and hard facts, the cause of the Union. Lincoln, we thought, would have been comforted by the long lines at the many polling places, and by the solemn faces of the people. One thought leads to another (work was now out of the question), and we strolled uptown, past lines in front of schools, churches, and shops, and into the American Wing of the Metropolitan. Our thoughts stretched ahead into the future, but we wanted to touch the past. We walked through the proud old rooms from Ipswich, and King George County, in Virginia, and Albany, and looked at the bright handmade silver, the Gilbert Stuarts, the mantelpieces, and the gleaming gold mirrors surmounted by eagles. Dusk was settling in when we left the Museum, and our path home took us again past those long, silent lines. When the polls closed, we settled down to await the returns.

The First Hoot

———————

We have our own method of telling when spring is in the air, and we pass it along for whatever encouragement it may give to others. One moment we are at our desk, glancing at the wall hook where our heavy winter overcoat hangs, an itchy wool muffler draped over one of its shoulders. Our umbrella hangs on the next wintry hook; beside it there's our drab, heavy gray felt hat. Beneath the hooks, at the base of a small cabinet, lies our emergency pair of galoshes, hideous objects whose name implies black slush rather than bright snow. There are aspirin bottles inside the cabinet. Our sinuses are engaged in some private and obnoxious festival to which nobody else would care to be invited. Our outlook, in short, is bleak, not to say wintry. And the next moment we suddenly hear the hoot from the North River—the full-throated, defiant, independent hoot of a liner that is setting out to sea. There may be other hoots all winter, but this particular hoot comes right through our window, jiggles our umbrella, topples the aspirin bottles, and breaks up the sinuses' party. We *know*, because we have just heard the hoot, and it is unmistakably the first hoot of spring, and filled—again, again—with promise.

Cat Show

We recently went over to see the cats, in their little cages, at the forty-fifth annual championship show of the Empire Cat Club, held in the 71st Regiment Armory. Some four hundred cats were on exhibit, but they barely made a dent in the huge expanse of the armory, and extensive infantry maneuvers could easily have been held in the area not devoted to cats. This surprised us when we first stepped out upon the armory floor, but after a moment's reflection we realized that cats are tidy, snug creatures, who, like sailors, can curl up almost anywhere and feel at home. We were also startled by the awesome silence. Then, here and there in the vast, fortresslike cavern, we detected faint, scattered miaows. These miaows were almost intrusions, as though a cat had somehow got into the Cat Show. The people (for the most part, elderly women) who were seated on little campstools in front of the little cages were as silent as the cats, and not appreciably busier. Many of them were dozing or staring into space; a few were knitting. Some were knitting cat comforters, cat woollies, or cat earmuffs.

We stopped in front of a cage occupied by a sleeping long-hair and guarded by a lynx-eyed lady, also a long-hair, who was struggling with a can opener and a can of cat food. "Have to stoke Pussy's little furnace," she said softly. "Vities make all the difference. Oh, the misinformation one reads about a cat's diet! I have actually heard experts urge garlic for cats. Garlic! That may be all right for an Italian cat, but out in Jersey, where I come from, garlic is unthinkable. This pussy rejects tuna, don't you, Pussy?" Pussy made no response; she did not hear the query. Pussy was asleep.

"And what do you have in store for Pussy?" we asked.

"Meat," said the lynx-eyed lady. "Rich, protein-filled meat, to stoke Pussy's furnace and make her coat shine."

We walked over to one side of the armory, where a lady in a pink dress was judging about ten short-hairs, all in separate cages. A small group had gathered to watch the judging. The tools of the judge's trade had been spread out on a long table covered with white oilcloth: a batch of blue, red, and yellow ribbons, a washbowl, a towel, a judge's book, a pencil, a bottle of Merthiolate, and a box of Band-Aids. A nearby sign read, "Don't get scratched! Don't get bitten! Don't touch any cat or kitten!" The judge stood between the cages and the table. Then she began moving silently from the front of one cage to the front of another. She crouched. She peered into the cages. She placed her hands alongside her eyes, like blinders, and stared at the cats. The cats looked the other way. She thrust a short metal stick into the cages and gently poked the cats. The cats rolled over. "Just like the doctor with his rubber hammer on your knee," remarked a man standing behind us. The judge reached into one of the cages, brought out a cat, and set it on the table. She ran its tail through her hand three or four times. "A lovely whip," she said. "A very lovely little whip, and a very lovely little cat." She put the cat back in its cage, washed her hands, dried them, and pulled another cat from its cage. "We check the age, but breeding makes the big difference," she said. "Only good breeding will give you tone and texture." She checked the cheekbones of the cat, looked into its mouth, looked under its mouth, and pushed back the skin around its eyes. "Only place in New York, except the Dog Show, where good breeding still matters," said an elderly lady beside us.

We moved away before the judge handed down her decision, and walked past long lines of cages occupied by cats who were not being judged. We passed the digs of Fluffy, Smokey Suzy, Dan Winky Dink, Muffin, Bag-O-Peanuts, and Ed-A-Puss. All the digs had colorful, individually styled curtains. Some cats were asleep in canopied beds. Some cats had pinups on their walls—portraits of cowboy cats, dancing cats, and folk-singing cats strumming guitars. We passed cages with artificial flowers in tiny vases, cats sharing cages with stuffed dogs, cats sharing cages with rubber mice. We passed a cage containing a miniature airline bag, next to a cage with a Coca-Cola bottle, next to a cage with a pagoda, next to a cage with a tube of shaving cream, next to a cage with a cat eating noodles, next to a cage with a cat eating pizza, next to a cage with a cat eating baby talcum, next to a cage with a cat who was trying on a sweater. A small patter of polite applause could be heard from the judging area. A short-hair had just won a ribbon. Miaow.

Mrs. Roosevelt Remembered

We first caught sight of Mrs. Roosevelt on a gray and blustery Sunday afternoon in the winter of 1929. We were very young. We had gone to a small community hall in the East Sixties to hear a brief address by Franklin Roosevelt, then Governor of the State of New York. The Governor did not speak from the platform. He sat behind a desk just below the platform, and Mrs. Roosevelt sat quietly beside him. The Governor spoke, as we recall it, of some social-welfare problems facing the state. He was concise, articulate, and human. But what we remember most about that far-off afternoon—the depression lay ahead, and the Presidency, and the war—was the departure of the Governor and his wife from the hall. The only way out was down a narrow aisle running the narrow length of the hall, past the camp chairs on which the audience had been sitting. The distance from desk to street could not have been more than a hundred feet, but it took the Governor an agonizingly long time to traverse it. His legs were in heavy braces, and he walked with the aid of two canes—first one foot and one cane forward, then the other. The audience, as though hypnotized, did not leave. It stood and watched the Roosevelts depart. Mrs. Roosevelt, walking alongside her husband, adapted her pace to his. The Governor was intent upon the task before him: to reach the street and the sanctuary of his limousine without help. Occasionally, she leaned over to whisper something in his ear, and he smiled and put the other foot forward. The slow procession became extremely impressive. Mrs. Roosevelt seemed to sense that we knew we should not stay but that we could not leave. Moving slowly along, she thanked many of us for coming, and expressed the hope that we had enjoyed the Governor's remarks. She greeted many of us with a wave of her hand. She turned again to say something to her husband, who smiled again, and moved forward. She never took his arm, and yet we knew that he was leaning as heavily upon her as upon his canes. Finally, the Roosevelts reached the street. The audience, still hypnotized, followed them outside. Mrs. Roosevelt and a chauffeur helped the Governor into his car. He put his head back against the cushions with the expression of a man who has accomplished his mission. Mrs. Roosevelt opened a window of the car and waved again. An audience of strangers had become a group of friends. "Goodbye!" she called out. "Goodbye!"

F.F.

While we were in Cambridge, the other day, we found it appropriate to venture into the austere confines of the Harvard Law School to see an exhibit devoted to the memory of Felix Frankfurter. Frankfurter, who was born in Vienna in 1882, was brought to the United States at the age of eleven without a word of English, attended the New York City public schools, haunted the Public Library, graduated from the College of the City of New York, received his law degree from Harvard, was a professor of law there from 1914 until 1939 (with time out for legal services in Washington during the First World War), and sat as an Associate Justice of the Supreme Court of the United States from 1939 (appointed by Franklin Roosevelt) until ill health forced him to retire, in 1962, three years before his death. Large events swirled around Frankfurter, and Frankfurter, a small, barrel-chested man, swirled around events, on and off the bench. Many of the chapters of this agile man's life have been laid out and put in spacious glass cases by Erika S. Chadbourn, the Curator of Manuscripts and Archives of the Harvard Law School Library, in an immensely long reading room in Langdell Hall. Mrs. Chadbourn, who calls her Frankfurter exhibit "A Passionate Intensity," has a passionate intensity of her own; she is a gracious, scholarly woman with a dogged determination to track down every scrap of available information about her chosen subjects.

We first met her several years ago, when she produced a stunning tribute to Judge Learned Hand. The other day in Langdell, we found her enthusiasm as contagious as ever. "Frankfurter was an

ardent Anglophile and I prepared a case called 'The Magic of Britain,' "
she told us, with a sweeping gesture in the direction of several glass cases
nearby. "In there you will see snapshots showing Balliol College, the
Bodleian Library, the Sheldonian Theatre, and a letter from Frankfurter
(everybody here refers to him as F.F.) to Justice O. W. Holmes in which
he says, 'O yes—I do some work, lecture, and have a seminar; but essentially my function seems to be to live.' I went over to the Bodleian myself,
in search of material, and climbed some extremely worn, mysterious
winding stairs to a room at the very top. I have no idea how they ever got
books up there."

We passed case after case of documents, photographs, clippings,
correspondence of F.F. with F.D.R., Brandeis, Niebuhr, Theodore
Roosevelt, Henry L. Stimson, and so on. A case labelled "Sacco and
Vanzetti" caught our attention. It contained the announcement of an
article by Frankfurter in the March, 1927, issue of *The Atlantic Monthly*
titled "The Case of Sacco and Vanzetti," and asked, "Is this the Dreyfus
Case of Massachusetts?" We also saw a letter from Frankfurter donating
his royalties from a book he wrote on the subject, under the same title, to
the Sacco-Vanzetti Defense Committee, and a letter from Benjamin Cardozo to F.F. saying, "Your flaming zeal for truth and justice is exhilarating and contagious." We saw many other letters, and it was as though
F.F.'s life were passing before our eyes. O. W. Holmes to F.F. in 1913:
". . . long to talk to you. I have longed often—feeling that there were
many observations, to wit, one or two, on life that I wished to pour forth
to you." An address by F.F. at the Centennial Celebration Dinner of City
College, in New York City, in 1946: "No one today, I think, would dare
to undo what the citizens of New York set out to achieve in 1846. . . ." A
letter to F.D.R. in May, 1935, when F.D.R. was encountering severe set-
backs in getting his social legislation past the courts: "I am, be assured,
as anxious as you are that you should not try to fool the American people into believing that you can do more than the Supreme Court permits
you to do. . . ." A letter to Professor Zechariah Chafee, Jr., of the Harvard Law School, in June, 1950, saying, "About one thing I could not be
more clear, namely, that reliance on the Court against the timidities and
the evasions of Congress is not the way to further habits of responsibility
in Congress."

Time to talk again with someone living, so we descended to the
ground-floor office of Professor Paul A. Freund, Carl M. Loeb Univer-

sity Professor Emeritus in the Law School and a devoted friend of Felix Frankfurter. We found Professor Freund where we had found him several years ago, almost entirely obscured by a thick jungle of thousands of books, papers, documents, and journals, piled from floor to ceiling, dangling over the edges of tables, and jutting from every available crevice and cubbyhole. When a way had been cleared for unobstructed vision, we noted that he seemed to be in perfect spirits and as patient and wise as ever. We complimented him on the glorious disarray of his quarters. He leaned back in his chair cautiously, to avoid colliding with several volumes of law journals, and smiled. "I like to think that a clean desk represents an empty mind," he said, and that was that. "One must remember that Frankfurter's most extensive influence was on people," he continued. "He won't be so much remembered for the inventiveness of his ideas as for his ability to bring out the best in people—capacities they scarcely dreamed they had. He was both warm and outgoing *and* pugnacious and contentious. Brandeis once said that he was 'the most *useful* lawyer in America.' Frankfurter cared terribly for people. I won't say that his ideas were original—he held to social democracy through law. He was a conservative, in the sense that he was attached to tradition. He carried on a lifelong love affair with Britain. We'd all be talking, for instance, and someone would mention France, and Frankfurter would say, 'Oh, yes, *France*. But France didn't give us habeas corpus.' Cases in which he became deeply involved—Mooney, say, or Sacco and Vanzetti—and which were causes espoused by liberals and radicals, he became deeply involved in because he saw them as miscarriages of justice. His procedural sense was outraged, because those decisions had failed his sacred legal system. His wife once said that when Felix spoke of 'the law' a distinct tone of awe crept into his voice. He felt that words were his business. English was his second language, and to my mind he used it with true artistry—the artistry of a Nabokov or a Conrad. He was a prodigious worker, and very sensitive. How furiously he would leaf through the entire transcript—page after page—of a court record. He was deeply wounded when President Lowell was once reported to have remarked that 'Frankfurter is too shrewd not to be accurate.' Historically, his reputation was at its lowest right after his death, in 1965. On the Supreme Court, he seemed to be a brake rather than an engine—something of a leaden foot. But his reputation is again rising. Doubts have been expressed as to the viability of all that the courts have attempted to undertake. Today, I think, he stands midway between the most active and the most reluctant of judges. At the height of the activist movement, this seemed to many a bad posture, but he yielded to no one in his insistence on human rights. A favorite pejorative of his was 'simple-minded.' He reacted to what he saw as the overreaching of the courts. He devoutly believed that courts must not act as legislatures. This often placed him in the position of spokesman for the status quo. He made certain difficult distinctions between state and national powers; he believed in granting more leeway to the states. There were grave conflicts in his personality. On the one hand, he admonished his judicial brethren to lead the monastic life. On the other hand, *he* was into everything—dining out, writing letters, giving advice. Such activities never concerned men like Holmes and Learned Hand. Holmes didn't read the newspapers, and Hand scrupulously kept his own counsel. Frankfurter was lost without constant news of the world. When he visited an old friend at the seashore in California, he almost frantically paced the beach until someone brought him that day's copy of the New York *Times*. And when he rented the summer place of another dear old friend, the phone company called the owner to say, 'We just thought you ought to know that your tenant is running up an *enormous* phone bill.' Essentially, he was the professor. He loved to teach, and some of the other justices felt they might do without the lectures of the professor. But as a teacher he was a refreshing bird—not in the dry, conventional mode. No such business as A giving property to B, subsequently stolen by C. For Frankfurter, a case always involved real people, and he presented it with all its disorder and its human elements. The three great influences on his life were Stimson, Brandeis, and Holmes. Felix was happy Monday, Wednesday, and Friday, but not every day."

In Bed with a Cold

We have received a letter from a friend home in bed with a cold:

This bed is a real mess—mountains of Kleenex, mountains of news-papers. You might say that on an extremely small scale I am fighting for survival, striving to keep from sneezing my precious life away, but between seizures I glance at the papers—especially at stories about Cos-mos 954, the Soviet nuclear-reactor satellite that blew a gasket and finally came to rest in the icy reaches of the Canadian north, spreading radioactive contamination over miles and miles—and I wonder if it is *worthwhile* to shake this cold. I mean, I'll get over the cold, with aspirin, fluids, bed rest, and the holding of many beautiful thoughts, but I am gripped by the fact that the Soviet Union has at least ten nuclear-powered orbs dancing through our skies and that the United States has nine. The newspapers are rather cozy about the matter, some stories saying that it will take six hundred years for one of the orbs to reenter the earth's atmosphere, and only adding sotto voce that even then the enriched uranium would be extremely radioactive. Another story says there's nothing to worry about for four hundred years. And another joyously speaks of four thousand years of grace. But aren't all these figures—six hundred, four hundred, four thousand—mere blinks in the long history of the human race? If so, I'm wondering who gave *anybody* permission, either orally or in writing, to tamper with the existence of Man, much less set a theoretical cutoff date for worldwide contamina-tion. One of the few things that have sustained me, through happy years and through sad ones, has been the thought that somewhere, sometime, a vigorous, intelligent, progressive, decent, perhaps freckled great-great-great-great-great-great-grandchild would put his or her shoulder to the wheel and roll the heavy stone one inch farther up the hill. Have to stop now. Aspirin time.

Eakins in Boston

We have heard from a friend who recently spent a day at the Museum of Fine Arts in Boston, where the huge Thomas Eakins retrospective— "Thomas Eakins: Artist of Philadelphia"—is being held:

Eakins has always spoken to me in a personal and peculiar way, and when Carol Troyen, curator of the show, invited me to come up on a day when the museum would be closed, I jumped at the chance. "You can have Eakins pretty much to yourself," she said when she met me at the museum. A tall, vivacious young woman, who that day was wearing a bright-red dress, Miss Troyen is articulate and swift-moving. She comes from Philadelphia, and she, too, has a special feeling for Eakins. "In a sense, this is a historic first for Boston," she said. "Boston has never seen more than a few Eakinses at any one time. He is a stranger here, as he was a stranger everywhere, all his life. The title of the show is ironic, for Philadelphia never took Eakins to its heart, which hurt him deeply, and caused him to write to a friend when he was fifty years old, 'My honors are misunderstanding, persecution and neglect, enhanced because unsought.' A funny business, art, for today many consider Eakins the very greatest American painter. You wander now, and I'll see you later," and she was off in a rush of red.

I noticed that I was not entirely alone in the gallery, for a discreet young man, hovering at some distance, was keeping an eye on me. (The museum prefers that when strangers are in the galleries alone, someone stand by, either to be helpful or just in case the stranger should go berserk and begin to nibble at the canvases.) At first glance, a room filled with Eakins seems dark, forbidding, and utterly Victorian. One wonders where the color is, and then slowly, almost imperceptibly, the color appears in odd, lighted places: the red toy wagon and the red-and-white striped socks of a playing child, a white hat and an exquisite crimson bodice trimmed with brown velvet on a woman, the monumental brown pier of a bridge. Eakins used his colors sparingly but with love and affection. He did not splash them around, or let his palette carry him away. All was control, and basic, sturdy melancholy. Suddenly, I found myself alone in a gallery (the anti-nibble man appeared to have taken a momentary break) with Eakins' two heroic-sized medical pictures: "The Gross Clinic" and "The Agnew Clinic."

They are fiercely dramatic pictures. "The Gross Clinic" was originally not scheduled to make its appearance anywhere but at the Philadelphia Museum of Art, but at the last moment Boston persuaded Jefferson Medical College, which owns the painting, to send it along. The clinic pictures are hung in natural light, and produce a staggering effect. Eakins' interest in science, facts, precision, measurement, a reality beyond reality gives us here two vast human sweeps. He also reveals great progress in medical science. In "The Gross Clinic," painted in 1875, all the figures are wearing dark clothes. "The Agnew Clinic" was painted in 1889, and the operating room has been sanitized. In each case, an actual operation is in progress, and there is not a suggestion of sentimentality or evasion. In both paintings, Eakins has concentrated not only on the surgical proceedings but on the memorable faces of the two surgeons—Dr. Samuel David Gross and Dr. David Hayes Agnew. As in so many of his portraits, Eakins is obviously trying to read the thoughts of his major characters. Dr. Gross, frock-coated, toweringly browed, with impressive clumps of gray hair, is staring into the distance. A leg is being operated on, but the eminent surgeon's thoughts are elsewhere. He has turned slightly away from both his patient and his intense young assistants, several of whom are wearing wing collars. Dr. Gross gives the impression that he is satisfied with the procedure and is willing to let his people carry on. His eyes are the eyes of a philosopher. Eakins has him pursuing surgery rather than a specific surgical procedure.

At this point, Miss Troyen reappeared. "I see you are deep in the clinics," she said. " 'The Gross Clinic' is a hard one for people to grasp, anatomically. Our curator of American paintings, Theodore Stebbins, often has to lie down on a bench and bend a leg to show viewers just what part of the body is being operated on. Incidentally, 'The Gross Clinic' has never before been exhibited in natural light. Also, it has been brilliantly cleaned for this exhibit." She was off at a trot.

In "The Agnew Clinic," Dr. Agnew, partly bald, ultra-patrician, dressed in a surgeon's white gown, holds a scalpel in one hand, and the other hand is in an explicative position. Above and beyond him are rows of medical students. Once again, Eakins has somehow removed his protagonist from the center of the action. Dr. Agnew, his eye on some medical future, appears to be thinking thoughts far removed from the immediate mastectomy being performed. He is unforgettable in his stark white surgical gown.

Eakins had a sly way of putting his own portrait into several of his paintings. In "The Gross Clinic," I caught sight of him, dour and unhappy-looking, far off to the right, hidden in shadows. He appears again in "The Agnew Clinic," again to the right and obscurely, but in a frankly melancholy portrait, this time painted by his wife, Susan Macdowell Eakins. I also spotted Eakins doing the breaststroke in the painting "The Swimming Hole." Like so many of us, he never seems to have been able to lose sight of his own uncomfortable self. I moved along to some male and female portraits. Being alone (in a sense) with him, it was quite apparent that he could not compromise one iota when it came to his judgments of other human beings. They interested him intensely and overpoweringly, but he had to respect them before any barrier could be breached. If he disliked the person, he spared no flaws, as in the portrait of A. W. Lee, a Philadelphian, who is painted, without a trace of sympathy, as a cold, frighteningly austere man. When Eakins liked his subjects, or even loved them, his mood changed. Heart and palette became unified, and the results are testaments to the wonderment and mystery of humankind. Eakins had a deep admiration for scientists, and especially for Dr. Henry A. Rowland, professor of physics at the Johns Hopkins University, and inventor of the concave diffraction grating, a device used in mapping the spectrum. In the portrait, Rowland is holding one of these devices in one hand. He, too, is staring into the incalculable scientific distance. He is serious, alert, intent. Eakins allowed his enthusiasm to run wild in the decorations on the picture's elaborate frame: physics formulas, selected by Rowland himself, are etched all over the frame, giving it the appearance of a blackboard in a laboratory.

Next, I found myself in front of the self-portrait Eakins painted upon being made a member of the National Academy of Design in 1902, when he was fifty-eight. I have always found it a heartbreaking picture, as brutally honest as Rembrandt looking at Rembrandt. Eakins is left with few illusions. He sees himself straight. One feels that *he* feels that he has failed, but failed with indefatigable defiance. (There's a wisp of hair straggling down the right side of his forehead, a devil-may-care wisp that betrays his inner defiance of a basically hostile world.) On this particular day, the defiance rather than the defeat captured me. The entire exhibit, after all, is a tribute to a victorious Eakins.

Miss Troyen returned silently and stood by my side. "As I said before, Eakins is new to Boston. Boston has always wanted things prettied up—an optimistic America," she said. "Incidentally, one of the great critical mysteries about Eakins is the reaction to his portrait of Walt Whitman. They were friends. They admired each other tremendously. Eakins often visited him across the river in Camden. Eakins took photographs and did sketches of Whitman, but his oil has never, ever been well received. Just recently, an eminent art critic referred to it as 'a summer-stock Falstaff.' " We looked at the picture together and shook our heads simultaneously. "Strange," she said, "how people misinterpret this picture, think it shallow. Before you go, let me quote you a few lines Whitman wrote a friend about this picture: 'Look at Eakins' picture. How few like it. It is likely to be only the unusual person who can enjoy such a picture—only here and there one who can weigh and measure it according to its own philosophy. Eakins would not be appreciated by the artists, so-called—the professional elects: the people who like Eakins best are people who have no art prejudices to interpose.' "

We Have Nothing to Fear . . .

Fifty years ago, on March 4, 1933, Franklin Delano Roosevelt was inaugurated president of the United States for the first time, and I was there, in the crowd. (This was the last of the March 4 Inaugurations; ever since, they have taken place on January 20.) I was eighteen, and I drove from college in Baltimore to Washington in a battered Ford owned by a classmate; the mere fact that he owned a four-wheeled vehicle gave him the appearance of being exceedingly rich. The times were desperate. Thirteen million Americans were out of work (including my own father); thousands of families were living in makeshift shacks in our greatest cities; farmers were rioting to prevent foreclosure of their land and homes; hunger was commonplace; and every bank in the nation was about to be closed. I was lucky: I had a scholarship that credited so many hours of work in the library against so much tuition. I was young and healthy and had my share of dreams.

The day was ominously overcast, and became more so as we approached Washington, forty miles south. Thick dark clouds hung over us; I was certain it would rain, and rain heavily. We had no tickets or credentials. The idea was to get as close as possible to the Capitol's East Front, within sight of the Inaugural stand, and find a citizen's perch for the ceremonies. My friend at the wheel knew nothing of the complexities of Washington traffic, and we drove around the city's circles and broad boulevards trying to find a place to park. Soldiers and policemen were everywhere; flags and bunting hung from every lamppost. But there was no hint of festivity in the air. Small knots of people had begun to line the sidewalks (it was late morning), but for the most part they appeared dispirited and sullen. We parked not very far from the Capitol, on a quiet, tree-lined street with neat, clean row houses with white stoops. It was a poor, black neighborhood. I was dressed for the day in the clothes of the time: a dark-blue vested suit (no jeans, of course), a long dark winter overcoat, and a snappy gray fedora with a huge brim. (The suit, as I recall, was a hideous shade of blue, and had come with two pairs of pants, for thirty-two dollars.) In my pocket I carried binoculars.

We worked our way fairly close to the Capitol before being stopped by a Marine guard. With extreme amiability, he asked for our tickets. He then gave us a friendly wink and pointed at a nearby icicle-laden, leafless tree. My friend and I scrambled into the tree and surveyed the special nexus of the nation that spread out before us. The white dome of the Capitol was gray, partly obscured by wisps of fog. The official grandstand was filling up with top-hatted dignitaries, all bundled up against the expected downpour. There must have been a hundred thousand people spread out over the vast Capitol grounds. For the first time, I examined my neighbors in our particular tree, each on a separate bare limb: an elderly gentleman in rumpled and ancient green tweeds, with patches; a beautiful redheaded young woman wrapped in a skimpy coat of rabbit, or of some other unfortunate domestic animal; a woman of indeterminate age who can best be described as dressed in rags, and whose face was lined with worry and pain. For the moment, at least, we were precariously snug in our tree house, waiting for a president to be inaugurated. President or no president, I had a hard time taking my eyes off the redhead; we subsequently became close friends.

The ceremonies were scheduled to start at noon. Noon came and went. The crowd was strangely silent. One could sense the unease. Rumors began to spread through the crowd, called up to the tree people by the less fortunate groundlings. Rumor: A mob somewhere along Pennsylvania Avenue had broken through police lines and surrounded the car containing President Hoover and President-elect Roosevelt. Rumor: Machine guns had been spotted along the route of the cavalcade from the White House to the Capitol. Rumor: Roosevelt had been wounded by an assassin's bullet, perhaps fatally. The lady in rags prayed quietly in the tree: "No more trouble, please, God. No more trouble." The man in the patched tweeds said that he had known all along that something terrible was going to happen on this day, and that one man's leaving office and another man's taking over would have no effect: only revolution would turn things right side up, once and for all. Nonsense, said the redhead; have a little faith, and don't fall out of the tree. Suddenly, there was a stirring in the crowd. The red-coated Marine band directly in front of the grandstand began to play. I pulled out my binoculars and focused straight ahead. President Hoover, glum and downcast, appeared and took a seat in a leather armchair to the left of the rostrum. A sound like the rustling of otherworldly leaves went through the crowd. Far away, through the giant center doors of the Capitol, appeared the president-elect. His face was totally without color. He made his way, painfully and slowly, along the ramp leading to the rostrum, leaning heavily on the arm of his son James. He seemed to be drawing on bottomless reservoirs of physical and mental strength to make the short journey to the rostrum and the presidency. The crowd held its collective breath. I doubt whether anybody, at that moment, knew that he was carrying ten pounds of heavy steel around his crippled and wasted legs.

I spotted the white-bearded chief justice, Charles Evans Hughes. He was wearing an odd black skullcap. As he delivered the oath of office, Roosevelt repeated every word of it in frighteningly solemn tones. Once power had passed into his hands, he seized it kinetically, with a vigor and force that stunned the throng. Both hands firmly gripped the rostrum. "This is preeminently the time to speak the truth, the whole truth, frankly and boldly," he said, in a clear and unforgettable voice. "This great Nation will endure as it has endured, will revive and will prosper. So, first of all, let me assert my firm belief that the only thing we have to fear is fear itself—nameless, unreasoning, unjustified terror which paralyzes needed efforts to convert retreat into advance. In every dark hour of our national life a leadership of frankness and vigor has met with that understanding and support of the people themselves which is essential to victory. . . . Yet our distress comes from no failure of substance. We are stricken by no plague of locusts. . . . Plenty is at our doorstep, but a generous use of it languishes in the very sight of the supply. Primarily this is because rulers of the exchange of mankind's goods have failed through their own stubbornness and their own incompetence, have admitted their failure, and have abdicated. . . . The money changers have fled from their high seats in the temple of our civilization.

We may now restore that temple to the ancient truths. . . . Happiness lies not in the mere possession of money; it lies in the joy of achievement, in the thrill of creative effort. . . . Restoration calls, however, not for changes in ethics alone. This Nation asks for action, and action now. Our greatest primary task is to put people to work. This is no unsolvable problem if we face it wisely and courageously. . . . We do not distrust the future of essential democracy. The people of the United States have not failed. . . . They have asked for discipline and direction under leadership. They have made me the present instrument of their wishes. In the spirit of the gift, I take it."

The crowd had come to life. It shouted approval. Roosevelt, still holding tightly to the rostrum, gave no sign of satisfaction. His expression was as grim as when he had started to speak. The ceremony was over. "I think we'll live," said the redhead as we climbed down from the tree. The man in tweeds burst into tears. "You know something?" said my college friend. "It never rained."

For many years, I have kept a tattered bulletin board in the kitchen, every inch covered with tacked-up addresses, memos, cards from loved ones, stray quotations from Shakespeare and Yeats (life-sustaining forces). Among them is an old, pockmarked newspaper photograph of F.D.R. leaning on a cane and listening intently to two ragged men who appear to have stopped him somewhere. I have no idea where the picture came from, but it is one of my priceless treasures. One of the men is small and scrappy-looking. His hands are in his pockets, and he is leaning into Roosevelt's face. The other man, larger and older, is wearing an ancient greatcoat, and is unshaved. Roosevelt's gray hat is somewhat smashed. He is being attentive to every word that is being said to him. The caption reads, "He knew how to listen."

Since that far-off Inauguration, I have learned that the family Bible on which Franklin Roosevelt took the oath of office lay open to the thirteenth chapter of I Corinthians—to "And now abideth faith, hope, charity, these three; but the greatest of these is charity."

Judge Hastie

As it happens, we've just received the following communication from a friend in New England who has a special feeling for jurisprudence:

Every once in a while, and quite by chance, one has the good luck to catch a glimpse of the life of a stranger and from that glimpse get some notion of great courage in the face of dreadful adversity and learn something of modesty, dignity, perseverance, and scholarship. This is a roundabout way of saying that I went over to the Harvard Law School one day last week to see its current library exhibit, commemorating the life and work of Judge William Henry Hastie (1904–76). It was an uplifting experience. Hastie's name was never a household word, but to those who labored year in and year out through morasses of bigotry and hatred for the advancement of black people within the framework of the legal system he represents a treasury of accomplishment. Hastie fought historic legal battles in the South during the thirties and forties, was dean of the Howard University Law School and then governor of the Virgin Islands, and became the first black appointed to a United States District Court and to a United States Court of Appeals; he sat on the Third Circuit (in Philadelphia) from 1949 to 1968, as Chief Judge from 1968 to 1971, and as Senior Judge from 1971 to 1976.

I like the feel of Langdell Hall, a massive, ivy-covered Law School building just off the Harvard Yard, where the exhibit was laid out in twelve glass cases, and I like to see Erika Chadbourn, the curator of manuscripts, who created this exhibit and earlier ones—devoted to Learned Hand ("The spirit of liberty remembers that not even a sparrow falls to earth unheeded"), Felix Frankfurter, and Oliver Wendell Holmes. Mrs. Chadbourn told me that she conceived the idea of the exhibit in 1979, when Judge Hastie's son and daughter presented Harvard with the Judge's papers. "Hastie graduated from Harvard Law in 1930 and came back for a Doctor of Juridical Science in 1933," she said. "One must remember the legal atmosphere into which he stepped." She read to me some words written by Professor Wade Hampton McCree, Jr., of the University of Michigan Law School, for the catalogue of the exhibit: "America's population in 1930 consisted of approximately a hundred million people, ten million of whom were black, but of her lawyer population of a hundred and fifty thousand, fewer than twelve hundred, or less than one per cent, were non-white. And small wonder, because in many communities, particularly in the South, black lawyers were not permitted to enter the courthouse by the front door or to drink from a public water fountain unless it was clearly marked 'colored.' The American Bar Association's application form inquired of race and a person who was not white was not accepted." Mrs. Chadbourn said that although two black persons had accidentally slipped through into the A.B.A. in 1915, blacks were not admitted until the nineteen-sixties. "Hastie was born in Knoxville, an only child," she told me. "His father had gone to Ohio Wesleyan Academy and Howard University, and become a pharmacist, but he found the prejudice too strong and went into the United States Pension Bureau. His mother was a teacher. Education was a driving force, and since there was no college-preparatory school for blacks in Knoxville, the family moved to Washington, D.C., so that the child could get a better education." He went on to Phi Beta Kappa and magna cum laude at Amherst, and, after graduating from Harvard Law (he received his doctorate later), went into the prominent black law firm of Houston & Houston, in Washington. Charles Hamilton Houston was a close friend, nine years older than Hastie; a true giant in the advancement of blacks in America; and one of the crucial forces in Hastie's life. Hastie, along with many others, revered him.

I wandered through the exhibit, in the vast, pillared library, past busts of Brandeis and Thurgood Marshall, in and out of a room with locked bookcases of incunabula, of laws and customs of England in Latin on vellum, and of statues of Henry VIII and Edward VI. But these things are for another day, and I concentrated on the documents, letters, photographs, and materials that gave a hint of Hastie's life. My attention was especially captured by:

> An editorial from the *Carolina Times* of April, 1933:
> This publication leads in applauding the courage of Thomas R. Hocutt, the student who applied for admission to the University of North Carolina [School of Pharmacy]. The courtroom deportment and technique of Barristers William H. Hastie, Cecil A. McCoy and Conrad O. Pearson won the respect of the white bar and of attendance at the meeting. Even our worst enemies admired their courage. They were also forced to concede the brilliancy of Attorney Hastie who most ably represented the student.

A September, 1933, press release from the National Association for the Advancement of Colored People stating, "A legal fight on the new salary schedules for Negro teachers in North Carolina will be waged. . . . It is the plan of the association to attack the unequal salary scale on the basis of its being a violation of the constitution. . . . William H. Hastie . . . will go to North Carolina to lay plans for court action."

A cabinet dealing with Hastie's stint as civilian aide to Secretary of War Henry L. Stimson during the Second World War, when Hastie recommended integrated housing and mess-hall facilities, and Colonel John R. Deane, Secretary in the Office of the Chief of Staff, wrote Hastie, "The intermingling of the races in messing and housing would not only be a variation from well established policies of the [War] Department, but it does not accord with the existing customs of the country as a whole." Hastie resigned.

An editorial from the Pittsburgh *Post-Gazette* of December 2, 1969, titled "Public Schools Threatened" and discussing the decision in Lemon v. Kurtzman, which upheld the constitutionality of a Pennsylvania law providing state aid to parochial and other private schools: "The dissenter in the three-judge panel, Chief Judge William H. Hastie . . . recognized the true effect of the parochial school law when he said it represented a 'legislative scheme' violate of the establishment clause of the First Amendment which has been held applicable to the states under the 14th Amendment."

I looked at enough of the following exhibits to see that Judge Hastie had subsequently been vindicated by the United States Supreme Court, and then went down some corridors to talk with Bernard Wolfman, Fessenden Professor of Law at Harvard and a compact force of intellectual energy at sixty. "You must remember that Hastie was involved in many of the most important breaking cases in the early civil-rights years," he told me. "He could have stood aside from the fray. He was a very quiet, extremely polite, very private person. The word for Hastie was dignity. He was not gregarious. Congenial but not convivial. I was never in his home, but we worked closely together when I was dean of the University of Pennsylvania Law School. I remember arguing a tax case in his court. He listened with *great* attention. Then he said, 'I would like to ask a question,' and the question was like a laser. He had mastered the case. Totally. That single question exposed the criteria. With Hastie, there was no elaboration, no pomposity, no big words. He wasn't thin-skinned and he wasn't self-conscious. Hastie and Learned Hand, for instance, were judges who regarded the cases before them as *their* cases. They felt *they* had the responsibility to reach a correct decision, and the lawyers were to be their aides in reaching that correct decision. Their questions went to the heart of the matter. I feel enriched by having known Hastie. By the way, I won that case."

Every few years, when I'm in Langdell Hall, I pay a call on the great constitutional scholar Paul Freund, University Professor Emeritus, and every time I step into his office, which resembles the crammed and cluttered theatrical set for Patrick Garland's dramatization of Aubrey's "Brief Lives," I have more difficulty locating the professor himself. I know that he is somewhere in that wilderness of books and manuscripts—the question is where. "Here I am!" he called out, and there he was, at a half-hidden desk, a large man of great affability. "Hastie and I were on the *Law Review* together," he said. "He was a year ahead of me. My most vivid memory is that he published more material than any other editor. There was a point system, a measuring scale for contributions to the *Review*, and Bill's was the greatest output. He was extremely efficient. He made a deep impression, although he was not a vivid personality, never tooted his own horn. There was nothing symbolic about Hastie. You know, I think you should talk to Charles Wyzanski, Senior Judge of the U.S. District Court here in Massachusetts. He was with us on the *Review*, too."

Professor Freund turned back to a Himalaya of papers, and I

stepped outside his office, passed an awesome bust of Learned Hand, and telephoned Judge Wyzanski. "I'm glad you called," he said, with great warmth. "On the *Review*, we would meet fortnightly with advance sheets of cases that might be considered for inclusion in the *Review*. We would discuss them—all the editors together—and each fellow would recite cases he felt were of importance. There was a *Review* chap from South Carolina, who shall be nameless, who would leave the room when Hastie began to recite. *Leave the room.* Hastie paid absolutely no attention to this man, disregarded him entirely. It wasn't long before I saw the two of them dining together in a well-known restaurant not far from the Yard, on Dunster Street. Hastie had a hard time with Stimson, trying to obtain better conditions for blacks in the armed services. Stimson didn't give him much support, but when he resigned he did it without trumpeting the story or hampering the war effort. He just felt he could perform better outside government. James H. Rowe, an adviser to Presidents Roosevelt and Johnson, once proposed his name to Johnson for appointment to the Supreme Court. Johnson said, 'He isn't known.' Rowe said, 'Nominate him and he'll be known.' He was a very good judge. He had forbearance, understanding, the judicial temperament. He had the copybook virtues. You will find nothing in his opinions that would enter a book of rhetoric. He wasn't a poet. But if you were a litigant you would want to appear before Hastie. He was a judge of the bar."

Sunday in the Park

Outdoors looked ravishing—a brilliant, cloudless, bright-blue sky, truly a benign day. Sunday, and home, I instinctively turned on the tube: governments paralyzed, assassinations revisited. A disgruntled group of commentators, sitting on their duffs in Washington, were engaging in their Sunday-morning litany of negativism and hopelessness. One of them, a cynical old codger with a voice that would curdle mother's milk, allowed that the City of New York was a *real* mess, millions and millions of unhappy people packed together in utter despair and gridlock.

The leaves must be turning, I thought. I snapped off the set and walked, in easy comfort, several blocks into Central Park—another world. A lone bagpiper sat on a bench, playing for his own pleasure. The sound was sobering, even mournful, but ended on a long, haunting upbeat note filled with wild hope. Quiet, strolling people were everywhere—lots of them. I headed toward Dog Hill, a paradise of unleashed dogs—from greyhounds to dachshunds—who race and frolic in a state of perfect freedom. Presumably cooped up all week, they have sense enough to relish these unfettered moments. "To heel, to heel," said the owner of an immense, shaggy beast, who, in turn, had his eye on a prim white poodle. Heated sniffing ensued. Swift human intervention prevented Senator Helms from swooping in and closing down the Park forever, on moral grounds. A cat on a leash was observing with amusement a group of elaborate picnickers, lunching on china plates. Someone was pushing a three-legged dog in a baby carriage. Two-legged babies in carriages were not in short supply. A leather-jacketed man with three earrings in each ear strolled past, a green parrot perched on his right shoulder. "Polly want a cracker?" I asked. "Polly want a cracker!" said the parrot. I wondered if this erudite feathered friend might have a sense of Central Park history. "Frederick Law Olmsted?" I asked. "Blast off!" said the parrot.

Joggers by the hundred, all sizes, shapes, and colors, trotted by. Bicycles moved along the Park Drive in an endless stream—some cyclists puffing, some almost at rest, some fiercely racing, others gliding by without using their hands. Everywhere, I saw newly seeded bright-green grass, much of it fenced off—Irish green, as green as the lamented long-lost spinach in the old Horn & Hardart Automats. There were more picnickers near a statue of the Polish King Wladyslaw II Jagiello. The inscription said he had turned back the Teutonic aggressors at Grunwald in 1410. I bought a slim hot dog on a roll, complete with mustard, relish, and sauerkraut that had been turned back by Teutonic aggressors in 1410. I also bought the obligatory bottle of ambulatory mineral water and took a long, satisfying swallow.

I walked and walked through the cosmopolitan crowd. I spied a silver plate bolted to a bench which read "Patty Loves Johnny," and a similar plate on a nearby bench reading "Please Sit and Enjoy the Park." And always the ballet of Rollerbladers moving forward, sidewise, backward—but no gridlock. Quite suddenly, I came across a combo of guitar, sax, drums, and double bass, playing soft music in the sunlit Park, under a linden tree. Someone passed the hat. My expenses for the outing: a buck and a half for the miserable weenie, a buck and a half for the mineral water, four bucks for the musicians. Total outlay: seven dollars. I looked at the gleaming skyscrapers, unbombed, on the horizon. I counted my blessings: an afternoon amid a passing semblance of peace.

Arriving

Another summer. Back to the old house in Wellfleet, on Cape Cod. Thoreau country. I think of "Little Gidding," from Eliot's "Four Quartets":

> And the end of all our exploring
> Will be to arrive where we started
> And know the place for the first time.

I open the door, glance around the old rooms, experience the strange sensation that I have been away not an entire winter but about twenty minutes. Old familiar steep and narrow staircase, old familiar pictures: the print of Ibsen; the print of the overfed, much too contented cat; the cherished oils of beach and woods by friends and neighbors.

Hey, buddy, knock off the aesthetics! Get real. You've got *problems.* Raccoons have been in the attic, living it up like Donald Trump. Smartest little creatures east of the Mississippi. Could run the whole damn country, just with their prehensile thumbs. I call the raccoon man for help; says he'll come. There's a dead mouse somewhere under the house, making its presence known. A domesticated squirrel, nowhere to be seen, has been dining on a window frame in the sitting room, near the Audubon reproduction of the belted kingfishers. (The female is swallowing a fish.) The squirrel has almost shaved down the muntins. My wife has gone upstairs. "Toilet's on the fritz!" she calls down. "Get the plumber!" (The equivalent of finding Jimmy Hoffa.) Mirabile dictu, I reach the plumber. "Look, Skipper," he says. "That toilet went through the Great Depression. That toilet is a dead toilet—once gulped five gallons of water every flush. I'll give you something new—flushes only a gallon and a half and you'll win an environmental medal." I order the toilet. Then I discover we're out of propane gas, but the gas man can't get his truck here until we clear away a giant felled beech tree that blocks the road to the tank. And there's bright-yellow pine pollen deeply settled everywhere. It's gesundheit time at the old homestead, and I forage for Kleenex.

To hell with dead mice, hungry squirrels, high-I.Q. raccoons, and pollen, too. Feel sudden need to reconnect with the outdoors. Take twenty-minute walk down to the Atlantic Ocean. Pass gleaming freshwater kettle-hole ponds, left over from glacial times. Pass small Herring River, and spy darting schools of alewives that have been spawning in nearby Gull Pond and are now heading toward Massachusetts Bay and the open ocean, so that, as the legend goes, they can make their annual trip back to Norway and joyous smorgasbords. Beach grass waving silkily, wild roses clumped near beach, beach itself, and high dunes, in resilient form. Walk back from the beach and reach the Old King's Highway. Some say that it ran from Boston to Provincetown, and if you look closely you can see deep ruts left by carts and carriages in bygone times.

Back to the house. A thousand bees are swarming around, near an attic window. They have been away two, three years, but apparently the queen also missed the old place and decided to come home. In a sense, I'm in Heaven. Perhaps I'm a bee. I think of Emily Dickinson:

> The Pedigree of Honey
> Does not concern the Bee—
> A Clover, any time, to him,
> Is Aristocracy.

Departing

In Wellfleet, on Cape Cod. A piercing-blue sky, gentle ocean breeze, low humidity, clean air. But what Seamus Heaney has called "the ache of summer" is increasingly palpable. Darkness will clamp down earlier and more suddenly this evening—one moment a rich, haunting Maxfield Parrish blue, the next pitch-black and night. Hard to face, but wouldn't you know, summer is ending and it is time for memories. Last year, the infants crawled and babbled, this year walked and talked, expressed ideas. Their fathers, brothers in their forties, not having got together for a year, fell upon each other like wild kids, pummelling themselves back into their pasts. As sage, I stood and observed with a comforting yet bittersweet sense of posterity.

And now the depressing thought of packing. Dragging the suitcases down from the attic, clump, clump. Which shirts should stay the long winter, which should head for city soot and the Chinese laundry? Certainly, some of the oils by friends and local artists must go back with us, especially the picture of a child's broken high chair, by the late Mary Hackett, of Provincetown, a painter fools might label "primitive" but whom those with eyes to see recognize as great.

What will be most missed? Those early-morning walks along unmarked sandy roads, past pitch pine being overtaken by climaxing oak, each walk a venture along undiscovered paths. Suddenly, one comes upon a shack in the woods, never before noticed, or an ancient roadside mileage marker, an arrowhead, a gentle snake. When one looks up, there is a bald eagle, rare, swooping and filling the glimpse of sky.

Departing

I will miss the bustling public library, brain center of the village (winter pop. 3,015, summer pop. circa 15,000), lectures, concerts, readings, expertly managed with a vestigial New England respect for learning. The local grocery, Lema's, has a permanent pervading odor of appetite: part vinegar, part scallion, part salami, part old wooden floorboards. And Charlie, the Scots butcher, always slicing, chopping off the fat, and singing, bagpipelike, songs of the Old Country. And Bayside Lobster Hutt, a scene of pure Bruegel: long wooden tables, whole families pigging out, cracking shells, dipping claws and tails into melted butter.

I will not miss the incessant, speeding, dangerous traffic on Route 6, the main artery connecting the Cape with the mainland. And beach picnics are a mixed blessing. There are elements of perfection—the expanse of beach, the pounding surf, the small, gleaming fires, the old friends gathered—but sand creeping into hot dogs, gumming up the relish, and clinging to the corn is not what the fancier places now call Cuisine Nouvelle New England.

Night is falling. There is a chill in the air. Winter will come. And go.

Summer Notes, Wellfleet, Cape Cod

SUNSETS: Summer visitors insist that, rain or shine, the sun sets gloriously and colorfully every evening in the east, owing to the Cape's odd configuration: sticking out into the Atlantic and winding around to face itself. Tell a visitor that the sun sets in the west and sparks begin to fly. Never argue with these people. They are dangerous, especially when racing east to catch a sunset.

DIPS: An essential accompaniment to an Art Opening, and there is an Art Opening every twelve minutes. Summer people occasionally, and inadvertently, glance at the pictures, but they concentrate on the dip: salsa, with crackers, or sour cream, chives, seaweed, and Elixir of Vincent, a stimulant designed to induce the purchase of paintings. Art dips, of course, are not to be confused with dips in the ocean, an entirely different situation, without crackers.

BEACH TALK: Juvenile Beach Talk—toddler to ten—is this summer almost exclusively confined to dinosaurs. Urchins who cannot add or subtract, read or write, discourse with authority about the distinctions, habits, and history of the huge, funky lizards.

Peggy (*five*): Tyrannosaurus, a carnivorous biped, is much nicer than a hyena.

Sam (*four*): The duck-billed iguanodon hates the armored stegosaurus. That's *my* shovel! (*Uncontrollable wailing and removal from the beach.*)

BIRD LIFE: Impatient, family-oriented catbirds sit on the edge of the picnic table waiting for you to finish lunch. Keep a catbird waiting and she does not disguise her irritation. Soft meows become strident, and the birds abandon politesse, jump over, stand beside your plate, and start to eat. This makes summer people feel that they are part of an eternal life chain, worth the entire trip.

TRAFFIC: Unbearable.

SIGNS AND PORTENTS: Old-time residents of the Cape (no summer people involved) are convinced that someone has been fiddling with the moon. "I can't find it anymore," a woman who has lived seventy-six years in Wellfleet told me the other evening. "And when I finally do it's in a strange part of the sky. Most unsettling." These same people often report that they have spotted Henry Thoreau walking along the back sand roads, hoping to have lunch with his mother.

Henry James probably had it right when he said that the two most beautiful words in the English language are "summer afternoon."

The Creative Life

I realize that any minute now my dear friend Al Hirschfeld will be ninety-five. I pick up the phone for a celebratory chat. Al is in his studio, on East Ninety-fifth Street, in his antique barber chair, drawing. Always drawing. "I feel wonderful," he says. "Absolutely wonderful." I suggest that work plays a part in his miraculous vitality. I hear a full-throated snort. "It isn't work, kid. It's luxury. Pure luxury. I don't call it work. I haven't a clue how one would retire." Al uses the word "retire" the way some people pronounce "Richard Nixon." "What's a man to do? Sit around some sun-soaked beach all day? Watching the waves? Or playing golf? Golf!"—same tone as "retire." "Human beings fascinate me. People," he says. "I used to love just sitting in the window of the Howard Johnson's at Forty-sixth and Broadway, drawing the constant parade of people passing by." Does he still make notes in his pocket during a show, in the dark? "Just for reminders," he says. "I'll draw a bow tie, or a cane, or jot down one word or make a sketch that brings back an entire scene."

I remind Al that he once said, "It would never occur to me to do a drawing of the Grand Canyon. It is just a decayed molar under a very dramatic light." Now Al says, "Still feel the same way. Nature is *there*. What are you going to do? It's movement that interests me. Movement in my drawing gives me total freedom. I can go where I want. I can take the line anywhere. I'm not governed by gravity." I venture that his line is stronger today than when he was a stripling of seventy-five. "It's the freedom," he says. "The exhilarating freedom." We talk a bit about kindness. In a mean world, there is never any meanness in a Hirschfeld drawing. "Nothing funny about a big nose, or a grotesque face, or making people look like an image in some Coney Island fun-house mirror," he says. "I once did a drawing of Jimmy Durante, and I left the nose out."

I remind him of the joyous weekly lunches we used to have at the old Lobster restaurant, on Forty-fifth Street, with S. J. Perelman, Joseph Mitchell, Brooks Atkinson, Harvey Orkin, Albert Hackett. "I'd like to start those all over again," he says. "Why don't we think about it?" He goes on, "Something has happened to humor. Out of fashion—I don't understand it. Jokes aren't humor. Something to do with economics and people incapable of satirizing the times in which they live." He's thinking back now. "I miss the great Miguel Covarrubias. Tremendous influence on me. I'd like to think I had some effect on him.

"But the fuss over this birthday! Hard to believe. Photographers all over the house, in every corner but the sandbox. We have a rabbi lives across the street, and I step outside the other day and there are *six* photographers on the rabbi's roof, snapping pictures of me. On the big day, Louise and I will go to her family in Larchmont for a barbecue. So long, kid. Much love to all at your place." Click.

PROFILES

The word "profile" is used these days to describe any piece of writing about any person, regardless of length, purpose, or quality. The Profiles in *The New Yorker* are not only spelled with a capital P, but are a highly specialized, compact form of biography. There is no magic formula, but an attempt to make the subject a living, breathing human being; hard factual digging; and humor. As for the time it might take to write one, Mr. Shawn was noted for remarking, "It takes as long as it takes." (By the way, I never use a tape recorder. I don't own one.)

The Bard in the Delicatessen

Rarely have a man and his environment been in greater harmony than Louis G. Schwartz and the Sixth Avenue Delicatessen. Both are physically small but spiritually colossal. The delicatessen, which is on Sixth Avenue between Fifty-fifth and Fifty-sixth Streets, is a hole-in-the-wall only nine feet wide and seventy-five feet deep, but it dispenses, over the counter and at tables in the rear, approximately a ton of corned beef and pastrami every seven days. The delicatessen mirrors its rich and sporty clientele, radio and theatrical celebrities who work or live in the neighborhood and a substantial backlog of merchants and their families. An order for one turkey sandwich is considered a chore, whereas an order for a thousand turkey sandwiches with Russian dressing and cole slaw, to go out, is filled joyously and considered an inspiring challenge. In this setting Louis G. Schwartz, one of the establishment's four waiters, is the glittering central jewel. For some years now I have known Schwartz and held him in high esteem, and I often drop into the delicatessen for the sheer pleasure of watching him at work. Schwartz, who is known to everyone in his acquaintance as Louie the Waiter, is a short, round blob of a man, with plump pink cheeks and a bouncy walk. He is forty-two. His customers and colleagues consider him a hero. They admire him as a waiter and respect him as a poet ("Send a Salami to Your Boy in the Army" is one of his more widely quoted rhymes), but they reserve their awe, as I do, for his ability to sell War Bonds in large amounts to customers who enter the store with nothing more in mind than a plate of chopped chicken liver. Singlehanded, he has sold almost exactly four million dollars' worth of War Bonds since Pearl Harbor. No other waiter in New York—or anywhere else, for that matter—can touch his record.

Louie's prowess has not gone unnoticed. For one thing, he has shaken hands with Secretary Morgenthau at the Treasury's office in Rockefeller Center; Walter Winchell buys bonds from him in unrevealed quantities and occasionally mentions him with enthusiasm in his column; he has appeared at bond rallies with Mayor LaGuardia, who is approximately his size and shape; he has been heard on the radio program "We, the People;" the American Women's Voluntary Services have made him their only male honorary member in the metropolitan area; and he has received an Award of Merit from the Treasury in the form of a scroll, along with a letter signed by the State Administrator and the State Chairman of the War Finance Committee. Louie always carries this letter with him, to establish his identity with new prospects. "You'll buy War Bonds sooner or later, so get them today from Louie the Waiter," he recently whispered in the ear of a startled newcomer to the delicatessen, a man who simply wanted supper. Then he pulled out the letter and read, " 'Just think what it would mean to the war effort if every waiter in New York City sold only twenty-five per cent of your total. Congratulations!' " Louie backed away and paused. "From the U.S. Treasury!" he cried, and wheeled off to another table. By the time Louie returned, the customer had about regained his composure. "A bowl of pot cheese, please," he said meekly, "and a fifty-dollar bond."

In many respects, Louie is the ideal salesman, a paragon of tact, good humor, and stubborn devotion to his product. The Treasury has prepared countless pamphlets, posters, throwaways, and elaborate sets of instructions to aid bond salesmen, but Louie considers all these devices unnecessary. His success is almost entirely due to the force of his personality. Being at peace with himself and with the world in which he works, he smiles often and radiantly. Furthermore, he has a constitutional inability to take no for an answer. "About drives I am ignorant," he told a customer who begged off buying a bond on the ground that he was waiting for the Fourth War Loan Drive to start. "Here every day is a drive going on." The man bought a hundred-dollar bond and went back to his noodle soup. Louie evaluates his customers as they study the menu. While they are deciding whether to take, say, the Sixth Avenue Special (a three-decker sandwich: tongue, hot pastrami, chicken-salami, Russian dressing, and cole slaw) or the Jack Pearl Special (a three-decker: spiced beef, tongue, lettuce, and tomato), Louie studies their clothes and their appearance in general. By the time they look up, he has made an estimate of how big a bond they're good for. He may revise this figure during the course of the meal, but generally he sticks to the figure he set for himself at the start. He may occasionally go up, but he rarely goes down. Several weeks ago a florid gentleman in a double-breasted pin-stripe blue serge beckoned to Louie and asked for an extra portion of butter. Louie, who had started to talk War Bonds to the man, had marked him down for a hundred-dollar one, but a certain quality of desperation around the corners of the man's mouth called for an instant revision. "That will cost you exactly three hundred and seventy-five dollars," Louie told him, then headed for the kitchen. When he returned with the pat of butter, the man's check was on the table.

Today, at the height of his powers, Louie is selling an average of seven thousand dollars' worth of bonds a week. On occasion he has taken in nine or ten thousand dollars over a brisk weekend and he has even made a couple of hundred-thousand-dollar sales. Since his clients do not receive the bonds until several days after they have paid Louie for them, his cash business is based on complete confidence between buyer and seller. Louie rarely carries less than four hundred dollars in cash in his pockets, representing purchases made by customers who merely hand him the money and do not ask for a receipt. "I would no more want a receipt from Louie the Waiter," one of his clients said a while ago, "than I would request myself to give me an I.O.U." Louie works a nine-hour shift at the delicatessen, from six in the evening to three in the morning, and he utilizes practically every spare moment, on duty and off, to extract bond money from his customers. He makes phone calls, sends notes, and collects cash on daily tours to the offices and homes of his clients. In his apartment he keeps a file of steady customers, alphabetically arranged in several notebooks, and consults it constantly to see who is due for another bond. He estimates that he spends about fifteen dollars a week out of his own pocket for postage, carfare, and phone calls to prospective buyers. Last Christmas all his regular clients received a greeting card bearing a rhyme composed, of course, by Louie: "Buying War Bonds helps a lot, To put the Axis on the spot." Louie is constantly hopping to the phone while he is on duty, to accept War Bond orders; when he is out of the store, the proprietors either take the messages or tell his customers to call him at home. To make matters easier for people who phone in for bonds while he is off duty, Louie has arranged to be listed in the next Manhattan telephone directory as "Louie the Waiter War Bonds 1370 6AV CI 7-6289." No. 1370 is his home address, three doors from the delicatessen. He and his wife have an apartment there.

Louie's devotion to War Bonds has been heightened by the war record of his son-in-law, Lieutenant Thomas Berschig. Berschig, a navigator in the Army Air Forces and a holder of the Distinguished Flying Cross, was on his fortieth combat mission when his plane was shot down over Foggia, Italy, in November, 1943. Observers saw him bail out, but there was no word of his whereabouts for several weeks. On Christmas Eve, the War Department notified his family that he was a prisoner in Germany. Louie passionately believes that every War Bond actually shortens the war, and after every sale he feels that he has brought Lieutenant Berschig one day nearer home. When we entered the war, Louie had merely a normal interest in bonds. He began selling them at the suggestion of a group of ladies from the War Bond section of the American Women's Voluntary Services who occasionally eat lunch at the delicatessen, their office being around the corner, on Fifth Avenue at Fifty-seventh Street. Four days after Pearl Harbor, Louie was serving corned-beef sandwiches to the ladies. One of them, a Mrs. Edell, admired his pale-blue waiter's jacket. Both lapels were covered with assorted insignia, including those of the Infantry, Medical Corps, and Signal Corps, all gifts from admiring customers in the services.

"A stunning jacket," murmured Mrs. Edell.

"How about an A.W.V.S. button?" Louie said.

"Sell War Bonds for us and a button is yours," Mrs. Edell said.

Louie agreed, and shortly after lunch Mrs. Edell returned to the delicatessen with a pile of green application blanks and a red, white, and blue enamel A.W.V.S. pin, topped by an eagle. "There's a fellow at the front table wants a hundred-dollar bond," Louie told her as she walked in the door, which should have given her some inkling of the shape of things to come. Mrs. Edell briefly instructed Louie in the fundamentals of filling out the blanks and put him on his own. She hoped he might sell perhaps three hundred dollars' worth of bonds weekly. He hit nine hundred the first week and seventeen hundred the second. By the end of January, every menu in the place bore the slogan, "You'll buy War Bonds sooner or later, So get them today from Louie the Waiter." That month's take was $10,875, and Louie remarked to Mrs. Edell that he felt he now had an established business.

Once a day, Louie takes the cash he has collected to his bank, the First Federal Savings & Loan Association, in Radio City, and waits there while the bonds are filled out; he doesn't clear his cash sales through the A.W.V.S. Checks, however, are delivered to Mrs. Edell at the A.W.V.S. headquarters. She turns them over to the Treasury and in due time the bonds are mailed to their owners. For a brief period during his early boom days, Louie felt guilty about turning over all his check business to one organization, and he began apportioning his receipts among the A.W.V.S., the local office of the War Finance Committe of the Treasury, and a bond booth at Sixth Avenue and Fifty-second Street. Louie felt that this wealth-sharing scheme was only fair, but Mrs. Edell couldn't see it. She finally collared Louie in the delicatessen one evening and almost brought tears to his eyes by recalling his humble beginnings in the bond business. "*Who* gave Louie the Waiter an A.W.V.S. button at a time when he desperately wanted one?" she asked. Louie stood silent, staring hard at a tablecloth. "*Who* ate a corned-beef sandwich four days after Pearl Harbor and suggested that Louie the Waiter sell bonds?" she continued. "You," said Louie. Two days later he appeared at the A.W.V.S. offices with a bulging envelope representing his total haul of checks for the week. Today, Mrs. Edell is mellow about the whole thing. "Louie strayed from the fold," she says, "but he's back home now."

A large pen-and-ink portrait of Louie by Al Hirschfeld, the cartoonist, hangs on a wall in the delicatessen. Hirschfeld, who is an old friend and client, drew the portrait for him one night as a sort of tribute to his war work. It faces a poster on the opposite wall that says, "The next $2,500,000 will buy 18 Thunderbolts." Louie feels that the achievement of this goal will compensate, in a small way, for the loss of his son-in-law's plane. The lapels of his blue waiter's jacket have kept pace with his business and are now completely covered with buttons and pins, including insignia of the Free French, the Junior Women's U.S.O., and an E (for Efficiency) given to him by a vice-president of Bendix Aircraft, a steady buyer of both bonds and meals. His decorations flop up and down on his lapels and jingle as he walks. Sometimes, as he bounces down the narrow aisle of the delicatessen, both arms loaded up to his elbows with plates, the sheer weight of the food and decorations give him a forward tilt. Old-timers at the delicatessen regard Louie's heavily laden lapels as no more than appropriate to his eminence.

Louie's affinity for delicatessens is a product of heredity and environment. He was born in an atmosphere of cold cuts. His father was something of an adventurer. He emigrated to America from Warsaw in his teens and soon afterward he joined Theodore Roosevelt's Rough Riders and saw action in the Spanish-American War. In 1900, he settled down in New York and married a girl recently arrived from Odessa. When Louie, the first of four children, was born the next year, his parents were living on the lower East Side and his father was waiting on table at Weinberg's, a well-known kosher restaurant on Grand Street. Louie's first job was peddling the *Jewish Daily Forward*, a newspaper published near his school, P.S. 147, on Henry Street. A schoolmate recalls that Louie sold more papers than any of the other neighborhood boys. "That Louie was a smart salesman," he said recently. "He made every paper sound like a bargain attraction." When Louie was ten, his father decided to go into business for himself and moved the family to Fourteenth Avenue in Brooklyn, where he established Schwartz's Family Restaurant, a combination delicatessen and eating place. It was a success from the start. Mrs. Schwartz rose at six-thirty to get breakfast for her children and for a shift of telephone operators who worked across the street. The Schwartzes lived next door to the restaurant. Mr. Schwartz took over in the late afternoon. When the restaurant first opened, it offered a seven-course dinner for thirty-five cents. The meal ran the gamut of fruit cup, soup, roast, salad, dessert, and coffee. Rising prices and growing fame gradually pushed the table d'hôte to seventy-five cents, but there were few complaints. The counter of the delicatessen was stacked with every kind of cold cut, salad, and sausage known to man, except pork products. Mrs. Schwartz's cooking became the talk of the Yiddish-speaking population of Brooklyn. The conversation grew most animated over her homemade gefüllte fish, kreplach (a kind of ravioli), poppyseed cookies, plum jelly, almond horns, potato pancakes, and twisted bread (called *challe* and served with gefüllte fish).

In Brooklyn, Louie attended P.S. 164 and then Manual Training High School. He always came home for a quick lunch and a few minutes in the kitchen to help with the dishes. After finishing school, he went to work full time in the restaurant. His father taught him to carve, cook, make triple-decker sandwiches, wait on table, and buy food. There was ample scope for his talents, for as the restaurant expanded it took over a second floor and then spread to the building next door. The place had fourteen regular waiters and could handle banquets for five hundred people. During the last war, the manpower shortage became almost as acute as it is today, and Louie was put in charge of the recruiting department. Driving a large red Flint, he would speed down to Court House Square in Brooklyn and try to tempt the bums snoozing on park benches to throw in their lot with Schwartz's Family Restaurant. Dishwashers were the hardest to corral. They got three dollars a day. In addition they demanded guarantees of unlimited coffee, apple pie, and corned-beef sandwiches, as well as transportation in the Flint from bench to restaurant and return. "They always had a piece of something in their mouths," Louie says, "but sum totalling, they were a blessing because they liked us and never broke dishes."

Business fell off after the war and Louie's father decided to sell the restaurant and retire. Today the elder Schwartzes live comfortably in Brooklyn on their savings and a Spanish-American War pension. Louie married a Brooklyn girl, had a brief fling at studying law in the office of an uncle, and finally went to work waiting on tables at Isaac Gellis's delicatessen, on West Seventy-second Street, in Manhattan. The Schwartzes have two daughters. Soon after their first one was born, in 1922, she showed signs of being asthmatic in the New York winter, so Louie shifted to an Isaac Gellis delicatessen in Miami Beach and took his family with him. For the next fourteen years, he alternated between Isaac Gellis Miami Beach winters and Isaac Gellis Seventy-second Street summers. Many of his customers went South too during the cold weather and he built up a considerable clientele, which used him as a sort of private post office. Friends up North wrote to friends down South, merely addressing their letters to the delicatessen c/o Louie the Waiter. By the time Louie returned to New York for good, in 1936, and accepted a post at the Sixth Avenue Delicatessen, he was known in the trade as a waiter of talent and personality.

From the outset, Louie was happy at the Sixth Avenue Delicatessen. His customers in part were old friends, people who had been served by him for many years. Because of their common appreciation of the fine points of delicatessen, a close friendship grew up between him and the man who then owned the place, Mr. Irving Asness. This deepened when Louie created a three-decker sandwich composed of sliced turkey, tongue, and corned beef, with Russian dressing and cole slaw, and suggested that it be called the Uncle Irving Special, in honor of the owner. Mr. Asness was pleased, and he was delighted when Louie began composing verse about the delicatessen's *schtickles*. *Schtickles* are small chunks of sausage—bologna, pastrami, and so on—stuck on toothpicks and generally placed out on the counter. They are traditional in Jewish delicatessens. *Schtickles* sell for five cents apiece and satisfy the appetites of hungry customers while they shop. People don't eat *schtickles*, they *nosch* them. *Nosch* is a Yiddish term covering the vast field of eating between meals. To Louie, the sight of a *schtickle* on a counter represented an entire way of life and cried out for a poet, or minnesinger, to do it justice. Louie's verses were written on the backs of the round cardboard tops of Tulip coffee containers and were placed beside the *schtickles*. He began, somewhat pretentiously, with:

> Oh Romeo! Where Art Thou?
> Said Juliet and sighed.
> At Irving's Sixth Avenue Delicatessen
> eating a
> Schtickle
> for a
> Nickel
> he replied.

It was not long before Louie's interest in the world outside the door made itself felt. There were hints of Louie the War Bond Salesman in his second and third poems:

> In most lands one may vote
> the way he must
> Here in America—We are thankful
> for our
> Schtickle
> for a
> Nickel
> And in God we trust.

Turmoil over there
Peace over here
The
Schtickle
for a
Nickel
Writer wishes you a Happy
New Year!

Customers of the delicatessen were delighted with the verses and, by popular demand, Louie turned out a fresh one each week. Many were merely gay doggerel, without significance, such as:

A tisket
A tasket
our
Schtickle
for a
Nickel
Is good for your bread basket.
Roses are red,
Violets are blue,
our
Schtickle
for a
Nickel
Is Good for You.

These days, Louie, preoccupied with War Bonds, has given up composing *schtickle*-for-a-nickel verse. He confines his versifying to timely adaptations of old works, which he uses to increase bond sales. Thus the one about Romeo and Juliet now goes:

Oh Romeo! Where Art Thou?
Said Juliet and sighed.
At the Sixth Avenue Delicatessen
Buying a War Bond

From Louie the Waiter
He replied.

Shortly before we went into the war, Louie composed a long narrative poem relating in detail the eating habits and idiosyncrasies of his more noted customers. It is entitled "Every Day but Monday" and is, in essence, the "Beowulf" of the Sixth Avenue Delicatessen. The title derives from the fact that Monday is his day off. Louie delights in reading it to friends around the fireplace in his apartment and interpolating extemporaneous remarks that increase the homespun flavor of the piece. "Listen to this!" he will cry, and read from his manuscript. " 'Belle Baker—the incomparable—likes nothing at all but chicken and matzoth ball! Then there's Alexander Smallens without his hat, He eats his sturgeon sandwich in one minute flat!' . . . Absolutely," Louie will interpolate. "The whole meal takes five minutes. He reads his mail and tears it up and gulps black coffee and whoosh! he's gone. Absolutely! Listen! . . . 'And Leon of Leon and Eddie's has one wish, for chopped herring, black olives, and gefüllte fish!' . . . Honest to God! He drinks Coca-Cola *and* celery tonic *and* tea at the same time! Listen . . . 'And Al Jolson hasn't come down a peg, Give him chicken—boiled—the leg.' . . . Has to be hot, *very* hot. . . . 'Here's Bobby Clark—but serve him quick— Real hot chicken soup with noodles thick!' . . . You like it?"

Today the Schwartz family is scattered, and Louie and his wife, Anna, live alone in a comfortable three-room, mahogany-and-chintz apartment. His elder daughter, Lieutenant Berschig's wife, lives in Hollywood, Florida. His younger daughter recently left for the West Coast to marry a sergeant in the Marines whom she met at a servicemen's party in the fall of 1942. Together with a girl she knew, who also had a Marine in tow, they had returned to the Schwartz apartment after the party. Mrs. Schwartz prepared a midnight supper of noodle pudding and platters of steaming chicken and spaghetti. Both Marines ate with gusto, and shortly afterward one of them married the daughter's friend. Miss Schwartz, a thoughtful type, did not act quite so impulsively.

Mrs. Schwartz, a buxom, friendly woman, has a talent for dressmaking and has for years made all of her own and her children's clothes. "Everything but the handbags," Louie says. She also knits the black bow ties he wears in the delicatessen. Louie is subdued and respectful in her presence. He often sits, small and unobtrusive, in his living room poring over his War Bond records, and Mrs. Schwartz, an intense house-cleaner, occasionally doesn't see him and almost sweeps him out. Her major activities are inviting servicemen to the house for dinner and worrying over her husband's health. She feels that he works too hard and too long. However, she is very proud of his accomplishments. "Is my Louie doing a wonderful job!" she will say to a friend over the phone. "Sixteen hundred dollars in bonds last night alone!" Louie is unsparing in praise of his wife. "My Anna," he often observes in the delicatessen, "is a regular one-woman U.S.O.!"

The Sixth Avenue Delicatessen is owned today by three men. Such an arrangement is common among delicatessen keepers, who generally take turns behind the counter and thus avoid large payrolls. Mr. Asness retired a few years ago in a fit of annoyance at the delicatessen business. "I decided to quit," he told Louie, "when I came out from behind the counter and saw thirty people at the tables and thirty mouths filled with pastrami sandwiches. Something inside me snapped." Mr. Asness sold out and went to Florida to recuperate. The new proprietors enlarged the place slightly and there is now room for forty-eight people to eat pastrami sandwiches. Rather extensive further alterations are in prospect, and when they are finished the restaurant will accommodate seventy-five. Old customers are none too happy about the impending changes; they feel that much of the delicatessen's character derives from its smallness. The most active of the proprietors, Mr. Ben Weisman, stoutly defends the improvements as being not only inevitable but also healthy signs of normal growth. "I'll know when to stop," he tells complainers. "*I* know that this business runs on memories, memories of old delicatessens from your youth. Stop worrying." Mr. Weisman keeps a careful watch on trends in his business and has concluded that cold cuts are far and away the most popular dish. This, he thinks, is solely because ninety per cent of his customers were weaned on them. "Start worrying the day we take out the cold cuts," he says. He is an analytical man, and he often gets concerned about Louie's future, especially since Louie recently began to show signs of restlessness. "In my love for Louis G. Schwartz," he has said, "I yield to no man. But the important thing for Louis G. Schwartz to remember is that someday, praise God, the war will end and people will sell their bonds and try to forget about the war. Many people keep telling him he should become a hot-shot insurance agent, but it is important for Louis G. Schwartz to remember that he is a fine waiter. I will go so far as to say that he is the *finest* waiter any-where. He's a fine waiter, and *that's* why he sells so many bonds."

Louie's day begins around noon, when he rises and hurries to his phone to start working on bond prospects. Leafing through one of his notebooks, he makes anywhere from six to a dozen calls before he leaves the apartment. One afternoon he invited me to accompany him on his collection route, and I arrived at the apartment while he was telephon-ing. "Yep, yep," Louie was saying. "I've been waiting to hear from you. Fine, fine. Be over in an hour." Louie put down the receiver and turned to me. "*He* apologized to *me*," he said. "He's a couple days late for his next bond."

After Louie had made several more telephone calls, we left the house and walked up Sixth Avenue. "One big thing a waiter must never for-get," Louie said as we walked along, "is to get the upper hand the moment he gives the customer the menu. Absolutely necessary for the waiter's peace of mind. Give the customer the upper hand and nobody has pleasure eating or waiting on table. Excuse me," he said suddenly, ducking into a bar. I tagged after him.

"Hi, Uncle Charlie!" Louie cried to a gray-haired man behind the cash register. "Saw you beckoning through the window. Got anything?"

"A thirty-seven fifty for me," said the man. "Cash!"

"Thanks, Uncle Charlie," said Louie, pocketing the money. "You'll get the bond in a few days."

Louie and I hurried out of the store and continued up Sixth Avenue. "Regular customer," he said. "Waits for me to walk by. Like I was saying, absolutely any customer gets the upper hand with a waiter is liable to get demanding. They want more of this and quicker of that. Then the waiter gets stubborn and there's trouble. It's human nature. Pardon me," he said, diving into a small jewelry store. The proprietor, a red-faced man in gray tweeds, was busy with a customer, who was poring over a tray of costume jewelry on the counter. "My friend Louie the Waiter!" the proprietor said, turning away from the customer and pulling a small white envelope from his cash register. "Two hundreds and a fifty. Total of a hundred eighty-seven fifty," he said. "Make out the hundreds for Malcolm and the fifty for Hilda. You got the names and addresses?"

"Sure, sure," said Louie, taking the envelope. "How've you been?"

"Dizzy," said the man.

"Likewise," said Louie.

"The whole family," Louie said to me when we reached the street again, "are very fine people. As for waiters getting the upper hand, I don't mean being tough, nothing like that. Is merely a matter of being in a good humor. You make the customer feel you know him and you like him and you're looking after him. Makes no difference how tired you are. You smile and the customer smiles. The customer smiles and he has an appetite. He has an appetite and he eats more. He eats more and the proprietor smiles. So everybody's happy and the waiter has the upper hand."

By six o'clock Louie had visited a cigar store, a clothing firm in a loft building, and a long list of clients in and around Radio City, including a fashionable diamond merchant and a theatrical agent specializing in name brands. In all, he had collected $2,365 in cash and checks, as well as a thirty-cent cigar. On his way to the delicatessen, Louie looked tired. The bounce had gone from his walk. With his hands in his pockets and his hat pulled low over his eyes, he looked like any small, harassed salesman. "My legs will hold out five years more," he said, half to himself. "How long can a waiter last if he walks all night and walks all day? Five years."

Mr. Weisman was behind the counter at the delicatessen when Louie and I got there. "Three people left these checks for bonds," he said. Louie stuffed the checks into a pocket and headed toward the rear. "Fred Allen was here for a sandwich," Mr. Weisman called after Louie, "and he asked for Edgar Allan Schwartz. He says you're a great poet."

I stood by the counter talking with Mr. Weisman, and Louie disappeared into the kitchen. He emerged a moment later, wearing his blue waiter's jacket, his collection of buttons flopping against his lapels. He bustled down the aisle, nodding right and left to customers. His round red face was beaming. His eyes had the quiet, happy look of a man who has come home after a hard day's work. "And what will the lovely lady have to eat?" he asked an elderly woman at a front table. "Pastrami on rye? Perfect. We'll make it hot, *very* hot." Louie cupped a hand to his mouth. "One pastrami rye for the lovely lady—*hot*," he called to the counter man. Then he turned back to the customer. "America's winning 'cause she's on the alert," he said. "Now you buy a War Bond for dessert!"

The Crier

Few public figures of our day, with the possible exception of Franklin D. Roosevelt, Winston Churchill, and Joseph V. Stalin, have been more deeply affected by the unsettled state of the world than Gabriel Heatter, the radio commentator. "My voice came to the people in the dark time," he often says. " 'Wake up!' it cried. 'Wake up, America!' " Unlike the average commentator or statesman, who can either take an event or leave it alone, Heatter appears stricken each time he discusses a piece of news on the air, whether it concerns a major amphibious assault or the restoration to normal civilian life of a dog honorably discharged from the Army. World crises often give him a Godlike feeling. Upon learning of Mussolini's downfall, he turned to a friend and said, "Heatter hounded the Duce like a dog, night after night—called him a clown, a gutter-snipe." He always delivers his commercials himself, causing some radio people to insist that he dispenses his emotion without discrimination. "Heatter makes an attack of gingivitis sound worse than the robots hitting London," one of them recently remarked. Nevertheless, six nights weekly, for fifteen minutes, over WOR and a hundred and ninety-five other stations of the Mutual Broadcasting System, he addresses an audience estimated by surveys at between eleven and fourteen million persons. He speaks with such fervor that many of his listeners make the mistake of thinking he is a clergyman and a large percentage of his weekly fan mail is addressed to "the Rev. Gabriel Heatter." Mondays, Wednesdays, and Fridays he works for Kreml, a hair tonic; Tuesdays and Thursdays for Forhans, a tooth paste; and Sundays for Barbasol, a shaving cream. His income is many times that of the average man of God. He grosses in the neighborhood of $800 a night, which amounts to about $250,000 annually. Of this, he nets, after taxes, about $30,000, enough to maintain a house on Long Island, a two-hundred-acre farm in Connecticut, and an apartment in New York. All in all, he has put anguish on a paying basis. "I was just a ham on a news program," he often says, "and I turned it into a crusade."

Heatter has nothing to fear from television. In appearance and manner, he could easily be mistaken for the pastor of a highly endowed suburban church. He is fifty-four, tall, and big-boned, with a broad, ruddy face, a prominent nose, dreamy, deep-set brown eyes, and a forehead that extends up and back a considerable distance before meeting the hairline, Kreml or no Kreml. His hair is gray. Tiny curled tufts jut from behind his ears, in the accepted ecclesiastical style. He is partial to loose-fitting tweeds, Byronic collars, and drooping bow ties. His voice is a clergyman's dream. It has a wailing, singsong quality that has led some of his listeners to suspect that he broadcasts from a swinging breeches buoy. Let him say, for example, "Guns blaze tonight in China as new frontiers are born of hate and force" or "May I respectfully urge you to try Barbasol?," and instantly it becomes a rich and resonant litany. He generally greets a stranger to whom he is introduced by saying solemnly, "I am humbled and honored," then grasping his hand and wringing it until the man's eyes begin to pop. For someone whose business encompasses the wide world, his existence is amazingly secluded. "I don't want to sound prim, but a person like myself has to lead an almost ascetic life," he once said. As a rule, all his work, including the preparation, writing, and delivery of his broadcasts, is done at home—whichever one of his three places he happens to be living in—but his traditional opening gambit, "Good evening, everyone!," and his closing remark, "Ladies and gentlemen, your friend and mine, Len Sterling!," which he makes when he turns the program back to his announcer, give the impression that he is broadcasting from a studio. His program is piped to WOR by telephone; Sterling speaks from WOR. Heatter finds working at home comfortable and relaxing, and he feels that it prevents him from catching cold. He lives in dread of getting a head cold as the consequence of expending so much energy during his talks. "I must admit," he tells friends, "that I wind up with some real perspiration." After each broadcast at home, he promptly takes a hot shower. On those rare occasions when he speaks from a studio, he takes more extreme precautions. At the end of his program, the audience is requested to remain seated, the lights are turned out, and Heatter, working swiftly in the dark, changes to dry underwear.

The time of day Heatter broadcasts has a lot to do with the uniqueness of his approach to the rôle of commentator. His Sunday program runs from 8:45 to 9 P.M., and all his weekday talks run from 9 to 9:15 P.M., a stretch of radio time not generally devoted to programs of cosmic import. He competes with Bing Crosby, Eddie Cantor, Frank Sinatra, and Major Bowes. Furthermore, H. V. Kaltenborn and Lowell Thomas, who also have tremendous audiences, speak their pieces during the supper hour, placing a heavy burden on Heatter, whose audience is presumably already in possession of the latest advices. He is thus compelled to wrap the bare bones of the news in dramatic garb, a technique which has resulted in his being known in the trade as "The Voice of Doom" and "The Crier." His major interests are the final defeat of Fascism and the formulation of a workable, democratic peace, but historians may someday record that he reached his peaks of eloquence and insight while speaking of dogs. Heatter feels about dogs the way Churchill feels about the British Empire. No man more staunchly supports those dogs who have laid aside their muzzles and gone off to war. "They have shared our great adventure, they must share our days of peace," he often says. Recently, eleven stray dogs found prowling around an Army camp were sentenced to death. Heatter paid tribute to an Army man who arranged for ten of them to be pardoned and adopted as mascots. "Only one, an old dog, had to go," Heatter said. "Now, some men wouldn't have cared about those dogs . . . and their dying. Outside your window tonight, tiny friends of man, birds and small animals, are fighting to live. . . . They will need food and they—they—will repay it handsomely a thousand times over." On another occasion, delivering a memorial tribute to the distinguished cocker spaniel My Own Brucie, he said, "I asked a man today who was always close to the dog, 'What was he like away from all the dazzling spotlight of competition where he won so much fame? And the man who knew him well told me he carried himself with the simple modesty which belongs only to the truly great— in men or dogs. . . . He was a dog of rare courage. He was in a car one day driving to Boston. There was a crash and a bad shaking up. Yet a few hours later he went into the ring and his poise and control were an amazing thing . . . and when they gave a dinner in his honor in Poughkeepsie, men who watched him said he looked up at everyone as if he seemed to understand and asked in all humility, 'Surely this isn't all for me?' "

In a recent film, "Once Upon a Time," starring Cary Grant and a caterpillar, Hollywood recognized Heatter's fame as a champion of dumb animals. In the picture, Curley, a dancing caterpillar, appears doomed to anonymity until Gabriel Heatter, a commentator, shows interest in his career, speaks well over the air of his achievement, and overnight brings him fame and fortune. Heatter did not play himself in the picture, but he got seventy-five hundred dollars for the use of his name. Together with his younger brother, Max, he saw the picture at the Music Hall. "Gabe burst into tears," Max told friends. "And why not? Has any man ever received such a tribute during his own lifetime?"

In order to justify the faith placed in his judgment by millions of people, Heatter feels that he must give his undivided attention to the perplexing problems of the world. Mrs. Heatter, a quiet, composed woman to whom he has been married twenty-nine years, makes certain that the wheels of the household spin noiselessly. Under her guidance, the Heatter kitchen provides a steady flow of her husband's favorite foods: clear soups, poached eggs, chickens, fresh vegetables, and puddings. Singlehanded, she turns into a studio whatever room Heatter wishes to broadcast from, flouting accepted acoustical practice by merely hanging two or three heavy sound-deadening curtains along the walls. Radio engineers are at a loss to explain her success. Heatter broadcasts from Freeport during the spring, fall, and early winter, from his New York apartment during the late winter, and from his farm throughout the summer months. The Heatters have two children—Maida, a serious-looking girl in her early twenties, who designs costume jewelry, is married, and has a daughter; and Basil, a twenty-three-year-old officer in the Navy. Ever since Basil was wounded last summer while commanding a PT boat in the Pacific, Heatter has kept his social engagements to a minimum. He rarely leaves the house except on Saturday, his only day off, when he may dine with a Supreme Court justice or an ambassador or take Mrs. Heatter to dinner at Longchamps. "No fancy gravies at Longchamps, nothing disguised," he says. Heatter has been on the air for eleven years. For the past eight, his brother Max has handled his commercial affairs, leaving him ample time to ponder. Max, a crisp, businesslike version of Willie Howard, lives with his family in Brooklyn and used to manufacture clothes. Gabriel ponders during practically every waking moment. He gets up at seven, drinks several cups of coffee, settles down with a batch of newspapers, and switches on the nearest of the dozen or so radios scattered throughout each of the Heatter establishments. As befits a mature seer, he selects the items for his broadcasts with great care. "The work humbles and mellows a man," he once told a friend. "I say to myself, what are today's Heatter stories? What will people be talking about at breakfast tomorrow? Will Russia fight Japan? Incidentally, I'm on record saying yes! *Where* is Hitler? Is the monsoon season over in Burma? Watch Burma! Heatter stories, *every one of them!* I read of hotels serving cottage cheese instead of butter, and I ask myself *how many people eat in hotels?* Not many. Not a Heatter story. But news of heroism—either of men or dogs—and of people holding to their faith, *these* are Heatter stories!" By eight in the morning he has selected three important items, and by lunchtime he has written a two-thousand-word script. During the afternoon, as the result of more ponderings and the arrival of more newspapers, he invariably discards his first draft and starts all over again.

Heatter has sources of information other than those available to the public at newsstands, and he generally considers them during the afternoon. He receives hundreds of mimeographed handouts each week from publicity agencies of the Allied governments, he telephones the Office of War Information, the British Information Services, and so on every day, and he subscribes to a news ticker service, which costs him about $10,000 a year. He insists that a phone call from Heatter is not treated as a routine matter. "I speak with men attached to the foreign departments of Britain and France," he says, lowering his voice, "and from time to time," he adds, glancing quickly about his study, "mysterious envelopes arrive bearing news—from—the—underground!" In the afternoon, Heatter will often answer the doorbell and talk with delivery boys or the mailman. "We have not yet scratched the surface of what people think, and I learn what people think from people," he is fond of saying. Max arrives at the house shortly after four o'clock, bearing more news of the outside world. "Max gets around, sees people, talks with them," Gabriel says. "He, too, is my eyes and ears."

At five-thirty, Gabriel sits down to supper with Mrs. Heatter and Max, and together they thrash out the manifold problems of the day. "What is the product for tonight, Max?" Heatter is likely to say.

"Kreml shampoo, Gabe," says Max.

"Impossible to follow the Burma jungle item with a shampoo," says Gabriel. "It will have to come after the Polish question."

"Definitely," says Max.

At six, Heatter retires to his study to make further revisions in his manuscript and Max takes his stand by the news ticker. If any momentous story comes over, Max promptly informs Gabriel. On his farm and in his New York apartment, the ticker is installed in a room next to his study, and in Freeport it is in a bombproof shelter in the basement. Fearing the worst, Heatter called in experts the week after Pearl Harbor to strengthen the walls and ceiling of the cellar and had it equipped with stirrup pumps, sandbags, and sufficient provisions to keep the family alive during a protracted siege. He turned down his wife's suggestion that the shelter be put in the back yard; he felt that it would create hysteria in the neighborhood if a man of his prescience were to be seen galloping from the house and ducking into his bombproof. Heatter never broadcasts from his cellar, but it was kept stocked with food for such a contingency until a year or so ago, when it was announced that the Nazis had shifted from bomber to fighter production. Ever since the robot bombs first landed in London, he has had the uneasy feeling that the shelter may come in handy.

Not long ago, Heatter invited me to attend one of his broadcasts from Freeport. I arrived shortly before eight o'clock and found him at a long maple desk in his study, looking somewhat haggard. He was speaking over the telephone. "Congratulations, old man, congratulations," he was saying. "Good work! Well done!" Putting down the phone, he told me that he had been talking with an official of the British Information Services. I sat down on a semicircular sofa and asked him why he had congratulated the man. "For the sinking of the Tirpitz," he said quietly. Then he turned to his typewriter and became engrossed in his manuscript. A tall man entered the room, walked to a red lacquer cabinet in one corner, pulled out a number of complicated pieces of broadcasting equipment, and put them on top of it. He told me his name was Nilson and that he was the engineer of the Heatter programs; he arrives each evening at eight, hooks up the telephone circuit to WOR, and handles the technical problems of the broadcast. In a moment, Max rushed up from the basement and put a yellow slip of paper beside the typewriter on Heatter's desk. "Ticker," Max said. "Western front!"

Heatter looked up. "Thank you, Max," he said. "The news comes to us wherever we are—New York, Freeport, Connecticut. Remember my vacation at Ponte Vedra, Florida?" Max nodded. "Ponte Vedra, Florida," Heatter continued. "The microphone fifty feet from the beach. I could hear the pounding of the surf. Ponce de León landed there, Max."

"He couldn't have picked a better spot, Gabe," Max said, and went back to the basement.

Nilson spun several dials on the broadcasting equipment. "Testing at Heatter's. Are you there, Ab?" he said into a hand microphone. "Zero woof, zero woof, zero woof." Nilson walked across the room and put another microphone on Heatter's desk. "Zero woof, zero woof, zero woof," he said. At eight-thirty, Heatter ran a hand wearily through his hair and walked out of the room with his manuscript, almost colliding with Max, who was coming in again, his arms loaded with a thick rubber mat, a pocket watch, a thermos bottle, a glass, and a red electric lantern. He placed the mat under the microphone on Heatter's desk, and the thermos bottle, watch, glass, and lantern alongside the microphone. "The mat absorbs sound," he told me. "It's squooshy because Mrs. Heatter washed it a couple of months ago and it never dried. Gabe needs the lantern in case the lights go out." He went down to the basement again. I was beginning to wonder what had happened to Heatter when Nilson explained that he was resting in his bedroom, a nightly custom.

For twenty-five minutes there was a profound silence in the house, interrupted only by an occasional faint tapping from the ticker. At 8:56, Mrs. Heatter came into the study with her knitting and sat down beside me on the sofa. "Zero woof, zero woof, zero woof," Nilson said into his microphone. Mrs. Heatter lighted a cigarette. I could now hear Heatter in his bedroom, down the hall, vigorously clearing his throat. At 8:59, he walked briskly into the study and sat down again at his desk. He took a box of Vicks cough drops from a drawer, put one on the tip of his tongue, poured himself a glass of water, and swished the lozenge back and forth in his mouth so hard that it clicked against his teeth. A few seconds after nine, Nilson wagged a finger at Heatter, who hastily maneuvered the lozenge behind his teeth, swallowed the water, spit the lozenge into a wastepaper basket, rested his elbows on his desk, and said into his microphone, "Good evening, everyone! My wires are open tonight for news from Tokio!" He was on the air. His face bore a solemn, dedicated expression. At 9:06: "This much, however, is certain—the dismal night can't last forever. . . ." Maida strolled into the room and took a seat near the window. At 9:10: "Forhans on your toothbrush, Forhans for your gums . . ." Max entered and shrugged his shoulders, which seemed to mean that there were no last-minute global developments. Maida strolled out. At 9:14, Max walked in a crouch in front of his brother's desk and held up one finger. ". . . and all the pain of that dog's dying," said Heatter. "Ladies and gentlemen, your friend and mine, Len Sterling!"

As far back as he can remember, Heatter, who was born in lower Manhattan in 1890, the son of an immigrant clothing sub-contractor, has never been at a loss for words. By the time Gabriel could construct a compound sentence, he had begun to frequent a neighborhood settlement house in Brooklyn, where his family had moved before he was three, and become one of the more voluble members of a group known as the Young Americans. Several nights a week grownup volunteer leaders led the group in discussions of Americanism and civics. One man, a manufacturer of gas appliances, often took him into vacant lots to instruct him in the fine points of public speaking, and as a result he won third prize (bronze medal) in a settlement-house declamation contest with his delivery of a passage from *Richard III*. "He was only a lad of ten," a neighborhood veteran recently recalled, "but he sure sounded like a mad old king." Heatter soon graduated from recitations to debates and mock trials. In one trial he was elevated to counsel for the defendant, but the accused was convicted, the result, Heatter insisted, of Heatter's arm being in a sling, which limited the scope of his gestures. Although he would have preferred to devote himself exclusively to preparing and delivering addresses, he attended P. S. 109 and then Boys' High School in Brooklyn, sold papers, delivered telegrams, and accompanied his father, every Friday afternoon, to a Russian bath. Father Heatter invariably took two loaves of bread and several herring with him to the bath. He and Gabriel would mount a tier of wooden benches and sit near the top, steaming quietly. Heatter feels that the conversations he had with his father during those weekly baths were the genesis of his social consciousness. "From time to time Father would tear off a piece of bread and take a piece of herring," Heatter remarks, "and hand them to me, saying, 'Gabriel, never forget that you are the son of a workingman!' "

Heatter had no opportunity to address the general public until 1905, when William Randolph Hearst, who was a candidate for Mayor that year, required the services of several boys to speak in his behalf on street corners throughout the five boroughs. Heatter received the Brooklyn appointment. He got five dollars an evening to take up a stand at places where Hearst was scheduled to speak, attract a crowd, and hold their interest until the arrival of the candidate himself. Heatter, on foot, preceded Hearst through Brooklyn by twenty minutes, jabbering almost incessantly. As the candidate approached, his chauffeur would loudly honk the horn of his car, a signal to Heatter to end his remarks and hurry to the next designated spot. Hearst ran on a platform of municipal ownership of public utilities, which gave Heatter ample opportunity to tell his audiences that he was the son of a workingman. His reception was mixed. He was often greeted with cries of "Get to bed!" and "Do your homework!" and once he was hit in the mouth with a tomato, but his picture appeared in Hearst's *Sunday American*, labelled "The Boy Orator of Brooklyn," and at the end of the campaign, Hearst, still only a publisher, gave him a ten-dollar bonus and got him a job on the Brooklyn *Times*. Heatter immediately left high school and for the next fifteen years floundered about in journalism, covering the courts for a series of Brooklyn and Manhattan papers, writing occasional human-interest stories about slum conditions, and trying to become an editorial writer. "I wished to improve the condition of the poor," he says, "but nobody seemed interested." For a while he attended New York University Law School, but too briefly to receive a degree. In 1915, he married a Brooklyn girl from his neighborhood, and after the war they went to Europe. He hoped to do free-lance articles as an observer of the effects of the war on humanity. A year later they were back in the United States, living in a small house outside Freeport. He had observed the effects of the war on humanity in Italy, Austria, and France, and had caught a heavy cold in London, but he had sold frighteningly few pieces. "As I look back," he says, "those, too, were the dark times."

For several months after his return, Heatter lolled about the house, took long walks, and fished. He was still determined to write, and while he was surf-casting one morning he got to thinking about the interest inherent not in tenements or the aftermath of war but in the relation between man and the great outdoors. A week later he got a job as a staff writer for *Forest and Stream*, a publication whose editorial offices smelled of pine cones. A man born in a canoe in the upper reaches of the Allagash could have written no more flavorsomely of Nature's wonders than Heatter did. "I spoke often in editorials of a boy sitting by a fireplace looking at the musket of his grandfather," he says. "I wrote, too, of the companionship of a man and a gun, or of a man and a rod, or of a man and a gun and a dog."

In 1922, Heatter left *Forest and Stream* to become editor of the *Shaft*, a monthly house organ published here jointly by three steel companies, Edgar P. Ward's Sons Company, the Summerill Tubing Company, and the Columbia Steel & Shafting Company. He found in industry, as in fish and game, the rugged, inspirational beauty of competition. Even though industry suffered from no marked inferiority complex, it felt the need of a prose poet sensitive to the glories of untrammelled private enterprise. "We were waiting in the outer office of a company president when a man walked by," Heatter wrote in a characteristic editorial. " 'There goes Smith,' explained someone. 'That fellow who never seems to strike out.' 'What does he do?' inquired another. 'I don't recall,' answered the first speaker, 'but I have seen him a hundred times and each time he was just as you see him today, calm, unhurried. The truth is I have never seen him excited about anything in all my life.' 'Well, he may never strike out,' replied the second man, 'but I never hear of him hitting any home runs either.' *He never struck out, but he never hit any home runs either! . . .*" Another editorial said, "Do you work for a living, respect your neighbors, believe in the golden rule, pay your debts, cut your hair, shed a real tear of sorrow for your fellow-man in his suffering? Do you believe in the white man's civilization, favor bathtubs, clean homes, and tooth paste? If you do then you are a Babbitt and your children will be Babbitts and so will your grandchildren—down to the last of your seed. . . . Ah, woe is us! The Babbitts!" Steel executives, almost to a man disciples of bathtubs and tooth paste, found solace in Heatter's remarks and urged him to address gatherings of steelworkers along the same general lines. During the twenties and early thirties, he delivered hundreds of inspirational talks at steel mills. "Men," he would say, "this steel has a purpose, this steel you make, these rivets you produce, this bright yellow flame—all have a purpose!" Heatter never quite knew what purpose he had in mind, but he feels that his words were prophetic. "I know now," he says, "that the purpose was to save the world in an avalanche of war production."

From time to time, Heatter took the text of his sermon from the animal world. In a *Shaft* editorial entitled "Faith," he said, "The scene of this story is an American home. The time—last night, tonight, or any night. And the characters are a boy and his dog. The boy's name is Jim and the dog is Bob . . . and during the day an automobile whirls around a corner, and a moment later a boy's world is brought to ashes as his dog lies dead at his feet. That same evening a friendly father places a hand on a boy's shoulder and tells him he must be brave and forget. 'Bob is dead and gone, never to return.' . . . 'But, Dad, Bob must be somewhere, a dog just can't go out like a light . . . and not ever be any more.' And his father struggles for words which do not come. . . .'"

The *Shaft* and its editorial writer met the depression with characteristic fortitude ("The Lord is reported to have sent famine and flood into the world of men in order to test their devotion or teach them to mend their ways. Who knows but that a . . . depression may have been designed merely to teach men a new understanding of the word— Friendship?"), but by 1932, Heatter had become militantly concerned with economic realities, though he still wrote for the *Shaft*. An open letter from Heatter to Norman Thomas appeared in the December 14, 1932, issue of the *Nation*. It ended, "You will find millions of followers if you will take the Socialist program, strip it bare of the verbiage it has gathered through the ages, and offer it to the people in language they understand and appreciate. If this is betrayal, let those who are living in the dead past make the most of it." Over the years the incident has grown in Heatter's mind, and he often talks about it as though he had engaged in a series of debates with Thomas comparable to those between Lincoln and Douglas. Actually, he got six dollars for the article and an invitation from Donald Flamm, then owner of WMCA, to elaborate upon it over the air. Heatter delivered his remarks with such majestic tonality that Flamm offered him the post of nightly news commentator at forty dollars a week. Sensing the hand of fate, Heatter accepted; he continued, however, to write editorials for the *Shaft*.

Within six months, Heatter had answered a call from the manager of WOR, and twice weekly, at seventy-five dollars a broadcast, he wrestled with the news under the auspices of the Modern Industrial Bank

("I could write a saga of human experiences on help and progress and new courage the Modern Industrial Bank has made possible for thousands"). His voice had a certain fascination for thrifty devotees of the bank, but he did little to distinguish himself until the winter of 1935, when the Mutual Broadcasting System, of which WOR had by then become a part, asked him to broadcast the trial of Bruno Hauptmann. The network offered him fifty dollars a week expenses but no pay, the program being unsponsored. He went to Flemington, at Mrs. Heatter's insistence, and established broadcasting headquarters in a pool hall across from the courthouse. "I saw the trial as a daily drama," he says today. "Here was a dead baby—nothing funny about this—and all the characters of a play." Heatter delivered three fifteen-minute broadcasts a day—at noon, 6 P.M., and 9 P.M.—and at the end of the second day he found himself sponsored, at eight hundred dollars a week, by Tastyeast, Grove's Bromo-Quinine, and the Modern Industrial Bank. (Mutual immediately cancelled the fifty dollars a week for expenses.) At the invitation of the presiding justice, Judge Trenchard, whose wife, a Heatter fan, had urged him to "make Mr. Heatter, the radio man, comfortable," he was installed at the court clerk's table. No reporter had a better view of the drama, but Heatter was far from comfortable. To push his way through the crowded courtroom and across to the poolroom, which he did three times a day, he required the assistance of a Jersey state trooper. It was eighty degrees in the courtroom, but the pool hall was unheated, and he had to deliver his broadcasts wearing fur gloves and with the collar of his ulster turned up around his ears. Snow lay deep in the streets of Flemington, and during the six weeks of the trial Heatter rarely removed his galoshes. "Colds," he says now, "were a continuing menace." He feels that he warded them off by almost incessantly munching bran biscuits with which he had filled his pockets. Mrs. Heatter occasionally went down to Flemington with a thermos of hot coffee. This led to additional health problems. "I deeply appreciated the thought," Heatter says, "but I invariably drank the coffee just after a broadcast, creating considerable perspiration. Then I had to sit fifteen minutes and cool off before going into the street. And over in the courtroom I'd begin to perspire again." Unaware of these difficulties, Heatter's radio audience enthusiastically followed his reporting of the trial. In his words, Hauptmann sat most of the time "with his lips pressed together" in a courtroom filled with "the whispering and humming of spectators," before a jury composed of "twelve good men and women true." From time to time, defense counsel Reilly's "red face turned crimson. His jowls quivered, the muscles in his neck stood out." The trial ended "on a note as strangely haunting and as mysterious as any a courtroom ever held," and it made Heatter an established commentator, the logical choice of millions to describe Hauptmann's execution.

On the afternoon of Friday, April 3, 1936, the day of the execution, Heatter went to Trenton and had a talk with the Governor of New Jersey. The Governor assured him that there would be no hitch in the proceedings—Hauptmann would die at 8 P.M. or a few moments thereafter. Heatter set up headquarters in a hotel room overlooking the state penitentiary. He spent the rest of the afternoon devising an intricate series of signals to ensure that he would be the first man to broadcast the news that Hauptmann had drawn his last breath; Heatter felt that his audience would settle for nothing less. Mutual was to install a man in the warden's office, who would carry the news to a man in the corridor, who would tell a man at the gate, who would wave a handkerchief three times to a man standing at a window in Heatter's room, who would turn to him and say, "It's happened!" To play safe, a radio would also be installed in Heatter's room—where other Mutual men would be standing by—and would be kept tuned softly to another network. Heatter expected, on the Governor's say-so, to be on the air for no more than five or six minutes. At eight, he began to speak. "I am in a hotel room looking at a certain window . . . as close as I wish to get to a room in which a man is about to die . . . could not bring myself to enter the chamber itself . . . merely waiting for a signal . . . will come in a moment . . . merely a moment . . . there will be no reprieve, of that I am certain . . . perhaps I am wrong, perhaps the cold, silent man has talked at last." Not for an instant did his voice betray that he had exhausted his prepared material and was beginning to ad-lib. At 8:12, a Mutual man put a note on Heatter's desk saying "Keep talking until it happens." Heatter cast an agonized glance at the back of the man at the window. "Wonder what's going on in that room . . . it wouldn't be a confession . . . no, that silent fellow, lips pressed together, would not confess . . . an accomplice? . . . type who works alone . . . reprieve? . . . doubtful if Governor . . ." Half past eight came, and Heatter had whipped up a monumental perspiration. He had visions of spending two or three months in bed with pneumonia. Barely pausing for breath, he launched into a recapitulation of the trial. He described the courtroom in minute detail. He analyzed the characters of the prosecutor, the defendant, Lindbergh, of several of the jurors. He discussed the rôle of Dr. Condon. ". . . yes, we are all in the same boat, you, I, judges, lawyers, Mrs. Hauptmann, the mother of that dead baby . . . the whole world waiting, tense, waiting . . ." At 8:47:30 the man in the warden's office signalled the man in the corridor, who ran to the man at the gate, who waved his handkerchief three times to the man at Heatter's window, who said, "It's happened!" but forgot to turn around. Heatter didn't hear him. ". . . all in the same boat . . . all of us tense . . . possible reprieve," droned Heatter, as the several Mutual men in the room turned pale and frantically waved their arms. Heatter snapped his fingers at the man at the window, who at last turned around. "Have you received the signal for which you were waiting?" asked Heatter, and the question was heard by millions. "Yes, sir," said the man. "Bruno Hauptmann," Heatter announced, "is dead."

Heatter was first with the news, a good ten seconds ahead of all other networks, and his forty-eight minutes of continuous ad-libbing had left his radio audience limp with admiration. "In this obscene muddle which was really more of an indictment of the human race than of the poor wretch who is now dead," Hendrik van Loon wired him, "your work tonight stands forth as the one relieving spot of dignity and decency." Soon after, Heatter was being sponsored, at various moments of the day and night, by Rogers Peet, Johns-Manville, Sanka, the Modern Industrial Bank, and a shirt called Big Yank. Suddenly finding himself an overwhelming enterprise, he called upon Max to take over his business affairs. Under Max's direction he cut down his work for the *Shaft* (for which he continued to write editorials until 1944), and, in addition to making his various news broadcasts, became master of ceremonies for "We, the People," a radio program on which he interviewed deep-sea divers, lady wrestlers, the widow of Dutch Schultz, and others. In 1941 he gave up "We, the People" and applied himself exclusively to the news, achieving his present eminence in a world at war.

Heatter occasionally finds surcease from the flow of news by evaluating himself in relation to recent historical events. I happened to be at his house in Freeport late one afternoon recently when such a mood came over him. He was typing a revision of his broadcast in his study, a cozy room hung with heavy curtains of green and yellow. Switching off the radio at his elbow and rising from his desk, he summoned the members of his family who happened to be at home. The first to respond was his granddaughter, Toni, who climbed up beside me on the sofa. "I'm two and one half," she said. Then Maida arrived, carrying a tray filled with olives, celery, and sliced carrots, which she put on a coffee table in front of the sofa. She sat down beside us. Max emerged from the cellar in his shirtsleeves, presumably having left the ticker unattended, and took a chair near the door. Heatter paced back and forth for several minutes along a panelled wall lined with bookshelves, one of which contained nothing but an autographed picture of President Roosevelt, in a leather frame. "Perhaps my influence," Heatter said suddenly, "is in the small American town, ordinarily suspicious, hostile to Europe. Because I saw this war coming—saw Hitler, Franco, Goebbels—I presented a realistic foreign policy. I spoke for the little man everywhere, the little man who would fight Hitler, the *people*. Some sneered. 'What do you mean, the *people*?' they asked." (Toni slipped off the sofa and made for the coffee table. "Toni want a carrot?" Heatter said. "Toni take a carrot!" Toni took a carrot and climbed back on the sofa.) "Tossing away all logic and military fact," Heatter went on, "I said again and again, 'The sky over England will never fall into Hitler's hands!' And in the bleak time, I said, 'Stalingrad will never surrender!' "

"Definitely," interrupted Max, "and competing the whole time with Burns and Allen!"

"You're right, Max," said Heatter. "With Holland, France, and Belgium gone, I still had hope. 'This is futile,' said the cynics. 'It is men versus machines,' I said. 'Men with hope—and help will come.' I remember the night France fell. Max brought the news at eight-ten. I went on the air at nine, and for one minute there was dead air, not a sound. *Heatter was crying.* I told the people what it meant to me personally to say that France had surrendered, but that very night *I began to fight back!* 'These are the Quislings who have surrendered,' I said, 'the traitors, not the people of France.' "

Heatter sat down behind his desk. "Pearl Harbor," he said slowly. "I must confess I didn't know it was coming. I had reservations for Florida—first vacation in years. That night I struck a solemn note. Five seconds of silence. I have always talked with a great deal of warmth about the people of China." (Toni tottered toward him, climbed into his lap, and began to hit the keys of his typewriter. "Toni want to play bing-bang?" asked Heatter. Toni shook her head, and he put her back on the sofa.) "And as the tide began to turn, people began to listen," he said, "began to take this man seriously. Now by the hundreds they write and say, 'Send Heatter to the trial of Hitler, let him broadcast the trial.' Oh, as I look back, suppose England had fallen and Stalingrad gone down?" He walked to the window and stood staring out. His hands were clasped behind his back. "Heatter," he said, "would have been a dead duck!"

From: The Perfect Glow

Invisible as his quirks may be, Oscar Hammerstein II is a major eccentric. "I am in love with a wonderful theatre," he often says. It is one of the monumental love affairs of history. He cannot enter a theatre without experiencing that acute aesthetic dizziness reported by travellers when they gaze for the first time upon the Taj Mahal. Hammerstein is six feet one and a half inches tall, weighs slightly less than two hundred pounds, and has the broad, hunched shoulders, the long, easy gait, and the ready, comforting, it's-going-to-be-all-right-fellows smile of a popular football coach, but passing through a stage door makes him feel weak and helpless. The sight of a bare stage illuminated by a single glaring rehearsal light sends sharp pains up and down his back. These sensations are nothing compared to the exquisite paralysis that comes over him when he stands at the rear of a packed theatre and observes an audience enjoying one of his own shows. Outwardly, he is calm, even indifferent, on such an occasion. Standing quietly, with his arms resting on the rail, he could easily be mistaken for a theatre manager. The only hint that the Furies are raging within is a slight droop at the corners of his mouth, which gives him the look of a man who fears, as Hammerstein feared at the Victoria when he was four, that he might any moment get sick to his stomach. Often, while one of his songs is being sung, he walks swiftly into the empty lobby and bursts into tears. Hammerstein has listened to "The Surrey with the Fringe on Top" at least five hundred times, but every time he has been reduced to weeping. "It's so beautiful that it makes a man want to cry," he explains.

From: *The Perfect Glow*

Hammerstein's overpowering devotion to the theatre includes not only an intense appreciation of his own lyrics but an equally intense appreciation of the music composed for them by his partner, Richard Rodgers. Rodgers is sometimes able to sit down at a piano and turn out a hit tune in a few minutes. His head is filled with an extraordinary collection of whistleable airs that require only a set of lyrics to bring them out into the open. Hammerstein is a slow and tortured writer. He often labors for weeks to produce a refrain of fifty words or so. He worked for five weeks, for example, over the lyrics of "Hello, Young Lovers!," in *The King and I*, and finally threw all his previous efforts aside and wrote the song, in a frenzy of creation, in two days. Once he has completed the lyrics for a song, he is spiritually and physically exhausted. As a result, he is exceedingly attached to what he writes, and when he listens to the words he has a tendency to recall the suffering he underwent while putting them together. Hammerstein is a tolerant man, but his tolerance stops short of letting anyone tamper with so much as a word of his lyrics. Some years ago, a radio singer, not quite sure of "Oh, What a Beautiful Mornin'!," inadvertently substituted "An' a li'l ol' willer is laughin' at me" for "An' a ol' weepin' willer is laughin' at me." Hammerstein was tuned to the program, his eyes full of tears. Shocked by the alteration, he switched off the radio, and swore that *that* particular singer would have a pretty hard time ever getting into one of *his* shows.

Although Hammerstein is sentimental about the theatre, his affection has a pragmatic base. "Oscar is a very careful dreamer," one of his oldest friends says. In Oscar's estimation, the public is the final judge of what is and what is not a work of art, and he has small patience with the experimental theatre. The test of a good play, for Hammerstein, is the length of the line at the box office on a rainy morning. "With my shows," he says, "I don't want to wake up in the morning and have to worry about whether or not the weather will affect the size of the house." In spite of his firm faith in the judgment of audiences, Hammerstein has been engaged for years in a strange personal struggle with them. "It's a matter of love and hate," he explains. He has evolved a method of evaluating an audience's reactions to a show, which he uses during the out-of-town tryouts of his productions. He stands at the rear rail and observes the backs of the heads of the audience. He believes he can pretty well figure out what is going on inside the heads. "There's a silent criticism felt by all actors, and everybody else who knows the theatre," he says, "but my method goes beyond that. And I don't pay any attention to coughs, either. They don't mean a thing. But if the heads are motionless, we're O.K. If they move either up or down or from side to side, we're in trouble. If people start rustling through the programs, we're in *real* trouble." Hammerstein does not confine his researches to the backs of heads. He often goes into a box and peers down at the faces of the audience. If the customers are enjoying a show, he feels, an indefinable glow comes over their faces. "I can't describe it, I just know it when I see it," he says. He may concentrate on one face and, crouched low in the box, await the arrival of the glow. If, instead of the glow, the face reveals dislike or, what is even worse in Hammerstein's opinion, no expression at all, the muscles of his stomach become even tighter. "There are faces that rise to haunt me," he says. "Years ago, a man sat in the third row in a tryout in Trenton, a big, fat, red-faced, snorey fellow, everybody around him laughing and laughing, and he just sat there, no expression, no nothing. I remember every line of that face. I would recognize him anywhere. My dislike is still quite active. I remember, too, a young woman once in Baltimore. What a glow! The perfect glow! A lovely, sweet face, responsive to everything!"

Hammerstein feels that the severest test of how a show is working out comes the moment the first-act curtain falls. Just before this moment, Hammerstein leans forward and cups a hand to one ear, then stiffens like a bird dog. "If that curtain drops and there is silence followed by silence—oh, we're in trouble!" he says. "If that curtain falls and there is silence followed swiftly by an excited buzz of conversation, a sort of ground swell of buzzy talk, we're probably safe." After only a minute or two of such listening, he rushes into the lobby. There, head down, he mixes in with the crowd. "I concentrate on a man and woman who spy another man and woman they know," he says. "If one pair approaches the other and says a few quick words about the play, and then there's general conversation about the play, we're O.K. If they merely say, 'Pretty good first act. When are you and Mary coming over for bridge?' we're in *real* trouble!" Hammerstein slips back into the theatre after the intermission and again is on the alert for the glow. He thinks that the glow is even more important during the second act. "If they glow when they get back into their seats," he says, "the chances are that the glow is permanent and we have 'em for good." Hammerstein feels that the glow induced by *Oklahoma!* may never be duplicated within his lifetime or anybody else's. "People returned to their seats for the second act and the glow was like the light from a thousand lanterns," he says. "You could *feel* the glow, it was that bright." . . .

Uppermost in Hammerstein's mind while he is writing a lyric is the larynx of the performer who will have to stand on a stage and sing the thing. "The larynxes of singers are limited," he has remarked. He tries to provide convenient breathing places in his lyrics, and to avoid climaxes in which a singer will be straining at a word that closes the larynx. "A word like 'sweet' would be a very bad word on which to sing a high note," he says. "The *e* sound closes the larynx, and the singer cannot let go with his full voice. Furthermore, the *t* ending the word is a hard consonant, which would cut the singer off and thwart his and the composer's desire to sustain the note." Hammerstein worries a good deal about closed larynxes, and he is inclined to brood morbidly over the times he has permitted his affection for a word to outweigh his concern over a closed larynx. For example, he often berates himself for ending the refrain of "What's the Use of Wond'rin'?," in *Carousel*, with "You're his girl and he's your feller, And all the rest is talk." He feels that if he were to write this song again, his last line would go something like "And that's all you need to know." "The singer could have hit the *o* vowel and held it as long as she wanted to, eventually pulling applause," he says. The song was not a distinguished success as sheet music or on records, and Hammerstein is convinced that the word "talk," which closed the singer's larynx at the finish, was responsible for this. The majority of his last lines are, he feels, forceful larynx-openers, conducive to applause-pulling, such as "Oh, what a beautiful day!," "Once you have found her, never let her go!," "Ol' man river, he jes keeps rollin' along," and "Bali Ha'i, Bali Ha'i, Bali Ha'i."

Hammerstein recalls with painful poignancy the problems he faced during the creation of certain lyrics. To a person who does not write lyrics, many of his dilemmas might seem elementary, but to Hammerstein they represent heroic struggles with the muse. "The problem of a duet for the lovers in *Oklahoma!* seemed insurmountable," he says. His leading characters—Curly, the cowboy, and Laurey, the young girl—are very much attracted to each other, but Laurey, who is shy, tries to hide her feelings. Curly does not like her attitude, and assumes a fairly belligerent one of his own. Instead of expressing their love, they take to bickering and squabbling. Since both Hammerstein and Rodgers wished to maintain the atmosphere of crackle and snap until at least the second act, it was impossible for Hammerstein to write a simple song in which Curly and Laurey said, out loud and with their larynxes open, "I love you." Hammerstein talked his dilemma over with Rodgers at great length. Together they hit upon the solution of having the two young people caution each other against demonstrating any warmth, since this might be construed by outsiders as an expression of affection. "People Will Say We're in Love" was the successful result. Hammerstein had another problem when he collaborated with Rodgers on the musical film *State Fair*. In the story, a young girl has the blues, for no particular reason, since her family is about to treat her to a visit to a state fair. Hammerstein wanted a song for her mood—it was time for a song, anyway—and it occurred to him, while he was pondering, that her melancholy condition bore a resemblance to spring fever. This thought made Hammerstein even more melancholy than the girl, since state fairs are held in the fall, not the spring. "I toyed with the notion of having her say, in effect, it's autumn but I have spring fever, so it might as well be spring," Hammerstein has said. He casually mentioned this possible solution to Rodgers. "That's it!" cried Rodgers. "All my doubts were gone," Hammerstein says. "I had a partner behind me." Out of this came the well-known "It Might As Well Be Spring."

Hammerstein thinks that one reason for his success as a lyricist is that his vocabulary is not enormous. A huge vocabulary, he is convinced, hampers a lyric writer; it might persuade him to substitute "fantasy," "reverie," "nothingness," "chimera," "figment," or even "air-drawn dagger" for the simple word "dream." He has discovered that a lyric writer seems always to have a supply of the word "dream" on hand, much as a housewife keeps salt in the house. Before composing the lyrics for *South Pacific*, he decided that he would avoid "dream." He felt that it had been turning up too often in his lyrics. When he had finished the *South Pacific* lyrics, he found that "dream" appeared with frightening regularity. "Bali Ha'i" speaks of "Your own special hopes, your own special dreams." "Some Enchanted Evening" says, "Then fly to her side, and make her your own, or all through your life you may dream all alone" and "The sound of her laughter will sing in your dreams." "Happy Talk" declares that "You gotta have a dream; if you don't have a dream, how you gonna have a dream come true? If you don't talk happy an' you never had a dream, den you'll never have a dream come true."

Even one of the songs withdrawn from *South Pacific* during the pre-Broadway tryout said, "The sky is a bright canary yellow . . . you will dream about the view." Hammerstein lost his dream of the view but retained the view itself—the bright canary-yellow sky in "A Cockeyed Optimist."

The word "dream" has worried Hammerstein in more ways than one. Not only has it turned up uninvited in his lyrics but its meaning, he feels, is not precisely clear to him. He is certain that he has never written a word in which he did not believe, which did not spring from the heart, and he is therefore disturbed by the fact that he and the word "dream" don't entirely understand each other. "The most important ingredient of a good song is sincerity," he has often remarked. "Let the song be yours and yours alone." He can put down such words as "love," "ain't," "feelin'," "rain," "yes," "forget," "home," "blue," "star," "believe," "arms," "nice," "little," "moon," "trees," "kiss," "sky," "dame," "beautiful," "baby," again and again, and he has been doing so for thirty years, and his only concern is whether they belong in a lyric, or at that particular point in a lyric. These words do not trouble him at all. The word "love" poses no problems for him, and he has no qualms about using it all the time. He will write down, "I'm in love, I'm in love, I'm in love, I'm in love, I'm in love with a wonderful guy" or "Dat's love! Dat's love! Dat's love! Dat's love!" without hesitation. He will even dwell upon the idea—"Love is quite a simple thing, and nothing so bewildering, no matter what the poets sing, in words and phrases lyrical. Birds find bliss in every tree, and fishes kiss beneath the sea, so when love comes to you and me, it really ain't no miracle"—eat a large supper, sleep eight hours, and rise the next morning to write another lyric about love. But the word "dream" perplexes him, even though he once went so far into dreamland in "Music in the Air" as to write, "There's a dream beyond a dream beyond a dream beyond a dream." It first made a real nuisance of itself seventeen years ago, while he was working with Sigmund Romberg on a motion picture. Romberg had turned out a waltz tune, and Hammerstein took it home to compose the lyrics. The moment he finished looking over the music, the first line, which he also thought would make a good title, popped into his head: "When I grow too old to dream." A moment later, a second line miraculously popped into his head, below the first: "I'll have you to remember." "I have it!" he recalls crying out loud. " 'When I grow too old to dream, I'll have you to remember.' "

Suddenly, and for perhaps the first time in his life, he was afflicted with a curious sensation that something was wrong with his words. He realized that he didn't understand what he had written. He remembers that he said to himself, "Too old for what kind of dreams? As a matter of fact, when you're old, aren't you likely to dream more than at any other time in your life, don't you look back and dream about the past?" For three weeks, he struggled with other words, but he kept returning to the original ones. "I loved to sing it to myself, alone in my study," he says. He decided to stick to these lines, and the song became a big hit, but its triumph shook Hammerstein deeply, since innumerable colleagues asked—and ask to this day—what the words meant. Before writing "When I grow too old to dream, I'll have you to remember," Hammerstein had religiously believed in simple, unambiguous lyrics. If he wanted to ask, "Why do I love you? Why do you love me?," he went ahead and asked it. Here, however, was a mysterious, perhaps meaningless combination of words, and they were commercially successful. The more Hammerstein brooded over the lyric, the more he felt that he had stumbled onto something bigger than himself. A year or so ago, still brooding, he brought the matter up in the introduction to his collection of lyrics. "Gertrude Stein has, of course, this unspecific approach to the use of words," he wrote, "and Edith Sitwell, in her group of songs entitled 'Façade,' has made a deliberate attempt to write words with special emphasis on sound and very little attention to meaning or clarity. I do not believe that the future of good lyric writing lies in this direction, but my experience with 'When I grow too old to dream' forces me to admit that there is something in the idea. It belongs with the general flight from literalism in all art expression—notably painting—which characterizes the creative works of this century."

From: J. P. Marquand

I have always picked my own subjects, and soon after William Shawn became editor I suggested a Profile of the novelist J. P. Marquand. For years I had admired his work: the incisive commentary on upper-crust America, with special references to the character and social mores of Bostonians. "The Late George Apley" is certainly one of the finest satires in our literature. What the late A. J. Liebling used to call "the boys in the quarterlies" gave little heed to Marquand, but the public loved his work and sent his books skyrocketing onto the best-seller lists. Shawn instantly agreed to the piece, and following his custom with me, he never mentioned the project again until I turned in the finished product. For this one, I decided to break the usual Profile mold, and write a parody of a Marquand novel—the Marquand style, the Marquand rhythms, the Marquand interests, with every fact in the piece absolutely accurate. To satisfy the novel form, and as a counterweight to Marquand himself, I invented a modest, self-effacing, somewhat overwhelmed character, Allison Craig, who had been assigned to write about Marquand for a mythical magazine. (By the way, Craig bears no resemblance to myself, or at least I hope not.)

I said nothing of my parodic plans to Shawn. He phoned me late in the evening after I submitted the piece to say that he was fascinated by it, but found himself strangely apprehensive. For one of the only times in my association with this great editor, he showed signs of editorial fear. "I'm relatively new in this post," he said, "and this is a radical change." There was nothing for me to say except to suggest that his fears were without foundation. He called the next morning. He had reread the piece, and was enthusiastic.

In the following excerpt, Marquand and Craig are on a train from New York to Boston.

The Leaves of Memory Seemed To Make a
Mournful Rustling in the Dark
—Henry Wadsworth Longfellow

Craig interrupted Marquand's thoughts. He leaned across the aisle of the parlor car, and said, "Tell me about your very first novel."

Marquand was ready for him. "Oh, no. I look back on it with horror," he said.

"I guess it was a foolish thing for me to ask about," Craig said. He sank back in his chair with such a defeated air that for a moment Marquand was tempted to talk to him. But then he returned to his thoughts of "The Unspeakable Gentleman."

He finished the novel, had it typed, and took it to Brandt & Brandt, the literary agents. They thought the story had merit, and sent it to the *Ladies' Home Journal*. The *Journal* bought it for two thousand dollars and ran it as a serial. At J. Walter Thompson's, Marquand had been making sixty a week, and the two thousand looked awfully big. "The Unspeakable Gentleman" began, "I have seen the improbable turn true too often not to have it disturb me. Suppose these memoirs still exist when the French Royalist plot of 1805 and my father's peculiar role in it are forgotten," and ended, many pages later, " 'Very much relieved,' he said, 'and yet—and yet I still feel thirsty. The rum decanter, Brutus.' " Marquand today found it difficult to read his earlier stories, and it was only with a good deal of will power, and rarely, that he ever did.

"The Unspeakable Gentleman" presented special problems and unique pains. A few nights after he finished his manuscript, he took it to the University Club, where he was meeting his old classmate George W. Merck. He and Merck started out together for an apartment house in the Thirties, on Park Avenue, where they were to call for some girls and take them to dinner. When Marquand entered the taxicab, he had the manuscript in a suitcase, which he placed in the doorless space alongside the driver (that's where they carried baggage in those days), and it was not until he stepped out of the cab that he realized, with a sudden wave of chill terror, that the suitcase had dropped off the cab. The manuscript

(104)

was not found for ten days—ten terrible days for Marquand—and then only after good old George had done some diligent private-detective work. Marquand was in despair and almost ready to abandon writing as a profession. He was never again to be without a carbon of his work.

The success of *The Unspeakable Gentleman*—it was published in book form by Scribner's after its magazine appearance—encouraged him to go on. The late George Horace Lorimer, then editor of the *Saturday Evening Post*, was enthusiastic about his work, and began to pay him five hundred dollars apiece for short stories. The late Ray Long, at that time editor of *Cosmopolitan*, who was not a man willing to see another editor develop a writer who seemed destined to reach popular heights, instantly began to compete with Lorimer. Lorimer responded, through Brandt & Brandt, with even higher rates. In those days, Marquand was just writing the best he could, and as rapidly as possible, and he aimed his products at the popular market without the slightest remorse. One lived and functioned as best one could.

Marquand's life now was to take a strange, and decisive, turn. While working in Cambridge, he had met Christina Sedgwick, the daughter of Mr. and Mrs. Alexander Sedgwick, and the niece of Ellery Sedgwick, the distinguished editor of the staid *Atlantic Monthly*. The Sedgwick family, although it came from Stockbridge, Massachusetts, where the frogs in the spring were all said to sing, "Sedgwick, Sedgwick, Sedgwick," was one of the intellectual prides of intellectual Boston—scholars, writers, teachers, ministers. They were among the select group who were final arbiters of taste. They were steeped in the traditions of the city, where American culture had been founded and had flourished, and they were nourished by their family traditions. They were a tightly knit group, proud, even arrogant, and to young Marquand from Newburyport and the *Saturday Evening Post* they had an indefinable, awesome quality. Marquand nervously crossed his legs in the parlor car. He tried to shake off his thoughts, but they persisted against his will. He rose and walked to the vestibule of the car, and stood for a moment looking out at the countryside of Rhode Island, but still the thoughts were with him. One can never dismiss some thoughts that lie most deeply within one; no effort of the will can do it. Christina, the mother of his first two children, was dead now. She had died not long ago—many years after she and Marquand were divorced. The marriage lasted nearly thirteen years, a tenderly happy and tenderly unhappy period for him.

He tried to shake the thoughts off, but they would not leave. The period with Christina seemed so far away and yet so near, so much like an experience in a different, delicate world and yet so full of pain and anguish. One can never explain such things. And still they mean so much to a writer—not at the time, God knows, when only the happiness and pain are present, but later, in retrospect. Flashes of memory—scenes and incidents—passed through his mind with the very swiftness of the train that was taking him to Boston.

Christina was a fragile and exquisite, almost otherworldly, person, and Marquand had fallen deeply in love with her. They became engaged in Rome—a classic spot for such an event—in 1922. At the time, he was travelling abroad to look with fascinated eyes at the cathedrals and paintings he had had no time to observe during the war, and she was travelling with her parents. The Sedgwicks moved about Europe with quiet, unhurried, *fin-de-siècle* elegance. Wherever they went, they ran into other Sedgwicks, or collateral Sedgwicks, or, at the very least, people from Boston. Journeying with the Sedgwicks through Italy, looking with wonderment at the glorious relics, at the Tintorettos and the Raphaels, and joining up at the end of each day in some hotel lobby or restaurant with a group of understanding Boston people, Marquand sensed the meaning of Boston and the hold it had on its own kind and on the world. Boston meant a great deal to Marquand, more than he could say.

Marquand and Christina were married back in the States, after the tour. They were married in Stockbridge, at the church where her Uncle Theodore Sedgwick—who was rector of Calvary Church in New York— occasionally preached. They returned for the reception to the old Sedgwick mansion on the main street, a red house gracefully fronted by an elm-studded lawn. The scene came back to him sharply twenty-six years later, when his own daughter, also named Christina, was married in the same church and by the same Theodore Sedgwick. Marquand was embarrassed about going. He had not seen the Sedgwicks since he and Christina were divorced, and he felt that his presence might cause uneasiness among many. Still, his daughter insisted that he give her away, a request that he had no desire to turn down. "I will come, Christina," he told her, "but don't ask me to attend the reception." She agreed that he could slip away immediately after the church service. His daughter understood his feelings. There were many occasions after

Christina's wedding when he thought about its fictional qualities: how he walked down the same aisle with his daughter, in the same church where he had been married, past pews filled with many people who had been at his wedding, seated upright and stately, and wearing on their faces that expression of solemn, half-expectant gaiety that one so often sees at weddings. Yes, it was an ordeal, giving Christina away, and when it was over, and Christina and her husband, Richard E. Welch, Jr.—he was a fine young man, with an excellent New England background, even if a year or so later he did absent-mindedly turn up one night at the Somerset Club wearing a tuxedo, green socks, and brown shoes—had been sealed in holy wedlock, Marquand was touched by the approach to his side of the elderly Ellery Sedgwick. He had rather thought that Ellery, who walked somewhat painfully with a cane, would avoid him. "John," Ellery said, "come back to the house with us. I want you to walk with me through the dog cemetery." Marquand said he would. It had been many years since he had walked through the Sedgwicks' dog cemetery, an ancient burial ground behind the house (the Sedgwicks themselves were buried elsewhere in town, in a pie-shaped burial ground known as the Sedgwick Pie; at the center lay an old ancestor, Judge Theodore Sedgwick, and other Sedgwicks surrounded him, their heads away from the center, so that when they rose they would all face Judge Theodore), clotted with small, well-tended graves, over which stood minute, handsome headstones testifying in Latin to the virtues of deceased Sedgwick dogs: Zozo, Kai, Benvenuto Cellini—a series of canine celebrities going back more than a hundred years and today resting in ancestral quiet. He and old Ellery walked through the garden behind the mansion—by that time rented from the Sedgwicks by a Stockbridge doctor, but put at the disposal of the Sedgwicks for the wedding ceremony—until they came to the dog cemetery. Ellery suddenly spotted a fresh, unfamiliar grave among the Cellinis. Two begonia plants stood beside a tiny, makeshift headstone, and a small American flag added a touch of poignancy to the scene. Ellery leaned heavily upon his cane and peered at the stone, and his face became pale. He read aloud the words on the headstone. " 'To Tubby,' " read Ellery, " 'the cutest dog that ever was.' " Ellery Sedgwick lifted his stick in the air and brought it down upon the begonia plants. "Blasphemy!" he cried. "Blasphemy!"

In a sense, that was part of the old Boston that he himself had known when he was married to Christina. He wished now that he could stop the flood of thoughts, but there was no turning back. He had done his writing at Wiscasset, in Maine, and in Newburyport, and in Boston, and in an apartment in Cambridge, and in 1927 he and Christina bought a house on Beacon Hill, at 43 West Cedar Street—a lovely three-story place. He paid twenty-nine thousand dollars for the house, and he told the real-estate man he felt the figure was high. The real-estate man seemed wounded by the comment. "You can't go wrong on Beacon Hill," he told him. Marquand sold the house in 1938 for eleven thousand dollars. Assuredly, you *could* go wrong on Beacon Hill. Many things had gone wrong on Beacon Hill. There could be no more strained relationship for a writer than the one Marquand found himself in vis-à-vis the Sedgwicks. To the Sedgwicks, there was only one magazine, the *Atlantic Monthly*, and only one type of literature, spelled with a capital "L." Christina's mother never read anything that her son-in-law John wrote, and she was not ashamed to tell him so. He wrote serial after serial, hot and heavy adventure stories, stories of China, of the Civil War, of families in a small New England town. He worked long and hard, and made no pretensions whatever about his work, and felt no condescension toward it, either. Years later, he was to remark that he always did the best he could at whatever he was doing. The Sedgwicks' attitude hurt him deeply. They looked down upon him as a popular fictioneer, almost a pulp writer. One winter, he and his wife stayed with the Sedgwicks in Stockbridge. The house had a broad hall with doors opening off it. Marquand was working in one room off the hall, and Christina's brother, A. C. Sedgwick, was working in another, directly opposite. Marquand was applying himself to a serial, Sedgwick to a novel called *Wind Without Rain*. Mrs. Sedgwick rapped on Marquand's door one afternoon and asked him if he would mind stopping work and taking her son's dog, Chou-fleur, out for its midafternoon walk. "He's writing, you know," she said. That same winter, Marquand went down to New York and returned with a number of tropical fish. Mrs. Sedgwick was puzzled. "Why did you present us with tropical fish, John?" she asked. "It seemed a bit chilly up here," he replied. Mrs. Sedgwick was not amused.

Marquand did everything that was humanly possible to bring in as much money as he could. He soon found that marriage was difficult in Boston for a writer. First, a cook was required, then a maid, then a nurse, then many evenings with Boston society. But he thought he was doing pretty well, pretty well indeed. "I ruptured myself in those days with slave ships and Java Heads," he remarked in later years. When his daughter Christina was a year and a half old, she had a bad bout of pneumonia, and then suffered a second attack of the illness. A rib had to be cut and the incision had to be drained, and she spent an entire winter in Children's Hospital, in Boston. Marquand worked feverishly on a serial called "Warning Hill" and received a thousand-dollar advance on it—a large sum, he thought—from Little, Brown. Before that, Scribner's had published nearly all his books, and the late Max Perkins had encouraged him, but Perkins' advances were somewhat meagre and he needed the money. (He had stuck with Little, Brown ever since.) In view of his industry, he was seriously hurt when one or another of the Sedgwicks would remark, "Why don't you write something nice for Uncle Ellery?" Write something nice for Uncle Ellery, indeed! And get paid handsomely with a check for a hundred dollars, and perhaps a silver inkwell!

And yet Boston charmed him in many ways. He worked at home, and ate his lunch at the Tavern Club, a men's club of considerable elegance, several mottoes of which make use of the word "bear," including "Bear with Us," and the symbol of which is a large stuffed bear. If one saw under the surface of Boston, one found that it had many wonderful qualities, many more than most American cities. He liked the notion of the Boston trustee—that unique Boston institution, perhaps closer to the notion of a London solicitor than anything else in this country. His own trustees, Welch & Forbes, took care of everything for him; he gave them an unrestricted power of attorney and they collected his royalties, paid his bills, handled ailing pets, and even bought him clothes on occasion. Their offices were austere, and contained a jawbone that had figured in the celebrated Dr. Parkman murder case—the firm had been Sohier & Welch then, and had represented Professor Webster—and overlooked the old burial ground off Park Street, where John Hancock lay, along with Paul Revere, James Otis, the mother and father of Benjamin Franklin, and old Sam Adams. (Old John Adams was buried in Quincy.) Marquand enjoyed his visits to the offices of Welch & Forbes; in fact, he enjoyed the company of Welch and Forbes themselves, two impeccably groomed young Boston men, souls of honor, with a sense of responsibility. He enjoyed hearing them say of him, "We are just hewers of wood and drawers of water for J. P. Marquand. We furnish logistic support to J. P. Marquand." He liked to look out over the old graveyard and recall that in the early days of Boston young sports from the fine houses on Park Street would emerge at night and sit on the tombstones, drinking champagne.

The Somerset Club pleased him, too, with its fantastically good, and cold, sweet Martinis, its corndodgers, its Madeira sauce with peppercorns, for sea food, its third-floor sign reading, "This water closet for emergency use only; other water closets available on the second floor." The Athenaeum, at 10½ Beacon Street, was a joy—a private library, the members of which owned shares in it, where tea or bouillon was still served in the afternoons: with three plain crackers, three cents; with three crackers and cheese, five cents; with one plain cracker and one sweet, three cents; with one plain cracker and cheese and one sweet, four cents; with extra sweet crackers a penny apiece; and extra plain crackers two for a penny. He relished the sign that had been put up many years ago in the Athenaeum and that read, "Copies of *Cosmopolitan* are available for the duration of the Coolidge articles."

When you came down to it, he supposed, Boston was an acquired taste. One had to know these people in order to appreciate them—people like good old Gardi Fiske, who was the only World War I ace to fall out of an airplane, catch hold of the rear struts, and clamber back aboard, and who worried not at all about the hereafter, since, as he once remarked to Marquand, "I know the Bishop, who is up there, and if there are any good clubs, he'll get me in." Marquand marvelled at the manner in which aristocratic Boston conserved the principal of its acquired wealth, and marvelled as well at its public spirit and its lack of extravagance or vulgar display of affluence. There was no shame in dressing tackily. Why bother about a run in one's stockings, or an old hat? Everybody knows you can afford better. Boston was symbolized once for Marquand when he recognized an elderly couple who were standing by the newspaper-and-candy counter at the Back Bay station. He knew they had recently given a million dollars each to Harvard. When he saw them, they were, in a subdued but firm way, arguing; one wanted a package of peppermint Life Savers, the other a package of orange Life Savers. They could not settle on which one to buy. Yes, there were times when, returning to Boston, just as he was doing now, he wished that he were living there again, even with all the memories. He knew the old feeling. He would look at the Esplanade, or walk through the Public Garden or past the Somerset, and he would think of the quiet of Beacon Hill and wonder why he didn't live there again. And then, if he stayed any time at all, the feeling of restlessness would start up. Something about Boston, perhaps its conservatism, perhaps its holding on to old ideas and its antagonism to new ones—the very things he loved about the place—would turn him against it, and within ten days or two weeks, like a man being smothered under a blanket, he would struggle desperately to get out. And he could not help remembering, although the thought pained him greatly, how he said to Christina, while they were still married, that he would like to—had to, in fact—write a book someday about Boston and the Boston type. He was thinking of a man to be called George Apley. Christina looked at him, startled, and said quietly, "We'll have to leave Boston, of course."

The porter gently tapped Marquand on the shoulder. "Back Bay station," he said. Marquand rose from his seat, and he and Craig stepped down onto the platform. "Mr. Marquand," said Craig as they picked up their bags and headed for the street, "I wish that sometime you would tell me a little something about Boston." Marquand smiled a peculiar smile. How could he ever tell him? How could he ever tell anybody?

From: All in the Artist's Head

Robert Beverly Hale is a beloved teacher. He is a tall, spare, somewhat rumpled patrician of seventy-six, with black-rimmed glasses and an El Greco face. He teaches two courses, Artistic Anatomy and Elements of Drawing, at the Art Students League, on West Fifty-seventh Street, and his classes are a continual, and almost legendary, celebration not only of the beauty and wonder of the human form but of Hale himself. Many people consider Hale the foremost teacher of artistic anatomy in the country, and perhaps the world. His classes are always oversubscribed, and students return year after year. When Hale enters a lecture hall or a studio, his students burst into applause. They do the same thing as he leaves. Hale is a modest, philosophical man, with a long view of history and of life, but he does not attempt to hide his pleasure at these tributes. "I have a flair for teaching," he often says. "The role of teacher fits me, and I play it. I never empty a lecture room." He does not attempt to hide his pleasure, either, at having recently received, at Alice Tully Hall, one of the Mayor's Awards of Honor for Arts and Culture, the citation for which reads, "Artist, poet, and teacher, he has inspired generations of ardent disciples at the Art Students League."

"Subtle and elemental forces are at work inside Hale," a former student told me not long ago. "There's an encyclopedic knowledge of art and artists, extraordinary humor, and the ability to make anatomical drawings with a piece of charcoal attached to a long stick which are miracles of precision and art." The young man paused for breath, but not very long. "I get extremely excited when I talk about Hale and his classes," he said. "So does everybody I know who works with him. There's a magic to the man as he stands up there drawing and talking. He's generous. He holds nothing back. He puts down everything he considers essential. Unlike some teachers, who assert themselves, he eliminates himself and concentrates on reverence for art and artists. There are no sly, arcane corners with Hale. He tells you what he knows. And in some inexplicable way it is always allied with the earth and with human beings, and with their survival as human beings on this planet."

Hale and I are friends. His company invigorates me and gives me a sense of purpose. I like to hear him talk, either formally, in front of a class or at some public function, or informally, at home. Hale enjoys talking. He talks quietly, in a dry, clipped tone, and each word emerges as though it had been leading a detached, private, educated life of its own. As he talks, his mind gracefully unfolds, and a landscape is dotted not with the delicate bridges, willows, houses, and carp-filled streams of a Chinese scroll but with ideas, fancies, memories—precise and embroidered—and technical details, wrapped in poetry, his own and others'. . . .

Hale is a chain-smoker, and he had now [I am in his apartment on West Sixty-seventh Street] filled several ashtrays. He started on another cigarette. "I went to the Metropolitan in 1948, when Francis Henry Taylor said that the trustees wanted an American Department at the museum. They had enormous funds—such as the George A. Hearn Fund—but not much taste for contemporary American art. The money was being spent on John Singer Sargents. Collectors hated contemporary American art. The trustees didn't think much of it, either, and the trustees held the purse strings. The market in modern American art had not yet started, and American paintings hung in the European galleries of the museum. Childe Hassam was with the French Impressionists. You could still buy a Mary Cassatt oil for five thousand, and a Winslow Homer watercolor for three thousand. I once took three Walt Kuhn pictures of clowns—*wonderful* pictures—into the boardroom and put them before the trustees. One of them flew into a rage and waved his arms around and shouted. 'If I couldn't paint better than that,' said this particular tycoon, 'I would shoot myself.' We did soon have three people on the board—Walter Baker, Elihu Root, Jr., and Sam Lewisohn—who appreciated contemporary American art, and Lewisohn, especially, was so taken aback by the attack on the Kuhns that he persuaded the board

to buy all three of them. The only thing that could produce more palpi-
tations, seizures, and hallucinations than American art was abstract art. I
brought a lovely abstract seascape around one day and showed it to the
trustees, and one of them remarked, 'I've had a yacht for forty years,
and, by God, I've never seen waves like that.' I was in with the last of the
Victorians. I always wore a dark suit to the Met, and a dark tie, so that I
could duck out at a moment's notice to a funeral, but that was a slow
process and didn't really solve my problem. My chance to indulge in a
little education came when a trustee suddenly said to me, 'I don't know
anything about these artists. I've never met one. Can you get some of
them together to talk to the trustees?' He gathered together a group of
tough old businessmen, and I got hold of Stewart Klonis, the executive
director of the Art Students League, and I got Eugene Speicher, William
Zorach, and Vaclav Vytlacil, and we met in a private dining room of a
midtown club. We had a full, pleasant meal, and some good wines. One
of the trustees then said to one of the artists, 'How can I tell a good picture when I see one?' There was a strange silence. One of the artists
said, 'Well, my method is to go to a gallery, look at the pictures, and then
say this one stinks or that one stinks. That's one way of doing it.' We
were getting nowhere. Another artist spoke up quickly: 'Have you ever
taken a walk by the sea and seen a wet and glistening stone that you particularly liked? Or perhaps a shell that you liked for its geometrical
qualities? Or a piece of tattered seaweed that had taken on a certain
shape? And you picked these up and put them in your hand. And sometimes you even took them home and put them on the mantelpiece to
look at and admire and cherish. You have a feeling about their goodness.
Have you ever done anything like that?' The trustee seemed quite bewildered. 'I don't believe I ever have,' he said."

While Hale was telling me this story, a strange sensation came over me. I
was peculiarly aware that the room in which I was sitting was quite
deceptive, and that what had at first seemed somewhat threadbare was
fairly bursting with a life of its own. I have often walked along a dark and
wooded path at night and thought that I was entirely alone, in a sound-
less, remote limbo—concentrating on something else—when suddenly
my ears were opened to hundreds upon hundreds of strange night
sounds: whispers, rustles, cries, mysteries beyond mysteries. I had been

listening closely to Hale. We had been talking so much that I had seen only a fragment of his room. Now I took a long look around, and intently observed the seashell or seaweed to which he had metaphorically referred. I noticed that the floor was tiled in white vinyl. The white vinyl had been there before, of course, but I had not seen it. A fire was blazing in the fireplace. The fireplace itself was capacious and baronial, of the outsize type still seen in some of the older, well-built West Side apartments. High on the mantelpiece stood a stuffed loon in winter plumage—a gift, Hale told me, from a friend. What appeared to be a medium-sized tree stood in a wooden tub not far from the fireplace. Hale could see that I was perplexed. "That's a Norfolk Island pine, from the Pacific," he said. "I brought it back from a store one Christmas Eve instead of the usual tree. I never thought it would last." . . .

We walked slowly back into the living room. The experience of the last few minutes had shaken me a bit. Once again, as so many times in my life, I had been made aware of the initial superficiality of one's impressions of things, of people, and of places. That room had been a comfortable, if somewhat alien, room when I first walked in. Now it had become a room of distinctive objects. And the scene and the leading character had merged and become one. I could never again look at the room without seeing Hale, or see Hale without thinking of the room. He was now speaking softly. "The beginner draws only what he knows exists," he was saying. "But there's an anatomy to everything—not just to the human body but to trees, for instance, and to all forms. What is required is detachment, the artist's detachment. A hard thing to learn. When someone bursts into tears is a prime time for acute observation. I say to my students, 'Observe. Observe the highlights on the tears as they course down the cheek.' And when some model faints at the League— the models range from eighteen to eighty, and someone periodically keels over—it isn't good enough just to rush forward to help, I tell them. 'Observe! Watch the changes in tone and value as the model changes position. Watch as the light on his or her face changes with the reflected light from the floor! Observe, as an artist must observe.' I have often thought how difficult it must be to remain non-human in one's sympathy after one has studied at the League and observed all those models. Young, old, tall, thin, and squat—all sizes, all shapes. Drawing from the nude is an enriching experience. Of course, the instant reaction of the square to the nude model is a sexual one. 'Aha,' he says. 'A naked body!'

But this has to be unlearned by the student. A most important lesson. This is the true beginning of observation and detachment. The experience is not unlike that of the medical student when he first dissects a human body. A difficult business, looking objectively at the human body. The student's fear of death is either overcome or changed. He *becomes* changed. I suppose I'm a humanist because I teach the human body. Extraordinary how much interest there has been in anatomy since Hiroshima." Hale crossed the room and toyed with some bones in the wicker basket. One of his wife's rugs, which an hour before had seemed to me a mild orange, now appeared to be a deep, rich, vibrating rust red. . . .

On many evenings, I have sat and watched this tall, very distinguished, very fragile teacher deliver lectures on anatomy. The chalkboard, the barely dancing skeleton, the long sticks, and the lectures themselves—on, say, the upper arm, or the elbow, or the head, or the features, or the rib cage—have become transformed in my mind, and my mind's eye, into one continuous, quietly flowing lecture, during which time and space and subject matter dissolve and are mysteriously reformed into another entity, with a distinct life of its own, which I think of as The Lecture. Hence:

Hale is holding the stick with charcoal at one end. He pours himself a glass of water from a pitcher on a small table. He says something into the microphone, and a great growling sound comes out. "Oh, Wash, Wash, something is wrong with the machine again!" Mr. Washington patiently steps onto the platform and performs some mechanical magic, and when Hale speaks again his voice is clear and firm. He is talking about the arm, and his own arm moves gracefully and slowly as shapes begin to form on the chalkboard. The members of the class are doing two things at one time: looking at Hale's drawings and making sketches of their own. There is the silence of study in the room. Hale is drawing and erasing—shoulder blades, collarbones. "See how the arm is closed," he says. "It is done with the biceps and the rib cage. . . . The ulna. All the ulna can do is go up and down, up and down." Drawing, erasing, drawing, erasing. "Artists have certain ideas of the arm. You can think of the arm as a three-sided prism. Goya did a drawing of a woodman and broke the sleeve into planes, and for this he probably put his own arm up." Hale does so. "Watch out for a model who may be tired, for then you will get a tired arm. Raise your collarbone if you want vitality. 'I like to draw what I see,' said a man to Whistler. To which Whistler replied, 'Wait till you see what you draw.' And watch out for literary terms in relation to anatomy. Very misleading. Such as 'Her breasts were like two young roes feeding among the lilies,' or 'Her nose was like a tower in Lebanon,' or 'Her lips are like scarlet thread,' or Emerson's comparison of Thoreau's arm to the bough of an elm tree. Practice, practice! Take a look at the lower arm—the length of the hand is one-fifth of the length of the ulna above." He rolls up one sleeve. "So many muscles in this arm," he says. "Many students look at the muscles and give up anatomy forever. The hand! A miracle! You can pull corks out of bottles, turn keys in doors. Your horse, however, is stuck. He can just go up and down. Your cat is stuck. He can't do much, either. Practice contour lines all the time." The stick crosses and recrosses the board. He is drawing lines, some delicately shaded, some thick, some eerily thin. "You can't draw a line unless you know where it's coming from and where it's going." Cylinders appear on the board, and cubes, rectangles and squares. The chamois cloth erases, and new drawings appear. "The positioning of the thumb is very difficult. Watch the planes and lines where they meet and change. A wrist is a block going in a certain direction. It's all in my mind. The artist watches the flow from place to place—the tendons that carry the flow, grasping and handling. It's all in the unconscious. Hang your baby on a gas jet at home and he'll automatically hang on. You can begin to see how subtle the body is. Hands can be as flat as the horizon"—he holds a hand out flat—"or they can stretch out to the horizon." He stretches his hand, making it look as though it were about to grasp the horizon. "Or it can look like a bird, with wings on both sides. Keep drawing, keep drawing. You'll do better if you have real bones to work with. Not too difficult these days. There were eleven murders yesterday in New York City." The board is filled up with the front of the hand, the palm, a side view, phalanges, wrists, thumbs. "Practice, practice—it's all hard work. But why should you think it would be easy? Remember Eliot," he continues:

> And so each venture
> Is a new beginning, a raid on the inarticulate

With shabby equipment always deteriorating
In the general mess of imprecision of feeling . . .

Hale briskly wipes the board clean and walks from the room. The class applauds again. Intermission. Students gather around the skeleton with their sketchbooks and continue to draw.

Hale reenters. A nose begins to take shape on the chalkboard, eyes begin to form. "The eye is a Ping-Pong ball. You run your lines over the forms you can see. Draw lines where planes meet." He discusses the muscles of the face. "Through time, gravity just pulls everything down, down into the grave. There are muscles of shape and muscles of expression. For shape, you have the temporalis in the head, and you can feel it by placing your fingers on your temples and chewing. The expressions are limitless, depending on the muscles used. Artists know these things. For a real smile—not an airline-hostess smile—you employ the zygomaticus major, the smiling muscle. The circular muscles of the eye must act for a sincere smile. Pain and grief—the muscles of the mouth operate as the mouth opens more and more in relation to the pain. For torture, you cease employing the muscles of the forehead—they are for attention— and open the mouth more for amazement. All these things artists know. Let's assume a banker receives a man in his office. 'Good morning,' says the banker. 'And your name, sir?' 'Getty,' says the stranger." Hale breaks into a broad and sickening smile. " 'Ah, Mr. Getty,' says the banker. 'Won't you have a seat? Please be comfortable. You must have a little oil business and many large problems to handle. Have a cigarette. Relax.' 'Well,' says the man, 'my name *is* Getty, but I'm on welfare, and I haven't worked in five years, and . . .' " Hale's expression changes to horror, to pain, to grief, to torture, to revulsion. "There is a muscle of irony and there is a muscle of anger," he says. "There is a muscle of sneering and a muscle of grief. There are expressions of sneering and of grief, and in New York they are often the same expression. Sculptors have a terrible time with eyelashes. Most of them cast them as shadows. The mouth itself goes over the cylinder of the teeth. Draftsmanship really resides in the mind." Hale is drawing a human head now, slowly, the features taking form as though they were emerging from a mist. I see a nose, a mouth. "The mouth is under the nose for a special reason—the smelling of food," he says. "Bridgman often speculated how inconvenient it would be if the nose were under the arm. Then we would have to put the food there and sniff before eating." Long hair is now flowing from the figure on the board. It is the face of an older man. The expression is sad and wise. Long, steady sweep of the charcoal. "Sausages pull down over old men's eyes as they grow older," Hale says. The class is intently leaning forward now, watching the drawing. "I'll put in sideburns, and a goatee," he says. "When I was a little boy, every doctor had a goatee, and they all made house calls. And I'll put in a mustache, and I'll make the beard longer, and fuzzier at the end. Everything is moving, always moving, in a perspective block, and finally into a block six feet under. There's a song of Leadbelly's about his days on the Louisiana chain gang, and it haunts me." Very slowly, standing in front of the wild and ancient figure with the long, flowing beard, Hale recites:

> Take this hammer
> And carry it to the captain.
> You tell him I'm gone,
> You tell him I'm gone.
> If he asks you
> Was I laughin',
> You tell him I was cryin'.

The lecture is over. Hale steps off the platform and heads for the door. There is a long moment of silence, and then long applause. By now, Hale is gone, but the class seems unwilling to leave, and many students move toward the chalkboard and stare and stare at the drawing.

From: Searching for Gregorian

The New York Public Library houses many treasures, but few are as colorful, complex, enigmatic, civilized, and stimulating as Vartan Gregorian, its president and chief executive officer. I have been looking things up all my life in the monumental Beaux-Arts building at Fifth Avenue and Forty-second Street, and one Saturday noontime not long ago I went over there to look up Gregorian, who holds a Ph.D. in history and is generally known as Dr. Gregorian. I had read of his somewhat legendary and magical work in restoring the library to financial and intellectual vigor—the strenuous fund-raising, the spotlight of publicity, the exhibits, the lectures, the unprecedented gala dinners—but I knew very little about the man himself. In a library, one thing leads to another, and each point of reference becomes an act of discovery, an extension of one's own horizons. My pursuit of Dr. Gregorian began in his office, on the second floor of the library—a spacious, high-ceilinged room with walls of green damask and dominated by an immense oval yellow oak conference table, which almost completely eclipsed a large desk in one corner of the room. The oak table was piled high with neatly stacked papers and books. Bookshelves and eighteenth- and nineteenth-century portraits—John Jacob Astor; Benjamin Franklin; Shelley's parents, by Romney—lined the walls. Tall windows opened onto Fifth Avenue, but the city seemed far away. The room is scholarly and noble, like so many spaces throughout the library, which was built by Carrère and Hastings, opened in 1911, and is universally acknowledged to be a classic structure. When I entered the room, Dr. Gregorian was standing by the desk going through some papers, and he didn't walk over to greet me—he bounced over, rapidly, with short, rolling movements. He is in his early fifties, of medium height, rumpled, and on the heavy side, with an anarchic clump of graying hair and an arresting short salt-and-pepper beard. I was immediately struck by his benign resemblance to the two sculptured lions, Patience and Fortitude, that guard the main steps to the library.

Dr. Gregorian whipped off the jacket of his suit and carefully hung it over the back of a broad-bottomed yellow oak chair that matched the big oak table. He beckoned to me to sit down in a similar chair, one of ten or so spread around the conference table. "We'll talk about library and Gregorian and have sandwich," he said to me. The prospect seemed to delight him. He speaks softly but quickly, with a pleasant Middle Eastern accent. "A library is a sacred place," he said. "My role is educator and teacher. For four thousand years, humanity has gone through dreadful horrors, dreadful turmoils, varied glories. How do we distill the past? How do we retain the memories? *Libraries.* The New York Public Library is one of the greatest in the entire world. Its research libraries contain some twenty-nine million items, and there are eighty-eight miles of stacks right here in this building. Millions of memories. We are a treasured repository of civilization. Sometimes I am overwhelmed when I realize what we mean to the city and to the world. Libraries keep the records on behalf of all humanity. We contain the unique and the absurd, the wise and fragments of stupidity. We mirror the world, in all its folly and wisdom. We serve the masses and the individual. A library must never be indifferent to the individual, must always protect him. Think of a lone person in one of our reading rooms, who has just read a book, a single book that has perhaps not been read in twenty years by another living soul, and from that reading comes an invention of incalculable importance to the human race. It makes a man tremble. Endless sources of knowledge are *here.* We have books in three thousand languages and dialects. I can take you through here from Balanchine to Tibet. There are esoterica on synthetic fuels, neglected maps of the Falklands that were suddenly in demand at the time of the Falklands War. And Warsaw telephone directories from the years of the Holocaust, often invaluable as the only source of documentation of who lived where, in order to substantiate claims for retribution. There will never be an end to this library. Never!" By now, I was quite aware that the Dr. Gregorian I was seeking was a vital, driving force, and I was happy that I had undertaken the journey.

Dr. Gregorian was still talking as he bounced again across the room and opened a door to an anteroom where a few people were working. "Sandwich and coffee for my friend, and sandwich and Diet Coke for me!" he called to someone just outside the door. He closed the door and sat down again. "I have the most extraordinary, loyal staff," he said. "They come in on Saturday. To *work*. You have noticed how quiet it is in my suite of offices, but we must not forget the hundreds of people spread all through this building who are reading, studying, digging into subjects, gaining knowledge. When I came here, in the spring of 1981, the library was in a crisis, the city was in a crisis. I was in a critical period of my own life. The city was under attack. I had been under attack. As it turned out, I was in the right place at the right time. New York is full of chutzpah. I am full of chutzpah. There has been an extraordinary revival."

The door to the anteroom opened, and a tall, energetic, and strikingly attractive young woman entered, carrying lunch. Dr. Gregorian introduced her to me as Maryann Jordan, his executive assistant. I could sense immediately that she must exercise a strong, calming influence on the president's office. She put lunch on the big table and quietly left the room. "Thank you, Maryann!" he called out to her. "When I first met the staff of the library, I was a total stranger to them," he said to me. "Naturally, they were somewhat suspicious of a man who had never been a librarian before, who had been provost of the University of Pennsylvania, who was a professor, who spoke with a foreign accent, who dropped his articles. I stood up in front of them, and my first words were 'Fellow educators.' This was appreciated. This gave people a sense of the dignity of their profession. I also told them I would go back later and pick up all the articles I had dropped. One of my greatest teachers was my maternal grandmother, a most remarkable woman, and one of the many things she taught me was that dignity is not negotiable. Dignity is the honor of the family. I have thought about it many times. She also taught me that envy is very bad. Envy will deform your character. 'You must not have a hole in your eye,' she would say. The hole in the eye was caused by envy. The hole would be insatiable and could never be filled."

We both eyed the sandwiches lying on the table. "I think it's time for lunch," said Dr. Gregorian. He handed me an egg-salad sandwich hermetically sealed in a plastic container. I began to struggle with it, attempting to find some chink in its armor, some vulnerable corner into which I could perhaps slide a nail to reach the sandwich. No luck. No luck whatever. Dr. Gregorian observed me closely. He seemed to understand my plight completely. "Some people have the knack of these things and some people don't," he said, with kindness. I realized that I was in warm and friendly hands. He took the package and, with a flick of a finger, had it open. We went on to other matters.

He said, "I am an Armenian, born in Tabriz, in Iran, in 1934. This was northwestern Iran, near the Russian border. My family had been in Iran for many years. I can trace Tabriz Armenians back some two thousand years. Where I was born was very cold—very high, very dry. Since I am a teacher, I like to talk about Armenia, and sometimes I like to use phrases like 'one, two, three,' and hold up fingers to prove points to the class. The capital of Armenia is Yerevan. Turkey is on the west, Azerbaijan on the east, Iran to the south, and Georgia to the north. Armenia is the oldest Christian state." He paused a moment, to take a bite of egg salad. "One learns only by learning about different cultures, different places, different peoples. A funny thing—I know a Soviet Armenian who has said that Christianity was founded in 300 B.C. There's history for you!

"We lived in a large house in what was known as the Armenian quarter of Tabriz. A middle-class section. The family was still speaking Armenian at home. I also spoke Turkish. Today, I can speak seven languages. Armenia was the first nation to accept Christianity as a state religion. There were two apostles who were said to have travelled in Armenia—St. Thaddaeus and St. Bartholomew—and thus the church was known as an apostolic church. My church, the Armenian Apostolic, is independent. The Russian Orthodox Church Outside of Russia remains czarist in its sympathies. As for my family, my grandfather was called Father, and my grandmother was called Mother. I called my father Samuel. He is still alive. He is seventy-eight and lives in Tehran. He telephones me occasionally, perhaps on a birthday, but we have never been close. How is that sandwich?"

I said that it was fine, now that he had found the way.

"Coffee for you," he said, opening a white plastic container. "I take diet cola. Back to Tabriz. It was in a Turkish-speaking province. They spoke an eastern Turkish. They also spoke Persian. Persian was the language of instruction, Turkish the language of population, Russian the language of occupation. One's early memories are vivid, yet scattered. My father's father had a caravansary—a sort of animal parking lot. No camels. Absolutely no camels. Mules and donkeys brought goods to the place where the animals were parked. I remember that my father's father had lost an eye—gored by a bull. A bad bull. When he died, my mother was determined that her father-in-law should have a Christian burial. She wanted to avoid his being buried in a Muslim shroud—the Muslims don't have coffins. My mother would have done anything to have her father-in-law buried in a coffin. The body had been brought home. Very important that the body come home before burial. My mother bribed the police chief and gave his wife all her needlework, and then my mother and I went to the bazaar and bought a coffin. She rented a phaeton and put the body in the coffin and the coffin on the phaeton and gave him a Christian burial. As they sprinkled water on the dead man, his good eye opened, and the people at the funeral cried out, 'Bala Beg is alive! Bala Beg is alive!'

"The house in which I lived in Iran, like other houses of the Armenian community, was designed for maximum privacy. They were interior houses—no display outside, small windows. Made of brick and mud." Dr. Gregorian suddenly stood up and moved briskly across the room. "There was a basement and a first floor. There would be a big knock on the door"—Dr. Gregorian knocked on the wall of his office—"Who is there?" he cried. "The answer would come from the street." He was back in his memories now, far from Fifth Avenue and Forty-second Street. He had a strange smile on his face, a smile of contentment touched with pride. "Then you would enter the house and descend to a courtyard and a basement with windows. On the right was the living room"—broad, sweeping gesture—"the Official Occasion Room. There was a rug here, and good china. This was, in essence, the foreign ministry. There was a huge kitchen—oh, a *huge* kitchen—with a huge oven. My parents' room was across from the kitchen. There was a large dining room, converted at night into a bedroom, with storage space for bedding. We slept on thick mattresses on the floor, under beautifully embroidered quilts. But the kitchen was the centerpiece—half the size of this big office of mine, which still makes it quite large. We cooked with charcoal. Bread was always being baked. The bread hung in the cellar on trays suspended from the beams by ropes. They were rounded loaves, drying there along the walls, and when bread was needed some-one would sprinkle water on a loaf. My grandmother had a small room to the right of the kitchen. Her name was Vosky; it means 'gold.' It meant gold to me then, it means gold to me now. She was known as Vosky Baji—a term of endearment, 'Baji' meaning 'sister.'

"Her influence was tremendous. She had no formal education, but immensely valued it. She lived her life with consummate dignity. She struggled. She coped. She never lost faith, was never cynical. She did not speak ill of others. She insisted that one must do good without expectation of reward. She believed that to think ill of others is to dimin-ish oneself. She was deeply respected all over town. When I went to the store for her, I never carried money. It was enough for me to say that Vosky Baji had sent me. I am not superstitious; she was dreadfully so. She knew about the evil eye and believed in it. *'You do not show your baby to someone with the evil eye!'* " Dr. Gregorian was pacing up and down his office now, speaking in what can perhaps best be described as circu-lar terms—never in a straight line. I sensed that I was experiencing a classic library phenomenon: search for one thing, and a moment later discover something new and beckoning.

Dr. Gregorian continued, "My mother died shortly after the death of my grandfather. She died in 1941. She was twenty-six or twenty-seven; I was seven. She died of pneumonia—the Russians were coming, and there were no medicines. There she was in her bed. Dead. But nobody explained it to me. They told me later that she had gone to America. Since she was very beautiful, I thought that America must be doubly beautiful—beautiful for itself, beautiful because my mother was there. But I find that I go back to my grandmother. When I went away as a young man, my grandmother sewed a blue bead inside my jacket for good luck. The color of lapis lazuli. When I think of her, I think of the strength of a wounded wolf. I still have some objects from my grandmother—for example, a piece of hair from my first haircut. She saved it, presented it to me. Also her picture—a woman with powerful eyes. A letter I wrote when I was eight or nine. She stopped going to church after one of her sons died. She felt that her children had been taken away from her—he was the seventh child she had lost.

"I must tell you that I was a choirboy. I felt very important, because I could look down from the altar. *I was on high ground.* And when a rich man died you carried the unlit candles and banners through the streets from his home to the church. It was Christ being resurrected. You walked around, but never across, the Muslim section of town. I was one of two candle bearers. I had a certain unity with the priests, a feeling of belonging to some metaphysical order. You know, I actually got involved with street gangs. Nothing serious, you understand, but there was trafficking in cigarettes when I was growing up. You would buy something for nine dollars and ninety cents and sell it for ten dollars and eighty cents. Big deal. But there was another road, and I took it. I landed in the local Armenian library, on top of the local archbishop's residence. Another big room. I *like* big rooms. I like working in them. My office when I was provost of the University of Pennsylvania was big, too— Victorian Gothic, a room as big as this one, with the trustees' big room next door and a large suite of offices outside for my assistants.

"But I am ahead of myself. I was a page in the Armenian library, with freedom to read and roam. Almost all the books were in Armenian, and there were translations of the classics. There were two Armenian monasteries that translated Shakespeare. I read Shakespeare. I read Dumas, *père* and *fils*. I read Victor Hugo. I was especially impressed by *Les Misérables* and the character of Jean Valjean, a man whose soul was touched. My own soul was touched. I also read Tolstoy, and didn't understand him. Another place in which I would read was a street bookstore, a sort of rental library. More books and still more books. There was the real world to face. So-called reality. Two events brought it home to me. On the streets of Tabriz, there was a madwoman who kept cats in her bosom. She would walk up and down the streets with those cats in her bosom, singing, singing, singing. It was a dreadful sight. One Sunday when she came to the church, the priests did not like her looks, or her madness, and they refused her Communion. This shocked me. Another important experience in coming face-to-face with reality took place when I saw my priest emerging one day from a men's room. Until that moment, I had felt that priests were a special breed, a higher order of humanity, which under no circumstances engaged in normal human functions. I went to an Armenian-Russian school. Russian soldiers were all over the place, but there was no massacre, no looting, no resistance. I remember going down to the main street to see the tanks. There was a tremendous wooden map in the center of the city—with arrows and illustrated military campaigns. I learned a good deal in Turkish about Russian subjects. One of the teachers in this school was an ignorant wise man. We treated this fellow very badly. He wasn't really qualified to teach Persian history, and we teased him unmercifully—sent up a dreadful humming that must have driven him to distraction. He would call us animals, but we kept on humming. He would punch two holes in his newspaper and pretend to be reading while we were studying, but all the time he was peeping at us through the holes. Corporal punishment followed upon infraction of the rules—whippings on the palm of the hand, where it hurt, with a whip carrying a ball bearing at the end. But this ignorant wise man taught us several important lessons I have never forgotten: One [finger in the air], if you see a donkey carrying gold, it is not a golden donkey. Two [two fingers in the air], if you see a donkey carrying a diploma, it is just a donkey carrying a diploma. And, three [three fingers in the air], if you see a donkey in Jerusalem, it is not a holy donkey. Useful information for later life. I was very bright, no question about that—straight A's all over the place. But once I hit the principal with a snowball that was intended, believe me, for someone else, and got a spanking. My grandmother instantly came to my rescue and defense. Down to the principal she went. She didn't know the word 'principal,' or what it meant, but she said to him, 'Have you fed him? Have you taken care of him?' And then she slapped him in the face."

Dr. Gregorian bustled over to the anteroom door, disappeared, and returned a moment later with another can of Diet Coke. "A key to my character was my physical smallness," he said. "I was very thin. I was not physically strong. But my survival instinct told me to go after the bullies in the school. This was my way of showing my strength of character, my sense of self. I was bloodied from time to time, but people said, 'Keep away from this fellow, he is somebody to be careful of.' I put up a curtain between myself and others.

"It was not an easy childhood. My father remarried, but my stepmother removed my mother's picture, and this deeply offended me and my grandmother. Just took the picture down. And I fought with my father, for I was caught in this messy situation with his new wife. My sister was studying in a local French school, and we had our private schemes. We collected matchboxes and filled them with ants. According to local legend, America was a sanitary, antiseptic paradise—so clean, in fact, that the anteaters of America were unemployed, totally without work. So my sister and I set about collecting ants for shipment to America. We envisioned making millions of dollars. We collected both the small ones, the Christian ones, and the big black ones, the Muslim ants. This was a venture that never got off the ground, and once we realized the enterprise was doomed we buried the ants under an almond tree. But it kept me occupied, and it removed some of the strain in the house. My grandmother had moved next door, and I was saved, in a sense, by three people in Tabriz with whom I could spend time and study—learning was becoming paramount, the main goal. One was an optometrist, another the director of a flour mill (my sister married his son), and the third a rug merchant. They were most important at the time. I profusely borrowed bicycles from them, not owning one of my own. My reading had unfortunately given me an exaggerated, literary view of a wicked stepmother, and it became fixational, something from which I felt I had to flee. In 1947—." Dr. Gregorian was interrupted by a knock on the door, and a young a woman appeared. "I hate to break in," she said, "but I think it is time for you gentlemen to have some brownies. We have outrageous brownies at the New York Public Library."

We both nodded, the brownies were presented, were tasted, and were pronounced outrageously good. The young lady silently departed.

"The people who work with me reflect my moods," Dr. Gregorian said. "If I am down, they tend to be down. When I'm up, they are up. Now, in 1947 there was a province-wide examination of scholastic achievement, and I did quite well—a sixteen-point-five average out of a maximum of twenty. About this time, an important figure came into my life. Important and helpful people have always mysteriously shown up at critical times. He was a French vice-consul named Edgar Maloyan, and since there were no good hotels in Tabriz he stayed at the home of a friend of mine, and I got to know him. We talked and talked, and he taught me to play chess—I would win one game in a hundred—and he told me of the exciting capitals of the world, and of the big world outside, and he said to me, 'Vartan, you are bright and must leave here and go to Petit Paris, to Beirut.' I cannot bear to think of Beirut today, where the shellfire and the bombing and the devastation have been so severe that the ancient Roman ruins are beginning to peep up from buried layers of earth. This man told me that even if I went to Beirut with no visible means of support I could still live on a banana a day. I didn't even know that you had to peel a banana in order to eat one! Beirut seemed impossible to reach—there was so much protocol involved in getting there—but this man volunteered to write a letter to officials in Lebanon. He would help in every way. My father was dead set against the idea. He told me that he would give permission if I could obtain a passport, feeling entirely certain that a passport was impossible. I brought a petition to the governor, at his official residence. I tried every avenue. I went to hearings. I was tenacious. I know how to be tenacious. Still, my father tried to dissuade me. 'It's a strange land,' he kept saying. 'A strange land.' Finally, after more than eight months, the passport came through. My father had one last ace up his sleeve. He told me to talk with my grandmother, the one I called Mother. He was certain she would persuade me not to leave home. She surprised them. Of course she surprised them. She said, very calmly—I remember it so clearly—'I would like my son to go and become a man. To become a man, he needs an education.' "

A week or so later, as we sat talking in Dr. Gregorian's quiet office, I could not help thinking of the many other people in the building, silent yet all around me, looking things up, pursuing facts, pursuing fancies, reading books, perhaps fulfilling dreams, reaching back in order to reach forward. I thought, What a curious world it is that places at the head of one of the greatest repositories of knowledge, in the center of the island of Manhattan, this exotic man from Armenia.

"You are shaking your head in a strange way," said Dr. Gregorian.

"I am astonished," I heard myself saying, "at the meeting of different cultures in this city and in this building. While you have been speaking of your grandmother, quite unexpectedly I have been thinking of mine. She was born in 1858, here in New York—then a city of nearly eight hundred thousand—on West Twenty-second Street, in Chelsea. And educated directly across the street from where we sit, at Rutgers Female College, on Fifth Avenue, in a series of Victorian Gothic buildings." This news excited Dr. Gregorian.

"Tell me something about her," he said.

"The paramount memory of her childhood, which she passed on to me, was of her father taking her to City Hall in April of 1865 to see the body of Abraham Lincoln lying in state, on its way to burial in Springfield," I said. "Hand in hand with her father, she climbed those beautiful curving stairs, with thousands of other mourners. When she was in school, the Croton Distributing Reservoir was right here, where the library stands, with high Egyptian walls of masonry and a fashionable promenade along the top."

"I imagine she walked there often," said Dr. Gregorian.

"I know that for a fact," I said. "I also remember how proud she was of Rutgers Female College. She studied Greek, Latin, French, piano, mathematics, art, and moral philosophy."

I had now had several visits with Dr. Gregorian. I knew something about him. He knew something about me. After all, we were in a library. On one of many other occasions, I was back in Dr. Gregorian's office, talking with him and struggling with an egg-salad sandwich. Once again, he mercifully came to my rescue, skillfully opening the stubborn wrapping. "I left for Beirut when I was fifteen, with fifty dollars in my pocket," he said. " 'Oh, you'll be back,' said my stepmother. *That* did it. I was determined to succeed. I stayed at the Hotel Lux. There was nothing luxe about it. It consisted of several rooms on the fifth floor of a building near the port. The guests were a motley assortment, all strangers to me. There were some poets, and everybody played pinochle, bridge, and poker. After about two weeks, someone asked me about paying a bill. I sold some silver cups and silver frames I had brought with me, and one of my blankets. There were some highly competitive bridge games. Because I was poor, I actually took seriously the advice I had been given to eat a banana a day, but learned rather rapidly to peel it. I began my studies at the Collège Arménien. A turning point in my life. The college was situated in the former headquarters of the French Admiralty—a good setting. Good teachers. A vital, all-important person now entered my life—Simon Vratzian, Armenian nationalist, writer, last prime minister of the Independent Armenian Republic. He was the principal of the college, and he took me under his wing, made me his protégé. To many he was a national hero. He managed to get me a small scholarship, and room and board. I would not be here today if it were not for Simon Vratzian." Dr. Gregorian rose and walked swiftly around the yellow oak table. Then he sat down again. "I wear on the fourth finger of my left hand a gold ring with embossed black stone given to me by Simon Vratzian. It pictures a shovel for the peasantry, a dagger for the revolution, and a quill for the intellectual life. At the college, I became secretary to Vratzian. His eyesight was bad, so I read all his mail for him. I was allowed to open it. I edited his memoirs. I became indispensable to him. The going was hard. I learned French. I picked up money where I could—different jobs, everything from busboy to dormitory assistant. People were kind, discreet, subtle in helping a young man—especially, once again, three families who gave me moral, and even financial, support. Someone would ask me if I would accompany him to his dinner engagement, and this would mean that I would then get a free meal. The approach would be indirect. The same with clothes. I would be provided with secondhand suits, but in a most civilized manner. Vratzian had been a close friend of Aleksandr Kerensky, and, as I say, was a national hero. As his secretary, I achieved a certain prominence. Wherever he went, there were demonstrations—flowers, speeches, outpourings of emotion. I am speaking of the Middle East and a demonstrative people. I returned to Tabriz three times to visit my grandmother. On one occasion when Vratzian was delivering a speech there, I introduced him to my grandmother. I felt so proud when Simon Vratzian said to her, 'I thank you for Vartan Gregorian.' When I left home, she had told me to go out into the world and become somebody, and now I *was* somebody. Whenever I visited her home, we ate a great deal, and I would take her to see American movies. She insisted on walking out on the *Ziegfeld Follies*. 'I want to go this minute,' she said. 'Nobody has invited those people to take off their clothes.' When I was twenty-two, in 1956, I began to feel that it was time to move on, to leave Beirut and head for the outer world."

He was teeming with ideas, he said, but had no set focus. He knew that he wanted to be a scholar, and to pursue knowledge to the fullest extent of his abilities. He began the study of Portuguese, with the notion that he might go to São Paulo, Brazil, and become principal of an Armenian high school there. The United States appealed to him. So did England. As for the United States, he had certain fixed notions of life there: everybody wore eyeglasses (all the American missionaries in Beirut wore them); everybody read constantly (this explained the eyeglasses); and the country had a strong, masculine, outdoor dignity (he had seen a lot of American movies). Some instinct told him that America was the place for him. He was attracted to Stanford University. He had read extensively about Herbert Hoover's relief work in Europe during and after the First World War, and he knew a good deal about the Hoover Library at Stanford. He was offered scholarships at both Stanford and Berkeley. The Stanford letter arrived by airmail; the Berkeley one had been sent as surface mail. First come, first served. Gregorian decided to go to Stanford.

New York, his first stop in the United States, overwhelmed him. "I felt like a yellow ant," he told me. He had very little money. He spent several nights at a YMCA, at two dollars a night, and rose at 4:00 A.M. in order to wash in privacy. His room, he recalls, was like a cell. His shyness was acute. Cafeterias and self-service stamp machines fascinated him, and signs reading "PED XING" bewildered him. He was totally confused by a sign that said "ANIMAL HOSPITAL." The notion of a hospital for animals was beyond his comprehension. He remembers an entry in the diary he was keeping that read, "Noise and noise! I have an eerie feeling as if I have lived in New York for many years," and one that read, "On Sundays there is a special breakfast that costs thirty-five cents (great!). It has a catch—I gather a Protestant minister will be giving a sermon during the breakfast. No, thanks." The sight of people poking through garbage cans made him sad. He gave a panhandler twenty-five cents, and noted in his diary, "I know too well what it means not to have any money." The girls on the street, he thought, were exceptionally well dressed. In general, he felt that Americans ate too much—heavy breakfasts and dinners. He wandered into the New York Public Library and headed for the Slavic section, but almost immediately he turned and walked out, stunned by the size of the place. "I simply could not believe that someone could walk up those big front steps and enter that extraordinary building without any questions, without any identification, no proving this or proving that, and no one asking are you liberal, conservative, or wishy-washy," he said.

On another occasion, I talked with Dr. Gregorian at an Armenian restaurant in the East Thirties. "We will have lunch where you will not have to struggle with the packaging," he said. "I will show you Armenian food." I arrived at the restaurant, a pleasant place with spotless tablecloths, promptly at eleven forty-five and was directed to a table at the rear, where Dr. Gregorian was surrounded by a cluster of waiters, who were obviously enjoying his company. I heard him say to one of them, "I like the Serbian expression 'Mrtvo Puhalo.' It means 'one who is dead and doesn't know it.' So many people like that are walking around."

All the waiters spread out through the restaurant except one, who said to me, "Your order?" I immediately made it clear that my knowledge of Armenian cuisine was less than rudimentary.

"You have nothing to say today, nothing whatsoever," said Dr. Gregorian. "I am doing the ordering. This is my table. I always sit here." An order was given, in Armenian, with considerable authority. The waiter smiled a smile of complete satisfaction.

"I am going to compress some of the next academic years," said Dr. Gregorian. "Undergraduate at Stanford with a bachelor's in 1958. Then a Ph.D. in 1964. I was scheduled to study English literature, but ended up a history major. My thesis was on 'Traditionalism and Modernism in Islam.' Although I spoke seven languages, I got mixed up in English from time to time. I studied extremely hard. I even shaved my head, to avoid social engagements. Perhaps I just wanted to save on haircuts. I mixed myself up in all sorts of campus activities at the same time that I was studying. I have always been extremely active. I studied geology, but it struck me as a mystical science, and I dropped it. I studied philosophy. There was an organization of foreign students on campus, and I became head of it, and acted as master of ceremonies on different occasions. Malapropisms dropped from my lips. Once, when I was told that the top brass of Stanford was coming, I rose and announced, 'Ladies and gentlemen, I wish to introduce the brass tacks of Stanford University.' Someone told me we were in the Year of the Dog, and I rose and announced that it was a dog of a year. That sort of thing, if you can stand it.

"I taught at San Francisco State part-time, and then full-time. I taught five courses a week. I taught European intellectual history and Middle Eastern history. I taught the history of Russia. I taught European history from 1914 to the present. I taught in the mornings, I taught in the afternoons, I taught in the evenings. I *loved* to teach. Then I taught at the University of Texas. Then, in 1972, I went to the University of Pennsylvania, and *that* is a history. I was the first dean of the Faculty of Arts and Sciences, and then I became provost. It was the most exhilarating and most painful experience of my entire life. It's on my mind a great deal. It was a searing experience. Sometimes I think I am over it, other times it still haunts me. I expected to become the president of the university." Dr. Gregorian put down his knife and fork and sighed. I could see that he was becoming agitated. He said, "When I start talking about the

University of Pennsylvania, my wife says, 'Please don't talk about it again.' Sometimes she tiptoes from the room."

Dr. Gregorian said that when Martin Meyerson, then president of the university, announced his intention to retire, in 1978, it appeared that a large proportion of the faculty expected that he would be named the new president. The trustees decided otherwise. Dr. Gregorian was deeply wounded. He feels that the manner in which he was rejected assaulted and violated his most basic dignity. During the height of the decision-making process at Pennsylvania, he was under serious consideration for the chancellorship of the University of California at Berkeley, which he has always considered one of the best academic jobs in the country. Thinking that he would get the University of Pennsylvania post, Gregorian withdrew his name from consideration for the Berkeley job—only to be passed over at his home institution. There are some differences of opinion in academic circles as to precisely how far the University of California went in its pursuit of Dr. Gregorian. Most of the scholars with whom I have talked are certain that he was one of two finalists for the post. Others seem to think that he was, in fact, definitely offered the post. Some of Dr. Gregorian's opponents in the fracas at Pennsylvania claim that he was never actually offered the chancellorship. A distinguished social scientist at Harvard who was asked about such matters replied calmly, "There are no blood battles anywhere, *anywhere,* that can compare with the blood battles of academia. Horrible is the word for the massacres." In any event, on September 15, 1980—the day the University of Pennsylvania trustees announced that Sheldon Hackney, the president of Tulane, would be named the next president of the University of Pennsylvania—Dr. Gregorian announced his resignation as provost.

"I felt devastated," Gregorian told me. "And now I am going to change the subject and talk about knowledge. I sit here and I look intelligent, but we must put our minds to real concerns. What is to become of memory? Orwell didn't realize the dangers of the computer: the possibility of being *overwhelmed* by undigested information, and the possible manipulation of that information by those who process it. Furthermore, he wasn't aware of acid paper, destroying the written word. I went down to Wall Street the other day and made a talk to some businessmen, and I scared them. I told them that information is doubling every five years— talk about explosions—but that the ratio of use to available information is declining. Availability has increased, but use has diminished. Technically we have managed to perfect retrievability, but the question remains how the general public will get the information. Presumably, the scholar will be able to make his way through the new technology, but what about the individual member of the general public? How will he master the methods of retrieving information? And the cost! Nobody knows how much information will cost. Knowledge will be there, but will it be only for the rich? It costs money to use computers. Will this mean that only those with money will have access to information? I worry about this. Believe me, I worry about this. The great fear for the future is the cry 'The computer is down!'—meaning you can't get the information until the computer is working again. This puts knowledge, in a sense, in the category of airline tickets. 'Sorry, we can't confirm your reservation now, as the computer is down.' When we say that the computer is down, we give the computer itself a say in the development of knowledge. Another thing that worries me is the loss of process with the computerization of knowledge. I am contradictory about all this, for I am wholeheartedly for the new system of computers, but I do see some of the dangers. I worry about the various drafts of a story or poem or essay, the material that has gone to build up libraries. What about all the revisions of *The Waste Land* that are in our Berg Collection? Will the computerization of knowledge wipe out evidence of the process of gaining it? All the systems are dangerous, but at the same time I have great faith in them. I am an optimist at heart." . . .

Dr. Gregorian took a sip of wine. "No question the Pennsylvania experience left a deep scar," he continued. "I am afraid I glamorized the Anglo-Saxon tradition of fairness. I still often wear the blue-and-maroon university tie. I still know the names of some one thousand Penn faculty members. But once I made up my mind to come to New York in 1981, that was it. New Yorkers are not afraid of passion. They are not afraid of flamboyance or panache. I was struck by the deep feeling the trustees of the library who approached me had for their institution. Their excitement infected me. I was feeling pretty bankrupt, and I said to them that when the lions are hungry you feed them starving Armenians. I told them that we would face monumental problems, that we could go either up or down. Yet I knew that I could not only run an institution but build it and make it stronger. All my life, I have wanted to know the rules of the game, and I felt that the people who ran the library knew the rules. I know that some people criticize me for all the social events we put on—the big, expensive dinners, the monumental fund-raisers—but they are ways of showing the flag. I have also noticed that at a literary cocktail party one requires a distinct, exaggerated peripheral vision in order to see who is coming in the door, who is talking to whom, and so on. Once here, to get a feel of the place, I went into active duty at the information desk in Room 315, the card-catalogue room. A terrifying experience. I answered the phone. I could not believe the way the inquiries poured in. A lady called wanting certain information about Flaubert. I was so flustered I couldn't find anything about Flaubert. I couldn't even find his name in the catalogue. The lady was nervous. She said, 'It's my first day on a research project.' 'Lady,' I said, 'it's my first day, too.' Finally, a seasoned employee took pity on me. 'Dr. Gregorian,' he said, 'the lady seems to be looking for an article, not a book. You will find it in Periodicals.' I learned what these people do from day to day. I learned how long it takes to get a book onto a shelf. I began to appreciate the details of the system. I have never forgotten something I heard in an exchange between Mike Wallace and Marlene Dietrich. Wallace asked what was the most important thing she had learned, and she said it was how to overcome the routine in order to do the essential. In the library, I discovered that someone must open the front door. Not everybody can be creative. The cogs in the wheel are vital. It is essential that someone spend forty years answering economics questions."

Gregorian's public life would be overwhelming for even the most hyperactive executive or politician—business breakfasts, meetings all day, lunches with donors, evening ceremonies at the library and elsewhere, the almost continuous receipt of civic and educational honors. "Personally, I don't see how he manages to keep on his feet," an executive of his acquaintance, with bags under his eyes, said to me not long ago. "I lead a pretty hectic life myself, but I cannot even imagine maintaining the Gregorian pace."

Somehow, Gregorian does manage. For one thing, he takes Sundays off, and spends a good deal of the day sleeping. "Sometimes I tiptoe into the bedroom with our sons and let them watch their father snoozing on a Sunday morning," Mrs. Gregorian told me recently. "It's one of the rare times they can see him in repose." Other times are those isolated evenings when nothing is scheduled—no lecture to attend at the library, no medal for good citizenship to receive—and on one such evening he invited me to dinner at his home. He lives in a sky-piercing high rise in the East Nineties. The lobby is flashy, with the razzle-dazzle décor that is said to inflame Bloomingdale's customers and turn them into frenzied buyers. Mrs. Gregorian greeted me at their door; she said that her husband would be home any moment. The apartment in which the Gregorians live is two apartments turned into one. As a result, the rooms are strangely shaped, with odd angles and unexpected corners. Round pillars are to be seen here and there. The floors are covered with stunning Oriental rugs. Books are everywhere, and on the walls are many framed maps of the Mediterranean area and the Middle East. "Vartan is very fond of maps," Mrs. Gregorian said, "but I honestly don't think he knows how to read one. He just likes to look at them." I noticed a great many record albums, and a stereo system. "I happen to love Fats Waller," she said to me. "That wonderful left hand. Nobody plays with the left hand anymore."

The front door opened, with a sudden gust of air. Dr. Gregorian had arrived. He embraced his wife. He gave me a bear hug. A golden retriever, which had evidently been waiting somewhere in the depths of the apartment for the arrival of its master, bounded into the living room. "Ah, Eliza," said Gregorian, embracing the dog. Mrs. Gregorian invited me to sit down at a brass coffee table that looked Middle Eastern. Gregorian said that it came from Boston. Mrs. Gregorian is a generous hostess, and she brought out and set on the coffee table a series of succulent hot hors d'oeuvres, all with a Middle Eastern flavor. There was a plate of smoked beef. There was a plate of blanched eggplant, which was surrounded by pita bread. "I use olive oil, pomegranate seed, and scallions for the eggplant dip," said Mrs. Gregorian. She was quite obviously proud of her Armenian dishes. We moved into the dining room, a corner room with picture windows, strange angles, and a lighted evergreen tree. Dinner was spectacular—a rich beef stew with a mysterious and tantalizing sauce, and a huge salad of lettuce, red peppers, Greek olives, and feta cheese. For dessert, Mrs. Gregorian had made a pumpkin mousse with fresh, pungent ginger spread over the top. "Clare does every bit of this, and I think it's wonderful," Dr. Gregorian said. He seemed deeply content, a man happy to be home.

As he had when we first met, Gregorian spoke a bit about his church, the Armenian Apostolic. "It goes back centuries, to a real split in 451, concerning a dispute on the divinity of Christ and his human qualities. The church in which I was raised uses classical Armenian in its litany. Nobody understands more than 40 percent of it, but it's used. There are few good Armenian dictionaries extant, and only a handful of Armenian phrase books, mostly out-of-date. I was looking at one the other night and came across the entry 'Can you tell me where I can find the nearest tenement?' "

I was given a choice of American or Armenian coffee. I chose Armenian. It was delicious and so thick that I could have floated on it. We moved back into the living room. The lights of the city outside the picture windows, and the Triborough Bridge, with its green illumination, lent the room a dramatic air. Gregorian told me again how much he had enjoyed teaching, and what it had meant to him. He missed most of all, he felt, the idea of being in a position to forge young characters. "I was nervous before every lecture," he said. "I was almost sick from nerves, but once I started talking I could go on forever. I recall a lecture, one day, about Faust. I went on and on. An entire class stood patiently outside the door waiting to get in for the next lecture. I was carried away. Teachers are governed by three things. One, they must be enthusiastic. Two, they must remember that the student has never heard any of this before. And, three, they must tell the truth. Above all, the truth." Gregorian pronounced the word as though it were Holy Writ. "Just a word about origins, before you leave," he said to me. "I want you to see this ceramic tile of Adam and Eve, copied from a ninth-century Armenian manuscript. Adam and Eve are fully clothed, and the serpent still has hands. You can see the serpent handing over the apple."

The evening was at an end. Dr. Gregorian insisted on riding down with me in the elevator, accompanied by Eliza. As we stepped into the lobby, he suddenly seemed like a visitor from another world, a bustling, compact figure distinctly removed from his immediate surroundings.

"There must be many times," I said to him, "when you are overpowered by the distance you have come from your origins."

"That happens many, many times," he said, with deep feeling. "The mysteries of my life multiply. The odd coincidences, the strange turns and twists. Things happen to me that simply cannot happen. For instance, in the very neighborhood where we live, a pastry shop has opened. Nooshin Pastry and Café. Can you believe that this is the same Nooshin Café that stood on Istanbul Avenue in Tehran—one of the first places I ate when, as a teenager, I went to the capital. Transplanted here! The odds of this happening must be several billion to one, and yet it has happened to me. Just the other day, I wrote my sister of this coincidence. My life is filled with such puzzles, endlessly beckoning, endlessly mysterious, endlessly fascinating."

A few days ago, I walked over to the library. It was the middle of the day and the middle of the week, and the library was crowded. Room 315 had been reopened, after being restored to its original appearance, as designed by Carrère and Hastings. It is a dignified room with big windows. The card catalogue was gone, of course, and I missed it. Some people were pulling the huge printed catalogue volumes from the shelves; others were standing in front of the thirty-two computer terminals. I tried my luck at one of them, hitting the keyboard of the terminal with my own name, which had been in the card catalogue. Green letters instantly flashed on the terminal screen. "Type HELP," they said. I realized that I was in the grip of technology and needed patience, perseverance, and an open mind. I felt blue about this until I walked into one of the enormous reading rooms behind the catalogue room. There sat hundreds of people, quietly reading. There was a slight murmur in the room, almost a whisper, and it sounded like low music of the spheres. As long as there is this reading room, these people, this murmur, I thought, we are safe. Perhaps.

CASUALS

I have no idea who came up with the term "casuals" to denote a certain type of piece for *The New Yorker*. There would seem to be no rules in this area. For the most part, they are short flights of fancy, and pretty much what the word implies. They can be fact, fiction, parody, or autobiography, and are meant to be read at one's leisure and enjoyed.

Some People Watch Birds

I do not wish to push myself forward as a municipal historian, but I think that I can shed some light on the habits of several recent mayors of the City of New York and their families. For the past ten years, I have lived in an apartment in a remodelled brownstone on East End Avenue, directly across from Gracie Mansion, the official residence of the mayor. From my living-room window, I look down upon the lovely old white house, with its imposing iron gates and fence separating it from Carl Schurz Park, in which it is situated. Beyond the Mansion lies the tidal turbulence of Hell Gate, where the East River becomes all churned up and behaves like an inland sea. Since I am by nature a lazy and easily abstracted man, I have spent an appalling amount of time during the past decade just staring out the window. If nothing is going on at the Mansion, I wait for a boat to come past. If no boat comes past, I wait for something to happen at the Mansion.

My first mayor was Fiorello H. LaGuardia. He was already in residence at the Mansion, along with his wife and his young son and daughter, when I took up my post at the window. LaGuardia was certainly the busiest of our recent mayors, and he spent, for a mayor, an inordinate amount of time at City Hall. Thanks to this perversity, I didn't see as much of him as I would have liked. He left the house each weekday morning shortly after eight-thirty, bustling down the steps from the porch and leaping into a police prowl car parked in the Mansion's circular driveway. (I never saw LaGuardia in a limousine, although I know that at one time he used one that was equipped with telephone, dictating machine, and fire hat.) The popular conception that he always wore a big black hat is, according to my observations, entirely correct. LaGuardia got home from work about seven-thirty. The lights in the Mansion, with the exception of one light in a room on the second floor, went out about nine-thirty. Some neighborhood gossips once pointed this lighted room out to me as the Mayor's bedroom; its light was doused by eleven. LaGuardia worked Sundays, too, heading for City Hall shortly before noon.

Mrs. LaGuardia was more in evidence. She and her Scotty strolled leisurely around the Mansion grounds almost every morning. Some days, they walked up and down East End Avenue, and at such times she was accompanied by the policeman who ordinarily sat in the small sentry box at the Mansion gates. The walks were uneventful. Some mornings she talked to the policeman, some mornings she did not. Some mornings she seemed to be talking to the dog. Often, in the late afternoon, the LaGuardia children chased each other around the lawn. One Sunday afternoon, the Mayor played hooky from City Hall and spent an hour or so on the lawn, batting out flies to his son. I have been told by neighborhood people that the LaGuardia boy fell from a tree near the house twice, and broke his arm each time. I am happy to report that I was not mayor-watching, or mayor-family-watching, on either occasion.

Once, during the LaGuardia era, I was interviewed by a newspaper-woman simply because I lived across the street from the Mayor. Somewhere in the Bronx, a lady had shaken her dust mop from her apartment window, a complaint had been lodged against her by some unfortunate who happened to be standing below, and she had been fined. Several days later, the lady phoned the newspaper *PM* to say that a friend of hers who lived near Gracie Mansion had seen a maid in the Mansion shake a dust mop from an upstairs window. How come, the lady asked *PM*, someone at Gracie Mansion could get away with mop shaking when she could not? Was there any justice or wasn't there? *PM*, which had a greased pole from its city room to the street, designed to speed reporters on just such urgent missions, instantly dispatched a young woman with a notebook to East End Avenue. She went from house to house in the row of brownstones on my block, ringing the bells of all the apartments. Had anyone seen a dust mop being shaken from a window of Gracie Mansion? Nobody knew, one way or the other; most of the people on the block weren't mayor-watchers. She was about to give up the story when she rang my bell. She had come to the right place. I assured her that, to my knowledge, no such incident had taken place, and that it was highly unlikely such an incident could have taken place without my knowing about it. She seemed reassured, stayed for tea, asked my wife how *she* shook out dust mops (onto paper, spread on the floor), and said that newspaper work was tough but that she loved every minute of it. The next day, she wrote a pleasant story about the mop episode, mentioning me by name. For the next week, I left the window only to eat and sleep.

In LaGuardia's time, the fence around the Mansion was fairly close to the house. There was plenty of lawn space to the east and north—on the river and uptown sides, that is—less space to the west, and barely any to the south. The southern part of the fence almost nudged the Mayor's dining room. I was astonished at the number of children and adults who gathered in Carl Schurz Park at the LaGuardia dinner hour and stared through the democratically unshuttered windows at the Mayor and his family while they ate. This upset me. For one thing, I didn't like the idea of anybody else mayor-watching. For another, I was sorry for the LaGuardias; there are few more disconcerting situations than looking up from the dinner table and seeing strangers peering in at you through the window. LaGuardia must have felt that this was part of the price of being in public life, for he did nothing about it. O'Dwyer, when he became mayor, acted with swiftness, moving the fence on the southern side to a sensible distance from the dining-room windows. The groups who had watched LaGuardia eating were incensed. They took up their stand behind the new fence and one could hear them shouting angrily, but O'Dwyer paid no attention to them and after a few nights they went away.

The LaGuardias didn't entertain much, or at least not enough for me. I get a real kick out of a first-class, bang-up party at Gracie Mansion. Early on the morning of a party, "No Parking" signs are strung up on all the trees and lampposts on East End Avenue from Eighty-sixth to Ninetieth Street. By the middle of the afternoon, parked cars are being joyously hauled away by large Department of Sanitation derrick trucks to some private resting ground the city maintains for delinquent automobiles. At dusk, lights blaze in every window of the Mansion. The gates are opened wide. Two antique carriage lamps, on top of the gateposts, are switched on. (In LaGuardia's time, the gate lights were precinct-house green, the traditional color of lamps outside the home of the city's chief magistrate. O'Dwyer changed the color to white, possibly because, being an ex-policeman, he felt uncomfortable with this reminder of his past just beyond his windows. Mayor Impellitteri shifted the color to highway yellow—the sort of lights one sees on express highways, which are designed, it is said, to dispel fog.) I can recall no large-scale parties when LaGuardia lived in the Mansion; after all, the war was still on. O'Dwyer, coming into office after the war, radically changed the Mansion's entertainment schedule. O'Dwyer was gregarious, and he loved to give parties. I watched some wonderful parties during his time, but none finer than the one he gave for Señor Alemán, the visiting President of Mexico. Alemán and O'Dwyer were close friends. The President had thrown a spectacular party for O'Dwyer once in Mexico City, and the Mayor was determined to outshine him. Throughout the morning of the party, caterers' trucks drove in and out of the driveway. Several hundred gilt banquet chairs were unloaded at noon and taken into the Mansion. Festive Japanese lanterns were hung all over the lawn. In the late afternoon, Cadillacs began discharging the distinguished guests. Red-coated musicians, standing on the lawn, serenaded them. I am somewhat confused about this party, for I have a recurring dream that I am attending it, and requesting that the song "Valencia" be played. It is played, and played again. I have a splendid time at the party, and the Mayor is extremely gracious. I often wonder if I *did* go to that party.

Whether I went to that party or not, I saw more of O'Dwyer than I did of LaGuardia. He seemed to have a genuine feeling for the Mansion, and on Sundays, especially in mild weather, he would often turn up on the lawn, in his shirtsleeves, and talk with passersby through the fence. Occasionally, he would sit outside Carl Schurz Park, on a ledge that runs alongside the park fence on East End Avenue, sunning himself, and chewing the rag with neighborhood people. After he married Sloan Simpson, he took her on walks in the park; they strolled about, the Mayor tipping his hat, and Mrs. O'Dwyer smiling and waving her hand to the burghers. There was an Old World quality to these promenades, and I always looked forward to them. O'Dwyer's romantic streak was real and touching, and it was evident to a mayor-watcher that he derived deep satisfaction from showing off his new bride. Although informal in a neighborhood sense, O'Dwyer was formal when it came to official limousines. He regularly used a long, black Cadillac, not the prowl car of LaGuardia's time. East End Avenue had never seen so many Cadillacs before, and will probably never see so many Cadillacs again. Few people came to the Mansion in anything but Cadillacs. One person, though, who did not arrive in a Cadillac was the Mayor's barber, John Vitale. He was an elderly Italian with a thick gray mustache, who operated a barbershop on East End Avenue near Eighty-fourth Street. Mr. Vitale showed up on foot almost every morning, making his way slowly and with tremendous dignity along East End Avenue and through the gates of the Mansion, swinging a small black bag. He went through the gates with something of the manner Gladstone must have employed as he arrived at Buckingham Palace for an audience with Queen Victoria. Mr. Vitale is no longer on East End Avenue. He has moved around the corner to Eighty-first Street, and his old shop is unoccupied.

O'Dwyer often visited Doctors Hospital, across the street from the Mansion and a few yards to the south. I guess he visited sick friends there. The Mayor always strode through the gates, crossed East End Avenue, shook hands with Mr. Cahill, the hospital's doorman, and entered the hospital. His Cadillac followed, and waited for him outside the hospital entrance.

O'Dwyer left Gracie Mansion for the last time on a hot summer day in 1950. He had resigned as mayor, and was headed for a rest in California and then Mexico City. A small knot gathered outside the gates to watch him leave. In the late morning, his Cadillac drove slowly out through the gates. The policeman at the sentry box saluted. The car turned south on East End. Suddenly, it stopped in front of Doctors Hospital, and the Mayor leaned out of the car window. Mr. Cahill came forward from under the hospital marquee and shook hands with O'Dwyer. Then the car drove off. I have not seen him since, and I don't suppose that Mr. Cahill has, either.

There isn't much to say about Mayor Impellitteri. Perhaps, as I have picked up more interests in life, I have mayor-watched less than when I first moved into the neighborhood, but Mayor Impellitteri is an almost nonexistent figure to me. The gates to the Mansion are closed most of the time. The lights aren't on much. Sometimes I think that nobody has been living there regularly. Occasionally, Mrs. Impellitteri drives off from the Mansion in the middle of the morning in a big car. Occasionally, the Impellitteris give a party, but without red-coated musicians or Japanese lanterns. Occasionally, the Mayor visits Doctors Hospital, but he doesn't walk across the street, he rides. A year or so ago, when he returned from his visit to Sicily, a station wagon piled high with luggage swept into the Mansion grounds. Perched on top of the luggage, in the rear of the wagon, was the Mayor.

As for the Wagners, who can say? They are young, they have two boys, they will move in the first of the year. I may be having an exciting era of mayor-watching ahead of me, and then again I may not. There is no way to predict this sort of thing.

Progress Report

My life as a mayor-watcher came to an abrupt halt a few years ago, when the building in which I lived, which lay directly across the street from Gracie Mansion, the building in which the mayor lived, was torn down. It was a shattering experience, the end of a personal era, and I felt as though the bottom had dropped out of my world—or, more accurately, out of the window through which I viewed the world. Overnight, my semi-official status was gone. I had prided myself on my ability to keep pretty close tabs on the city's chief executive. I had been a conscientious mayor-watcher. In fact, I can safely claim to be the first mayor-watcher on record, and I recorded my findings in these pages about a decade ago. If the mayor summoned a group of his top commissioners to a breakfast conference at the Mansion, I was there, at the window, watching the long, black, official limousines swing into the driveway. If the mayor's children came home for Thanksgiving, Christmas, or Easter, I shared their joy at being home again. (After all, I had watched them grow up.) If the mayor was about to hold a huge reception on his spacious lawn, I stood transfixed as the caterers' trucks, bearing thousands of little sandwiches, rolled up to the kitchen door. If the mayor's wife walked the dogs, I, at my post, observed the simple scene. And so it went, year in, year out—a rich, full, vicarious life. There was a good deal more to mayor-watching, however, than mere mayors, and I missed most the moments of blessed relaxation, when there was a lull in events at the Mansion and I could temporarily shed my duties and stare beyond the white, eighteenth-century house to the swift waters of the East River and the massive tidal ebb and flow of Hell Gate. From time to time, mayors bedded down their dogs, turned out the lights in their children's rooms, and went to sleep, but the life of the river, with its tugs and barges and pleasure craft—and they, in turn, with their hoots and sea cries and blinking running lights—never ceased. It was a wonderland of sky, water, and mayors, and I loved it.

Well, the building was torn down, and I moved several blocks inland, to the west, to Lexington Avenue. The first thing I did, of course, when I moved into my new apartment, was to head for a window and look out. I drew back, shaken. My instinct was to pull the shades, and devote the rest of my life to rereading the collected works of Emily Dickinson. Summoning up my courage, I took another look. The vista was unpromising—a nice, quiet, genteel, respectable, middle-class vista: a newsstand, a drugstore, a bar-and-grill, a furrier's shop, a custom shirtmaker, a butcher shop, a shoe-repair place, a delicatessen, an apartment house, a spidery assortment of fire escapes, and a bus stop. There was no sign of a mayor, and no rational expectation that one would turn up, even at the bus stop. I stood in the window for some time, evaluating my situation. My mayor-watching days were over, that was certain. I had been cut off from my major preoccupation in the prime of life and cast adrift in a new and alien locale. My transplantation could not have been more complete had I been set down in a window in the heart of Des Moines, Iowa. I felt pretty blue. Nothing, certainly, was ever going to happen *here*.

I resolved never to wash the windows in the new place. I would let the dust and grime of the city accumulate until they completely obscured the view, or non-view, across the street, leaving me alone, inside, with my memories of LaGuardia, O'Dwyer, Impellitteri, Wagner, and the Moran tugboat company. Even while I entertained these unhealthy and melancholy thoughts, I noticed, with a flicker of interest, that a long, gray Cadillac had drawn up at the bus stop in front of the butcher shop, and that a long, gray man, wearing a gray fedora and a gray Chesterfield, had emerged from the car, gone around to the back of the car, opened the luggage compartment, hoisted a side of beef onto his shoulder, and headed into the store. This man, I told myself halfheartedly, would bear watching. Not only was he debonairly parked at a bus stop, but he was the first butcher within my experience to bring his produce to his store in a Cadillac. I shuddered at the thought that I might become a butcher-watcher, but anything seemed better than nothing, and I went about my private affairs for the rest of the day, and retired early.

I awoke to the sound of shattering glass. I glanced quickly at the clock beside my bed, noticed that it was three in the morning, and bounded to the window. Lights blazed in the bar-and-grill across the street—an establishment that I shall call Mother Machree. Two men were rolling around on the pavement, pummelling one another. Two other men, in front of Mother Machree, were dazedly and stiff-leggedly circling each other, as though in a trance. The butcher's car was still parked by the bus stop, and a man sat on the hood of the car, his body racked with sobs. There was a gaping, jagged hole in the plate-glass window of Mother Machree, and as I stood watching, a rather small man crawled through the hole in the glass, reached the street, and began to brush himself off. He was obviously a fastidious man, deeply humiliated by his situation. His appearance instantly brought all the others to attention. The men who were rolling around rose, the dazed pair stopped circling, and the sobbing man slipped off the hood of the car. They surrounded the small, fastidious man, picked him up, and threw him back through the opening in the store front of Mother Machree. Then they began to hit each other, wildly. The small man, whose courage must have been the courage of ten, once again crawled through the opening, and began once again to brush himself off. He was immediately tossed back through the opening from which he had emerged. Four police cars, their sirens wailing and their red lights sweeping the night, materialized in front of Mother Machree. Within minutes, all the men had been whisked off by the muscular arm of the law. I went back to bed and fell into a deep, satisfied slumber. A new life had begun.

The next morning, when I rose, refreshed, and looked out the window, workmen were already on hand installing a new plate-glass front on the bar-and-grill. The butcher's car was gone. When I went downstairs, later in the morning, and asked the doorman if he had heard about the excitement across the street, he seemed singularly unmoved. "Some sort of brawl," he said, casually. "Some fellows stayed up too late and had too much to drink and tossed someone through the plate glass. Happens all the time at Mother Machree." By the time I got back upstairs, the butcher's car was parked again at the bus stop. The same gray-clad gentleman was busily removing boxes of what appeared to be chickens, in various positions of repose, from the luggage compartment and taking them into his store. Buses had to fend for themselves, grinding to a halt alongside his car. On the roof of the building that housed the shirtmaker, a young lady in blue shorts was hanging wash on a line. It was a warm day, and she went about her work slowly and meticulously. When she had finished hanging up the wash, she lay down in a beach chair and went to sleep. She was prettier by far than any mayor I had ever watched. Looking directly across the street, I could see into a modestly appointed living room, lined with books and prominently occupied by two baby-grand pianos. Two small boys were seated at the pianos, obviously practicing. I watched them for some time, until a woman (whom I took to be their mother) came into the room, clapped her hands, and signalled the end of the session. I decided to have my windows washed at least once a month.

One picks up the strands of a new life slowly, a thread here, a thread there. Women shrieked pitifully, on disturbingly frequent occasions, in Mother Machree. "He's killing me, he's killing me!" became a familiar night cry, rousing me and sending me to the window, only to see a man and woman emerge, arm in arm, and head into the night. The plate-glass window was shattered again (although nobody was tossed through it), and the prowl cars arrived again, but could locate no culprits. The police milled about for a while, chatting with the bartender in the red glow of a neon sign, and drove off. My older son, an inquisitive young man in his teens, came into my room one night, after an especially hectic Donnybrook in front of Mother's, and announced that he was glad we had moved and hoped we would never move again. "This is *life*!" he said. "This is real *life*! I'm learning more than I ever learned over by the river." Then he went back to bed.

The man who ran the newsstand fell ill. His wife struggled to carry on the business for a few months, and then sold out to a laundromat. *Nothing* ever happened at the laundromat. Women brought their bundles of laundry, put them in the machines, and just sat around, waiting. In the shoe-repair shop, the old Greek shoemaker with the face of a poet opened his place daily at eight and closed it daily at seven, spending the intervening hours in the window tearing off soles and heels and replacing them with soles and heels. I found the rhythm of his motions comforting, as he pounded away with his tiny hammer and kept removing what appeared to be an endless supply of nails from his mouth. One winter night, the wind howled furiously and the plate-glass window in the furrier's place suddenly blew out. Simultaneously, a series of shrill alarm bells automatically began to ring. Expensively draped mannequins stood in the window giving the impression that they were violently shivering. It was a golden chance for someone to come by, reach in the window, and remove a mink or two. The police were prompt. A battalion of them arrived and stood guard throughout the night in front of the exposed window. They must have had difficulty locating the store owner, for it wasn't until dawn that a harassed man turned up, wringing his hands, and took the furs off the mannequins, leaving them looking colder and more forlorn than before.

I began to sleep lightly, and at the first tinkle of an alarm bell I was up and at the window. One night, someone broke through the front door of the drugstore. I was at the window in time to see a shadowy figure race from the store and head down a side street. This time, a division of police arrived. Once again, they milled around, apparently getting nowhere. Next morning, the doorman had a grave look on his face. "Dope fiend," he said. "Dope fiend broke into the drugstore and made off with dope. Dope fiend." An iron grille now guards the front of the drugstore, and I sleep more lightly than ever.

About a year ago, a man I will call Mr. Lazzeri, who runs the delicatessen, fired his first shot. At least, it was the first shot by Mr. Lazzeri that I heard, and it was the full-fledged, insistent, percussive shot of a shotgun. I was at the window before I knew it. Mr. Lazzeri is short and stocky, he stays open almost all night, and he wears an old-fashioned long white apron. He was out in the street, firing to the north. He then broke into a run and headed north. The prowl cars arrived almost before the sound of the shots had died away. They slid silently up to the front of the delicatessen, their sirens stilled and their red lights extinguished, and swung into position at right angles to the curb in a crazy-quilt arrangement. A few minutes later, Mr. Lazzeri returned, gun in hand. He climbed into a prowl car and was whizzed off. Next morning, I went around to his place to buy a bottle of milk. He was uncommunicative. There is a mind-your-own-business look about him. His eyes are small and red, his cheekbones are high. His face is perpetually flushed, and he has a mouth that spells vengeance. "How are things?" I asked. "Thirty-one cents," he said. I did not intend to be put off quite so easily, and I bought a carton of cigarettes, a tin of anchovies, and a loaf of Italian bread. I noticed a slight thaw in Mr. Lazzeri. "Heard the noises last night," I said, cautiously. "Robbers," said Mr. Lazzeri, in a sudden gush of confidence. "They come in here at night, because I am the only light on the block except for the bar, and they want to steal, and they want to kill me, and I will kill them." He reached behind the counter and produced the shotgun. "They think they'll get me first. *I'll get them first!*"

I warned my wife and children never to buy anything at Mr. Lazzeri's after dark, and went back to watching the occasional fist fights in front of Mother's. A month later, another shot, another glimpse of Mr. Lazzeri out in the street, gun, apron, and all, and another rendezvous of prowl cars. During the past six months, the tempo has accelerated at Lazzeri's, and I have found it necessary to spend most of my time watching his place and neglecting the others. I hear the shots, but I have yet to see the robber, or robbers, or even catch a glimpse of them. About two weeks ago, there was a mighty fusillade. Mr. Lazzeri, I could tell, was beside himself. He kept firing and firing indiscriminately down a long, sloping block that runs past a group of fashionable brownstones to Third Avenue. I happen to know that a distinguished cultural adviser to the United States government, a world-famous photographer, a noted lawyer, and an internationally celebrated abstract painter live on the block, which is tree-lined. The street was pitch dark, and I had the sinking feeling that if anyone should stick his head out of his door to see what the shooting was all about it would have been blown off by Mr. Lazzeri. Nobody stuck his head out, and the prowl cars once again arrived, and the police led Mr. Lazzeri back to his delicatessen. Just the other night, he was at it again, filling the neighborhood with his explosions. His mind is made up. He is going to kill the robbers, any robbers. Nothing can stop him. Lazzeri is a man possessed, and I, unfortunately, am also possessed. Fate has decreed that I will be at the window when Lazzeri gets his man, or men.

Meanwhile, life is not all shrieks and shattered glass. Mother Machree seems to be catering to a less turbulent crowd; it has dressed itself up, somewhat, and installed a brightly colored, filigreed wooden canopy across its frontage. (Mother Machree was forced to this move several months ago, when its overhead neon sign fell to the pavement one morning, bruising a passerby.) The canopy is inhibitory and has quieted things down. It has lent Mother's a curious status that discourages mayhem. The shoemaker continues to pull little nails from his mouth, and the mannequins, behind their window in the fur shop, look sleek, reasonably happy, and warm. People stand in clusters in the mornings at the bus stop, waiting to go to work. If the butcher's car is not there, they board the bus without inconvenience. If the car is present, they race around it to catch the bus. Nobody seems to mind, one way or the other. The two boys across the street, I gather, have gone away to school. In any event, they are visible only during holidays, at their pianos. They are growing up nicely. I have the feeling that they are fine lads, perhaps even fine pianists, and that everything will work out well for them, unless they happen to get in the way of Mr. Lazzeri's shotgun.

The Doorbell

(A Dramatic Exercise in the Manner of Harold Pinter)

———————

The action of the play takes place in a flat off the Tottenham Court Road, London. A large room with skylight. Bare white walls. Scattered chairs. A bright-red bentwood hatrack. A long narrow refectory table set with single brass candlestick.

Evening. Winter.

Beatrice and Allen enter through door, stage right. They are in their forties.

BEATRICE: Mauve.

ALLEN: Purple.

Pause.

BEATRICE: Which purple?

ALLEN: Light. Dark. Vivid. Very light. Very dark. Royal. Imperial. Balkan.

Long silence.

BEATRICE: Mauve. (*Hangs up hat and coat. Sits in chair.*) Every bloke in town thinks mauve. Charwomen think mauve. Chimney sweeps think mauve. Turf accountants think mauve. The Prime Minister thinks mauve. The Maharaja of Boohoolie thinks mauve. And you think purple! If you can't think mauve, flake off. My mum warned me when you first came around. Warned me, she did. Wrinkled old bag was so messy you couldn't tell the mum from the mop. But she warned me. Watch out

The Doorbell

for him, she said. He'll twist your liver, she said. He'll pound your pancreas, that one will.

Pause.

ALLEN: Not half so bad as all that, not really half so bad. (*Hangs up hat and coat, sits in chair at far end of room from Beatrice.*) Riding around in the tube, at least, was fun. Reading the stations was fun. Goodge Street, Warren Street, Euston, Mornington Crescent, Camden Town. Adventure, you said then. I'm in Arabia, you said. I'm on a flying carpet! (*Pause*) You were perky. When the announcer cried Mind the door! Mind the door!, you stuck out your little tongue and said Mind the door yourself! I admired that. Within my limits of looking at the matter, I thought that took spunk. (*Long pause*) Got off at The Striped Carrot. And you read the leaves.

Silence.

BEATRICE: *You* read the leaves. You always read the leaves.

ALLEN: Not that time, I didn't, mate. Not at The Striped Carrot. If you're talking about Cuckfield or Leighton Buzzard or High Wycombe, those leaves I did read. Soggy they were, too. And bad. Especially High Wycombe. Beware aunts and uncles, they said. Beware sisters, brothers, cousins, adopted nieces, foster parents, and wards of the court. Beware the whole last bloody lot of them, the leaves said. (*Pause*) I can remember I was quite shaken by the reading.

Long, long silence.

BEATRICE: The nurse was kind. She had a dog face. Big red ears, long red nose. She inspired confidence. I felt at ease. When she asked me to rinse, I rinsed. When she said open, I opened. When she stuffed the cotton wadding, I smiled. The surgeon was the bad one. I hated the surgeon. I disliked his manner, so to speak. I felt threatened in his presence. Relax, he said. This will only take a minute, he said. This will hurt me more than it hurts you, he said. I wanted to scream, do you understand my meaning? I wanted to flee. I wanted to kick him in the privates. We have ways of making you laugh, he said. They say I laughed a great deal while he was working on me. They say he worked on me very quickly. He must have gone right to work on me. He was very deft and cunning. I think he was Spanish.

Long pause.

ALLEN: What became of the tooth? I seem to remember something

(157)

about your giving me the tooth. For safekeeping. Put the tooth away, you said, with all the other teeth.

Silence.

BEATRICE: I had a special feeling for teeth in those days. Molars, pre-molars, canines, incisors, it didn't matter. My bureau drawers were full of them. They represented something important to me. What I am driving at is that those teeth were my teeth, they weren't somebody else's teeth. They weren't the landlord's teeth. They weren't Mum's teeth, you can count on that. She didn't have any teeth.

Long, long silence.

ALLEN: I am the last person in the world to quarrel about small things. Such as me reading the leaves at The Striped Carrot, or you reading the leaves. But there is such a thing as elemental justice. The bedrock, you see. The base. Either a thing happened or it didn't. No two ways about it. Men understand these matters. I am inclined to be set in my ways about this sort of thing. I don't shift ground easily. All my old friends know this about me. They are very well acquainted with this side of my character. They prefer not to cross me. They know that I am capable of giving a good account of myself. (*Pause*) My old chums would call something a footstool. They would point at an object and say, That's a footstool. Oh, no, I'd say, that's an ottoman. And then I would look round the room very slowly to see if I had convinced them or not. And if anybody still thought it was a footstool I would reluctantly be forced to flatten them. Flatten them cold. From time to time, we would get off into history, topics of cultural interest, broad general reading, wide background, preparation for life, and all that. Test one's mettle. Jog a bit about the mental track. Sweep out the cobwebs, you understand my meaning? I would give them a very simple lesson. Lads, I'd say, the order of succession went Edwy the Fair, Edgar the Peaceful, and Edward the Martyr. Some camel face from the provinces would open his blooper at this point and say, Are you not forgetting Ethelred the Unready? (*Long pause*) I would fracture his skull. He was attempting to place Ethelred the Unready where he least belonged. I can cite other examples, some of them too numerous to mention. But at The Striped Carrot, I didn't bring my glasses, and I didn't read the leaves.

Long silence.

BEATRICE: I suppose it wasn't you at Clapham Common, when we walked past the cemetery in the rain? And you took my hand and I went wet inside. And I said, There will always be room for you in the family plot, Puss in Boots, lying beside me forever under the elms in the green moonlight, next to the Skipper, God rest him, and alongside my mum, if she'd just shove off. And I suppose it wasn't you mucking about on that damp slab, breathing heavy and saying you would consider it an honor and a privilege to be lying with me under this sod in eternal bliss, surrounded by all these distinguished cheesers.

Long pause.

ALLEN: It wasn't me at Clapham Common. It was me in the train. I will admit that. The Night Scotsman, London to Edinburgh, sleeping cars, and all that. Slip me the time, you said. Just slip me the time. Eleven-thirty-five, it was. King's Cross. Slip me the time, you said. You're a saucy bugger, you said, and I fell out of the upper at Doncaster. Or Selby. Or York. Near three in the morning, it was. We reached Edinburgh at six-fifty-seven. Slip me the time, you said.

Silence.

BEATRICE: That wasn't the train, and it wasn't you. That was the Fishguard-to-Cork ferry, and it was your brother.

The doorbell rings. They do not seem to hear it.

ALLEN: I suppose it wasn't me at Brighton, eh? You looked like a sick sparrow then. You were wafer thin. Your bones jangled. If you had sneezed, you would have died. (*Rises, walks to refectory table, picks up candlestick, holds it menacingly over Beatrice's head. Long pause. Allen replaces candlestick, resumes seat.*) I fattened you up. I walked you up and down the beach in the salt air. And all the while I was looking into your face, close up.

Silence.

BEATRICE: That was Harry, close up, at Brighton. That wasn't you. I admired the cut of Harry's jib. There was nothing lumpy about Harry.

The doorbell rings.

Long, long silence.

ALLEN: I can remember the Governor saying to me when I was a nipper that he didn't think much of me in general, in a manner of speaking. We were on Route 705 of the Green Line. Chiswick or Bromley, Westerham Hill or Osterley. Maybe Catford. Maybe Catford.

The doorbell rings.

At Barking, I took you to Dr. Wu's for dinner. Fu sent me, I said, and they gave us a table near the parrot. You were impressed. Holus-bolus!

screamed the parrot. You were amused. You gave me your first teeth. I'm glad you brought me, you said. I don't give a fig about Harry, you said. I ordered the won ton and I told you I loved you.

The doorbell rings.

I ordered the egg rolls and I told you I loved you.

The doorbell rings.

I ordered the lobster Kew with bean sprouts and tiny button mushrooms and I told you I loved you.

The doorbell rings.

And I said, Let's settle down. (*Pause*) Let's build a nest. (*Pause*) Let's thatch the roof. (*Pause*) Let's amalgamate the porridge.

The doorbell rings.

BEATRICE: That wasn't me and it wasn't you.

Allen seizes candlestick, holds it aloft menacingly.

ALLEN (*coolly approaching her*): I don't think you understand my meaning.

The doorbell rings continuously.

The curtain falls.

Double Vision

(Some notes inspired by the New York Times *Op. Ed. Page, which bravely sets out, as far as one can tell, to present every conceivable side of every conceivable question)*

THE PLUS OF POLLUTION

By George Sylvester Burberry

Too many people these days go around taking it for granted that pollution per se is a bad thing. They hear about air pollution and water pollution and just jump to the conclusion that it's harmful. I disagree. In my opinion, the worst part about pollution is the propaganda against it that the media have been spreading. I base my argument in this space on intensive research studies undertaken by the Willis Harlan Olburn Institute of the Environment, at Grand Union College, which first used vitaminized gerbils as guinea pigs. The findings revealed:

1. Gerbils, with no prodding or *outside* tactile stimuli, and during their leisure periods, displayed more creative energy (e.g., imaginative building-block formations, improvised tunes on their recorders, and so on) when waves of carbon-monoxide gas were blown into their cages than during periods when these same cages were systematically filled with purified air.

2. Four small plates were placed in the cages of the gerbils, each containing a different ingredient. Plate No. 1 held the candy-coated dry cereal Flourpower, possessing two hundred per cent more direct protein fulfillment than is generally required for a family of four gerbils; Plate No. 2 held emulsified sateen ochre; Plate No. 3, enzyme nuggets; Plate No. 4, "poison" liquid mercury in a cream sauce. Statis-

tics showed that the gerbils not only devoured every last particle of the mercury "poison" but came back for seconds. Systematic checking of the height and weight of the gerbils further confirmed the health-giving qualities of the ingested "poison." "Frankly, they never looked better in their lives; nor have I ever seen them in better spirits," said Dr. Ernest R. Laudendorf, the Institute's *Gerbilmeister*. "If what these gerbils have been subjected to is pollution, I say let's have more of it!"

3. The Institute enlisted the help of the Exhaust Fumes Committee of the American Academy of Automotive Freedom, in Detroit, for some additional tests. The committee needs no endorsement from me. Thanks to the generosity of several of the largest manufacturers of motorized vehicles, a fascinating experiment took place in New York during the hottest days of last summer. The guinea pigs in this case were not gerbils but old people—seventy and up—with chronic bronchial disorders, congested sinuses, broad-gauged allergies, and certified ulcers. Volunteering their services in the public interest, a large and representative group of the above-named stood for three consecutive hours on Fifth Avenue, stepping off the curb behind a bus each time one stopped, and only stepping back on the curb once the bus had started up again, to that delightful amalgam of keening sound, swirling gases, and grinding gears that means so much to real New Yorkers who cherish the essence of their city. Trained technicians were on hand to test the pulse, blood pressure, and other vital responses of the oldsters. Following exposure to the "noxious" fumes, 93.6% of the subjects showed marked ruddiness of complexion, 87.5% showed "positive" attitudes toward life, and only 4.6% died on the spot.

Statistics don't lie!

Mr. Burberry's forthcoming book, "Smokestacks and the Yeast Culture," will be published next month by Constellation House.

WAR: MAN'S HIGHEST CALLING

By Richardson (Rickey) Dakota, Maj. Gen., USA (Ret.)

The flabbiness of peace is what appalls me, the sheer *sissyness* of it. A new generation comes along and suddenly tells us that the thousands of years of sacrifice, of strength, of wile and cunning required to crush one's enemies should be thrown in the ashcan. Holy cats! Each year, my work takes me to hundreds of high schools and junior colleges throughout this broad land of ours, where my illustrated lecture, "Kill or Be Killed," has attracted a following. The moment I step onto the platform of one of those auditoriums, I can instinctively tell whether or not I am in the presence of red-blooded American boys and girls. If I am, I get an ovation; if I am not, I am booed—in which case I give the V sign (with both hands) and step down. When, under better circumstances, I proceed with my lecture, I start slowly with Daniel Boone hacking his way across the Cumberland Gap, cutting down the tall trees, spearing the big fish, building the log cabins, rassling the fox and the bobcat. "Was Daniel Boone a peacenik?" I ask them. "How long do you think that brave man would have lasted in the hostile wilderness wearing beads and a peace button? Kill or be killed!" I tell them about Washington crossing the Delaware, dodging the big chunks of ice, his greatcoat wrapped around him, and I talk about the need for getting from one side of that river to the other side of that river. "Was George Washington a peacenik?" I ask them. "Do you think this nation was built by young men sitting cross-legged playing East Indian music on old cigar boxes? Kill or be killed!" Then I get to the glories of battle—the call of the bugle, the rumble of the tanks, the whine of the missiles, the starbursts as villages are blown up, and later, when the battle has died away, the unforgettable experience of gathering around the campfire with your buddies, arms linked, singing "Buckle Down, Winsocki." Then, for a windup, I tell them that one manly American boy is worth a hundred gooks and I get back to my philosophy—"Kill or be killed."

General Dakota is the recipient of four Silver Stars, three of them currently under congressional investigation.

WHO NEEDS PARKS?

By Wil J. Cork

America has been put through some desperate hoops by charlatans of "liberalism" and "human rights," but no crueller joke has been played upon the gullible general public than the widespread notion that cities are better off when a certain percentage of their acreage is devoted to park space. Central Park, in New York City, represents perhaps the outer limits of the folly to which anti-business, anti-free-enterprise, rural-oriented, nature-faking groups have led us. The facts are chilling. Eight hundred and forty-three acres of the richest imaginable land—pay dirt of unparalleled magnitude—have been set aside in the very heart of the world's business capital as a permanent haven for squirrels, tiny tots, toy sailboats, and *grown* men and women riding bicycles. Touch so much as a leaf of a tree, dig so much as a small hole, and swarms of organized, militant locusts blindly descend, screaming "Desecration!" What is their real game? What lies behind the amiable smoke screen—the soft talk about whole families' strolling together on Sundays under the trees, breathing fresh air, the visionary picture of kids in the big city having room to play, of picnicking on the grass, of listening to music under the stars? The real game is obvious: As long as the eight hundred and forty-three acres of Central Park are reserved for non-commercial use, bearing no interest, producing no revenue, they stand for all to see as a symbol of the Socialist "utopia" the park-lovers have in store for us.

I propose:

1. The immediate abolition of the Department of Parks, and the formation of a quasi-public Inner City Authority, empowered to exercise the right of eminent domain over parkland, issue long-term bonds, and sell to the highest bidders and at the earliest possible moment the bankrupt equipage of the Park: benches, swings, slides, carousels, rowboats, statues of deceased writers and poets, fountains, skating rinks, and one- and two-room suites formerly devoted to caged animals.

2. The immediate establishment of a People's Acreage Zoning Commission, to divide the eight hundred and forty-three reclaimed acres in order to best serve the most pressing practical needs of the city. Experts will differ, of course, but I think an honest, free-for-all, democratic give-and-take between conflicting real-estate interests in the city would come up with a formula something like the following:

(a) Forty per cent of the land to be devoted to the construction of strictly commercial buildings, with the ironclad proviso that no structure exceed fifty stories in height.

(b) Thirty per cent of the land to be utilized for the construction of what have been popularly mislabelled "luxury apartments" but are in fact high-return, self-liquidating edifices; these should face Central Park South, Central Park West, and Fifth Avenue, with an Observation Wall to be constructed across 110th Street, with pay telescopes.

(c) Thirty per cent of the land to be turned into the most daring, innovative real-estate venture in the United States: well-tended acres devoted to single-family Georgian houses, in the utmost taste, and for the most discriminating people, to be erected in a series of small, tightly knit individual communities, such as Bethesda Village, Belvedere Hills, Shakespeare Town, and Reservoir Vue. No one with whom I have discussed this venture has any doubt that these communities would soon become the most desirable—and tax-producing—communities in the nation.

And one small last, but not unimportant, item: Crime in our parks is a shame and a disgrace for each and every law-abiding citizen of our city. Think of the decrease in park crimes that would result from the elimination of the parks!

Mr. Cork is chairman of the Finance Committee of Atlantic States Mortgage Brokers, a horizontal conglomerate.

Contemporary Writers VI: An Interview with Grip Sands

The interview with Grip Sands, three-time winner of the coveted Alma M. Halloran Fictive Award (for his novels "Lud," "Fust," and "Drime"), was held at five-thirty one morning in his loft workroom-bedroom-living room on Manhattan's lower East Side, within sight of the ever-poetic span of the Brooklyn Bridge. Sands works at night and sleeps by day, and the interview was conducted between the hours of his most intense concentration and his hours of rest. He appeared exhausted yet exhilarated. He is short, squat, and somewhat dishevelled, with thick eyebrows and piercing green eyes. He was dressed in black leather pants, a black leather jacket, and highly polished black boots. Sands and his boots are inseparable, as inseparable as Sands and the strange, private lexicon of obscenities he employs in ordinary conversation. Sands wears his boots everywhere—to literary conferences, to prize conclaves, and to bed. Bed consists of a mattress on the floor of the loft, with no pillow. The loft is sparely furnished: an unpainted worktable piled high with supplies of green copy paper, on which Sands writes in red ink, and, in one corner, a refrigerator. The floor of the loft was covered with crumpled mounds of discarded pieces of copy paper. They lent the otherwise barren room the appearance of being a mossy glen in a thick forest. Sands was seated on the mattress, reading galleys of his forthcoming fictive effort, "Zwer." Several volumes of Proust were visible on top of the refrigerator, lying beside a half-eaten pomegranate.

INTERVIEWER: You have been accused of a certain deliberate obscurity, not only in connection with the time continuum but with relation to the personnel of your novels. Your non-beings appear to have more life-force than your beings, and even at times to be interchangeable with them. What are you saying to us?

SANDS: I should like very much to get my hands on the blarfs who accuse me of obscurity, much less deliberate obscurity. Their watchword would appear to be crand. I am saying what I am saying, and each driggle must figure the matter out for himself, depending on the time, the place, the barometric pressure, and the nearest horoscope. To read "Fust," for instance, without a horoscope would be sheer groozle. And yet many try, and sink. I lay great store by horoscopes, mostly for their paramorphic value. They cut through the paninvisibility of non-being. We are left with the dark shadow of cartilage. The nub of the matter.

INTERVIEWER: We know that each writer secretly whispers to himself in his innermost places, awake or asleep, that this time he has touched the truth—zeroed in, you might say.

SANDS: To me, eternity is eggshells. The whites are pure mag, and the yolks—well, I won't even consider the yolks. They are beneath contempt. But the shells present an entirely different problem. We have the problem of poise—absolutely essential—and, with it, the delicate elaboration of personality, or, in the case of "Lud," non-personality. One exudes. Otherwise, there is nothing—not even the void.

INTERVIEWER: Do the city streets inspire you? I mean, do you prowl?

SANDS: Inscrutably. Inscrutably, rather than haphazardly or continuously. The inspiration, once again, is eggshells. They rise beneath the feet and touch off myriad images. The prowling must be done under cover of darkness, and the feet themselves provide the motivation. One either senses this sort of thing or one doesn't. The eggshells are everywhere, but one must feel them. Lower Broadway bleeds with eggshells. There the poise requires deftness, murim, and a calm spirit. If one is unhurried, collected, one is safe, one's inspiration is safe. Jar the balance and there is a crack in eternity.

INTERVIEWER: That would be irreparable?

SANDS: Irreparable. There are no second chances. The wheel turns and stops—red or black, good or ill. And, of course, there is the question of money. The foundations and the grants help. I loathe them, and I loathe the gurds who sit in boardroom splendor and award them, but I never turn one down. The first grant is always the hardest. Then they pour in; some blick recommends me one year, I recommend the blick the next. It is a question of poise, almost vegetable. They say travel to England, France, Spain. I say no. I stay here. My terms. Fleep!

INTERVIEWER: Do you revise much?

SANDS: As an exercise in the art of interregnum. The floor of the studio attests to the continuously heightened and renewed perceptions and non-perceptibles.

INTERVIEWER: Do you mingle much with other writers?

SANDS: Sparsely.

INTERVIEWER: But you do mingle occasionally—conferences, creative-writing gatherings, and so on. Do you derive much inspiration, if any, from these encounters?

SANDS: The average writer is a brape. I observe them to renew my contempt. And to replenish the wellspring. The fallow times, you know, are not kinsel. Bears do it. Inspiration often derives from one's low opinion of those around one, so I occasionally drive to the gas station and ask the man to fill up the tank. Then back here to aloneness and the eternal, internal me. You are the first person I have talked to since beginning "Zwer," and you may be the last.

INTERVIEWER: "Zwer" has already evinced almost universal interest. Can you tell me something about it—its themes and goals?

SANDS: In "Zwer," the root is the branch. It will win all the prizes, but for all the wrong reasons. In "Zwer," the personae ascend in descension. The interstices become the corpus. Form follows reason to the city limits, and then explodes with malevolent magnanimity. The bulldozers appear to triumph, but the squeak of the mouse is heard over the land.

INTERVIEWER: Where would you say the novel in general is heading? I mean, this would come down, I suppose, to shape and form and content. You must have given this a good deal of thought.

SANDS: The problem centers acutely on the extricular. Gravy boats, bronzed booties, canoes—that sort of thing. Try to avoid these tactiles and the novel will foist. Slowly at first, but with increasing blushes. That is one thing I am certain of, up to a point. Characters must become egressors. The costume is without meaning, the setting a mere ball of fire, and the dialogue quirp. People often halrow and urge you to try that one on your cigar box. I tell them to emerge, shed, blacken with soot.

Cold cream is dodo. Definitely. "Zwer" 's most powerful scenes are illuminated with the passion of an underwater gazebo. The inundated summerhouse! It is a summing up, and nothing will ever be the same. Follow the green arrow and take the wrong turn. Most of them are rotten.

INTERVIEWER: In other words, you are optimistic.

SANDS: Insofar as the circle bisects the square and leaves it dangling. And with respect to the pastoral mutations. The rest is queel. But there are some bright spots—Lipton in Kansas City, struggling with his penetrobes, and poor Kenneeley being bitten alive in Algiers.

INTERVIEWER: Kenya, I believe.

SANDS: You are right. Kenya.

INTERVIEWER: Can you tell me something of your origins?

SANDS: Bridgeport was pure treem. The noxious workmen and their hardboiled eggs. Puget Sound was drave, and New Orleans grob. Heady stuff. My parents were one-burner electric stove, here today and gone. St. Louis, Denver, the transcontinental bit, and then the breakaway. Collapse and recovery and the dusty road to the center. The self-initiated self. It came one night and knocked, and I said, "Enter." And here I am.

INTERVIEWER: A complete man?

SANDS: Ragout.

The Diaries and Letters of Sir Gerald Woolton

(Introduction by Cavendish Woolton)

Sir Gerald Woolton,[1] distinctly a man of his time and place,[2] penned his diaries—generally in the mornings, between rising[3] and tubbing[4]—throughout his long and distinguished career in the differing yet tangential worlds of people, journalism, diplomacy, people, literary salons, politics, people, and club life. If anyone was worth knowing, Sir Gerald Woolton knew him. One can put it down as a rule of thumb that Sir Gerald Woolton did not know people who were not worth knowing. His standard was a relatively simple one: if Sir Gerald Woolton knew someone, that person was worth knowing. To people worth knowing, he was generous, kindly, warmhearted, benevolent, tender, understanding, sympathetic, and friendly. His attitude towards the remainder speaks for itself. In all, Sir Gerald Woolton penned twelve million six hundred

---

[1] My uncle, Sir Gerald Woolton, shall be referred to throughout the Footnotes as GW, a purely arbitrary decision on my part. In the Letters, NG refers to his old nanny, Nell Grit, who lived to be ninety-eight and who played an abiding and comforting role in his emotional life.

[2] The Diaries cover roughly the second quarter of the turbulent twentieth century, give a decade, take a decade, when GW, an Englishman, had reached his middle years.

[3] 6:32.

[4] 6:51. The drawbridge at Lower Woolton is often washed out.

thousand two hundred and forty-six words in his diaries, and I have edited (without reference to specific years) what I consider to be a representative selection from the crowded times. On with it!

DIARY

23RD FEBRUARY

To the Chop and Chowder for lunch. Winnie[5] there, also Neville,[6] Lord Nelson,[7] G. M. Trevelyan, Doodles Baltic.[8] Doodles just back from Austria, convinced that Pfernig is entirely sincere, if mad, in his determination to proceed with the *Aufgrab*. Winnie, inexplicably silent, concentrated on his mutton chop. G. M. Trevelyan eloquent, brimming with historical analogies, something about the Trojans, the point of which was lost in the grinding noises made by Neville's teeth. Too bad, but irretrievable. Lord Nelson spoke with conviction of sea power. I walked home slowly through Green Park, pondering on success and failure in life. Quite pleased with myself today. But it will pass.

DIARY

6TH MARCH

At Hollyhocks.[9] Gardens radiant, but cannot keep my mind off the *Aufgrab*, should there be one. There is far too much wickedness in the world, it would seem. Following breakfast, I shall retire to study to work on novel, novella, lectures, reviews, biography, and address to be delivered to All-Bowdoins[10] Sunday night. I am such a bundle of marmalade! Perhaps Crunchy was right when he said years ago, at lunch at the Hip and Thigh, "You are an exalted water bug, skipping about, never settling." Could it be true? All in all, a glorious year so far, and I have never been happier, except when miserable.

[5] Winston S. Churchill. British statesman and descendant of the Duke of Marlborough. Winston Churchill's mother was an American—"a fact," as GW often remarked, "over which he had little or no control."

[6] Neville Chamberlain. British statesman and prominent son of a prominent father, whose grandfather is said to have misplaced his umbrella at the Battle of Waterloo.

[7] Prominent sea dog.

[8] Known for his mauve landscapes, with bulldog faces peering from the lower-left corner. They are not to be found in the Tate.

[9] GW's country place at Bleemes-on-Bleemes. Hollyhocks was second only to Nell Grit in the affections of GW.

[10] An arcane offshoot of the Society of Good Chaps.

GW to NG

7TH APRIL

I think of you all the time and shudder to ponder what life would have been like without you. I shudder.

NG to GW

14TH APRIL

Always dry behind the ears after tubbing.

DIARY

18TH APRIL

Standing for Parliament for West Grind. A loathsome spot, filled with workingmen. Much soul-searching on my part. Lady Braumont-Greaves[11] says I simply must, that I owe it not only to myself but to my country. Strong words. Visited West Grind over week-end, and got hopelessly lost on way down. Many wrong turns, detours, culs-de-sac, and so on. Mingled with people, a searing experience. I am devoted to beautiful and lovely things, both in nature and in art, and would do much to overcome my sense of intense loathing for the unattractive, in animals, people, and plants. I know it to be a failing, but I treasure it. Dinner at Grouse-Neck—a glittering assemblage: Great Farr,[12] Lesser Far,[13] Winnie, Neville, Tony,[14] Lord and Lady Muff,[15] young B. S. Blinden,[16] and an assortment of dull, apathetic Americans. Why are Americans so crude, and their eyes so watery and lacklustre? A Mrs. X, from Eltoona,[17] Pennsylvania, totally incapable of manipulating her knife and fork.

[11] Prominent widow of Lord Braumont-Greaves, who lost his life, inexplicably, while serving as Falconer to H.R.H. George V.

[12] Kenneth Courtney Beardsley Farr, prominent M.F.H. to H.R.H. George V. Something of an eccentric, he was noted for standing on his head throughout dinner.

[13] His Scotch terrier, and constant companion.

[14] *His* Scotch terrier, and constant companion to Lesser Farr.

[15] Of the prominent toffee family.

[16] The poet, then sixty-two, and, as GW repeatedly said, "full, so full, of promise."

[17] GW was in error here. Mrs. X came from Scrunton.

DIARY

23RD APRIL

Elected for West Grind by two votes. Received returns in drab hall with dark walls, amidst strange people. My constituents. A very wee bit of cheering at the conclusion of the counting, and the crowd broke up within minutes and headed for their cottages, or whatever.

DIARY

9TH MAY

Splendid lunch in the Commons dining room. Brilliant conversation throughout. How I love these luncheons amidst all these clever lads, such a considerable contrast, alas, to the electorate. Will there be war? Grebinger[18] says no. He could be right. He could be wrong. Savoured the savoury.

DIARY

12TH SEPTEMBER

In America, lecturing on "Life in the Cotswolds" and "Elegance: The Vanished Art," two subjects of sufficient simplicity to grip the attention of the heathen. I am to be shipped about amongst eighteen cities, like a burlap bag, delivering one lecture one night, another the next.[19] Crass commercialism, I suppose, but someone must keep the eternal flame alive. So far, at public lunches where I have been Guest of Honour the same fare is presented: chicken à la King,[20] often in patty shells; bright-green peas; and ice cream. I think this has been remarked upon before by other visiting lecturers, but I am not entirely certain. My evening meals have been partaken of in the home of the richest person in whatever township I happen to be. By and large, the rich give me pleasure, but not here. The American hostess is intensely interested in the art treasures of the Old World, and I feel it incumbent upon myself to enlighten them, for example, upon such matters as the Gioconda Smile.[21] I have met no American Indians, who live, I am told, in quarries.

[18] Hans Grebinger, confidant of Lesser Farr.
[19] GW went, in his words, "from the sun-kissed shores of Maine to the rockbound coast of California."
[20] Edward VII.
[21] An oblique reference to the Mona Lisa.

DIARY

6TH OCTOBER

Still in America. I keep asking myself, What is Man? No ready answer, and no reason to expect one in a nation devoid of sparkling give-and-take and brittle bons mots. Much deep-dish apple pie in the provincial townships, and obligatory ice in drinks. A cardinal axiom of my upbringing is never to hurt the feelings of a host, especially in his presence. Little sense of international tension here. I can get nobody interested in the Schnallberger Crisis. Poor, dear things, they dream of their wheat fields and their corncobs. I do wish I could remember the names of some of the people I have met. But no matter.

DIARY

4TH NOVEMBER

Hollyhocks. Home again! Stopped in London, for delightful salon evening at Lady Falmouth-Cowpers'. Not a soul missing: Cranshaw, Winnie, Lord Piedmont, Lord and Lady Graze, the Viscount,[22] the Maharaja of Bradnipah. At midnight, My Sovereign[23] arrived, elegantly turned out in sandals, kilt, and naval tunic, complete with dazzling ribands. The ladies curtsied, the men fell prone to the floor—an ancient custom, and one that I take pride in perpetuating. Lord Piedmont had fallen to the floor some five minutes before My Sovereign arrived, for private reasons. My Sovereign, ever so approachable, said to me, "We like your stuff." Kraundorf, of the Netherlands Foreign Office, remarked cryptically, *"Auch!"* Did he mean war? If so, small credit to our national pride. Barely any good Yorkshire pudding to be found anywhere.

[22]I have searched hundreds of records and cannot locate the precise viscount. Gildsley was known to have been in London that evening and he must have dined somewhere, although he loathed maharajas.
[23]Edward VIII. Ah!

GW to NG

29th December

I live in the great bright world, and mingle continuously with the clever ones, and at year's end I reflect upon matters both weighty and small, and my most abiding joy derives from you, my old Nanny.

NG to GW

31st December

Tidy up the nursery!

One Man's Vote

All through the intense Presidential campaign, two lines from "Waiting for Godot" kept running through my mind: Estragon says, "I can't go on like this," and Vladimir replies, "That's what you think." I have voted in fifteen Presidential elections, the first in 1936 (for Franklin Roosevelt, of course), but never before have I or those near and dear reached such heights of pre-election anxiety. Rightly or wrongly, we felt that if our man lost, our country would be lost, too—Supreme Court, jobs, racial reconciliation, abortion rights, you name it. (Even had Hoover been reëlected in dark 1932, we would have kept in the White House a President who had appointed Charles Evans Hughes and Benjamin Cardozo to the Supreme Court.) Damp hands, poor appetite, short temper—all telltale signs covered by that irritating Teutonic word "angst." I watched the Republican conclave in Houston with a friend and neighbor who was born in Berlin—a scientist of international renown, driven from his native land by primal hatreds. During Pat Buchanan's preliminary tirade, this man sat silent and rigid, but when Buchanan called for a religious war he leaned over, his face ashen, and said, "I see the armbands."

We devoured the papers, hugged the tube. I noted a fascinating development in the technique of the Big Lie: someone would tell a vicious whopper (implying, with no sustaining facts, that Clinton had been buddy-buddy with the K.G.B., say), and then, the next day—or perhaps just hours later—deny that such a statement had been made. Lying about lying, I hope, will turn out to be a political ploy without a future.

There were bright, even encouraging moments, especially when the tube showed us the excited, smiling faces of thousands who had stayed up long past midnight in small towns all over the map to catch glimpses of Clinton and Gore as they came through on the bus. . . .

As November drew closer, tension increased geometrically. Daily, we were whipsawed by the polls—it's narrowing, it's widening, it's narrowing, it's widening—and by the ubiquitous pundits. There was a sickening sense that the high office of the Presidency was being demeaned by self-inflicted wounds.

At long last, that memorable Election Day. Teeming rain. At 7:30 A.M., I walked to my usual polling place, to find unprecedented, uncomplaining lines. An interminable wait, only to learn that my polling place had been changed to an old-folks' home four blocks from where I stood, dripping wet. Two instant thoughts. One practical: the lines at the old-folks' home would be so long that I should accept fate, throw in the sponge, and prepare to live there. The other, paranoid: the entire election process was a fraud, everybody's venue had been secretly changed, and New Yorkers would be robbed of their votes.

At the home, more long lines, but only three machines. Many citizens, like me, found themselves in an unexpected voting place, and there was great commotion. "I'm a doctor, and I have patients waiting, but nothing is going to stop me from voting," a young man standing next to me said. "You bet your sweet life," said a businesslike brunette behind me. "I'm voting today if I have to stay here through the night." Democracy was rescued by a fragile wisp of a woman, a volunteer poll-watcher who called herself Connie. Connie had arrived at six: no officials on hand, no registration books, and one of the three machines was broken. "I stood on a chair and shouted for calm," she said. She then methodically reached election headquarters, had the broken machine repaired, and, clutching a neighborhood list of addresses, directed people to the proper booths. Finally, I voted. Now that it's over, my friends and I have not yet unwound. We are smiling again. Warily.

FOREIGN PLACES

Dorothy Thompson, the correspondent, invited me to dinner one evening early in 1945. To my delight, she seated me next to Harold Ross. He knew my history: that I had been rejected for the draft (poor eyesight); that I had left his magazine immediately after Pearl Harbor and gone to Washington to work for Archibald MacLeish, head of the Office of Facts and Figures (a small writing unit peopled, among others, by Arthur Schlesinger, Jr., McGeorge Bundy, and Henry F. Pringle, which eventually became the Office of War Information); that one of the pieces I turned out, *Divide and Conquer* (an analysis of Nazi propaganda techniques), had attracted wide attention, been distributed in the millions by the government, reprinted in full in newspapers all over the country, and had resulted in a totally unexpected and forever memorable congratulatory phone call from President Roosevelt; and that I had returned to *The New Yorker* in 1943 to write Profiles and Talk stories. Sometime during the meat course, Mr. Ross suddenly turned to me and asked, "What do you want to do next?" I said my heart was set on going abroad as a correspondent. A few days later, I was told that Mr. Ross was sending me to Rome.

The End of Mussolini

Letter from Rome
May 8, 1945

Having lived for a year in a troubled semblance of peace, Rome has accepted the news of peace itself with the helpless and tired shrug of the defeated. My guess is that few cities are sadder today. V-E Day has pointed up an unpleasant fact many people here had tried to forget: that Italy lost the war and can advance no claims for the rewards of peace. To the Italians I've talked with, peace in Europe means at the moment little more than a dreary continuation of their present misery—fantastic prices, black markets, unemployment, the struggle to regain national pride, and the even more difficult struggle to get people to think for themselves after two decades of stupefaction. The German surrender seems to have increased the Roman's capacity for introspection; his comprehension of the situation his country is in is almost morbid, and his personal problems have suddenly loomed larger and become more pressing: how can a young man get to Turin to discover whether his parents survived the German occupation; does the American know someone who will deliver a letter to a lady's husband, a Partisan, in Milan; please, will the United States permit Italians to leave home and settle in America; at the far end of town a wealthy friend has food enough for his friends tonight, but can the American arrange to get them there and back by jeep?

Today, Tuesday, is V-E Day, but the bars and restaurants are deserted, the streets practically empty. No more bells than usual have been rung. To be sure, some flags are out and the sirens have sounded, but something is lacking. Occasional noisy groups of young Italians parade the streets, trying with almost pathetic desperation to crash the gate of victory, but the victory is not theirs and the enthusiasm is hollow. One such procession—fifteen to twenty poorly dressed young men, a boy beating a drum, and another boy carrying a large red flag—straggled down the Via Sistina this afternoon and stopped before a British mess. Through the door they could see men laughing and drinking. *"Finita, finita, la guerra è finita!"* cried the paraders, and a British sergeant, glass in hand, stepped outside, bowed gracefully, and thanked the parade for stopping by. "Good of you to come," he said, and went inside. The procession slowly moved down the street a few doors to a hotel where some Americans live. *"Finita, finita, la guerra è finita!"* the Italians cried. Several Americans stuck their heads out of windows and yelled "Hooray!," and one man with a camera leaned out and said, "Hold it till I get this!" Then everybody stuck his head back in again. The parade disappeared around a corner, the drummer half-heartedly sounding a roll. Of all the troops in town, only the British seem to be in a rejoicing mood. Arm in arm and six or eight abreast, groups of them have been marching through the city, singing. Victory in Europe appears to have accented only the homesickness of the American troops, and knowing very well that for most of them the end of one war means simply the beginning of another, still farther from home, they have shown little enthusiasm. Tonight I saw hundreds of them sitting alone on curbstones staring into space or ambling along the streets, hands in pockets, looking into shop windows.

Italy last week was Milan, and, unlike Rome, Milan had its victory, a victory all the more pleasant, perhaps, because it came from within rather than from without. Our troops were greeted there almost with hysteria, but this exhilaration had already been touched off, first by the Partisan uprising in the city and then by the execution of Mussolini and his most infamous henchmen. When the Germans in Italy finally surrendered, the news went almost unnoticed in Milan. The newspapers welcomed the capitulation in modest headlines but continued to devote their biggest ones to Partisan activities. On the whole, the efficiency and triumph of the Partisan tactics seemed to stun even the Partisans, and for the first three or four days after the liberation large groups of them—

almost all of whom were dashing around town in captured German cars, rounding up or finishing off lingering Fascists—could be seen embracing one another in the streets.

Because Milan is in the plains and would have been difficult to defend against any reinforcements the Germans might send in to aid the garrison troops, the Committee of National Liberation had to move slowly. Nevertheless, from the beginning of the German occupation, in September, 1943, at least fifteen thousand copies of clandestine newspapers were circulated every week. The newsprint for them was bought on the black market. In March, 1944, the Committee put on a successful eight-day general strike in Milan. In September of that year the Partisans began to attack the Fascists and Germans in the mountains of northern Italy, but they knew that it would be futile to attempt a fight in Milan yet. "Justice and Liberty" squads—one squad to almost every block in the city—were formed and told to provide themselves with arms. The main source of weapons was the garrison of twenty thousand Fascist troops, many of whom were willing to sell their arms if paid high enough prices. Many others were killed at night and robbed of their arms. The acquiring of arms was accelerated last December, when the Allies gave the Committee of National Liberation the task of leading the resistance movement in northern Italy. The Allies not only began to supply arms but also gave a lot of money to a trusted Partisan in Rome, a banker. By intricate financial maneuvering, he was able to transfer the money to the north.

Meanwhile, in Milan, the Partisans shifted their headquarters about once a week, settling now in the office of an obscure razor-blade distributor, now across town in a dismal restaurant. Mussolini, who had a villa on Lake Garda, north of Verona, appeared less and less frequently in Milan. When he did appear, he and his heavily armed cavalcade usually raced through the city, bound for somewhere beyond. By last January, work in the factories making supplies for the Germans had almost entirely stopped because Allied bombing of the Brenner Pass had cut the railway over which coal was sent into the country. In April, the Committee of National Liberation ordered railroad and tramway workers in Milan to strike, snubbed the Fascists when they suggested that everybody let bygones be bygones and that one big brotherly "sacred union" of all Italians might be created, formed a Committee of Revolt, mobilized the Justice and Liberty squads, and finally, on the twenty-fifth, told its ten thousand armed and ten thousand unarmed Partisans to start taking over the city. By noon the following day, a hundred Fascists had been killed and the Committee was in control of Milan. The Germans fought in the suburbs until the twenty-eighth, the day of Mussolini's execution, but those inside the town barricaded themselves in several hotels and refused to come out and fight, preferring to await the arrival of the Allies and to surrender to them.

Although many Romans—and quite a few American correspondents—deplore what went on in the Piazza Loreto on the morning of Sunday, the twenty-ninth, to the Milanese these events will probably always be symbols of the north's liberation. To an outsider like myself, who happened to be on hand to see Mussolini, Clara Petacci, Pavolini, Starace, and some of the other Fascists dangling by their heels from a rusty beam in front of a gas station, the breathless, bloody scene had an air of inevitability. You had the feeling, as you have at the final curtain of a good play, that events could not have been otherwise. In many people's minds, I think, the embellishments of this upheaval—thousands of Partisans firing their machine guns into the air, Fascist bodies lying in a heap alongside the gas station, the enormous, pressing crowd—have been overemphasized and its essential dignity and purpose have been overlooked. This is best illustrated by the execution of Starace—the fanatical killer who was once secretary of the Fascist Party—who was brought into the square in an open truck at about ten-thirty in the morning. The bodies of Mussolini and the others had been hanging for several hours. I had reached the square just before the truck arrived. As it moved slowly ahead, the crowd fell back and became silent. Surrounded by armed guards, Starace stood in the middle of the truck, hands in the air, a lithe, square-jawed, surly figure in a black shirt. The truck stopped for an instant close to the grotesque corpse of his old boss. Starace took one look and started to fall forward, perhaps in a faint, but was pushed back to a standing position by his guards. The truck drove ahead a few feet and stopped. Starace was taken out and placed near a white wall at the rear of the gas station. Beside him were baskets of spring flowers— pink, yellow, purple, and blue—placed there in honor of fifteen anti-Fascists who had been murdered in the same square six months before. A firing squad of Partisans shot Starace in the back, and another Partisan, perched on a beam some twenty feet above the ground, turned toward the crowd in the square and made a broad gesture of finality, much like a highly dramatic umpire calling a man out at the home plate. There were no roars or bloodcurdling yells; there was only silence, and then, suddenly, a sigh—a deep, moaning sound, seemingly expressive of release from something dark and fetid. The people in the square seemed to understand that this was a moment of both ending and beginning. Two minutes later, Starace had been strung up alongside Mussolini and the others. "Look at them now," an old man beside me kept saying. "Just look at them now."

No city could long remain in the emotional fever of the first days of liberation in Milan, and by the middle of that week there were signs of weariness. Fewer Partisans roamed the streets, and they were less rambunctious. Only isolated shootings took place, and these at night. The slow process of rounding up the twenty-four hundred Fascists in the city continued; they were placed in San Vittoria Jail, in cells recently occupied by their captors. A good many Partisans dropped their clandestine names and resumed their own, which created some confusion among the Partisans themselves, who had never known one another's real names. It suddenly became apparent that the days ahead, like any morning after, meant a slow and complicated readjustment.

As for the city itself, its population has, in a few years, jumped from a million to a million seven hundred thousand. A sixth of Milan's buildings were bombed, a considerable number of them in the center of town. The Duomo, however, has survived; only two of the hundreds of delicate statues along its sides were chipped by bomb fragments, although five of its seven organs were wrecked by the concussions of nearby explosions. On the first day of liberation, a crude sign over the door of La Scala (whose roof had been bombed out) said, "We Want Toscanini," but someone took it down after the entrance of the Allied troops and substituted the American, British, and Russian flags. Most of the church of Santa Maria delle Grazie and all of its cloisters are now rubble, but there are hopes that da Vinci's "Last Supper," in the refectory, is intact. Before the first bombings of the war, the fresco was lovingly buttressed with heavy wooden scaffolding and bags filled with stones. The framework withstood the bombings and looks sturdy enough from the outside, amid the wreckage, but so far, understandably, no one has had time to begin the painstaking work of removing the wood and the bags of stones to find out whether da Vinci's masterpiece has survived the second World War.

A Reporter in Switzerland

WHAT TIME IS IT?

By and large, American soldiers are wristwatch-crazy. Cuckoo clocks and alarm clocks attract them, pocket watches bring a gleam to their eyes, but wristwatches drive them mad, especially if the dials are like the instrument panel of a B-29 and tell not only the time of day but the day of the month, the month of the year, and the aspect of the moon. Watch craziness may be an occupational disease of all armies; Russian troops are reported to be paying their American colleagues in Berlin and Vienna five hundred dollars for drugstore Ingersolls and a thousand dollars for watches with Mickey Mouse dials. (What happens when one watch-crazy soldier sells his watch to another watch-crazy soldier is clearly a problem for the advanced seminar.) This horological phenomenon has had a lot to do with the opinions the American soldiers now hold about Europe. Next to wanting to go home, our troops want to go where the watches are, and the watches are in Switzerland. There are apparently millions of watches in Switzerland, a good many of them with dials like the instrument panel of a B-29, and Switzerland, to our soldiers, is becoming the most popular country on the Continent. Before the Army is through over here, at least three hundred thousand members of it will have had a chance to find out about it at first hand. Every week, some six thousand American soldiers—three thousand from the Mediterranean Theatre, three thousand from the European Theatre—are visiting Switzerland on seven-day tours under the auspices of its government. Moralists may feel that a nation whose wartime philosophy appears to have been that every country has the right to be an island unto itself does not deserve such attention, but moralists have probably never heard of watch craziness. Furthermore, Switzerland is the first European country the American soldier has had a chance to see whose cities do not lie in ruins and whose population has not been beaten down by war. A veteran of the Salerno landings said to me one day in Interlaken, pulling up a sleeve and exhibiting an intricate piece of machinery with two second hands and a bell, "Even if I couldn't have bought this, I'd still be enjoying myself. The place has railroads and milk!"

I found out exactly how this craving for watches and unbombed cities operates when I went on one of the tours last week with a group from the Mediterranean Theatre. The point of departure is a Special Services building in Milan, covered with Swiss posters showing cable cars dangling from mountaintops, obviously contented cows on hilltops, and electric trains whizzing into tunnels. Every day about four hundred enlisted men and officers (the proportion is about ten enlisted men to an officer) on leave from units in Italy turn up in Milan and are assigned to one of three set tours—through eastern Switzerland, including Davos; through central Switzerland, including the Jungfrau, Bern, and Zurich; or through southwestern Switzerland, including Montreux and Geneva. So many men have shown a preference for the second route—bigger cities, more watches—that lots are drawn to see who goes where. Before they start off, the tourists deposit thirty-five dollars to cover expenses, pay thirty-four dollars and ninety-seven cents for a hundred and fifty Swiss francs (the maximum allowed), have a temporary Swiss visa stamped on the back of their travel orders, and are addressed briefly by a Special Services corporal who informs them that they are among the first foreign soldiers in uniform to enter Switzerland in this war. "Even though the war is over, make no mention of troop movements," he says, and adds, "And take no towels from Swiss hotels."

A hundred and thirty-nine soldiers and I drew the popular Tour No. 2. We left next morning in comfortable third-class coaches, passed through a cursory Swiss customs examination at Chiasso (the St. Gotthard tunnel is the only route currently open between Italy and Switzerland, the

Simplon tunnel being closed while mines are being removed), and stopped for lunch at Lugano, a lakeside resort with huge, empty hotels, delicatessens piled with cold meats and cheeses, and shop windows full of watches, to say nothing of cuckoo clocks. Later, on our way to Lucerne, practically the only topics of conversation were watches and the physical condition of Switzerland compared to that of Italy. A tall, lanky sergeant from Texas who sat opposite me was amazed that any country in Europe was still able to present what he considered a civilized appearance. "A clean country!" he said. "Did you see that station in Milan this morning, with all those people scrambling around in all that dirt? No, sir, nothing like that here in Switzerland. And the scenery! I'm coming here on my honeymoon." I asked him if he had bought anything in Lugano. "Hell, yes," he said. "Spent a hundred and forty-eight francs on a wristwatch that would have cost about five hundred bucks in Italy. I've got two francs left." I suggested that he might find himself a little short before the journey was over. "Don't *you* worry," he said. "*I'm* not worried."

For the next few days, the enthusiasm remained high. Every place seemed more enticing than the one before—Lucerne and the Lake of the Four Cantons; Interlaken and the Alpine foothills; the snow-covered Jungfrau, with its astonishing cog railroad, which climbs more than eleven thousand feet and runs through four miles of tunnels; the village of Grindelwald, in the valley below the Wetterhorn. We rode to all points on tiny, swift electric trains with big open windows, and everywhere there were the immaculate hotels, the cool milk, the cool beer, and the good cheeses. There were walks through the countryside, bicycle trips around lakes, lighted shop windows, clean streets lined with brightly painted houses, and all the hundreds of gimmicks and gewgaws that Switzerland puts on display for the tourist trade. Switzerland seemed the most beautiful of all possible places, with the exception of home. Money ran short, of course. A hundred and fifty Swiss francs can't get a man much more than one wristwatch. But lack of cash only temporarily deters a man who is watch-crazy. Cash can be raised in all sorts of ways—a package of American cigarettes will bring one franc thirty centimes, a field jacket twenty-eight francs—and commodities can always be acquired by old-fashioned barter. Most of the soldiers' baggage turned out to be disproportionately full of razor blades and fountain pens that the tourists, evidently tipped off in advance, had lugged in from Italy. In the matter of trading, colonels were no less interested than sergeants and were often sharper. One middle-aged colonel swapped all his woollen clothing for three wristwatches for his wife and a toilet-paper holder with a music-box attachment that played part of "The Blue Danube." "I had to get it," he said. "I just had to get it." On top of the Jungfrau, I saw the Texas sergeant, in his shirtsleeves, shivering as he gazed down at the beginnings of the Grosser Aletsch-Gletscher. "Mighty pretty glacier," he said, "but I certainly would appreciate it more if I hadn't sold my blouse and my underwear." His musette bag by now contained not only watches but innumerable bottle corks surmounted by carved figurines.

American tourists are American tourists, whether they are rich civilians or soldiers on leave. Today, as ever, there are the cliques: the inseparable three sergeants from Colorado, for example, who look with contempt on even the biggest Alps, reducing them to mere hillocks in comparison with their native Rockies. There are the incidents, momentarily so important and hilarious, that are recounted ad infinitum at the dinner table: the story of the pfc who bought eight music boxes during his first fifteen minutes in Switzerland and spent the rest of his tour in hotel rooms, with the boxes spread about him, all playing at once. Or the one about the night the party slept in a hotel halfway up the Jungfrau. A lieutenant had rather liked one of the girls at the hotel, had spent the evening dancing with her and buying drinks, and toward midnight had offered to escort her to her room. "That would be wonderful," said the girl. "I live in the next village, just down the mountain." So the lieutenant spent fifty minutes going down the mountain and three hours scrambling back up. Besides all this, there are snowball fights in the middle of summer (always good for a laugh), rides in sleds drawn by Eskimo dogs, and the luxurious sense of eating, sleeping, and being treated like civilians.

I cannot say exactly when the change in attitude took place, but it seemed to me, along about the fifth day, that there was a stiffening among the soldiers I was with, a reawakening of the critical faculties, less of a tendency to praise everything Swiss indiscriminately, whether a mountain, a hotel, a main street, or a girl. There was certainly no slackening of hospitality; everywhere the tourists were made welcome, were given free drinks, were met at railroad stations by townsfolk who invited them to their homes. It was not a matter of food or accommodations, which were better than satisfactory throughout the trip. It was not a matter of the weather, which was glorious—cool and crisp in the mountains, sunny and warm in the valleys. It had something to do, I guess, with the Swiss themselves and their conversations about neutrality. Neutrality seems to have left the Swiss in an unsettled frame of mind: they have their homes and their cities, their industries and their public utilities—in short, the fruits of their neutrality—but something appears to be lacking. You are not aware of this at first, for the Swiss appear at ease with themselves and the world, as comfortable and well ordered as their houses. It was an Air Forces captain, a pilot with a record of many missions, who was the first to piece together his scattered impressions of Switzerland and draw some conclusions. We were in a compartment on our way back to Italy. "You know," he said to a group of officers and men, as the train rolled south, "every magazine I've picked up this week has been filled with war pictures—*Swiss* war pictures. Maneuvers in the mountains, maneuvers in the valleys, Swiss soldiers leaving home for training, soldiers creeping out of foxholes or throwing grenades. And every street was so filled with soldiers it looked like San Antonio back in '43. And every Swiss I've talked to has told me how they planned to retreat to the Alps and how all the big tunnels were mined and what a fight they would have put up. I'm beginning to think they think they actually were in the war."

A sergeant laughed. "I've been noticing that, too," he said. "But they sure make certain you know they were neutral, whatever that is. The owner of that hotel where we stayed last night—he talked and talked about neutrality and what a tough spot the Swiss were in, alone in the middle of Europe, and I kept saying, 'Did you help the Germans?,' and he said, 'Well, we had to haul German coal through Switzerland to the German armies in Italy or we wouldn't have got any coal for ourselves,' and I said, 'Did you help them in any other way?,' and he said, 'Well, we had a rest camp for German soldiers, but you must never forget that we took care of the American fliers who crashed on our soil.'"

Another Air Forces officer, who had been peering out a window, turned around. "That's the bunk," he said. "I did some looking around while we were in Bern, and I got a little sick of that guide on the walking tour through town. On one corner he was delivering speeches about Swiss gratitude to Americans for saving them from tyranny and on the next corner he was asking us for American supplies. I ran into some American friends of mine who lived in Switzerland during the war and I asked them about the American fliers who had been interned. It's a hell of a story. When the first crews crashed in Switzerland, the Swiss wanted to put them on road gangs. It was only after the American government made strong protests that they got sent to those big hotels you hear so much about. And when some of our fliers escaped and were captured by the Swiss before they could get across the border, they were tossed into lousy jails as common criminals and held there, incommunicado, for as long as two months. Maybe our Minister was afraid to offend the Swiss, but he finally got off his tail and registered a loud complaint."

"Let me tell you something," said a short, stocky major. "It's a matter of money. I'm a fellow likes to trade. I brought a knapsack full of stuff in here and I'm taking two knapsacks full of stuff out, so I know what it means to make a dollar. But these people are dollar-nuts in a different way. With them, a dollar is like two dollars, they want it so much. I was talking with a fellow this morning in Locarno, a merchant type who I was doing a little business with, and he was giving me the line about neutrality, so I said, 'Tell me the truth,' and he said, 'The war's over, so you might as well know—we sold everything we could to the Germans, including munitions, but we put our foot down on one thing.' I asked what, and he said, 'The Germans shipped hundreds of tons of stolen goods from northern Italy through Switzerland to Germany and they asked us to carry so much that we finally protested. We said we couldn't take the stuff unless it had certificates of ownership. So the Germans set up a big office down in Como, made out certificates of ownership for every bit of stolen property, and sent it through. Those Germans are bad, but you must admit we maintained our neutrality. After all, a franc is a franc and what happens to other countries is none of our concern.' That's what he said."

The officer who had been staring out the window turned around again. "Look," he said, "one thing you should remember—the Swiss people wanted us to win. At least, that's what I think. Most of them don't even know what their government did during the war, the censorship was so bad. Our government has got wise and won't unfreeze Swiss funds until the Swiss tell us about all the German dough that's hidden in Swiss banks under false names. We've got them on the hot spot and they know it, and they're worried and that's one reason why they've asked us on these tours."

The lanky sergeant from Texas was present. He crossed one long leg over the other. "Well," he said, "I guess maybe we'll be glad to get back to Italy again. A little honest-to-God dirt never hurt anybody." He stared lovingly at his wrist. "My, my, what a beautiful watch," he said.

From: Hooray!

I was in Rome when the war ended, and I had a strong desire to visit Yugoslavia, then under the iron heel of Marshal Tito, who had not yet broken with the Soviet Union. Tito disliked American journalists (unless he had a guarantee of their political persuasion), and the American authorities disliked Tito. Wherever I turned, the answer was always the same: don't waste your time, you will never obtain the proper papers. Of course, this only whetted my appetite and increased my desire. Somehow, with help from friends, with help from the British, and with journalistic luck, there was a sudden concatenation and permission was granted to enter a distinctly hostile environment.

As an art form, the spontaneous demonstration has reached new heights under Marshal Tito of Yugoslavia, as I discovered not long ago when I spent a few weeks in and around Belgrade. Spontaneous demonstrations kept popping up at all hours of the night and day. They are a matter of high policy, an integral feature of Marshal Tito's government, which solemnly refers to them as "spontaneous," especially when describing them to visitors to the country. The lack of spontaneity in a spontaneous demonstration does not, in the government's eyes, detract from its restorative and invigorating qualities. Marshal Tito and his colleagues evidently feel that a good, long, well-planned spontaneous demonstration is just what the doctor ordered for Yugoslavia, and that four or five doses a day will make the patient really sit up and take notice. For the most part the demonstrations involve civilian adults, but thoughtful provision has also been made for the kiddies and the army, which consists largely of ex-Partisans, to demonstrate spontaneously as well. That takes care of everybody, and on a fine, clear day in Belgrade, men, women, and children, both in and out of uniform, are to be seen spontaneously demonstrating all over town.

The ordinary, or civilian, demonstration is generally in the nature of a parade—not a parade as we know it, with plenty of brass bands and drum majors, but a sad, slow, solemn procession, or shuffle. At the head of the column walks a fellow carrying a large Soviet flag, flanked by two men struggling to hold aloft huge cardboard portraits of Marshal Tito and Marshal Stalin. Then comes a group of about fifty men and women in ragged ranks, then a man supporting a large Yugoslav flag, then several hundred more men and women, many carrying banners reading, "Long Live Tito," "Long Live Stalin," "We Want Trieste," "Hooray for the Glorious Soviet Union," "Death to the Enemies of the People," and so on. At approximately four-minute intervals, everyone shouts, *"Živio Ti-to, Živio Ti-to, Živio Ti-to!"* This means "Hooray Tito!" or "Long live Tito!" and it is uttered mechanically, with the accent on both the "ti" and the "to." When several hundred people take to chanting in this manner, "Ti-to" becomes a meaningless and yet somehow frightening sound. Hearing it again and again and again, I lost all sense of its connection with any living man; it might just as well have been "Bi-bo, Bi-bo, Bi-bo!" or "Wi-wo, Wi-wo, Wi-wo!" or *"Sieg heil, Sieg heil, Sieg heil!"* Except when the marchers are shouting *"Živio Ti-to!"* they make little noise. They pad along, reading newspapers as they walk or talking quietly with one another. These parades are forever wheeling suddenly around corners and tangling with unsuspecting strollers and with the horse-drawn carts that fill the streets. Now and then two parades turn into a street from opposite directions, and there is considerable delay while the outriders decide which has the right of way. Meanwhile, the marchers mark time by turning the pages of their newspapers and sounding off at intervals with salvos of *"živio"*s.

Some of the army's marching can probably be classified as spontaneous, by government standards; the rest of it is more openly in line of duty, for armed soldiers stand guard at all public buildings and utilities. They are constantly coming and going between their posts and their mess halls and barracks, and occasionally units of them march to eastern Serbia to round up bands of from thirty to forty still belligerent Chetniks who, under Mikhailovitch, collaborated with the Axis. Whatever the reasons for the troops' marching, it gives them ample opportunity to express fealty to the boss, and the military demonstrators, like the civilian ones, shout their *"Živio Ti-to"*s once every four minutes. The soldiers march briskly, in close formation, swinging their arms and thrusting their legs forward in a stride that is almost but not quite a goose step. During the war singing played a large part in any Partisan march, and sing the army does today—lusty, violent songs, with the music of traditional folk tunes and words born of the recent fighting. One can be translated, roughly, thus:

> Through forest, villages, and cities
> Partisan battalions are marching
> Against the German bloodsuckers and dirty dogs.
> The working millions are rising up.
> We are the young army of Tito.
> With us is coming the whole of our people.
> Our country will be free; only Ti-to, Ti-to, Ti-to,
> Let him be alive and healthy!

And the refrain of another goes:

> We don't want wealth, we don't want money.
> We want freedom, work, and justice!

My room in the Hotel Moscow overlooked Belgrade's main street, where, at night, the clip-clop of soldiers' heels on the pavement often awakened me. From my window, I would watch units of the vague, shadowy, automatic figures marching past in numbers that seemed excessively large to dispose of a handful of Chetniks. I heard two theories concerning the purpose of these nocturnal exercises. In the opinion of many persons in the city, they are a hangover from the days of guerrilla fighting, when all Partisan mass movements had to be undertaken at night. Another school of thought holds that people march at night only when they don't want other people to know where they are going.

The children demonstrate spontaneously in a variety of ways. For one thing, not too surprisingly, they march through the streets singing. The songs the children sing are hardly less martial than those of their older brothers in the army. This is natural enough, for most of the children between the ages of five and fifteen have been mustered into a juvenile army called the Pioneers.

Among the songs the youngsters sing is this one:

> When the National Army passes,
> The country will be called happy.
> Happy time, happy. Come with us to war.
> And you, the old, where are yours, your sons?

And this:

> Comrade Tito, when are you going to Russia?
> Please convey our gratitude to the Red Army
> And tell them all the youth is for them.

The words of a haunting melody sung by soldiers on the Salonika front after the First World War began:

> Far over there, by a seaside,
> There is my dear village, my sister, my love.

To the same tune, the Pioneers now sing:

> Far over there, by a seaside,
> There is the leader of the workers,
> The great comrade, Stalin.

Although there is a severe shortage of clothing in Yugoslavia and many of the citizens go barefoot, the Pioneers have complete uniforms. Every unit of the organization has its own chief of staff, an assistant chief of staff, and a youthful commissioner in charge of each ten members. Children who do not join the Pioneers are not allowed to participate in mass sports, receive lower and lower marks in their classes, and are deprived of the delicious privilege of spying on their parents, required homework for Pioneers. Nonmembers are also not allowed to attend

From: *Hooray!*

such spontaneous mass demonstrations as the one in a Belgrade park last April that I was told about. On this occasion, the Pioneers gathered to swear allegiance to Tito. "We will fight to the end for Ti-to, Ti-to, and never spare our lives," they shouted in unison. Nor could nonmembers join in a program of war games that was held in the park a week later and that involved hiding behind trees, crouching behind rocks, leaping forth to surprise enemies, and, in general, having the devil's own good time.

The streets of Belgrade, through which these interminable processions pass, are littered with the wreckage of four years of war. The German bombing of April 7, 1941—a memorable day, on which the Yugoslav people, while Tito was still holding hands with the Axis, arose on their own in a heroic, if hopeless, revolt against the Nazis—ruined a substantial part of the heart of the city. Belgrade is situated at the confluence of the Danube and the Sava Rivers. Its one bridge across the Danube is down, and the only bridge across the Sava is a temporary one that will support pedestrians and motor traffic but not trains. This leads to the fertile and relatively unravaged agricultural area known as the Voivodina, to the north. For some reason, the American Air Forces bombed Belgrade on a number of occasions, notably on Easter Sunday of 1944, when several thousand persons who had run out into the streets to wave at what they thought were friendly planes were killed. Belgrade suffered further, and willingly, during its liberation by the Red Army from the Nazis, who, intent on destroying whatever they could not dominate, fought violently for every foot of ground. Russian and Partisan soldiers were buried where they fell, and their graves, surmounted by small red stars, now dot the city.

Belgrade's citizens show the effects of what they have been through. Everywhere you go you see one-legged men and women, often with the stumps of their limbs merely wrapped in soiled rags. The children have the drawn, gray, tight little faces of the very old. With a terrible frequency, former Partisans suffer seizures on the streets, falling down in a frenzy, waving their arms and screaming. When this happens, a number of passersby instantly and almost casually sit on the stricken man, pin down his arms and legs, and hold open his mouth to prevent him from biting off his tongue. After several minutes of writhing, the veteran, apparently recovered, gets up and walks off. He remembers nothing of the seizure. Some doctors, in spite of the similarity of this ailment to epilepsy, call it "war sickness," a reaction to the awful tension of guerrilla fighting; others call it "postwar sickness" and consider it a reaction to the disparity between the ideals for which the Partisans fought and the realities of Yugoslav life today.

I thought it odd that a government would permit its citizens to spend their energy marching through a shattered city rather than clearing away the rubble, but I found the parades interesting at first and, during the early days of my stay there, I stopped to watch a considerable number of them. I soon noticed that few people, except for myself and those waiting to cross the street, paid any attention to them. I was fortunate in having a sketchy familiarity with the language, which enabled me to understand some of the remarks I overheard in my wanderings around town, remarks that, though casual, led me to wonder further about certain aspects of the Yugoslav government. One afternoon, for example, a large, handsome, elderly man sat down beside me in a park and, looking straight ahead, said in a tone of utter resignation, "May they take away everything I have, and I have nothing, but merely because I am tall, please do not always force me to carry one of those damn banners!"

After my first week or so in Belgrade, I began to get the impression that I was being followed by small, dark men in dirty raincoats. Now, this is a dangerous frame of mind to fall into anywhere, especially in the Balkans, and I resisted the thought, but the more I tried to shake it off, the more the small, dark men in dirty raincoats seemed to be following me. Eventually it became quite evident that I *was* being followed, and also that Yugoslavs follow not only foreigners but many of their own countrymen as well. The men who did the following were of a curious uniformity; all were around five feet four, with ferret faces and hungry expressions. They followed at a respectful distance, usually about thirty feet. They worked in shifts, one man stalking his prey for five blocks, then giving way to another man, and so on. The switch points were generally unoccupied storefronts, where four or five other men with ferret faces and hungry expressions lounged, smoking and talking. After the person being followed had walked past, one of the loungers would leave his companions and start down the street, while the man whose place he had taken would sidle up to the store, lean against its window, and casu-

ally light a cigarette. The process was painfully naïve, its variations
pathetically limited. Cross a street and your follower would cross it;
recross and he would recross. Stop short and let him glide past, and you
would observe the swift, panicky twists of his head and his frantic efforts
to maneuver into position again. Then off once more—the hunted and
the hunter!

Since coming home from Yugoslavia, I have often wondered about the
dossier of my activities that is unquestionably on file in the offices of
Ozna, the Yugoslav secret police. Ozna is short for Odelenje Zastite
Naroda, or Committee for the Protection of the People. My feeling is
that the people would willingly settle for a little less protection, since
Ozna has succeeded in creating the widespread impression that it spies
into every phase of Yugoslav life and that its agents are wicked and all-
powerful. The success of secret police as a political weapon depends
less on what the police actually do, I have concluded, than on what people *think* they do; a Yugoslav who merely suspects that Ozna agents are
watching him can hardly be more terrified if he suddenly discovers that
they actually are on his trail. Since all of Ozna's activities are secret, the
organization has become the subject of many rumors, the most widely
circulated of which is that its agents are trained by N.K.V.D., the Russian secret police. This suspicion is part of a current tendency to blame
all evils of the Tito regime on the Russians. I ran across one man in Belgrade, though, who believes the issue is not quite as simple as that.
He told me that he thinks Yugoslavia is a case of the tail trying to
please the dog by wagging on its own, often wagging so violently that it
causes the dog some embarrassment, if no real displeasure. Physically,
the Russians are not much in evidence. Red Army officers help with the
training of the army, but there are no longer any Russian troops in
Yugoslavia.

However that may be, if the Ozna men who traipsed behind me
turned in accurate reports, they must have wasted the taxpayers' money
in some such way as this: "American C-3 left Hotel Moscow in rain at
4:30 A.M. and went to marketplace to watch long lines of citizens waiting
to buy food. Stood first by a vegetable line, then by a fruit line. Talked
with citizens and was told that acute food shortage in Belgrade is partly

attributable to unenlightened attitude of peasants, that with few excep-
tions peasants have refused to bring produce into town because government cut produce prices 30 percent, and that peasants have demanded
similar cuts in prices of consumer goods. Housewives said they stand in
line until 8:30 or 9:00 A.M. and sometimes go home with apples and
potatoes, or a few grapes, and sometimes not. Best scheme, they said, is
to bring several members of family along, thus covering all lines at once.
Most people manage to survive because friends and relatives in countryside give them extra food.

"American had breakfast at shop near hotel—bread, ersatz jam, and
coffee. Asked proprietor what coffee was made of and was told dried
acorns, for one thing. Did not take second cup. Went to Ministry of
Information and asked again to be allowed trip to devastated area in
Bosnia to see government work of reconstruction; also asked for interview with Marshal Tito and answers to questions submitted to Ministry
three weeks ago on wages and prices. Man in Ministry said he had misplaced questions but would have answers in due time. He reiterated that
trip to Bosnia is absolutely guaranteed sometime soon but suggested
this was awkward moment to leave Belgrade. Told American mass press
conference is being arranged by Ministry to prove conclusively that anybody opposing Marshal Tito is reactionary Fascist collaborator. Also
said that interview with Marshal is most difficult to arrange, that Tito
has upset stomach. American asked how come sixteen Polish journalists
had interview with Tito the day after their arrival in Belgrade. Ministry
representative suggested visit to exhibit of Partisan activities from 1941
to 1945, now open at Prince Paul Museum.

"American said exhibit sounded fine but he preferred to stay at Ministry and ask a few questions. He and Ministry man talked about Yugoslavia for two hours, and American learned things quite possibly he
should not have learned. Man in Ministry is not too bright. He talks too
much, gets excited too easily. To him, as to so many other sincere and
hardworking Yugoslav officials, everything done under Tito is so fine
and so wonderful that he admits to activities that may be questionable to
many outsiders. Man admits that people are forced to participate in
spontaneous demonstrations of loyalty to Marshal and new Yugoslav
government; that orders are issued by government to all shops and
offices, naming hours and starting places of processions; that those who
fail to turn up are subject to severe questioning by Ozna; that failure to

From: *Hooray!*

participate often results in loss of civil rights, including disfranchisement for not only culprit but his family, as well as loss of job, confiscation of property, and inability to procure medicines, shoes, clothing, etc.; that same penalties apply for failure to attend weekly block meetings addressed by political commissars, or for expression of unsound views at weekly discussion groups held in all shops and offices; that Yugoslavs who talk to Englishmen or Americans are liable to questioning by Ozna; that superintendents of Belgrade apartment houses are instructed to report fully on goings and comings of tenants and friends; that keys to front doors of apartment houses have been taken away from tenants, so anyone entering or leaving must have door opened for him by superintendent; that, although country has been devastated by war and disease, new national budget allots only ten million dinar to Ministry of Health and ninety-three million to Ministry of Construction but provides four billion for Ministry of War and National Liberation Army; that right now Tito is almost exclusively concerned with consolidation of his political power, rewriting of history to give himself credit for revolt against Axis in 1941, and denouncing all opposition, liberal or otherwise, as Fascist. American left Ministry and returned to hotel. Looked slightly ill." . . .

From: Winds off the Pampas

Having experienced a left-wing dictatorship, I was curious to examine life under a right-wing dictator, Juan Perón of Argentina. I quickly learned that there is little difference between left and right dictators. Both are intolerable. For obvious reasons, I had to protect my sources, especially Victoria Ocampo, one of the most prominent and courageous anti-Perón intellectuals, editor of the literary journal Sur, *and close friend of everyone, from the editor of* La Prensa *to Jorge Luis Borges.*

The terrible notion that Hitler, Eva Braun, Martin Bormann, and other choice Nazis are alive and breathing somewhere in Argentina has been gnawing at the Argentine imagination since the end of the war in Europe. Like practically every other notion in Argentina today, it is nourished by accumulated rumors, national anxieties, and scraps of circumstantial evidence. The chances are that few of the many people who tell over and over again the same anecdotes about Hitler's presence in Argentina believe that the flesh-and-blood Hitler is literally on the premises. He is, rather, an obsessive symbol of their deepest fears and frustrations. Stories about him turn up wherever one goes, and he is unexpectedly injected into the most unlikely conversations. Not long ago, travelling in Argentina, I heard the Hitler stories. When I began to hear them again and again, from different groups in different places, their meaning became somewhat clear to me. For one thing, they serve to bring closer together segments of the population that formerly had l tle in common and communicated with each other hardly at all. The law student, the elevator operator, and the owner of an *estancia* (or ranch) are united by a body of Hitler lore. Through him, they all share the same fear, mainly that if he were indeed in Argentina, nothing official would be done about it. Moreover, many high-minded Argentines are uneasily aware that the wartime conduct of their country made it the sort of place Hitler might well have chosen for his postwar residence. And although the Argentina of Perón today cannot reasonably be compared with the Germany of Hitler, the very fact that the stories are told carries the painful implication that the Führer would not totally disapprove of the current course of Argentine events.

The origin of the Hitler stories is obscure. They appear to be based upon the mysterious and unheralded, and possibly legendary, arrival of two U-boats at the popular seaside resort of Mar del Plata, two hundred and forty miles south of Buenos Aires, in the latter half of 1945. Some people say that the submarines surfaced at sea before docking, while others say that they came alongside the big quay there before rising. As some tell it, the landing was made in daylight; others claim that it happened after dark. In the daytime version, knots of the curious flocked to the oceanfront as word went around that U-boats had been spotted. Police prevented anyone from getting any nearer to the scene than the top of a high bluff overlooking the quay. Onlookers are said to have watched several people pop out from the submarines' hatches, scramble onto the quay, and enter waiting automobiles. All the men were wearing the type of greatcoat worn by German field marshals. One, who walked with a limp and had one arm that dangled loosely at his side, was approximately the size and shape of Hitler, while the one woman looked like Eva Braun. The group was driven away at high speed, the crowd was dispersed without getting answers to any of its questions, and no mention of the incident appeared in the newspapers. The nocturnal version has even more sinister overtones. The submarines arrived by moonlight, disgorged the same group—including the lady and the man with the limp—which entered cars and was driven away at a normal speed. A young policeman, patrolling the waterfront, observed all this, unknown to the participants. As one of the cars drove past, he saw, seated inside, a man who looked like Hitler, and beside him a lady who looked like Eva Braun. He reported the episode to his superiors, who passed it along to *their* superiors. Within a few hours, he was summoned to headquarters, discharged from the force for being intoxicated on duty, and sent, under guard, to his home. The next morning, he was removed to an institution for the incurably insane, and its doors closed permanently behind him. . . .

The Hitler stories have filtered through layer after layer of Argentine society. Who is to vouch for their truth, and who is to deny it? In any country, the people can weave and twist and enlarge upon a rumor. In Argentina, which is such a curious combination of the real and the fantastic, the odder an idea is, the quicker it takes hold. After travelling about that strange country, so different from the rest of the world, so far removed and other-planetary, I was quite willing to believe not only that Hitler was there but that I, along with several million others, had actually seen him.

Hitler intruded himself into a visit I paid to Mar del Plata. I had settled down in a large, modern, impersonal hotel in the center of Buenos Aires when, one morning, a lady of my acquaintance invited me to spend several days at her villa in Mar del Plata. (For fairly obvious reasons, the identities of all the characters in this article have been disguised.) She is wealthy, the proud bearer of an old and honored name, and related to almost everyone of importance in pre-Perón Argentina. Her roots are deep in the rich, black soil of the pampas from which her money is derived. Cattle and wheat are her heritage. Her father, a Spaniard, came to Mar del Plata more than half a century ago, drawn by the soil and by the fertile warmth of the days and the bracing chill of the nights. Mar del Plata is on a point of the coast exposed to winds from the antarctic. On a map, it is parallel with the southernmost tip of land in Australia, halfway across the world. The lady's father, like other enterprising Argentines of his generation, set about conquering and molding his environment, to make it fit his needs and fulfill his desires. Inland from Mar del Plata are the pampas, and in her father's time their section of the pampas was treeless, except for a few ombús, majestic shade trees of tremendous girth, whose wood is too soft even for firewood. Their leaves, which are poisonous, were often prescribed for the very sick by herb doctors in ancient times. Wherever he settles, man requires trees, it would seem, not only for shade and shelter but to provide some sense of permanence. Her father planted non-native trees by the thousands, and his friends and their friends planted others, and millions of them now grow in and around Mar del Plata and on the great ranches that lie on the long, lonely, sometimes flat, sometimes undulating sea of plains and grazing lands that stretches inland. The sons and daughters of the tree planters and *their* sons and daughters are considerably different. Many of them have been educated abroad, in French, Italian, or English schools. The wealth from the land has brought the opportunity to pursue one's leisure and turn it into one's profession. Thus, my friend became a painter and, although possessed of a passionate fondness for the land, grew away from it and from those who work on it. She is typical of those Argentines who visit the United States—rich, cultured, sophisticated, avant-garde in a curiously laborious and defensive way, and with an extreme sensitivity that betrays itself in an intense, nervous, easily aroused pride. Some time later, the Führer again broke through the thin crust of conversation. I was spending an afternoon at a celebrated *estancia*. I had gone once again to my friend's villa at Mar del Plata and had expressed to her my desire to see such a place, and she had promptly and graciously arranged it for me. The *estancia*, which was owned by a cousin of hers, had been visited a quarter of a century before by the then Prince of Wales, who had spent several days around the place, admiring the high-spirited horses and riding polo ponies. During his stay in Argentina, the prince had visited many celebrated *estancias*, and those at which he had fallen from polo ponies were thenceforth considered to be Very Distinguished. He had tumbled off a pony—no harm done—at the one I visited.

I was driven to the *estancia*, which was an hour or two away, in a chartreuse-colored limousine by one of my hostess's men, who wore a tight-fitting livery the precise color of the car. We bounced and jiggled across the dusty pampas, and along orange dirt roads, in swirls of dust. The day was painfully close, and the dust seeped in around the windows of the car and caught in my throat. Ahead of us were threatening black clouds. Before long, day turned into night, and storybook thunder and lightning boomed and crackled. Still there was no rain. Suddenly, there was a nasty, jagged flash, and the car swerved and then came to a halt before a big and forbidding log gate. The stop and the flash were so close together that for an instant I thought we had been struck. To my left, just inside the gate, was a structure that was pure Humperdinck, with a slanted, colorful tile roof that might have been gingerbread trimmed with sequins. Out of the house, as in a dream, ran a little girl with long blonde curls, wearing a calico dress. She swung open the big gate and we drove on. We had passed the gatekeeper's cottage, the driver said. For at least a mile, the road twisted under an archway of great oaks. We seemed to be passing through a deep forest, and yet, until we had got to the gate, there had been scarcely a tree. Soon there were breaks in the forest wall, and I could see pastureland stretching to the horizon, with cattle grazing in the distance. Then the forest closed around us again. Then more views of pasture, more forest; then the road widened, and curved gracefully past a park of lush lawn bordered with box hedges to an ivy-covered Tudor castle, complete with turrets, casement windows, a massive oak door, and a broad flagstone terrace with steps leading up to it.

At the top of the steps, where I half expected to see Henry VIII, stood an El Greco in modern dress, a singularly tall and lugubrious gentleman with a long, dark face, sunken cheeks, and a thin, high-bridged nose. He had on a brown-and-white sports jacket, gray flannel trousers, and heavy brown sandals. I got out of the car, and he descended the steps, one hand in his pocket, the other outstretched. He was the owner of the *estancia*, and he had been expecting me. The imminence of the rain, he said, had upset some of his plans for showing me around. He told me that I was about to have an encounter with a *pampero*, one of the famous southwest winds of Argentina, which blow with a cold and awesome violence, often accompanied not only by rain but by hailstones large enough to crush a man's skull. He thought that we should make a rapid tour of the grounds and then repair to the house. There was another crackle of lightning and another boom of thunder, and he said we had better get going. He dismissed my car, telling the driver to take it off to the garage behind the house. Then he pointed to a beautiful, serene willow at one end of the terrace. I noticed a maze of roots curling over the ground near it, running every which way. My host suddenly said, "Yes, it's become a troublesome tree. It is one of the first I planted here. It has always stood at the foot of the terrace, almost like a flagstaff. When I built here in 1902, not a tree. Now, as you can see, hundreds of thousands of trees. I imported the seeds from all over the world—from England, from North America, from Java and the Indies—and set my trees out in little pots. I set out oak and pine, blue spruce, chestnut, maple, hickory, hawthorn, Lombardy poplar, black acacia, plum, cherry, peach, paradise. I landscaped everywhere, set banks of small trees below balconies of large ones, grouped them here in a semicircular design, there in full squares of green. It took time and imagination, and, I fancy, some artistry. The small rocks directly ahead"—my host thrust out a hand—"are a perfect prospect from the terrace of my house. Those small rocks were there when I came, standing oddly among the grasses, and it was here I decided to build. Then I put the willow in its pot and it grew, and now these roots have broken through the earth around the tree and crept under the terrace, and perhaps under the house. I walked out of the house one morning several months ago and saw these roots coming out of the ground, and decided to cut down my trees, all my trees, every tree on the place." He looked at me—somewhat desperately, I thought—for some slight sign of agreement with his decision. "If I do not destroy them, they will destroy me. The willow roots are a portent. I must cut down the trees. We are at the business now. Every day, the men are out chopping them down." I have rarely seen a man look as sad as this man looked then. . . .

We returned to the dining room for tea and found my host's wife, an ample, stately woman in her middle sixties, sitting at the head of the table. She was distressed. In the middle of the morning, she said, she had rung for a servant and asked him to bring the teacart to her room. The message had been passed along downstairs. By the time it reached the kitchen, it had become an order to hitch up the pony cart for the Señora so that she could ride about the estate. The pony cart had been instantly made ready, and a man had stood alongside it for several hours, waiting to help the Señora in. He had gone without lunch. In fact, he had stood beside the cart until an hour before, when the Señora's mother had gone out for her regular afternoon ride. The servant was understandably indignant, the other servants had discussed the matter, and, all in all, the help, from top to bottom, were behaving peculiarly. She had spent the past half hour trying to patch things up. "These days, our inside people are mostly Central Europeans—Czechs and Poles," she told me. "One never knows whether the orders are misunderstood or deliberately twisted. Incidents like this, whatever the reason, are unpleasant." She was further distressed because her mother had not yet returned from her ride and had unquestionably been caught in the downpour. She had dispatched a man in a car to get her, but she was afraid that her mother would catch cold.

We chatted for several minutes. I had a glass of dark sherry and some small cucumber-and-watercress sandwiches and had just asked for another glass of sherry when through the door from the great hall came a stooped, tiny-boned woman of advanced age, dressed in black lace. Her face was a torment of wrinkles—so numerous and running in so many directions that the effect was one of cynical good humor rather than of antiquity.

"Mother!" my hostess cried. "You are soaking!"

"A Scotch-and-water, please," said the old lady. We shook hands and she sat down beside me.

"Mother," her daughter said, "you must not sit in those wet clothes."

"First my Scotch-and-water, then my story, and then I will go upstairs, like a good girl," the old lady said. Her son-in-law handed her a highball and she took a sip.

"You are a stranger here," she said to me, "and perhaps you do not know what troubles us. Many of us think Hitler is here."

Her daughter got up and quickly walked around the table to the mother's chair. "Not that again," she said.

"It is *not* nonsense," the mother said. She patted my knee. "The old often know a great deal. They say I dwell on this, but they all feel something, too. It's only that I am willing to speak out. Just now, I was riding in my pony cart. It is my daily custom, and I went quite far with my pony today. The light was interesting and the shadows led me on, and I reached one edge of our place, far down at the end of the woods, close on the village, and I saw him."

"Saw whom?" asked her son-in-law.

"Hitler, of course," she said. "He went past in a car."

I looked at my host. His face had the expression I had noted when he glanced down at the roots of the willow tree beside the terrace.

"If it was not Hitler, then it was a man who looked very, very much like him," said the old lady. She patted my knee again and rose. "I have had some Scotch-and-water, I have told my story, and now I will go upstairs."

The conversation petered out, so I finished my sherry and a few minutes later was on my way back to Mar del Plata. The storm was over, but for the entire distance we ploughed through ugly thick mud.

Buenos Aires provided small relief from the odd sense of doom I encountered on my trips to the country. It seemed an extraordinarily gloomy city. The *porteños*, as the residents of Buenos Aires call themselves (the term means "people of the port"), try anxiously to convince visitors that the city is gaiety incarnate. I had the feeling that they were trying to convince themselves, too, and not entirely succeeding. . . .

The *porteños* take an elaborate pride in their fine, clean city, but they seem to be reaching for something more. Their constant emphasis on a gaiety that does not exist gives them away. I had the impression that, having settled down and grimly and studiously created a city—again, much as one would build a stage set—they are lonely and confused in it, and dubious about the drama being enacted upon the stage. Practically all Argentines are of European stock, and Buenos Aires derives from European cities. It has the sidewalk cafés of Paris, the drawn shutters of Madrid, and the polite suburbs of London. Europe was the model, and Europe is far away. One has the feeling that, having turned their backs upon Europe, the *porteños* feel a disturbing sense of remoteness from it. I took long walks through the city at night and fancied that I *saw* their loneliness. A great deal of it is inarticulate. Argentine husbands have a habit of going out after supper and heading for a *confitería*. One sees them sitting by themselves at tiny tables on warm nights, toying with glasses of beer or vermouth, motionless and abstracted. By the act of leaving the house, they have asserted their manhood, and yet such self-conscious posturings of independence appear to bespeak a deep uncertainty. Evenings when they go forth with their families to cabarets, the sense of collective loneliness is almost unbearable, and suddenly someone will raise his voice in song. Others will join in, and a sad melody will momentarily bring them together. The professional entertainers themselves seem to be victims of the prevailing gloom. They leap to the bandstand and, in voices so sorrowful they are almost ludicrous, begin to chant the lyrics of popular tangos. One evening when I was making the rounds of some cabarets, I collected the words of three of these tangos. They translate, roughly:

All my life, I have been a good friend to everyone. I have given away everything I own and now I am alone, ill, in my dirty and gloomy small room in my neighborhood slum, coughing blood. No one comes to see me now except my dear mother. Ah, now I realize my cruelty to her. I am at the point of death and I recognize my love for her. She is the only one who really cares for me.

Do you recall, loved one, that sable coat I bought for you when we were both poor and I loved you in our neighborhood slum? Do you remember how I went without cigarettes for months and borrowed from all my friends? I even went to the usurer. Do you remember? And just last night I saw you leave a nightclub with a fashion plate, and I could not help but think that our love is a dead thing, but I am still paying for the sable coat.

Ah, beloved, do you recall when you were a poor seamstress, trying hard to eat every day and dodging poverty in our neighborhood slum, and you bestowed upon me tenderness and love such as you will never give another? And now you have been deceived by some stupid playboy, and you have all the money one could desire, and you play with him as a cat plays with a poor mouse. But the day will come when you will be just an old, worn-out piece of furniture. On that day, dearly beloved, should you need a friend, advice, or any kind of help, remember that you can come to me, there will always be an old friend willing to risk even his skin for you, should the occasion present itself.

... At five the next afternoon, a North American friend, in Argentina on business, telephoned me to say that if I would join him right away at the Casa Rosada—the government house—I stood a chance of meeting Perón. He expected to be closeted with the president and several other North Americans for half an hour, and then he would ask the president to greet me. I walked the short distance across the broad Plaza de Mayo to the Casa Rosada, a graceful, elegant pink brick Spanish structure. My friend and his group were just arriving as I got there. We all went in together, past several soldiers with sabres who were standing at attention. An attendant whisked us into an elevator. When we got out, he led the way down a long, wide corridor, through several salons, and into a cream-colored anteroom with brocaded sofas and chairs. My friend and his party were ushered down another long corridor, to the president's office. A middle-aged colonel, whom I took to be some sort of protocol officer, requested that I wait in the anteroom until summoned. There were four other colonels in the room, all drinking black coffee from demitasses. I wandered into the corridor leading to the president's office. The corridor ran half the length of the building, had many big windows overlooking the waterfront, and was lined on both sides with stiff little Empire chairs and tables. Some fifteen bright landscapes hanging along the walls gave it the air of a dignified private gallery. On one small table was a framed quotation from the Argentine epic poem *Martin Fierro*: "If you make a great deal of money, be modest about it—don't show off. Just be quiet and don't act like a rich man; this is a virtue." Obviously, the president was conscious of the role he felt he should play in these surroundings.

My turn came quickly. A door at the other end of the corridor swung open, and a blue-uniformed majordomo beckoned. As I crossed the threshold of the president's office, I saw Perón standing at the far end of a very long and impressive table, at which my friend and his party were seated. Perón bounded toward me and embraced me in typical South American fashion; he put one arm around my shoulder and squeezed, then pounded my back, then drew me toward him and squeezed again. Not until he had led me to a seat at the table did I have a chance to really get a look at him. He is a bit above normal height, and has thick shoulders and a red and slightly pudgy face, somewhat disfigured by what appears to be some form of acne. His eyes are small and very active. He was wearing a brown Palm Beach suit. He seemed ill at ease, and his smile seemed mechanical. Five white telephones and a small bottle of pills were at his side, and behind him, on a desk, I saw a photograph of Señora Perón, etched on glass. At one side of the room was an enormous do-or-die picture of some of Perón's *descamisados*, or "shirtless ones," in revolt. With nervous movements, Perón sat down at the head of the table, took a Chesterfield from a pack in front of him, tapped it several times, lighted it, and took several quick puffs. Someone asked him what he felt were his greatest accomplishments. He did not have to grope for a reply. "My social and economic reforms," he said immediately. "Close behind them are my judicial reforms. Of what use would the other reforms be without accompanying judicial reforms? Our judicial system needed overhauling. We require new laws, new judges. After all"—he paused and winked—"we are in the age of the stratosphere." He added that there was much work yet to be done before his term of office was over. He sighed. "One must have plans for all phases of life," he said. "This takes time." He told us that he was working harder than any other president of Argentina had ever worked, and that it was not all fun. Most other presidents, he said, had come down to the office for an hour or two to sign papers and then gone back home. "Education is our next great step," he said, almost angrily. He leaned forward. Now the president of Argentina seemed about to unburden himself. "I have gone from one university to another and seen no scientific spirit of inquiry. The old professors just walk into a classroom, sit down, read from a book, and walk out. Education must mold and apply." He began to clasp and unclasp his hands. "This is not a matter of putting my own people into the universities. It is a matter of getting politics out of the universities. I am accused of dismissing professors from the universities. This is not true. A group of professors addressed insolent messages to the revolutionary government and resigned, and that was a fortunate thing, since it saved me the trouble of getting rid of them."

The president then stood up, to signify that the meeting was over. "Of what use is it to develop just the arm?" he asked. "One must mold and develop the *entire* organism." He reached behind him to his desk, picked up a jar of sour balls, and held it out to us. Several of us helped ourselves. I passed by his desk and saw that Señora Perón's photograph showed her in a long white "Gone With the Wind" dress, while another picture of her, ingeniously etched on the opposite side of the glass, showed her with a bandanna tied gaily around her head. The president stood fondly in front of the picture for a few moments, popped a sour ball into his mouth, led us to the door, and opened it.

There, outside, surrounded by a hushed group of officials, was Señora Perón, in a fluffy pink dress with a large bustle. Her hair was arranged in a series of golden quoits, one above another. Her skin was strikingly pale, and her eyes were heavy-lidded and lowered. I noticed that, without raising her eyes, she was glancing rapidly from one of us to another. She stood there, a figure in a pageant, as though she had just made her entrance as a young, hard, fanatical queen, poised, supremely confident, all-powerful. She played the role to perfection. She began to shake hands with us, one by one. Her expression never changed. She held out her hand to me, and I took it for an instant. It was stone cold.

Letter from Berchtesgaden

Like the Reich that Hitler built to last a thousand years, his Berchtesgaden is now a grotesque and instructive heap of rubbish. A visit here can be highly rewarding, especially to archeologists, anthropologists, isolationists, and anyone who has ideas of sometime becoming a Führer. Better still, it makes nice sightseeing for American troops, hundreds of whom swarm over the charred grounds every day and poke through the dismal relics of the man who brought them to Europe in the first place. I have been doing a little poking myself.

To begin at the beginning, or at the foot of the Obersalzberg, you drive through the village of Berchtesgaden, pass American Army signs reading "To Hitler's Home," cross a simple, rustic bridge at the edge of town, and shift into low gear for the steep climb up the mountain. The glistening concrete highway is intact and very smooth. The vistas are breathtaking—now acres of pine forest, now snowcapped Alps, now green valleys below—and all along the roadside you see neat fences and dainty flowers. The first gatehouse is disarming, a naïve wooden chalet-like structure with an archway across the road. Except for two M.P.s standing guard, this could be the entrance to the estate of a gentleman, a gentleman with an appreciation of the countryside. The second gatehouse is more ominous. It is of wood and stone, standing forbiddingly on the hillside, and it is the first break with the setting, the first hint that perhaps the master of the estate was afraid of someone. Turn sharp right, inch up a steeper grade, and the road becomes broad and level as it runs along a shelf of the mountain lined on both sides, as far as you can see, with a vast tangle of camouflaged, bombed-out buildings, all green. Instantly you realize that, even when these buildings were intact, they were a desecration of the surroundings, utterly without beauty—a bulky, brutal set of structures thrown together in haphazard fashion, spreading every which way, as though to satisfy a boundless and ugly dream. "In the name of God," said the corporal who drove me up, "who ever called this place a retreat?"

There are few signs that Hitler had, or wanted, solitude. On the contrary, he seems to have had a passion for providing accommodations for hundreds of his cohorts. Above and behind his house, the Berghof, he constructed a massive, rectangular barracks to house eight hundred S.S. men. The barracks are badly in need of repair; there are gaping holes in the roof and piles of debris in the courtyard. Large sheets of ragged green metal, once used for camouflage, have been blasted from the roof and lie scattered over the ground. In the basement are garages, with their gasoline pumps and "No Smoking" signs. Except for one Mercedes-Benz, telescoped and fallen into a bomb crater, the cars are gone. The S.S. men are gone, too. According to German workmen around the place, they were the last to leave, after the heavy bombardment of April 25th. Adjoining the barracks are the remains of a long, low administrative building, and across the road is a hothouse, which catered to Hitler's love for flowers. Also on the estate were another building for S.S. men, close to the master's house; a guest house; a home for Goering, which is now crushed and silly-looking, as though stagehands at the Metropolitan had taken hatchets and ripped apart a setting for *Hänsel and Gretel*; a home for Bormann, successor to Hess, and reputedly commanding officer of the estate in Hitler's absence; a nursery for the sturdy *Kinder* of the élite (the little Führers of the future); tunnels connecting all these buildings with one another and with Hitler's house, and leading up the hill to the final proof that privacy was certainly not wanted—a three-story hotel known as the Platterhof, with three hundred and fifty rooms and hot and cold running water.

Important visitors—field marshals, satellite premiers, high Party officials, and so on—were put in the guest house, but lesser Nazis always stopped at the Platterhof. The Führer's hospitality didn't include free room and board for the guests at the Platterhof; they paid their way. Now the 101st Airborne Division, Army of the United States, occupies its low-ceilinged, cell-like rooms, each with two pine beds and a desk lamp. Most of the furnishings were destroyed by the French troops who were the first to break into the place and who, apparently under the impression that it was Hitler's house, smashed most of the windows and made off with china, glassware, wall decorations, and the hotel's plentiful stocks of fine wines. (Senator Wheeler, who came along several weeks later to view the wreckage of an establishment where he might easily have been made to feel right at home in the old days, was seen by someone tearing a telephone from a wall as a souvenir.) Behind the desk in the bare, uninviting lobby, a sergeant divides his time between acting as room clerk and passing out, to visiting troops, maps of the estate politely labelled "Obersalzberg, Hitler's Mountain Retreat." A model of the unsuccessful camouflage plan for Berchtesgaden, designed by a Munich architect, stands in the lobby; it is dotted with tiny buildings, trees, green nets, and so on.

Guests at the Platterhof ate their meals under gold-and-white wooden chandeliers in a vaulted pavilion adjoining the hotel. It sits on a bluff overlooking Hitler's house and has a large hat-check room, a kitchen with a *caffè espresso* machine, some deep-freeze tubs for ice cream, and a beer tap. A German electrician detailed by our Army to clean up some debris told me that Hitler's final military conference at Berchtesgaden took place in the pavilion last June, after our invasion. Two hundred generals, including Keitel and Guderian, attended. The meeting went on for more than two days, almost without pause. Hitler shouted so loudly that workmen in remote parts of the estate could hear his rasping voice as it pierced the clear mountain air. "He kept banging so *verdammt* hard on the table," the electrician said, "that on the second afternoon he knocked a heavy lamp onto the floor and I had to rush in with a new bulb." While the bulb was being put in, the Führer stopped his harangue and the generals watched the electrician in silence. The moment the electrician stepped outside, the Führer resumed.

The right wing of Hitler's house received a direct hit in the great raid. The resulting fire spread to the rest of the building, destroying all the fittings in the main entrance hall except some squat red marble pillars. The big front room, with its famous large window, is charred and empty. There is only the frame of the window and, at the opposite side, a large wrought-iron fireplace decorated with the figures of three German soldiers. The main staircase is in fairly good condition. Where its marble balustrade is chipped, you can see that the marble is no more than an inch-thick veneer on concrete. Hitler's workroom, upstairs, runs the width of the house; its walls have been thoroughly scorched and only the sockets of three windows and a hideous brown *Kachelofen* remain. His bedroom, which adjoins the workroom, has also been burned. The Führer's bathroom is in better shape. It has green tiled walls, in the best *Good Housekeeping* tradition.

In the basement, I came upon a narrow, gray-walled shooting gallery, the sort of thing you'd expect to find in an F.B.I. school. There are also numerous pantries and kitchens; the entrances to many tunnels, mostly blocked, into which vast quantities of food were put in the last months before Germany's defeat; a room cluttered with overturned chairs and tables, phonograph records, birth certificates, X-ray plates, and piles of old magazines, including a November 15, 1930, issue of the *Kölnische Illustrierte Zeitung* containing an article violently demanding that outworn treaties be discarded.

The German workmen I have talked with here agree that Hitler left the Berghof last June, after his meeting with the generals, and never returned. "Eva Braun drove off in June, too, with a captain and lots of luggage," one of the men said. Goering hung around the place long after Hitler had gone, prowling through the hills in Alpine shorts and with a hunting gun. During the bombardment of April 25th, he took to his bomb shelter. "He trembled tremendously," this man said. The last gay times at Berchtesgaden came shortly after the conference, when Eva Braun's sister married a colonel general and then five hundred guests went to Hitler's Adlerhorst, or Eagle's Nest, on the Kehlstein and got plastered. In March of this year, after Hitler consulted a stomach specialist in the nearby town of Bischofswiesen, orders were given to install a diet kitchen in the Berghof; this started the rumor that he would soon return. Some people thought they saw his car in Berchtesgaden shortly afterward, but nobody saw the Führer.

During his last weeks at the Berghof, Hitler walked with a slight limp and carried a cane. He occasionally visited some Gestapo cronies at the nearby Schloss Klesheim, once the castle of one of Franz Josef's brothers. When he did, all roads in the neighborhood were closed off. He also enjoyed short walks down the mountainside to a summer house known as Mooslahner Kopf, adjoining some farm lands he owned. He was invariably preceded and trailed by three or four hundred Gestapo men. Inside the Berghof, Heil Hitlers were forbidden. His housekeeper, a

Frau Middelstrasse, was instructed to say *"Grüss Gott"* whenever she encountered him. *"Führt euch Gott,"* he would reply, sweeping past. Just before his final departure, he told her, "Now that I am going away, you will no longer have to bother with my needs and you can busy yourself with many things about the house."

Four o'clock on Sunday afternoon was the Führer's brooding hour. He was driven rapidly up the Kehlstein, past long lines of Gestapo guards, and then took the elevator to the building on its summit, the Adlerhorst, known to everybody on the estate as the Tearoom. While he brooded, as many as a thousand S.S. and Gestapo men surrounded the place.

I went up to the Adlerhorst. I drove along the twisting mountain road (hundreds of Yugoslavs are said to have died building it) until I reached the end, a thousand feet below the summit. At this point, in a broad pocket cut out of the mountain, I faced two bronze doors leading to the elevator which reaches the building itself. An inscription over the doors says *"Erbaut 1938."* The day I was there, the elevator wasn't running and Army engineers were in the shaft removing mines, so I took a footpath to the peak. It was a brisk fifteen-minute walk, past ice fields and small, snow-covered shrubs. Perched on the top of the mountain and surrounded on all sides by the jagged peaks of other mountains is the Adlerhorst, a hexagonal granite structure from which an L-shaped rear juts out. Both inside and out it reveals Hitler's madness and his exquisite bad taste. Taking Nietzsche's words literally—Superman lives on the mountaintop—the master of Europe went into the clouds. And what did he build? From the outside, the place could be the guardhouse of a state penitentiary. Inside, everything is out of proportion or off key—ceilings too low, windows too small, bronze doors here, wooden doors there, some rooms right out of an ad for Men of Distinction, others designed like a cheap bar-and-grill. Clouds sweep in through the doorways and windows. The master went so high that for only a few hours a day, and then only when the weather was very good, is there any view at all. The elevator opens on the entrance hall, and beside it is a metal panel with thirteen lights to show the position of the car. On it, too, are the words *"Vorsicht! Aufzug!"* and the information that the capacity of the elevator is 1125 kilograms, or fifteen persons. Twenty-four bronze hat-and-coat hooks hang in the hallway, and opposite them are lavatories large enough to handle a Music Hall crowd. At one end of the hallway is a taproom with a bright-blue table and seats with bright-red leather cushions. In the kitchen are shiny pots and pans, stoves, and a meat block that has never been touched; there isn't a cleaver mark on it.

Off the main hall is a long conference room with an oak table, twenty-six chairs, and blackout curtains, and off that is a huge hexagonal room—the brooding room, the room where Hitler could think his long, lonely, megalomaniac, bloody thoughts. And into this room he crowded forty-six chairs, one more ugly than the next—low-slung chairs covered with sickly blue imitation needle point. On the floor is a machine-made imitation Chinese rug. Before a massive red marble fireplace stands an overstuffed rust-colored sofa that no Kansas farmer would allow in his house. A huge white circular table is in the center of the room. The wall lights are garish gold strips arranged fanwise to simulate tongues of flame.

Furthermore, the Adlerhorst had mice. In a closet I found a half-empty cardboard box of powder. An absolute guarantee against *Feld-mäuse*, the label said.

MUSIC

Around Christmastime in 1948, Harold Ross suddenly asked me if I would be the music critic of *The New Yorker*. Robert Simon had been conducting the weekly column "Musical Events" for many years but was rumored to have wearied of the job. Ross would seem to have had one of his unexpected, somewhat intuitive instincts about me and music. Both he and Shawn knew from conversation that I went to a great many concerts, and talked about them later to anybody who would listen. But he didn't know much more than that. Neither did I. I possess a deeply felt amateur appreciation of music. I know what I like and what I dislike. But I have never studied music and cannot read music. I mentioned all this to Mr. Ross, who didn't seem the least disturbed. "Just listen," he said, "and write." I said I would accept the post on two conditions: first, that I would perform the task for no longer than one year, on the logical assumption that I could disguise my ignorance for just about that length of time. This notion appealed to Ross. My second condition pleased him even more: I said that I felt a music critic for *The New Yorker* required a certain degree of elegance. Would he buy me a black homburg hat to wear to concerts? That wrinkled, wonderful, gap-toothed face broke into a grin. "Goddamn good idea," he said. "Go to Brooks and buy a Lock and send us the bill." I had become a music critic.

What I call my appreciation of music started, I suppose, while I was growing up in Wheeling, West Virginia, where I was born in 1914. We lived in a big white house on Maple Avenue, with a broad porch, swings, turrets, nooks and crannies, but a favorite haunt was a dark panelled room which my grandmother liked to call "the music room" because it had an old-fashioned wind-up Victrola with that picture of Nipper, the spotted terrier, sitting around listening to music coming from the horn of the Victrola—His Master's Voice. I had the impression (I still have it) that every civilized family in America in those days had houses bulging with Caruso records, and that a large segment of the population spent many of its waking hours, tears streaming down their cheeks, as Caruso sang out his broken heart with arias from "Pagliacci."

We moved to New York City when I was about seven or eight. My musical appreciation deepened in elementary school, at P.S. 165, a remarkably progressive establishment allied with Teachers College. Every Friday morning around eleven, the sliding doors of each class-room went into action, and the entire school became one huge audito-rium while we listened as "Papa" Walter Damrosch, the former head of the New York Philharmonic and the New York Symphony, in his gentle dulcet tones led us via phonograph through the wonders of classical music, with emphasis on Wagner. "And now, dear children," he would say, "we vill listen to 'Looowengrin.'"

Well, I bought the Lock homburg and gained a certain degree of self-confidence. New York being one of the great musical capitals of the world, there were myriad concerts to choose from, and almost every night I would dash from Carnegie Hall to Town Hall to Times Hall (long gone, but then on Forty-fourth Street) to hear one concert or another. Carnegie Hall was, and still is, my favorite. There is no place to which it can be compared. Saved by Isaac Stern, and now owned by the City of New York, it is an oasis of calm and beauty and permanence in a hectic city. I love going to Carnegie Hall, and have often felt that I could sit there, in perfect happiness, for hours on end, concert or no concert, just admiring its huge proscenium, its soaring balconies, its red seats, its glittering rosette of lights high above. I often go quite early, the moment the doors open, and enter the empty auditorium. I sit quietly and let my mind wander over a strange notion I have had since childhood: that all beautiful sound waves go out into the universe, travel about, hover in space, never lose their sound, and if I or someone smart enough would find a way of getting out into space, he or she could retrieve those sounds and hear those concerts all over again.

Both Ross and Shawn liked what I turned in each week. So did read-ers. Janet Flanner told me that Virgil Thomson enjoyed the way I wrote about music, and this made me happy. I just went to concerts and lis-tened. There were those who considered the reviews irreverent. I espe-

cially recall reviewing, and deeply admiring, the appearance of Dame
Edith Sitwell at the Museum of Modern Art, in a remarkable performance of her "Façade" poems, in ragtime rhythm, set to music by
William Walton. Dame Edith was delighted with my review, so much so,
in fact, that she invited me to lunch at the St. Regis, where she was staying. When I arrived at her suite, I met her brother, Sir Osbert, and her
other guests: Katherine Anne Porter, Monroe Wheeler, of the Museum
of Modern Art, and the novelist Glenway Wescott. Dame Edith, austere
and turbaned, sat at a large round table, topped by a huge bowl of martinis. It was a heady crowd, and a sight to see. As Dame Edith imperiously
stirred the deadly gin, the talk turned to "that new music critic on *The
New Yorker*." "He is dreadful, simply dreadful," chirped Wescott.
Wheeler turned pale and sprang into action. Wildly pointing at me, he
cried, *"C'est lui! C'est lui!"* and Wescott became silent. I also vividly
recall the aftermath of a review of a concert at Town Hall by the pianist
and master teacher Ania Dorfmann. I wrote a negative review of the proceedings. On the morning of its appearance in print, Ross burst into my
office. "So she took a swipe at the piano, and the piano swiped her
back?" he said. "That was my impression," I said. "Do you know
who she is?" he asked. "Ania Dorfmann," I said. "No, no," said Ross.
"Who she IS?" I had no idea what he was talking about. "Well," said Mr.
Ross, "she would appear to be a very special friend of Arturo Toscanini, who has been on the phone all morning and is outraged by your
review. He would appreciate your departure." "You plan any action?" I
said. "Of course not," said Ross.

DECEMBER, 1948

"Otello," Maybe

There is very little that can be said about the opening opera. There is a good deal to be said about the Opera Opening. I hope that someday Mr. Edward Johnson, or his successor at the Metropolitan, will meet the problem head on and open the Opera one night before the Opera opens. In other words, the evening before the singing starts, throw open the Opera House to the hand-painted dowagers and their red wigs, to the prancing young bucks in their tails, to the pails upon pails of iced champagne which Sherry's so conveniently places at the red tables in the Buffet on the Grand Tier. Move the Buffet to the stage for the evening, put the Audience on the stage, raise the Great Golden Curtain, and let everybody wander about to his heart's content, drink, even sing if he likes, but, for God's sake, have no opera. Dinner music in the pit might be quite suitable, but no selection more profound than "Carry Me Back to Biarritz, Baby" should be attempted.

The opera at this year's Opening was, I am told, Verdi's "Otello," and, to be candid, there *were* isolated moments during the evening when, through cracks in the wall of bodies moving in and out of seats in front of me, I was able to identify the voices as those of fair Desdemona, wicked Iago, and poor old Othello. For the rest of the time, it might have been "Aïda," or possibly "Sweethearts." Serious criticism of the performance would be an insult to the performers, since they were engaged practically throughout in what amounted to a pitched battle with the audience. Not until the stirring and tragic last act did Othello and Desdemona have even half a chance, the frivolous elements among the

(224)

patrons by then having either departed the building or nestled down in the Buffet with their champagne. Mr. Vinay, the Othello, seemed to get a grip on himself and on his voice, and Miss Albanese, the Desdemona, sang with touching beauty. Mr. Warren's Iago was, I imagine, the only completely satisfactory performance. Iago is such an evil man that not even an Opening can faze him, and Mr. Warren was admirably evil and in good voice. The décor of the last act had elements of style, if only in contrast to the earlier acts, which displayed the type of scenery one often encounters at summer camps for little boys and girls.

The Opera came into its own on the second night, perhaps proving my point. The presentation was Donizetti's gem "L'Elisir d'Amore," and it was difficult to believe that the same Opera Association that had been in charge on Night One was in control on Night Two. For me, the evening was one of sheer pleasure. Even the scenery was bright and fresh and engaging. Mr. Antonicelli conducted with enormous relish. He quite obviously loves the music with a passion. The audience was composed of people who had come to enjoy an opera rather than to admire a tiara, and they were infected with the joy of the singers. I have nothing but praise for Miss Sayão, Mr. Tagliavini, and Mr. Valdengo, and for that tremendous compound of outlandish comic gesture and superb bass voice that is known as Salvatore Baccaloni.

Mostly Positive

The Metropolitan laid another of its big, heavy eggs last week with the first subscription "Rigoletto" of the season. I was more puzzled than pained by the performance. The question that came to mind was: How is it possible to make "Rigoletto" sound dull, thick, interminable, sticky, and sick? Little boys playing airs from "Rigoletto" on combs could gather crowds on a side street any day. Organ-grinders who turn their instruments over to "La donna è mobile" run the risk of suffering contusions of the scalp from the fifty-cent pieces dropped on their heads. But leave "Rigoletto" to the Metropolitan and the trick is miraculously done. A large share of the blame must rest on Miss Pons, the Gilda of the evening. I am afraid that Miss Pons has reached a point, operatically, where she should be seen and not heard. She was admirably decorative, but when it came to the singing—well, let's talk about network time and package deals. The orchestra deferred to her at every juncture, slowing its pace, becoming obsequious, almost silent, and still the voice of Gilda seemed unable to cope with the music. The Quartet was pitiable. It was a trio, really. For all that one could hear of her, Gilda might have been back at the Ducal Palace in Mantua rather than outside Sparafucile's unsavory roadhouse. Mr. Cimara, the conductor, led the band as though he and his men had fallen victim to pernicious anemia. Mr. Warren, the Rigoletto, had his moments of glory, to be sure, but they were defeated by the prevailing humidity. Only Miss Elmo, as the red-blooded and womanly Maddalena, was adequate. She was alive, and she was acting and singing well, and no man could ask for anything more.

The Little Orchestra Society is to be congratulated for its stimulating evening a week ago Monday at Town Hall. Some of our Big Orchestra Societies would do well, I think, to take a look at the programs that Mr. Scherman, the Society's conductor, gives us. Last week, he gave us the world première of Schubert's Overture for Strings (a fetching piece written by Schubert, a bright boy, when he was fourteen), the world première of Alexei Haieff's Concerto in One Movement for Violin and Orchestra (an interesting number, superbly played by Miss Fredell Lack), Prokofiev's Piano Concerto No. 3 in C Major (played to what seemed to me like perfection by Frank Sheridan), and Chausson's Concerto for Violin, Piano, and Strings (in which Mr. Sheridan also performed brilliantly, with Miss Lack demonstrating somewhat less lustre than she did in the Haieff piece). In all, a musical pleasure.

I shall not soon forget, either, the Philharmonic-Symphony's playing, last Thursday, of d'Indy's Symphony on a French Mountain Song, for Orchestra and Piano. Carnegie Hall tingled with Gallic joy and wonderment. The incomparable Robert Casadesus, the soloist, was so much a part of the music that he did everything but conduct, while Mr. Münch, the conductor, became so enraptured with events that he did everything but sit down and play the solo part. Mr. Münch belongs to the ballet school of conducting. He hops, leaps, and jumps, and is wonderful to behold. More important, he gets the best out of his men, though I'll bet they are exhausted by the time they get home.

I feel sorry for anyone who missed the Oratorio Society's performance of the uncut Handel "Messiah" at Carnegie Hall last Saturday night. What can one say of the "Messiah" other than that it would appear to justify the creation of Man? It makes the whole experiment seem worth while. The Oratorio Society's rendition was so much a labor of love that, in a sense, criticism would be a quibble. Alfred Greenfield, the conductor, has a noble conception of this noble project. There were some numbers by the contralto, Miss Dinwoodey, that I did not feel measured up to the words or to the music, and some tum-te-tumming by the chorus in the glorious "Hallelujah," but Miss Faull (the soprano), Mr. Kent (the bass-baritone), and Mr. Jarratt (the tenor) could not have been much better and still remained earthbound. As a matter of fact, Mr. Jarratt's "Thou Shalt Break Them with a Rod of Iron" contained intimations of something beyond the walls of the Hall.

Hark!

There was more music in Grand Central Station last week than in any other place in town, including Carnegie Hall. The station was a festive sounding board of Noel, Noels, Come, All Ye Faithfuls, and Little Towns of Bethlehem. It was impossible to walk through the upper level during the late afternoon or early evening without hearing one or another choral group singing away on the east balcony to the glories of the season. The groups came from all over. There were, to name a few, the Summit, New Jersey, High School Chorus; the Trenton Collegiate Glee Club; the Lord & Taylor Choral Group; the Mamaroneck High School Chorus; the Continental Can Choral Society; the Borden Choral Group; and the Good Shepherd Choir. All of this was sponsored by the New York Central and the New Haven Railroads, and I think it was a fine thing for a couple of railroads to have sponsored at this time of the year. Some of the singing wasn't so good, but then some of the singing at Carnegie Hall isn't so good, either. The advantage the station singers had over singers in more orthodox concert halls was a sense of oneness with their audience. There was a striking rapport between the groups up on the balcony overlooking the busy concourse and the sweeping, rushing, pushing holiday crowds below. I saw one man—and what I took to be his whole family—nearly miss the Wolverine because he became engrossed in "Hark! the Herald Angels Sing" and lifted his voice in accompaniment. Luckily, a woman in his party came to her senses and dragged him through the gate with a few seconds to spare.

No higher tribute could have been paid to the power of song, except having the fellow actually miss his train.

I will not be unhappy if I never hear Tchaikovsky's Concerto for Violin and Orchestra in D Major again. Nathan Milstein played the piece with the Philharmonic-Symphony last Thursday, Charles Münch conducting. I don't think Mr. Milstein, a truly great violinist, was too happy with the music, either. It's such a noisy, sentimental, bravura thing, and quite empty, and Mr. Milstein seemed to be saying, "Look, I can do this with my eyes shut, but is it worth the time and effort?" The rest of the program was scarcely more satisfying. Mr. Münch gave us Lalo's overture to "Le Roi d'Ys," which, as far as I'm concerned, could be renamed "The Ride of the Rockettes." Then, there was Ravel's "Valses Nobles et Sentimentales," led by Mr. Münch as though he wanted to get home and start to trim his tree, and Roussel's Symphony No. 4, the only music of the evening that interested me. Incidentally, why are the names of the Philharmonic-Symphony players not printed in the program? Such consummate musicians deserve something better than anonymity.

The Metropolitan's first "Madame Butterfly" of the season was delightful. Miss Kirsten, her voice in splendid condition, was a fetching, lovable, tragic Butterfly. A wonderful singer, Miss Kirsten, and a fine actress, too. She was what some critics call "ably supported," especially by Mr. Brownlee, as the consul—the sort of man we should be proud to have in our Foreign Service—and Miss Browning, as Suzuki. Mr. Kullman was Lieutenant Benjamin Franklin Pinkerton, and I liked him a good deal better than I had two weeks before, in "Louise." He seemed more at home in a United States Navy uniform than wearing a droopy bow tie in a Paris garret. People can talk all they want about East's meeting West and never the twain, etc., but the fact remains that Pinkerton is a blot on the escutcheon of our Navy. Nonetheless, Mr. Kullman led me to believe he was the victim of conditions beyond his control, and that was a feat of which he can be proud. The entire opera was, as it ought to be, exceedingly pleasant. One can just sit and let the score pour over one, or one can look at the stage and see human beings, their faces not covered with matted hair, registering human emotions. Mr. Antonicelli, the conductor, had the orchestra obviously excited over the beauties of the music.

Pierre Fournier, the distinguished French cellist, was in top form at Town Hall last week. His concert was somewhat marred for me by the excesses of his accompanist, George Reeves, who played with such volume that at times it was difficult to know whether the evening had been planned as a cello recital with piano accompaniment or as a piano recital with cello accompaniment. Mr. Fournier triumphed, of course, for he is a musician of transcendent talents. He and his cello give the impression that they were spawned simultaneously. Mr. Fournier provided a rich evening of Francœur, Bach, Beethoven, Martinu, Schumann, and Chopin. I enjoyed his Bach Suite No. 1 in G Major, performed with vision and purity, better than the other numbers. Mr. Fournier, out there alone with his cello and Bach (not so alone, when you come to think of it), was something to remember.

One other thing: Brandy should be provided with every ticket to Carnegie Hall and Town Hall these nights. They are as drafty as windswept heaths. The blasts that come in the rear door and sweep through the auditorium could give a head cold to a French horn.

Ouch!

———————

The influence of the Keystone cops hung heavily over the Metropolitan's first presentation this season of "The Barber of Seville." I will confess to a certain pleasure at witnessing the cops in seventeenth-century Seville, but it was a short-lived pleasure. There was so much aimless and absurd running about, so much to-ing and fro-ing, that throughout the evening the voices of the singers were forced to compete with their leg muscles. This is not a fair test for singers. It is a pity that Mr. Tajo, the Metropolitan's new basso, had to make his local operatic début under such athletic circumstances. He is obviously a man of superior talent. As Don Basilio, he was vocally quite fine, if occasionally a little winded by the race. He has a pleasing, firm voice, somewhat lacking in power. To look at him, one would expect a voice that would bring the sets down, for he is a tremendously tall beetle of a man, with a huge head, a face that expresses ages of experience, and hands that leap, flutter, point, and do everything but sing. Mr. Baccaloni, the Dr. Bartolo, was not consistently at his best. He appeared to be embarrassed by the presence of another funny basso, and attempted to outcomic him. There were moments when I was afraid that Mr. Baccaloni would resort to parlor tricks. Toward the end of the evening, after he had become reconciled to Mr. Tajo, his spirits rose and his voice showed a parallel improvement. Miss Pons, the scheduled Rosina, was indisposed. Miss Gracias, who sounded somewhat indisposed, too, took her place.

.   .   .

Ouch!

I have rarely encountered such pretentious humbuggery as "The Rape of Lucretia," the Benjamin Britten music drama, at the Ziegfeld Theatre. Perhaps the Ziegfeld, one of the largest theatres in town, is not the place for so intimate an opera. (Even in this wicked day and age, rape is something of a private matter.) Britten's work was first performed—in 1946, at the Glyndebourne Festival—in a small opera house. It is scored for only twelve instrumentalists, another fact that would seem to call for smaller quarters. Big house or little, the score does not appeal to me. I found it sketchy, elusive, and weak, with only isolated moments of vigor and commanding beauty. Not much can be said about Ronald Duncan's libretto, either. It is as high-blown as a radio script with a college education, and no more profound. Mr. Duncan has invested Lucretia's rape, in 509 B.C., by Tarquinius, with deep religious significance and some outrageous verbal nonsense, but the night I was there the principals played to the crowd, not to the cathedral. Miss Kitty Carlisle, as the violated one, was sadly miscast. Her voice is for the musical shows, and I hope she finds herself a nice one soon, with a good, hot score. A mimeographed handout sent to me before the opening hinted that in order to understand fully what was about to occur at the Ziegfeld, I should visit the Etruscan Wing of the Metropolitan Museum of Art. Agnes de Mille, the director, apparently visited the Wing and got trapped there. All through the first scene, in front of a tent outside Rome, the actors kept slapping at their faces and waving their arms, and I was puzzled until I realized that Miss de Mille's researches had uncovered the presence of mosquitoes in the Pontine Marshes some twenty-four hundred years before Mussolini. Only Miss Piazza, as Lucia; Mr. Tozzi, as Tarquinius; and the elegant and striking sets of John Piper—true masterpieces of art in the theatre—achieved the high level toward which the entire production groaned and struggled.

Among the Living

Dr. Koussevitzky and his Boston Symphony Orchestra swept down from the North and into Carnegie Hall a week ago Wednesday, and by the end of the evening I was a good deal wiser and enriched musically. The evening had several remarkable aspects. For one thing, Dr. Koussevitzky's program was made up entirely of modern—and for the most part good modern—American music. There was no compromising, no hedging, no "Flying Dutchman" overtures or dudelsackpfeifers to soften the blow. For another, every composer represented is still alive and breathing, and, furthermore, was alive and breathing in Carnegie Hall that night. Present were William Schuman, Lukas Foss, Samuel Barber, Henry Cowell, and Walter Piston. Not one among them is past fifty-five, and three are still under forty; Mr. Foss is only twenty-six. With the exception of Mr. Foss, who took over the baton to lead his "Recordare," all the composers sat in one upper-tier box and graciously acknowledged, at the conclusion of their respective works, the scant applause of the audience. And this brings me to another aspect of the occasion. The only warmth granted to those composers—aside from the affectionate enthusiasm of Dr. Koussevitzky and his men—was the body heat they must have engendered sitting together in the box. The audience, a huge and dressy throng, rather ostentatiously sat on its hands. A Boston Symphony concert is One of Those Things People Go To, and go they did, but they didn't seem to enjoy it. Listening to the splendid music and then to the driblets of applause, I was reminded of the old Irish gentleman who, finally encouraged to leave a wake at dawn, stood in the doorway and shouted at the deceased's family, "I'm going, but before I go, let me tell you this—you've no respect for the living!"

All the music was interesting, and some of it struck me as being of considerable stature. I think I enjoyed most Mr. Piston's Symphony No. 3 and Mr. Cowell's "Hymn and Fuguing Tune No. 2," for string orchestra. Although the music by Mr. Piston, who was born in 1894, is, in the twentieth-century tradition, starkly cerebral, it has about it an air of strength, hope, and form. One can hear Mr. Piston thinking aloud in his Third Symphony, and his thoughts—for me, at least—are beautiful ones. Mr. Cowell—he's of the Class of '97—has also written a piece in which the glass is not completely shattered. Mr. Foss's "Recordare" was given its first local presentation. He began to compose it on the dark day, a year ago, when Gandhi was murdered, and he was evidently affected, along with articulate and inarticulate millions of others, by the dreadful portent of the violent end of the world's least violent man. Unfortunately, his music seemed in spots to demonstrate an unrestrained pessimism that tended to defeat its solemn purpose.

The following night, and in Carnegie Hall again, Leopold Stokowski conducted the Philharmonic-Symphony in the sort of program that brings the folks off their hands. All by himself, Mr. Stokowski is enough of a spectacle to arouse, if not applause, at least stunned admiration. That familiar head of hair is worth one movement of an unfamiliar symphony any day. Last week, Mr. Stokowski surprised us with the overture to "The Flying Dutchman," the polka and fugue from "Schwanda" (Schwanda was a bagpipe player, or dudelsackpfeifer, and, for my money, a fool), Brahms's Fourth Symphony (for the steady trade), and, to prove that he was still among the living, Hindemith's "Philharmonic Concerto." This was another first local presentation. Although I listened attentively, I can remember very little of what I heard, and I consider this a bad sign.

None Better

———————

Until a week ago Wednesday evening, Jascha Heifetz had given no local recital for almost two years. According to newspaper interviews, he had gone off to think things over—to aerate his mind and to ponder about himself in relation to music and the world in general. I can imagine that Mr. Heifetz, now somewhat past the middle of the journey, was faced by some very real problems. I feel certain that he came smack up against the dilemma that faces (but is too often ignored by) all truly great interpretive artists who have mastered their instruments and wonder whether they should rest there or try for something more. For a man possessed of Heifetz's keen and restless intellect, to be acknowledged as the world's greatest violinist was obviously not enough. It might have been enough for his concert managers and the manufacturers of his records, but it was not enough for Heifetz, and he was the only party, in this instance, who mattered.

Well, Heifetz returned to Carnegie Hall last week and cast a spell over his audience, which seemed to sense that during his two-year absence he not only had maintained his preëminence as an interpreter but had reached for, and attained, a creative status. There was the music, and there, with his violin, was Heifetz, as outwardly distant and unimpassioned as ever, but he seemed to be doing things to, and with, the music that were beyond the music itself. The entire evening gave me the feeling that here in this hall a man was fulfilling himself. I was especially moved by Heifetz's performance of the Bach Sonata No. 3 in C Major and of the familiar Vieuxtemps Concerto No. 5. His playing of his own transcription of Ravel's "Valses Nobles et Sentimentales" (Nos. 6 and 7) gave that music more depth and delicacy than I had thought possible, and the Debussy-Hartmann "Il Pleure dans Mon Cœur" was played with such stirring artistry that I could swear that *il pleurait dans mon cœur, aussi.*

I am grateful to Leopold Stokowski for introducing Ralph Vaughan Williams's Symphony No. 6 to this city, at last Thursday night's Philharmonic Symphony concert. Vaughan Williams, now seventy-six and living outside London, wrote this symphony something over a year ago, and it betrays the tenderness, the aspirations, the exalted vigor, and the terrible wisdom of a genius who has grown old only in the arbitrary arithmetic of the years. There is always danger in reading anything into music such as this, but I found the "Epilogue" filled with solemn hope, with promise for all of us.

Minority Report

The Metropolitan's production last week of Richard Strauss's dismal old turkey "Salome" was probably the most inspired and well-integrated one that we shall see for a long time. I use "we" in a broad sense, since, unless I'm dragged to "Salome" by seven or eight of Herod's guards, I look forward to many happy years away from this opera. For one thing, I have a prejudice (purely personal) against operas that depict an ancient court, complete with bowls of fruit for the king, hypersensitive court flunkies pressing their faces against the pillars of the court at every wail from the orchestra, gold goblets, flares, solemn Moorish attendants with gleaming cutlasses, wigs dipped in mercurochrome, great, high chairs for the brooding monarch, and so on. A collection of such trappings—and "Salome" has them all—just makes me want to go home and reread "The Voyages of Doctor Dolittle." For another thing, Strauss's "Salome" music has always struck me as being bargain-basement Wagner, of a singularly repulsive nature. Herr Strauss's score, of course, revolves around the advanced necrophilia of Fräulein Salome, and in dealing with so obsessed and frantic a young woman he was entitled to go pretty far with the morbid qualities of his music. It seems to me that he went a good deal farther than was required, and began to tell, musically, some sly and dirty little stories of his own.

In this happy frame of mind, I went to the Metropolitan's "Salome," and I must confess that I came away almost stunned by the intensity of the performance. Fritz Reiner, conducting opera for the first time in this city, had the orchestra sounding like an ensemble of talented demons. If "Salome" must be presented, Mr. Reiner is obviously the man to direct the orchestra. His passionate control of the proceedings both in the pit and onstage was something to sit back in the presence of, and admire. As Salome, Miss Ljuba Welitsch (the occasion marked her operatic début in this city, too) was overpowering. She never for an instant lost her sense of drama, and her voice throughout was nothing short of wonderful, except for an occasional shrillness of tone. Mr. Berglund sang Jokanaan, the Prophet, with superb dedication, but physically he was so detached and immobile that I felt matters had changed hardly at all when the Prophet's head was served up, toward the close of the ceremonies, on a platter. Mr. Lorenz sang Herod with the properly horrified inflections, and Miss Thorborg, as the cold-blooded mother of Salome, was adequately depraved. The evening, however, belonged to Mr. Reiner and Miss Welitsch, who, almost as though propelled by private devils, turned in wild and unforgettable performances.

The Best Things in Life

On one of those hot nights last week that made strong men whimper—Wednesday, to be exact—I went over to hear the Goldman Band play on the Mall, in Central Park. Within a matter of moments, the world had been set right again; the tension and the sweat and the feeling of what-the-hell had passed away. For me, there is a magical quality in any concert of the Goldman Band, a feeling compounded, now that I think of it, of many elements. For one thing, Edwin Franko Goldman and his band have lent a beautiful sense of permanence to our summer lives. There is the fine, white, acoustically perfect bandstand, and there is the band, summer after summer after summer, and there, white-topped, spry as a cricket, and seemingly inexhaustible, is Edwin Franko Goldman. There, too, is the setting, a curious one in a city of cement, exhaust fumes, jarring horns, and a heat more tropical than the city boosters might care to admit—an almost Parisian setting of leafy trees, comfortably uncomfortable old-fashioned green benches, and a slow, nostalgia-filled twilight. There is the audience—thousands upon thousands of people, from every corner of the city, some in their shirtsleeves, others in their baby carriages—all come to relax and to listen to and enjoy the music. (Even the babies applaud at a Goldman Band concert.) Above all else, I suppose, there is the generous, happy notion of Daniel and Florence Guggenheim, who endowed these free outdoor concerts as "an annual gift to the people of the City of New York."

Last Wednesday's concert, I am certain, would have pleased the Guggenheims and made them aware of the happiness that their gift has brought to a great many people. Mr. Goldman, never a man to shirk a piece of music simply because its composer intended to have a few strings on hand, presented a rich program: some stunning excerpts from "Die Walküre," "Parsifal," and "Lohengrin;" a jolly, sprightly "Suite of Old American Dances," by the arranger and composer Robert Russell Bennett; "Finlandia;" "Aase's Death;" and Liszt's Second Hungarian Rhapsody. Mr. Goldman played "Finlandia" with such feeling and attention to tonal detail that I dropped my Popsicle, and the lady alongside me, who was about to reach the bottom of her Cracker Jack box, held off searching for her prize until the end of the piece. (She finally fished out a decalcomania.) One of the major pleasures of the evening was a march written by Mr. Goldman, "The League of Composers," first played a year ago last January at a concert in honor of his seventieth birthday. It is filled with the bouncy, rhythmic joy of living that Mr. Goldman puts into not only all his marches but all his concerts. For those of us who were weaned on his "The Third Alarm" and "On the Mall," there is nothing quite like an Edwin Franko Goldman march, except another Edwin Franko Goldman march.

REPORTER AT LARGE

"Reporter at Large" is a broad rubric denoting a somewhat lengthy and in-depth factual experience, distinct from a biographical Profile or critical essay. "At Large" means exactly what it says, and since the world is a large place, a reporter at large was given free rein to go many places, carrying his curiosity with him. Some of these stories appeared under the headings Our Footloose Correspondents and Onward and Upward with the Arts.

From: Toscanini Train

One recent sultry midnight, in Richmond, Virginia, I stepped aboard the special fourteen-car train carrying Arturo Toscanini and the N.B.C. Symphony Orchestra on an eight-thousand-mile six-week transcontinental concert tour, and into a small, bright, affectionate world dominated by the Maestro. Earlier, in New York, I had asked some officials at N.B.C. if I might join the tour, and they had agreed, suggesting that I meet the train at Richmond and travel with it to Atlanta, where Toscanini was to give one of twenty concerts.

In Richmond, I had gone to the Broad Street Station, walked through a gate over which there was a sign reading "Toscanini Train," and then down a steep ramp onto a long, deserted platform, alongside which stood the Toscanini Train. The shade on every window was drawn, and the entire train was silent except for occasional hissing bursts of steam from beneath the cars. I had been assigned to car RCA 5, and in its corridor I found a wide-awake, smiling porter, who, even before he took my bags, made it clear that Toscanini was uppermost in his thoughts. "Oh, that Toscanini!" he said. "He is a sight to see. He is a very elegant, old-fashioned gentleman." I followed the porter to Compartment A. He shoved the bags under the berth. "You know what he ordered for lunch the first day, when we left Pennsylvania Station?" he asked. "He ordered chicken à la Maryland. That chef in his car—the Columbus, at the rear—man, that chef is still singing. Nothing he'd rather prepare than chicken à la Maryland. He feared he'd be cooking nothing but porridge and soft-boiled eggs for the old gentleman, and right off he's cooking chicken à la Maryland." The porter lowered his voice. "The Maestro said his car was swaying and bumping, so the train's been slowed down to fifty miles an hour for his better comfort. Did you hear about his soup? Man, that Maestro eats soup at every meal—soup for breakfast, lunch, and supper!" He scratched his head in wonderment. "Imagine. Eighty-three years old and soup for breakfast! Thick soup, too. He must like soup. The galley in that private car, that's a regular soup kitchen!" The porter broke into laughter. "And his pajamas! Bright silk ones, they tell me, and he's got special cases of fizz water sent over from Italy. Won't drink the regular water." The train gave a slight lurch. "We're beginning to move," he said. "Man, I've seen trains and trains. We almost had a television set for the Maestro's car; they tested one out between Philadelphia and Washington, but she wouldn't work. But he's got a bathtub in his car. There are some gentlemen in the lounge, two cars back, waiting for you." . . .

The rear door of the lounge swung open, and a scholarly-looking man in his early fifties, wearing a rumpled gray suit and a gray tie, entered and sat down opposite me. He was Walter Toscanini, the Maestro's son. He wiped his brow with a handkerchief.

"How's Maestro?" asked Walker [Albert Walker, N.B.C. executive assistant].

"Finally got to bed," said Mr. Toscanini. "He will kill us all yet with his energy. He wears me out, really. The moment we reached his car after the concert tonight, he insisted on walking through the train, said he wanted to see the musicians. 'Father,' I said, 'the musicians have not yet arrived at the train.' But no, he goes through every car, first one way, then the other. Then he had some soup and red wine, and *then* he said, 'Walter, I will show you a trick,' and he stood in front of a divan and jumped up on it backward. I am exhausted."

"How did Maestro enjoy playing 'Dixie'?" said Walker.

"Father said 'Dixie' was *molto bene*," said Walter Toscanini. "He came offstage while they were still cheering, and said, ' "Dixie" is the end of the knockout.' " Walter got up and said good night.

"Walter shares the private car with Maestro," Walker said to me. "We keep someone on guard back there at the door twenty-four hours a day, either the porter, the chef, or a waiter." He smiled. "We stayed over last night at the John Marshall Hotel, in Richmond, and when we left for the concert this evening, coming down in the elevator, Maestro said to me, 'Walker, how many steps from the lobby to the street?' 'I don't know, Maestro,' I said. 'Fifteen, Walker, fifteen,' he said. And he was right. He knows exactly how many steps there are in every auditorium from the wings to the podium, but I didn't realize he counted steps in hotel lobbies, too. He broke another pair of glasses yesterday. We have glasses in repair shops everywhere. Maestro keeps sitting on them. He gets absorbed reading a score, takes them off to think, and before you know it, he's sat on another pair."

Williams [Jack Williams, of RCA] stood up. "I'm concerned over the swaying of Maestro's car," he said. "Think I'll sneak back and see if slowing down to fifty miles an hour has helped."

Shortly afterward Walker and Dine [Josef Dine, N.B.C. press director] went off to bed. I picked up a magazine, and read for a half hour before the rear door opened and Williams came in. He looked pale and shaken. "Maestro's up," he said. "Gave me one hell of a start. I tiptoed through his car and sat in his sitting room, with all the lights out, to test the rocking of the car. She's moving nicely. A light flashes on in Maestro's bedroom, and before I know it, there he is in the doorway, in his pajamas and bare feet. He smiled and said, 'I'm thirsty. I'd like some rocky water.' I ran to the galley and told the porter to open some fizzy water fast. Peeped into his sitting room just before I left, and he was sitting in a chair reading scores. I think I better sit up most of the night, just in case something goes wrong. We want Maestro to be comfortable." I wished Williams good luck and went to bed. . . .

When I had finished breakfast [next morning], I walked to the lounge and found Walker sitting there smoking a cigarette and beaming. "Maestro's taking a little nap," he said. "He was up some during the night and read a few scores, but he fell asleep about three and slept until seven. Then he had a big bowl of soup and some Italian coffee with bread sticks. Walter makes his coffee for him in a special, portable *espresso* machine. Maestro started to read a guidebook of the Southern states sent him by his grandson Walfredo—he's at Yale—and then dozed off in his chair."

A tall, elderly, distinguished-looking man with a florid face burst into the car. "Maestro's awake," he said. "Wants to buy a gray hat when we get to Atlanta. Says his black Homburg is too dull for the South." Walker swiftly headed for the Maestro's car. The tall gentleman sat down beside me and said he was John Royal, a vice-president of N.B.C. He had travelled thousands of miles with the Maestro, he said, including his trip to South America in 1940. "Everywhere he goes, adoration," said Mr. Royal. "He gave eight concerts in Buenos Aires and the streets were lined from his hotel to the Teatro Colón, both going and coming. Maestro loves to travel. He just told me, back in his car, that he feels forty-five years old again. He remembers conducting 'Aïda' and 'La Gioconda' in Atlanta in 1912, with Caruso, Amato, and Destinn. A fantastic man. There was a rehearsal last year when he stopped the orchestra and pointed to a violinist in the second section and said, 'You are not using your own violin,' and the man blushed and said, 'You are right, Maestro, I have borrowed someone else's. Mine is being repaired.' Startling, startling. He's a great showman, too. Ever notice how he times his bows? It's unconscious, but it's great showmanship. Straw nights everywhere from here to the Coast and back!" I must have looked puzzled, for Royal said, " 'Straw night' is an old circus term—when every seat is sold, they put straw on the floor and people sit on it. Full houses in Baltimore and Richmond, full house coming up in Atlanta! We're going to stop this train for fifteen minutes at Athens, Georgia, so the Maestro can stretch his legs. We've wired ahead for permission, and all's clear. Hell, he can use a little leg-stretching. He's been on this train since before midnight last night."

Walker came back. "Maestro says he will require two pairs of special cuff links in Atlanta," he said. "Wants the kind that snap together. Damn hard to find."

"Still want a gray hat?" asked Royal.

"Definitely," said Walker. "Says it must be an *extremely* light gray."

The train almost imperceptibly began to slow down. "Athens," said Royal.

"I better get back to Maestro's car," said Walker. . . .

When we got to the hotel, Walker moved me up front beside Mr. Adams [the driver] and told me to sit tight for the drive with the Maestro to the rehearsal. He disappeared inside the hotel, and a few minutes later Toscanini came out, followed by Walker and Walter. He was wearing his new gray hat, a blue jacket, and gray trousers. Several people standing in the driveway applauded. Toscanini smiled and walked over to the car. He and Walter got in back, and Walker slipped in front beside me. I was introduced to the Maestro.

"To the auditorium," Walker said to Mr. Adams. He looked back at Toscanini. "How do you like your new hat, Maestro?" he asked.

"It needs to be stretched," said Toscanini. "One size more, otherwise a fine hat." His voice was resonant and throaty. "Atlanta is the city for hats," he said. "New hats. I remember in 1912 I bought a lovely straw hat here."

For the remainder of the ride, Toscanini was silent. I turned around once or twice to glance at him. He seemed to me the ideal of graceful, vigorous, even beautiful old age. The flesh of his face is firm, and his complexion has a healthy, ruddy tint. His eyes are more deep-set than any others I have ever seen, with an arresting far-off expression.

"*Santo Dio!*" cried Toscanini as the car stopped at the side door of the auditorium. He pointed to a group of men with cameras.

"They are our own men, Maestro," said Walker quickly. "Members of the orchestra. No flash bulbs, Maestro. Don't worry. They just want to take snapshots."

"*Santo Dio!*" said Toscanini. He walked swiftly past the men with the cameras, into the auditorium, and to his dressing room, followed by Walker and Walter.

The orchestra gathered onstage and began tuning up. In a few minutes, Toscanini emerged from his dressing room in a black alpaca rehearsal jacket, buttoned up to his throat. He walked slowly to the podium, as though he were asleep, and a hush fell over the orchestra. He gave a swift but courtly half bow, said "Brahms, please," raised his baton, and launched into the rehearsal.

For the next two and a half hours, I stood in the wings, watching Toscanini as the orchestra rehearsed the entire Brahms First Symphony and short pieces by Rossini, Dukas, and Saint-Saëns. He was a compelling sight. From time to time, he accompanied the orchestra in a low, husky voice, carrying the melody. His beat had the precision and force of a drop hammer. His face became fiery red, and beads of sweat appeared on his forehead. "*Cantare, cantare,*" he would cry, or "*Molto, molto,*" placing his left hand over his heart in a beseeching gesture or stopping the music entirely to cover his face with his hands in a gesture of agony. He signalled for the orchestra to stop, by shaking his baton violently, and asked it to repeat one section of "Danse Macabre" seven times, pleading for a bit more shading here, a tiny emphasis there.

At one point, Walker tiptoed past me, carrying the Maestro's gray hat. "Going down to have it stretched," he said. Twenty minutes later, he was back. "Hat's stretched," he said.

Walter Toscanini wandered about backstage, listening attentively to the music. Every time the Maestro ordered the music to stop, Walter walked swiftly to an open door leading to the stage and stood anxiously watching his father. "Father must have it perfect, always perfect," he said, with an air of immense pride. "Nothing is ever *exactly* right with Father." Part way through the rehearsal, the Maestro called for a five-minute break, and at least half of the orchestra instantly produced cameras, surrounded him, and began to snap pictures. He looked bewildered but did not object.

When the five minutes were up, the Maestro led the orchestra through a couple of short pieces, then suddenly dropped his baton to his side, said "Thank you," and walked offstage. "Good," he said, to no one in particular, and started toward his dressing room. Walker told me to stay where I was.

Fifteen minutes later, Walker stuck his head out of the dressing-room door. "Maestro's coming," he said to me. "Wants to take a drive in the country. Tag along."

Once again, at the curb, a group of musicians stood snapping pictures. *"Santo Dio!"* said Toscanini, getting into the car.

"Start her up, for heaven's sake, man," Walker said to Mr. Adams. "Drive into the country somewhere. Maestro wants to see the dogwood."

For the better part of an hour, we drove in a leisurely way about the environs of Atlanta. The Maestro dozed or looked out the window, occasionally talking in a low voice, in Italian, to Walter. I caught snatches of the conversation. Mostly, Toscanini spoke of Italy—of his promise to an Italian general, in 1916, that if he won a certain battle, he, Toscanini, would take a band to the battlefield and play for the men, and of fulfilling his promise; of cancelling his subscription to the *Corriere della Sera*, the celebrated Milan newspaper, the moment it espoused the Fascist cause; of his wish to see the musical museum at La Scala in a building of its own. Each remark was short and came to a sudden stop. When we reached the hotel, some musicians were waiting in the doorway to greet him. "Good evening, Maestro," they called. Several of them bowed and waved. He smiled benignly, tipped his hat, and walked to the elevator. . . .

At seven o'clock [on concert day], I was told, Toscanini, in his rooms, ate an egg, boiled one and a half minutes, and drank some Italian coffee. At seven-thirty, he left for the auditorium, where the concert was to begin an hour later, and about eight o'clock I went there in a taxi. Just before the concert got under way, I met Royal, who was standing near one of the entrances counting the house. "Another straw night!" he cried. "Fifty-four hundred people!" When the Maestro appeared onstage, the audience rose, but they sat down quickly, sensing that he was impatient to begin. They listened in the deepest silence I have ever encountered at a concert. The people sat up straight; even their heads barely moved. I had the impression that Toscanini—he was a tiny, almost immobile black speck from where I stood at the back of the hall—represented an idea of perfection to the audience, and that they felt that even a stifled cough would destroy the spell. After the intermission, I went backstage. Royal, Walter Toscanini, Williams, and Walker were seated on trunks in the dark, their heads in their hands, listening to the music. Now and then, Walter would rise, keeping time to the music with his hands, peep through the wings, nod approval, and tip-toe back to his trunk. I looked out at Toscanini. He was much paler and more intense than he had been during rehearsal. But for his flashing hands, he might have been in a trance. Walker beckoned me to the dressing room, and, standing in the doorway with one finger to his lips, pointed to a table. On it were the four towels, the two bamboo fans, the picture of the Toscanini family, and the silver box containing rock candy.

At the end of the last number, Toscanini came offstage looking exhausted. Walter embraced him before he walked back onstage. The audience was shouting as he ascended the podium again, lifted his baton, and began to lead the orchestra through "Dixie." The shouts became louder, and then the audience started singing. When "Dixie" was concluded, Toscanini came into the wings, headed for his dressing room, hesitated, wheeled around, walked onstage, and again led the orchestra in "Dixie."

"Good God!" said Royal. "I never thought I'd live to hear Toscanini play 'Dixie' twice in one evening!"

Toscanini came offstage slowly. The audience was cheering even more loudly than before. But the concert was over. *"Basta, basta,"* Toscanini said, and walked to his dressing room without turning around. Royal called out to an electrician, "Maestro says enough! Turn up the house lights!" A half hour later, still looking tired, Toscanini walked out to his car. A quiet crowd of perhaps five hundred was gathered in the street. Many of them were perched on lampposts or the tops of cars. They burst into applause as he appeared, and several of them cried out, "Thank you, Maestro, thank you!"

Royal had invited me to an after-concert dinner in the Maestro's rooms. Having snared a means of locomotion somewhat swifter than the one provided by Mr. Adams, I arrived a moment or two ahead of Toscanini. A heavyset, dark-complexioned man in a chef's hat was hovering over a table in the sitting room. The table had been laid for a banquet: fine china and silverware, bowls of spring flowers, and champagne, wine, and brandy glasses at each place. "I am Chef Serpe," the man said, "and tonight's dinner for Maestro will be the classic dinner. For three hours, I have personally supervised the preparation of Maestro's dinner. The antipasto is a special delicacy. You can imagine the care that I have taken with this dinner. Here comes Maestro—I must step outside." He left through one door as the Maestro, Walter, Walker, Williams, and Royal entered through another.

"Molto bene," said the Maestro, admiring the table.

"Champagne for the Maestro," said Royal, pouring him a glass and pouring me one, too.

Toscanini clinked his glass against mine. Most of his weariness seemed to have left him. *"Salute!"* he said.

I complimented him on the wonderful performance of Brahms' First Symphony.

"Of course," he said, shrugging his shoulders impatiently. "It was Brahms, Brahms. I played it in response to popular demand in Atlanta. One woman wrote me to play Brahms. Royal!" he called out. "Turn on television!"

Royal hurried over to a television set that was in one corner of the room, and tuned in to a wrestling match. Toscanini took a seat at the table near the television set and drank another glass of champagne. The rest of us sat down, too. "This Antonino Rocca who wrestles in New York," said Toscanini, "why, he finds his opponent's weakness in five minutes and then he *kills* him."

Two waiters began to serve the dinner. Toscanini ate sparingly of antipasto, finished a bowl of thick *vichyssoise*, did quite well with some breast of chicken, washed down with red wine, and had some strawberries. He neglected entirely a large mixed green salad and a plate of asparagus hollandaise. "I have no idea how the music will sound while I am conducting it," he said. "I have no idea."

"Father wants perfection," said Walter, "and he brings out perfection in others. That lady today at the Cyclorama, delivering her lecture, she wanted to outdo herself to make it perfect for Father. It was that way always at La Scala, too. Everyone did their best, even the people who polished the brass."

"I never wear gloves," said Toscanini. "And yet my hands never seem to get dirty. I don't understand it. When I was a young conductor in Italy and rode everywhere on the trains, everyone else's hands would get dirty but mine would be as clean when I stepped off a train as when I stepped on. Very strange."

Serpe appeared in the doorway and cleared his throat several times, but Toscanini didn't see him. He walked over to Toscanini's chair. The Maestro looked up and began to applaud. "Ah, Serpe!" he said.

Serpe's eyes filled with tears. He took one of the Maestro's hands. "Maestro Toscanini," he said quietly, "we honor you tonight not only as the greatest conductor in the world, not only as a beloved doctor of music, but as a glorious Italian who shall live forever throughout the ages." He leaned over and touched his right eye and then his left eye to Toscanini's hand. He was sobbing. He backed to the door, turned, and walked out of the room quickly, his head high, his chef's hat bobbing.

The Maestro watched him go out. "Serpe is part Italian, part French," he said. "His cooking is flawless." For a few moments, he was silent. Then he said, "Royal! The only trouble with this tour—we're not giving enough concerts. We should give a concert a day, have more music." He was silent again. "More music," he said suddenly, rising from the table. "I want to go to the train."

Walker hurried to his side, the Maestro's overcoat in his hand. "All ready, Maestro," he said. He helped him into his coat and handed him the light-gray hat. Toscanini walked to the door with Walter and Walker, and then turned for a moment, smiling. He was not only the oldest man in the room but the youngest. "Good night, my dear ones," he said.

From:
The All-American Breakfast

In a release issued by the American Broadcasting Company, Don McNeill, master of ceremonies of the "Breakfast Club," is described as a "righteous family man, God-fearing, orthodox in every way. He is not at all slick and could never be a sharpy." His audience, the document continues, consists of "the great middle class—the solid citizens, the churchgoers, the 'squares,' the butcher, baker, and candlestick maker, the Eds and Ednas." The document then recounts the various reasons for the program's enormous appeal to Ed and Edna: "Inspiration Time presents McNeill reading a poem or a 'message' . . . calculated . . . to improve the outlook of those who are dejected and heavy laden; Prayer Time . . . a brief interval in which listeners and the studio audience join in silent prayer . . . the sight of heads bowed in the Studio is something you won't ever see in connection with any other air show; March Time . . . the audience . . . led by members of the Breakfast Club cast . . . march around the so-called breakfast table . . . Cruiser Crooning Time presents Jack Owens . . . crooning a torch song while he roams through the studio audience with a mike. . . . This gimmick supplies the only sexy note on the show—and it's in the sugary, 'postoffice' tradition and not remotely concerned with adult passion."

Chicago is the home of the "Breakfast Club," but McNeill often takes his troupe on tour. In the words of one student of radio, these tours are "a sort of portable Lourdes." Stirred by the prospect of seeing

McNeill in person, thousands of his followers rise at dawn and storm the doors of whatever auditorium he is appearing in. Some weeks ago, on the occasion of a morning appearance by McNeill at Madison Square Garden, the doors did not open until eight, but many of the faithful stood in line throughout the night. By eight-thirty in the morning, there were seventeen thousand people in the Garden. McNeill did not disappoint Ed and Edna; the program, which had a circus motif, was on a stupefying scale. Before McNeill made his entrance and the program went on the air, the crowd was entertained by several circus acts. Trained seals blew horns; a juggler tossed fiery torches into the air; elephants circled the arena, wearing signs honoring the sponsors' products, Swift's Premium Hams and Philco Refrigerators; clowns rollicked about, bearing placards that read, "To be a comedian you gotta be hambitious!" and "If you read Swift's backwards, you're nuts!" Many of the more fortunate among the audience were hit in the face by tiny, cellophane-wrapped chunks of ice cream, provided by Philco and tossed into the stands by the clowns. A band played martial music. After a fanfare of trumpets, McNeill entered, aboard a huge float labelled "King of Corn." "There he is!" shouted the crowd. "It's Don! It's him!" He waved graciously in acknowledgment.

Alighting from the float, McNeill joined some half-dozen members of his troupe behind a breakfast table set with dishes and a tablecloth, in the center of the Garden floor, and the program went on the air. No food was served to any of them, then or later. Before long, McNeill got up and was hoisted to the top of the balcony, seated in the claw of a steam shovel, from which, precariously balancing himself, he interviewed members of the audience through a portable microphone. Jack Owens, the Cruising Crooner, was strapped into a boatswain's chair and elevated to a point at which he could conveniently serenade two young women who had been hanging upside down from a trapeze for some time. A silent prayer was offered up for the United Nations, and everyone lowered his head while searchlights played over the hushed throng. McNeill read an inspirational poem by Charles Hanson Towne. He then urged his audience to drop postcards to the patients in the State Hospital for Crippled Children at Elizabethtown, Pennsylvania. "Where's Aunt Fanny?" shrieked the crowd. Aunt Fanny is one of the program's staple characters. "She's coming," said McNeill. At nine-thirty-five, a two-door sedan drove onto the Garden floor, disgorging fifteen to twenty midgets, clowns, giants, and animals, and finally Aunt Fanny. She turned out to be a young lady dressed like an old lady and was carrying an umbrella and wearing high, buttoned shoes. The crowd laughed loudly as she shook hands with McNeill and sat down at the breakfast table. "It's Aunt Fanny! It's her!" they cried. An elderly employee of Swift greeted a new employee of Swift. "It's a great company," he said, "and someday you may be president." The whole house sang "Auld Lang Syne," in honor of the elderly employee. Many people wept. Sam Cowling, a comedian in McNeill's troupe, suggested that the difference between a tiger and a panther is simply that a tiger is a big cat "but panther what you wear." At ten o'clock, breakfast ended, and Ed and Edna, as in a dream, stumbled out into the street. . . .

A radio official I know slightly, an assistant chief program director for a large network, recently let me attend a conference in his office at which he planned to clarify for several of his subordinates the philosophy underlying breakfast-hour programs. The office of this man, whom I shall call Thurman Pratt, is a large room with orange walls and floor-length curtains of green and yellow. Hanging on the wall behind his massive oak desk is a sign that says, "Abusive language strictly prohibited." Pratt has four telephones on his desk and three more on a small table at his side.

When I arrived, Pratt's associates were already seated on chairs arranged in a semicircle in front of him. He was standing behind his desk, fingering a slip of white memo paper. He is an athletic-looking man of forty-five, with a year-around deep tan. He was wearing white flannels and a green-and-white-checked sports jacket. His tie, with a knot the size of a fist, was of turquoise silk. "Gentlemen," he said, "sociologically and psychologically speaking, breakfast programs unify the American home. What could be more important?" Nobody said anything. Pratt glanced down at his notes. "I'm desperately serious about this," he said. "*Desperately* serious. People are still all tensed up from the war—nervous, run-down, their heads ache, their stomachs hurt—yes, Mr. and Mrs. Citizen get into some pretty nasty scraps around the breakfast table. But they turn on a program while they're eating and their minds are distracted, *because you just can't listen and fight at the same time!* That's sublimation!" There was a buzz of approval. "It's a kind of sociological stabilizer, and that's the public-service angle and it's absolutely top-drawer. Moreover, most citizens never touch the hem of a celebrity's garment. But they can listen at breakfast to people who know Douglas Fairbanks, Jr.!" He sat down at his desk and put his chin in his hands. For several moments there was silence. "I'm desperately serious about this, too," he said suddenly. "Talk about hominess. Psychologically, most men don't wear the pants. They may wear the pants at the office, but not at home. On some of these breakfast programs, by God, the man wears the pants, and it's a psychological fact that a fellow at home who doesn't and hears a fellow on the air who does feels better." Pratt took a deep breath. "I got another angle, and I'm *desperately* serious about it," he said. "People ask, 'Who listens?' Poor people go to work early. Granted. Commuters have to watch the time pretty carefully to catch a train. Granted. But the wealthy folks are home, and the women, and don't forget the paralyzed and the shut-ins." He rose and paced the floor behind his desk. "What I'm trying to say," he said, "is that it's a matter of income groups and community levels and keeping up with the Joneses, but that underneath the whole kit and boodle is the fundamental animal instinct to eavesdrop. Listen to Brown next door or little Mrs. Kelly up the street or Mike around the corner. Just ordinary folks. Just like everybody else. I'm saying that, sociologically, people are eavesdropping bastards. That's it—eavesdropping bastards!" With a smile of triumph, he sat down.

From: Good of You to Do This for Us, Mr. Truman

I first met President Truman while preparing a Profile of Dean Acheson, the Secretary of State. We met in the Oval Office, just the two of us. This memorable (for me) occasion was arranged through the good offices of my friend Stanley Woodward, who had been Chief of Protocol under F.D.R. and Truman, and subsequently Ambassador to Canada. But there had been a personal and prophetic epiphany between myself and Truman during the 1948 Presidential campaign, a moment about which Truman knew absolutely nothing. I had walked over from The New Yorker *offices on Forty-third Street with my colleague John Bainbridge to Broadway and Forty-fourth, where we stood opposite the old Astor Hotel. The President was scheduled to come past this spot in an open car (an open car!). The throng was so huge that a stranger might have thought it was New Year's Eve. The Presidential cavalcade rolled past at a normal speed, and it seemed to me that there was an almost magical connection between the President and the people. There was dignity in every motion of his hand, an aura of controlled power and kindness. He appeared to be looking at individual persons, not at a crowd. I turned to Bainbridge and said, "Everybody expects Dewey to win, but something is happening here and I sense a Truman victory." In fact, there was an office pool and A. J. Liebling and I, alone among the resident pundits, cleaned up to the tune of several hundred dollars: we were the only ones who put their money on Truman.*

Some years later, I met with then former President Truman at the Carlyle Hotel in New York. As I was leaving, he asked if I had any children. "You bet I do," I said. "Two fine boys, one six and a half, the other ten." "Bring them around tomorrow morning," said Mr. Truman. Next day, a Saturday, around we went, the boys in and on their best. Mr. Truman treated them as old friends, playing with them, asking about school, signing autographs. Later, he wrote me from Independence, Missouri: "It was a very great pleasure to meet the boys. If they enjoyed it only half as much as I did, they had a good time."

A friend of mine who works for Doubleday and Co., which has just published the first volume of former President Harry S. Truman's *Memoirs: Year of Decisions*, called me up a couple of weeks ago and said that Mr. Truman was going to autograph copies of the book on Wednesday, November 2, in the grand ballroom of the Muehlebach Hotel, in Kansas City, Missouri. "I think you'd have a lot of fun out there," he said. "It's the first time, as far as we know, that a president or an ex-president has agreed to sit down and sign copies of his book. Mr. Truman says that he'll start at ten in the morning, stop at noon, resume at two-thirty, and stop for good at five-thirty. May I read you a letter he wrote me just the other day?" I urged him to fire away, and he said, "Mr. Truman wrote, 'I will set aside one day near the book's publication date, and I will autograph as many as I can. I am not an expert with a machine, and I would rather do it by hand. As you know, I am accustomed to signing my name a great many times a day. I cannot possibly enter into a program which would look as if I were selling autographs instead of a book. I want the book sold on its merits. If it cannot be sold that way, then it's not worth having. I have a very strong feeling about any man who has had the honor of being an occupant of the White House in the greatest job in the history of the world and who would exploit that position in any way, shape, or form.' "

I decided that I'd like to go out to Kansas City. . . .

"Well," said Mr. Truman, appearing in the doorway of his office. "I'm sorry to have kept you waiting. Come into the office." He led me down an interior hall that was crammed with photographs and into a large, comfortable, warmly furnished room. Books filled one wall. Along the other walls were pictures of Andrew Jackson, Franklin Roosevelt, Miguel Hidalgo y Costilla, San Martín, and Bolívar. Also on the wall, I noticed, was a framed letter from Lewis and Clark to the War Department; it had something to do with an expense account for a hundred and sixty-one dollars. A couch was piled with copies of the New York *Times*. In one corner of the room was a bust of Chaim Weizmann. Several flags, all furled, stood behind Mr. Truman's desk. Mr. Truman sat down at his desk, and I sat down across from him. He looked fine. His complexion was pink, his face was firm, and his eyes gleamed behind thin-rimmed bifocals. He was wearing a brown suit, a brown-figured tie, and light brown shoes. "That was the Greek ambassador out there ahead of you," he said. "He wants me to come to Greece." He sounded as pleased as could be. I told him that I liked his book very much. "I hope you won't be disappointed with the second volume," he said. He sounded like any writer. He told me that he had dictated at least 60 percent of the book. "Right here in this room, too," he said. "It was a tremendous job, with all those documents and files to go through. I'd spend several hours each morning dictating. I called in a great many of my friends, such as Dean Acheson and John Snyder, to go over the manuscript, and we would sit and discuss disputable points. All in all, I must have dictated a million words or more, and we threw out a half million when it came time to publish the book. I'm not getting any tax break on this book— I'm paying 62½ percent. But that's not the point." Mr. Truman leaned across his desk. "I wanted to get the facts straight," he said, moving his hands up and down, parallel to one another and about twelve inches apart, in his familiar gesture of emphasis. "I have been misrepresented— outrageously misrepresented—and I wanted to put the truth down. I wanted to get the facts on record. Of course, the columnists who mis- represented me at the time will continue to do the same thing, and they won't like the book." He swung around in his chair toward a globe standing beside his desk. "There's the trouble spot now," he said, indi- cating the Middle East. "I'd do something about that. The trouble there goes back two thousand years. The Jews and the Arabs—they're like cousins, and, like cousins, they hate each other. Come along," he added, and he rose abruptly and led me back into the reception room.

Mr. Bailey [private secretary], a self-possessed young man wearing tortoiseshell glasses, was there. "Gene," said Mr. Truman, "let's open that cabinet." Mr. Bailey opened a file cabinet standing against a wall. Mr. Truman reached in and brought out a thick packet of letters, in envelopes of different sizes, bound together with a couple of rubber bands. "These are the letters to my mother and sister," he said. "The ones I put in the book as the 'Dear Mama and Mary' letters. And across this room," he said, with a sweeping gesture, "is the bulk of the files that went into the book. Now I want to show you something else." He led me down the hall toward his office. "I've got something here I'm very proud of," he said, pointing to a photograph on the wall of the corridor. It was of him and Prime Minister Churchill. They were standing in front of a painting of a naval engagement, and an inscription, in Churchill's hand, read, "To President Truman, whose decisive stroke against aggression in Korea turned the fortunes of the Free World to the sure hope of peace." "That was taken aboard the presidential yacht, the *Williamsburg*," Mr. Truman said, "and I maneuvered Mr. Churchill in front of the painting." The painting depicted the sinking of the British vessel *Guerrière* by the *Constitution*, the forty-four-gun frigate known as *Old Ironsides*, on August 19, 1812. "Just as we were having our photograph taken," said Mr. Truman, "the old man turned to me and said, 'You put one over on us that time.' " Mr. Truman chuckled.

In his office, I asked him if he was worried about the autographing party, and he said no—he was used to signing his name, and he had often signed six hundred documents a day in the White House. "Once, in 1930," he went on, "when I was presiding judge of the Jackson County Court, I signed three thousand county bonds in two and a half hours. Of course, that's different from books, because the bonds are all lined up for you and you just run down the list." I asked him about the flags behind his desk. "That blue one is the presidential flag," he said. "That belongs to the presidency. I will always keep it furled, because it goes with the high office."

"Mr. Truman," I said, "in your book you mention the time that you were sworn in on the night President Roosevelt died. You say it was 7:09 P.M. I was wondering how you could possibly have remembered the time on that dreadful day."

"It *was* a dreadful day," he said. "Dreadful, dreadful." He led me out into the corridor again and showed me still another picture on the wall. It was a photograph of his swearing-in at the White House. There were Mrs. Truman and Margaret and Chief Justice Harlan Stone and members of the Cabinet, and there was Mr. Truman, his left hand on the Bible and his right hand in the air. "See that picture?" Mr. Truman said. "The very moment. And you will notice that the clock above the mantel, right below President Wilson, says seven-nine." He glanced at me and then broke into a grin. "But I looked at the clock at the time," he said. "I looked, all right." We went into the reception room again, and Mr. Bailey joined us there. I said that I wanted to go out to Independence and poke around. Mr. Bailey instantly volunteered to lend me his car. "It's fully covered," he said. I thanked him and said I'd take a cab. . . .

On the day of the signing, Mr. Truman walked into the Muehlebach's grand ballroom, looking as though he were having the time of his life. His bearing was military, and he marched with quick steps to the platform, where he sat down. Mr. Bailey took a seat at his right, and a stocky gentleman with dark glasses took a seat at his left. It was evident that Mr. Truman was attacking this task with great seriousness; he had obviously figured out his approach in advance. There were some eight hundred people in the room now, and the autographing was about to begin. The lines looked like the lines you see on Election Day—neighborhood people whom you know, but who keep their distance, because they have come to the polling place on a special, private mission.

Five hundred roses had been provided by the Floral Industries of Kansas City, Missouri, and these were distributed to the first five hundred women in the crowd. Mr. Randall Jessee, a jolly gentleman who works for Station WDAF-TV, in Kansas City, took hold of a microphone and said, "Ladies and gentlemen, welcome to Harry Truman Day." He then led his five-year-old daughter to the platform. She was carrying a copy of the book, and Mr. Truman signed it. It was evident that he was eager to get along with the signing. People stepped up, Mr. Bailey took their books, opened them to the page before the title page, handed them to Mr. Truman, who signed them and passed them on to the gentleman at his left. He signed "Harry S Truman" and nothing else, doing this with astonishing swiftness and mechanical precision. Whenever he looked up, he flashed a smile. Whenever anyone spoke to him, he answered. A good many of the people were shy when they reached the platform, and said nothing. Others spoke up. A lady came by and said, "Will you last?"

"I've lasted many harder days, and I have worked overtime, too," Mr. Truman said.

The trio [accordion, violin and guitar] broke into "Tea for Two." The ballroom now had at least a thousand people in it. I walked around and noticed that there was a large number of small boys in the lines, some of them carrying as many as ten copies of Mr. Truman's book. At ten-twenty, the B'nai B'rith arrived, in a group, and presented Mr. Truman with an award.

"The B'nai B'rith Women's Division of Greater Kansas City proudly presents this distinguished-service citation in honor of his outstanding services in the cause of human relations," a lady in the group said, reading aloud from a printed document. Mr. Truman rose and accepted the award. "I may not deserve all the fine things you are saying about me now," he said, "but I hope to be worthy of them before I die." He still had a fixed smile on his face as he sat down and went back to the grind of writing "Harry S Truman," "Harry S Truman," "Harry S Truman." The long lines moved forward. "Good of you to do this for us, Mr. Truman," said a lady with a book.

"You're more than welcome," said Mr. Truman.

"I had eight boys in the service, Mr. Truman," said a lady with a book.

Mr. Truman looked at her and said nothing, and went back to autographing.

Shortly after ten-thirty, an assemblage of gentlemen wearing flowing cloaks of green and yellow and large turbans of green, yellow, and red arrived, and took up positions behind the president. There was a moment of genial and general handshaking. The Oriental-looking gentlemen were members of the Ararat Shrine of Kansas City, and they had just dropped in to pay their respects. They stood around behind Mr. Truman for quite a while. His pace seemed to be picking up. "I'm doing nine a minute now," he whispered to Mr. Bailey. "It was eight a minute a while back."

"The crowd goes all the way down the stairs to the lobby," a man from Doubleday said to me, "and out into the street, and it's *snowing*! They're standing out in the street in the *snow*." It was evident that he thought he had another *Ben-Hur* on his hands. A second group of Shriners arrived, and they, too, took up positions behind Mr. Truman. These gentlemen wore fezzes, rather than turbans, and together the two groups made quite a backdrop for the machinelike autographing that was going on at the table.

From: *Good of You to Do This for Us, Mr. Truman*

"I've come five hundred miles," said a gentleman to Mr. Truman, "and I would have walked every inch of the way."

"My thanks to you," said Mr. Truman. "I hit ten a minute there," he whispered to Mr. Bailey.

"Hello, Harry," said a gentleman.

"Hello, John," said Mr. Truman, signing John's book.

The lines moved on. They were endless. There was a sudden burst of noise as some thirty men marched into the room to the tune of "The Caissons Go Rolling Along." It was Battery D, 129th Field Artillery—Mr. Truman's battery from the First World War. Mr. Truman looked up and smiled, but he kept on signing. He was in the rhythm now and he wasn't going to stop. The turbans and the fezzes departed, Battery D took up its place behind him, and the signing went rolling along.

"My feet are killing me," said a lady to Mr. Truman.

"I'm sorry that you have to stand up," he replied.

A rather elegant lady in a purple dress and a fur piece stood in front of the table. "This is a great privilege, sir," she said, "and it is the only autograph in my sixty-three years of living that I have ever sought."

"Thank you," said Mr. Truman.

I thought that the lady's remark was extremely graceful, and I followed her to the ballroom exit. She was a Kansas City, Missouri, lady, and she knew a good deal about the Trumans. "People from the East don't know that the Trumans are aristocrats," she said. "And people from the East don't understand that the aristocrats of Independence are more aristocratic than the aristocrats of Kansas City. Independence was the gateway to the West—to the Santa Fe Trail and all the rest—and was where the covered-wagon trains started. They went to California from Independence. The mules and the oxen got rested up in Independence, and got put in shape. My daughter, who lives in Alabama, wrote to me when Mr. Truman was elected president in 1948 and told me how tickled she was, and I sent the letter along to Mr. Truman. He wrote back that the letter was a dandy. He also said that he had known he would be elected, because he could see it in the faces of the people. Take a look at him now. He's watching the faces, and the faces are watching him, and he isn't missing a stroke of his pen. He's always been that way. I've got to get home now."

There was a hubbub of excitement at the platform end of the grand ballroom. The lines had broken and people were crowding around Mr.

Truman. An official of the hotel went to the platform and announced in a soapy voice, "You folks just going to have to stand around with love in your hearts and wait your turn." That did the trick.

Mr. Truman was scheduled to stop the morning session at noon. At noon, however, the ballroom, the staircase, and the lobby were still filled with people carrying books to be signed. Someone had the sense to close the ballroom doors, but that still left several hundred people inside. A man from Doubleday went over to Mr. Truman and told him that it was twelve o'clock. "To hell with it," said Mr. Truman. "I'm going to sign for everybody in the room. Lunch can get cold."

The man from the hotel again took the podium. "Don't let another soul in, Officer!" he cried to a Kansas City policeman at the door.

Mr. Truman made a brief speech. "I agreed to sign only one book a person," he said. "Lots of people are bringing in more than one book. I'll sign for everybody in this room, but just one copy. I'm hungry." There was applause. I caught sight of Mrs. Truman at one side of the room. She was talking with Thomas Hart Benton. Shortly before one o'clock, Mr. Truman had signed books for all the people left in the ballroom. . . .

[After lunch] I noticed a tall, eager-looking gentleman who was keeping people in line, and I introduced myself to him. "I'm Tom Evans," he said. "I'm one of Mr. Truman's oldest and dearest friends. Why don't you stay over a couple of days?" I told him I had to catch a train. "Oh, hell," he said, "the trains leave every day." I asked him what he did for Mr. Truman, and he said, "Twenty-five years ago, Harry Truman put me in charge of his wearing department."

"His what?" I asked, and he said, "For the past twenty-five years, I've been in charge of Harry Truman's wearing department."

I didn't have the nerve to ask him what he meant, and after a few minutes he turned back to the line. A reporter from the Kansas City *Star* was standing beside me, and I asked him if he had overheard the conversation. "I did," he said. "I did indeed, and he wasn't shooting you any bull. He's been in charge of Harry Truman's wearing department for at least twenty-five years." I asked if he would mind spelling the word. "Wearing," he said. "W-o-r-r-y-i-n-g."

The line was still endless, and the trio played on—mostly the "Missouri Waltz." At four-twelve, Mr. Evans closed the doors. There were hundreds of people in the ballroom. I spotted Norm Dygon, the pianist from the hotel's Terrace Grill, standing in line with a book. "The least I can do for Mr. Truman, who is willing to sit here and autograph the book, is to stand here and have him autograph one for me," he said. A gentleman said to Mr. Truman, "We saw Margaret on television last night and she was fine."

"I'm prejudiced in that department," said Mr. Truman. He nodded toward his wife. "Stop by and see the boss, who's sitting over there. She'll be tickled to death."

At five-thirteen, when, according to a Doubleday man's estimate, Mr. Truman had signed very close to four thousand books, the last person in line appeared in front of the desk. His name was David Nasaw, and he was twelve years old. He lived at 7520 Eaton Street, Kansas City, Missouri. Mr. Truman signed his name in the book, and he did something else, too. He wrote, "With best wishes to David Nasaw." The boy's father, Irving Nasaw, who was standing nearby, was almost overcome. "That's what we hoped you would do, Mr. President," he said.

Mr. Truman looked up. "If he hadn't been the last one in line, I wouldn't have done it," he said. "I haven't done it for the others." He put down his pen and threw his arms in the air. "Finish," he said.

From: That Great Big New York Up There

Friends Talking in the Night, *a Reporter at Large, was my first encounter with William O'Dwyer, about a year after his election in 1945 as Mayor of New York City. We became good friends. He also became a close friend of Harold Ross, and these two exotic, colorful men loved to sit on the porch of Gracie Mansion, gossip, joke, and swap tall stories of their youth—one man from Ireland, the other from the Far West. For this book, I have adopted the title of the first O'D. story, but am including my second story, when he was ex-Mayor, living in Mexico City. Shawn jumped at the idea of my visiting him there. "We'll do this one for Mr. Ross," he said.*

Not long ago, it occurred to me that it might be rewarding to go down to Mexico City and spend some time in the company of William O'Dwyer, former Mayor of the City of New York, whom I first met shortly after he took office, in 1946. O'Dwyer has been living down there since the fall of 1950, when he resigned as Mayor to become United States Ambassador to Mexico. He resigned as Ambassador two years later, but stayed on in Mexico City—acting as consultant to the law firm of O'Dwyer, Bernstein & Correa. Many charges have been made against O'Dwyer and his regime as Mayor, and many people have concluded that he lives in

Mexico City because he can no longer live happily in New York City, but I assume that he lives where he does because he likes the place. However, I had no wish to discuss any of this with O'Dwyer. I simply felt that a man of his perceptive qualities and wild conversational powers who had twice been elected Mayor of one of the largest cities in the world might have some unusual observations to make on that strange and terrifying office, especially after having the time to reflect and the chance to see the city from the vantage point of a foreign land.

Late one afternoon, therefore, I picked up the phone in my office and put in a call for O'Dwyer at the Hotel Prince, where he is currently staying in Mexico City, and ninety seconds later we were saying hello. I told him that I wanted to come down and talk with him. "Wonderful!" he said, in a voice that sounded pretty much the way it had when I last talked with him, some seven years before—rich and rolling, and with a pleasant suspicion of a brogue. "Want to see a ball game? Remember when we were on our way out to Ebbets Field one rainy night, and I said there was nothing gloomier than a jail unless it's a ballpark on a rainy night?" . . .

The Prince ("a very good hotel with reasonable prices," according to a standard guidebook to Mexico City) is a seven-story building, surmounted by a roof garden called El Ranchito—an unpretentious stone terrace with several small tables and chairs scattered around it. Centrally located on the bustling Calle Luis Moya, in a district occupied by many stylish hotels, it stands just off the Paseo de la Reforma, the capital's main boulevard, and within easy reach of the old section of the city and its widely known park, the Alameda. O'Dwyer, who has been married twice but has no children, lives alone in a three-room penthouse at one end of the roof garden. The day after I arrived, I went around to the Prince at the appointed hour, gave my name at the desk, stepped into the elevator, and, on the way up, examined a menu posted in it. Among the specialties of the hotel's dining room, I noted, was curried chicken à la Victor Sassoon, and I was speculating on what a dessert listed as "Cha-Cha" might be when the elevator stopped and the operator informed me that to reach the roof garden I would have to walk up a short flight of stairs. As I stepped out onto the roof garden, I saw

O'Dwyer standing in the doorway of his penthouse, wearing navy-blue trousers and a light-blue sports shirt. "Hi, there!" he said. "Come on in."

Entering, I found myself in an attractively turned-out combination living room and dining room, with a light-blue ceiling, brownish-violet walls, a tan carpet, and beige window curtains. The principal furnishings were an ample couch flanked by a couple of chairs and with a handsome coffee table in front of it; a small dining table, set for lunch; and a sideboard holding a long-playing phonograph and a high stack of records. "Four Great Tragedies by William Shakespeare," a paperback, lay on the coffee table. Off to one side were a bedroom and bath, and near the entrance was the kitchen.

"You sit here on the sofa, and I'll sit in this chair alongside," said O'Dwyer. "We close down our offices—they're not far from here, on the Paseo de la Reforma—from one to three. We open at nine in the morning, and we close for good at six-thirty. I keep a neat desk down there— no papers. I never kept papers on my desk at City Hall, either. From my office, you can look right down the Paseo de la Reforma, which was modelled after the Champs-Elysées by Maximilian. It is said that the Empress Carlota, the wife of Maximilian, could lie in her bed in Chapultepec Castle and watch his carriage as it headed toward the National Palace, just down the line here in the Zócalo—the great square with the Cathedral. I have a long glass-topped conference table in my office, and under the glass I keep a map of Ireland labelled 'First Families of Erin'— a green one showing all the counties and listing the names of the families who have lived in each. Pishta!"

A tall, thin, angular man with a nervous reddish-brown mustache emerged from the kitchen. He was wearing a chef's cap and apron, and a white shirt with an open collar. Addressing him in Spanish, O'Dwyer said, "Pishta, let's have a drink before lunch." Pishta bowed slightly, and retired.

"My cook," said O'Dwyer. "He understands a little English, but he can speak only one sentence in it—'Shut up, baby.'"

Pishta came out with two Scotches and set them on the coffee table.

"Tell my friend here your English sentence," O'Dwyer said. Pishta grinned broadly, and I had the impression that his mustache was smiling, too. "Shaddup, bay-bee," he said, and went back to the kitchen.

O'Dwyer roared, and then abruptly became serious. "There was some danger of Pishta's being sent back to Hungary," he said. "He was working for an embassy here, and going back to Hungary would have meant death for him, so I gave him asylum. But about that map of Ireland. It was given to me by a man called David Owens, and that reminds me of some of the problems of being Mayor of the City of New York. I was presiding one day at a meeting of the Board of Estimate when we were discussing departmental appropriations—the municipal cupboard was bare, by the way, and I had to worry about the comrades in some departments who would ask for two hundred and forty million for a department they'd got into, where Tammany used to give their families an occasional bag of coal. . . . Well, I was presiding. I was bending my ear to all sorts of grievance committees when suddenly a man with a huge mustache, who looked as though he had stepped out from behind a rock in the eighteenth century, stands up and says, if my memory serves me right, that he represented seventy-five watchmen of city buildings."

At this point, Pishta announced that lunch was ready, and O'Dwyer led the way across the room to the dining table, where an orange-colored soup awaited us. "Carrot soup," said O'Dwyer. "You need a stout heart to cook it."

I dipped my spoon into the soup and tasted it. Out of this world. Pishta was hovering about, and when I smacked my lips and smiled at him, he burst into Spanish.

"He's telling me about the soup, and I'm telling you about the Board of Estimate," said O'Dwyer. "He says it has carrots in it, and grated onion, garlic, parsnips, and silander, a local herb."

Pishta grinned, and went back to the kitchen.

"Now," O'Dwyer continued, "David Owens—for that is who it was, David Owens—standing there in front of the Board of Estimate in that courtly white Colonial room in City Hall, in New York, insisted that he could not possibly compete with the high-pressure groups that had previously appeared before us. To plead his case for the neglect that the city was showing toward its watchmen, he told the story of the watchman of a building between the two Calvary cemeteries out in Queens."

Pishta, reappearing, directed another burst of Spanish at us.

"The soup again," said O'Dwyer. "He says there's flour in it, too—to make a paste—and salt and pepper, and something the size of a nut. Also bouillon cubes. Also water. Don't forget the water. As the soup is boiling, take an egg and mix it in. Then throw the egg out the window. O.K., Pishta. Many thanks."

After Pishta had gone back to the kitchen, O'Dwyer said, "These interruptions are like being Mayor of the City of New York. Well, Owens said that this man who worked in the building between the two grave-yards guarded heavy machinery. It was truly what could be called a dis-mal place, and at times there was not even the sound of a branch blowing in the wind over the tombstones. This man—this city watchman—would look to the right and he would look to the left, and there would be tomb-stones, and he would pull out a little handkerchief and put it on his shoulder, and then he would rest a violin he had against it and he would play to himself to keep himself company out there in Queens. A supervi-sor arrived one night and heard the sound of this violin, and docked him two days' pay. That was the lot of a city watchman, as told to me by David Owens. Some years later, when I was leaving for Mexico, Owens arrived at a farewell party for me at my brother Paul's, and I said to him, 'I wish I could have heard that fellow who played the violin between those two graveyards.' And Owens said, 'He's outside in the hall,' and he brought the man in and the man played."

Pishta arrived with a dish of pork, hot peppers, and tomatoes. He started to tell us all about this one, too. "I think we'll let the recipe go this time, Pishta," said O'Dwyer. Pishta subsided and left us.

"As you may have gathered, he says you start out by cooking the meat in *agua* for an hour," said O'Dwyer. "Then drop in a thousand herbs, conduct the operation under a slow fire at 305 degrees until all the grease is absorbed, and throw an old *shoe* out the window. To get back to being Mayor of the City of New York, the problems are truly monumental. The administrative problems alone are enough to make a man drop dead. I lost my health at it. My doctor told me I would not live through another spring if I tried to stick it out for my sec-ond term. The problems of highways, bridges, traffic, and housing alone would stagger a man. Departments had to be built up. In Hospi-tals, we had fifty-two beds for one nurse to take care of, with that nurse working twelve hours a day and not being paid enough. I wanted to set up a municipal outpatient department, to avoid this business of putting people who didn't have to stay overnight into city beds when we didn't have the space. I was sick myself at the time this thought came to me. I wanted a health center where sick people could bring their medical records, have the benefit of a large staff and facilities, without fee, and then be returned to their own doctors. I was told this was an encroachment of rights. I tell you, there were times when, as Mayor, I truly wanted to jump. You would look out over the city from some place high above it, and you would say to yourself, 'Good Jesus, it's too much for me!' There was the public-relations job, too, along with the job of running the city—two separate things. Let's move back to the other side of the room."

I went over and settled myself on the couch again. O'Dwyer, after putting a record called "Show Biz" on the phonograph, took his place in the chair beside me. "Great stuff, that record," he said. "Lots of lovely, dirty, naughty New York in that record. I love it when Franklin Bauer sings, 'I'm living up in the clouds, chasing a rainbow of a girl.' Lots of Fanny Brice and Helen Morgan and Eddie Cantor in it. Everything happens to the Mayor. Ed Flynn once wanted a fellow named Hymie to be made a magistrate. Hymie Something-or-Other. So one night I am on the dais at the Concourse Plaza Hotel, up in the Bronx, near the Yankee Stadium, when Hymie turns up. It was some sort of banquet. Hymie has been dipping into the grape, and he starts over to me across the floor. 'Are you going to make me a magistrate?' says Hymie, standing before and below me. 'Right now,' I said. 'Right now, Hymie. But you got to do something for me first.' 'And that?' asks Hymie. 'Stand up straight,' I said. So Hymie tried to, but fell on the floor instead. One of the troubles of being Mayor, you couldn't go anywhere. Or I should say you had to go where you were expected to go. I like it here in Mexico because I can go anywhere I want to. Now, you take all the nice and lovely people who wanted to do something sweet for the city. There was a gentle lady who was in charge of the Outdoor Cleanliness Association—Mrs. Throckmorton Updike, or something. Somehow or other, she got through to see me. Miss Holley, my secretary, would fix up the appointments, and she let this woman in. Miss Holley, by the way, would always say, as she led a delegation in through the door of my office, 'Now we're ready for the pho-toe.' "

O'Dwyer shifted in his chair. "Well, Mrs. Throckmorton Updike came in and she was as nice as could be," he went on. "She was in charge of flower beds on Park Avenue, as far north as Fifty-seventh Street. She wanted to plant forsythia inside the Park Avenue railings. 'Well,' I said to her, 'why *don't* you plant forsythia inside those railings?' 'Well,' she said, 'for one thing, it is Parks Department property, and, for another thing, it will cost ten thousand dollars. I had the notion,' she said, 'that you would know of some worthy organization that would come to our help in such an aesthetic undertaking.' I said to the lady, 'I think I know an organization that is hungry to enjoy respectability of this nature— Tammany Hall—and I feel sure that if you approach them with your lovely spirit, they will float your aesthetic undertaking for you. Mr. Sampson is the head of the organization at the moment, and he is a noble man with a pretty woman." The lady departs. All hell breaks loose. New York, New York! First thing I know, some fellow in the Parks Department calls up to say that forsythia blooms only one month in the year. Sampson, at Tammany Hall, phones to say that he has received a request that if any forsythia is to be planted, it must be planted in a Democratic neighborhood. Another fellow from the Parks Department volunteers, 'There's wibrations from the railroad under Park Avenue.' Then it turns out that Brooklyn is the Borough of Forsythia. The Delancey Street Chamber of Commerce takes umbrage—'Why Park Avenue for forsythia?' they ask. Somebody else says there's too much dust on Park Avenue. Mostly, Brooklyn made the fuss, claiming forsythia was a Brooklyn bloom. The lady came back to my office later, after all her trouble, and remarked, 'How lovely of Tammany!' "

O'Dwyer clasped and unclasped his hands, and I noticed that he was wearing rectangular silver cuff links with a simple "O'D" inscribed on them. "Oh, my God, the characters!" he said. "There was a man who was professor of Romance languages at one of the local colleges. Somehow or other, he got into Housing. Personally, after I met him, I thought he sniffled too much ever to have talked French, but somebody wanted to dress him up as George Washington and send him around the world. It was promotion for the City of New York. Americanism. In Tokyo, he sat on a nail and wrecked his pants. The man was back in a week. It was a fiasco. Listen to Franklin Bauer!"

We listened to Bauer intone, "Nothing but the stars and Mars and Venus coming between us. I'm living up in the clouds, chasing a rainbow of a girl." O'Dwyer shook his head in admiration and said, "He *sings* it! One of those songs we heard last night at the restaurant, it has a line that goes, 'You have the poison that fascinates.' Mexican songs are beautiful; they are all beautiful." I nodded. "Oh, that great big New York up there!" said O'Dwyer. "The delegations that would come through the office! They march right into City Hall and into the Mayor's office, and they really talk harsh and nasty to you when they first enter. If they get belligerent, and they often do, you call in the newspaper boys from Room 9. But if they are just reasonably aggressive, you wait quietly for an opening, and when some spokesman or other pauses for breath, as pause he must, you say, 'Don't you think we should do something about the children?' That usually stops them. And, actually, the children are on your mind a good deal of the time. What do you do when people come in—groups of citizens—and complain that you are turning an ice-skating rink in Flushing into a temporary headquarters for the United Nations? 'Where will the children skate?' they ask. There is a true conflict of interests, and you have to weigh and weigh. And then there are the tugboat strikes. They usually take place in February. Good and cold, and need for the transport of coal. You put your Health Department to work, and you alert your Hospitals Department, and then you proceed to whack both sides. A dear friend once said to me, 'You'd be a great Mayor if only you'd have time to think.' You don't *have* time to think in that job."

Charles King, on "Show Biz," was singing. "A million lights they flicker there, A million hearts beat quicker there, No skies are gray on the Great White Way, That's the Broadway Mel-o-dee." O'Dwyer hummed a bar or two of the tune, and said, "If you wanted truck loadings after 6 P.M., the unions would holler. They wanted a thirty-three-and-a-third-per-cent raise. The city is more than unions, after all, and the idea was dropped, and a pity, for from six o'clock on in New York you have streets wide open to the stars. I wanted a highway from the Hudson to the East River—through the sixth or seventh floor of the Empire State Building. But the real-estate boys came down and raised hell. Whenever the real-estate tax is about to be jacked up, someone organizes the homeowners of Queens, a borough of retired Tammany politicians. My Lord, I saw a lot of people in the course of a day! At the Mansion, I usually got downstairs for conferences at ten. I was shaved every morning by John Vitale, who kept a barbershop in the neighborhood. He would come every morning, and there was a great dignity in this man. At nine-fifteen, he would come through the gates of the Mansion—with his razor and his clippers in his black bag, and his slow, splendid walk—and he would mount the steps of the porch to enter, and it was always a pleasure. I would never keep John Vitale waiting. It would have humiliated him. But about those conferences. Tuesdays, it was always Trygve Lie, Robert Moses, Wallace Harrison—all United Nations business. The Board of Estimate work was mostly done in executive session the day before each public session. I couldn't possibly see all the Commissioners every day—out of the question. Too big a city! I remember, after I was elected, I went down to City Hall to pay my respects to Fiorello LaGuardia, and he jumped up from his chair and he said, 'Sit down in that chair,' and I did, and he shrieked, 'Now you'll have a perpetual headache!' Oh, those Waldorf dinners! I'd eat at home, and have the cops phone me from the Waldorf at the end of the second course, and then I'd zip down. Why, once I even had to ride on a tallyho, to celebrate the hundredth anniversary of something or other, and they brought this tallyho right into the driveway of the Mansion. They had brewery horses, and Sergeant Burke driving them. I had to climb aboard the damn thing, and the horses started to get out of hand as we were heading west on Eighty-sixth Street. Now, this fellow Whalen—the Honorable Grover Whalen—was riding behind, in a car, waving and smiling and bowing, and the horses pulling the tallyho were about to break loose and kill the Mayor. Whalen brought Winston Churchill through the city once and ordered the procession to proceed at six miles an hour. It would have made Churchill a perfect target for a pot shot. I cancelled *that* order. But those tallyho horses—Burke got them under control at last. He was an old sparrow cop, once rode a horse himself."

We sat in silence for a moment, and then O'Dwyer shook his head incredulously and said, "The funny thing about all these things—they happened. My Lord, the opening of Idlewild Airport in July of 1948! President Truman was coming, and we were sent all sorts of instructions from Washington. We were told that when the President arrived at the airport and put his left foot on the runway, a twenty-one-gun salute was to be fired. We had Lieutenant O'Hara posted at the airport with binoculars to give the signal the instant that left foot touched the runway. Then, all of a sudden, a whole lot of other directives turn up. These came from Mr. Cullman, of the Port of New York Authority. He said that Governor Dewey and his party would be escorted to the Admirals Club at LaGuardia Field, arriving there at twelve-eleven. Governor Driscoll, of New Jersey, would be in the party. All hands would then proceed to Idlewild by plane. There is a lunch, too, that is off again, on again. Everybody gets into the act. One directive reads, 'Commissioner Pope shall return home in the company of his wife.' For the Governors, there are to be eighteen-gun salutes. There are to be nineteen-gun salutes for various Secretaries—Cabinet officers. I said to Whalen, who was buzzing around, 'Say, there's going to be a lot of shooting going on around here. Who's got the gun?' Cullman had arranged for some sort of gun to be brought over from Governors Island. Well, in the end the ceremony came off. They always did, and the city kept on going. Funny thing is, these things happened. I can laugh now. . . .

The next day, I again had lunch with O'Dwyer in his penthouse atop the Prince. Since by now I knew my way, I just walked in, and found him seated in one of the chairs beside the sofa, reading the paperback copy of Shakespeare. He was wearing a gray shirt, gray flannel slacks, and black loafers.

" 'Macbeth'!" he said. "What a story!"

Pishta, his chef's cap at a sharp angle, came tearing out of the kitchen and raced through the door leading to the roof garden, where we could hear him screeching in what I took to be Hungarian. "Pishta's wild today," said O'Dwyer. "Something to do with a stolen empty Coca-Cola bottle. He was knocking himself out in the kitchen making something special, and while he was at it, I gather, a small errand boy he knows sneaked in and swiped the bottle. Pishta always prides himself on returning cases of empty Coca-Cola bottles with every bottle in its place. He is jarred. He is upset. Things like this distract Pishta from his cooking."

Pishta came back in from the roof garden. His mustache was quivering. He threw up his hands in a gesture of utter helplessness, and sidled into the kitchen.

"Shaddup, bay-bee," O'Dwyer whispered to me, then said, "What do you think of Henry Fink?" (a Cuernavaca chum).

I said I thought Henry Fink was an impressive man.

"Henry is a true friend," said O'Dwyer. "There were times when I was Mayor when I wanted to jump, and I was a sick man, and I had lost my army. Henry proved himself a true friend. You know, the city's too big. It's too big for one government. I have always found that you can do more by talking directly to people than any other way. All those reports! You can't rely on them. You have to get your information in person. You can take that Andrew Green—the fellow who was responsible for unifying the five boroughs, back in 1898—and you can build him a statue, and then, as far as I'm concerned, you can cut off his head and you can cut off his tail and blow the rest of him up."

Pishta tore out of the kitchen again, and onto the roof. More Hungarian invective—or what I took to be Hungarian invective.

"He'll get that missing Coca-Cola bottle back if he has to go to hell for it," O'Dwyer said, and then he cried out, "Hey, Pishta! How about lunch?"

Pishta reappeared, and grudgingly went back into the kitchen.

"Oftentimes, a disturbance like this makes him rise to new heights in the culinary art," said O'Dwyer.

A few minutes later, Pishta stuck his head out of the kitchen door and told us that lunch was ready, and we moved over to the dining table. O'Dwyer was right—the missing Coca-Cola bottle had not diminished Pishta's skill. The meal began with shrimp-and-avocado salad—luscious avocados and small shrimp, mixed with mayonnaise—and proceeded to the finest roast lamb I have ever tasted, served with string beans and carrots, and washed down with a superior red wine.

"Bring me a whole platter of carrots," O'Dwyer said to Pishta, and Pishta brought him a whole platter of carrots. O'Dwyer polished off the platter. "I love carrots," he said. "I'm against a centralized city. I have always felt that the city's police should be under the jurisdiction of Albany. By that I mean I'd have the State Police run right down into New York City, taking care of every town and hamlet in between, too. I think it's the only way you'll ever lick crime. After all, Murder, Inc., wasn't just a Brooklyn affair. I found that out, all right, when I was D.A. in Brooklyn. Pishta! More carrots!"

More carrots were brought in, and O'Dwyer dug into them. "A Mayor of the City of New York is bound to have trouble with Albany," he said. "Especially if the Governor belongs to the opposition party. That

Albany! Do you think Albany will tell City Hall the percentage of the liquor tax that comes from the city, where the people are heavy drinkers, and the percentage that comes from the upstate counties, where they drink milk? I should say not! I haven't worked it out in my mind, really, but, as I say, I think I would have a centralized police, operating out of Albany. I know it sounds strange, but I believe in it, and I might even favor running it over into Connecticut and New Jersey."

Pishta brought out some delicate pancakes filled with almond paste. "Pishta should lose a Coca-Cola bottle every day," said O'Dwyer.

Coffee was served, and O'Dwyer poured a great deal of milk in his. Then, slowly stirring it, he sat back, and said, "Happily, politics is all behind me now. I've got time to read and reflect and live a bit. I'm tired of bluenoses. I'm tired of people who think it's O.K. to place a bet at a track but are dead set against off-track betting. I'm tired of public life. I have memories, thank God, that mean more to me. I went back to Ireland once in the twenties to visit my mother and my sisters, and there was a great party, and everybody turned out. There was this old lady of eighty-five—a friend of the family—and she asked me to accompany her home at three in the morning, when the party was breaking up. Her entire family, as I recall it, was left-handed. She was blind, totally blind. The night was black—no stars, even—and the road was rocky, and she held a lantern for me. She knew the way, every step of it. The lantern blew out in the wind, and I told her that, and she said, 'Hold my hand. I will show you the way.' The house she wished to reach had been her home for eighty-five years—all her life—and she held me by the hand and led me to it. She told me to sit down in the kitchen, and she walked over to the fireplace and she struck a flint, and turf in the fireplace flared up. 'I would like to talk awhile,' she said. 'You have seen my children in the United States.' She asked me about Patrick, and about the noble one, Shamus, who had fallen into a well in Chicago, and about Kathleen and Michael, and I praised them all. Two of the others had become gamblers, but I said nothing of that. 'Oh, Bill,' she said, 'I remember when my husband—he was a great man—I remember when he said he was going to England on a Tuesday, and I wanted him to take the Friday boat, so I hid his whipcord pants and his jacket in a haystack, because he couldn't go to England without them, and on Friday he had a pain, and on Saturday he was dead, and the neighbors, who were good neighbors, built a little coffin and they buried him, and on the way home from the funeral, back to this very house, I sat on a stone. I was carrying Agnes, and I began to cry. I quickly dried my tears, and I said to my children, who were with me, "I must not cry before innocent ones, it will only make it worse," and I moved on to the house and sat on the very stool where I now sit, and I summoned my children around me, and I said, "Now I must be both father and mother to you, and I will put any of you in a coffin and bury you alongside the coffin we just lowered, and I will wear a flower in my hair, if any one among you turns out to be a black-guard." And the noble one spoke up, and he said, "Mother, you will not wear a flower in your hair, because we will not become blackguards." Ah, Bill, it is a true friend like yourself who will come back and tell me nothing but beautiful things about my own. But I have death in my bones, and I will never see you again.'

"Thank God, I've got those memories, too," said O'Dwyer. "But, you know, most of the time I can't get New York out of my head. All the scenes swiftly pass in my mind these days. I am sixty-seven. Pishta!"

Pishta appeared.

"Pishta," said O'Dwyer, "open that trunk in my bedroom, please. I'd like that old policeman picture." Pishta raced into the bedroom. He reappeared and placed a photograph on the dining-room table. O'Dwyer studied it. A moment later, he said, "Look at this picture of me with the nightstick when I was on the beat at Bush Terminal in 1917. Police Shield 6406. I'll never forget that number. I'm not holding the nightstick too well." Pishta was standing by. He'd evidently forgotten all about the missing Coca-Cola bottle. "I think I'd like my magistrate's robe, please," said O'Dwyer to Pishta, and a black magistrate's robe was produced. O'Dwyer stood up and put it on. "Not bad," he said. He smiled, and touched one of the sleeves. "Not bad at all. And now the police badge, Pishta, please." Pishta disappeared, reappeared, placed a glittering gold-spangled badge on the table, and left the room. In gold, embossed on blue, were the words "Police Department City of New York." The seal of the city, in gold, was in the center of the badge. The word "Chief" rested below an eagle. There were five silver stars under the word "Chief."

"I like to think of this as the Mayor's badge," said O'Dwyer softly. "It was given to me by my friends in the Police Department after I became

Mayor. The badge of the Mayor of the City of New York." He picked up the badge and stared at it in silence for a long moment. He put it on the table and slipped off the robe. "Pishta!" he called. Pishta came in, and O'Dwyer handed him his robe. Then he pointed to the badge and the photograph. "Put everything back in the trunk," he said.

Train of Thoughts

Visiting in Washington. Came home on Amtrak's sleek new Swedish-built, high-speed tilt train, X2000, which cuts minutes from regular running time between capital and Big Apple. First step toward President's goal of high-speed rail travel. Fast or slow, I love trains: no manic airports, no twisted seat belts. Room to sit back, look out, not down, at Mother Earth, reflect on lifelong traversal of same route. Up at dawn to catch 6:50 A.M. train, No. 202. Washington like small town—eerily quiet, still snoozing. Passed White House, gray in dawn. Flag flying from roof. Residential second floor completely dark—no Bill, Hillary, Chelsea, cat. Union Station almost deserted. Onto train at 6:43 and into spacious, elegantly appointed coach. (Ninety dollars one way, a hundred and eighty round trip.) Soft blue seats, pull-down teak-like desks at each one, attractive beige carpeting with rust-colored squares. Coffee bar in middle of car: on the house. Car almost filled with dignified, highly professional-looking men and women, many already with spread-out papers, laptop computers. People smiling reservedly at one another. This no Love Boat. Digital clock in front of car read 6:50. Without fuss, feathers, jiggling, or sound, we were gliding out of station right on time.

Almost instantly, attendant came by. Did I want breakfast at seat, she asked, or prefer bistro car—fancier stuff? Said I'd sit tight. Attendant fount of information, proud to be part of test run of train. Told me train had been rented for eight months from Swedish owners. Said, "We're zipping along now at a hundred and thirty-five miles per hour. We pay extra attention to curves. Curves are *important*. Ordinarily, you take a curve or you leave a curve alone, but where regular trains take curves at a hundred and ten miles per hour, X2000 goes around at a hundred and twenty-five. Or takes a ninety-mile-per-hour curve at a hundred and fifteen, or a hundred-and-five at a hundred and twenty-five, or a hundred-and-ten at a hundred and thirty-five."

Docent momentarily interrupted by tinkle of loudspeaker system, followed by voice announcing train would make only stop of entire trip: New Carrollton, Maryland, 6:59—gentle stop, gentle start.

"Highly technical, this business of curves," attendant went on. "On regular trains, cars have rigid axles, so when the train goes around a curve, the axles remain rigidly parallel. The higher the speed, the more the tendency of wheels to overrun the rails. That won't do. The X2000 axles are computerized, and assume their natural radial position on each curve, redistributing and minimizing forces exerted by rigid frames. Am I spoiling your appetite?"

"Not at all," I said.

"This means," she said, "that an X2000 undercarriage might exert barely more force taking a curve at a hundred and fifteen miles per hour than a regular train at eighty miles per hour. Also, we have a complicated tilting system: X2000 tilts at the proper angle and time as we take a curve. If we tilted a hundred per cent of the curve, people might feel uncomfortable. So we settle on a seventy-per-cent tilt, and people aren't confused by changing horizon line."

Clock said 7:15. Obviously, time to eat. Attendant brought tray to seat. Yummies included orange slices, hard-boiled-egg slices, raspberry preserve, prune Danish, croissant, grapes, coffee. No charge. Top of coffee cup still as millpond. Sliding non-stop through Baltimore: 7:21.

Familiar city. Father born here. Can't say I miss stopping at quondam Pennsylvania Railroad's Union Station. Always preferred romantic Renaissance Baltimore & Ohio Mount Royal Station, furnished with rocking chairs. Rocking chairs! In old days, Mount Royal pure Manet painting: great shed, clouds of smoke from steam locomotives. I spot Maryland Institute, massive old Belvedere Hotel. Tunnel, then East Baltimore. Almost deserted streets, legendary row houses, spotless white marble steps. Catch glimpse of dome of Johns Hopkins Hospital. Almost lost precious friend years ago; saved by brilliant medicine at Hopkins, medical team led by my uncle (who was, incidentally, in first class at Hopkins Medical

School). Constant vigil, loving care. "It's touch and go," uncle said to me. "Be strong, be prepared. As Osler would say, Aequanimitas." Grant E. Ward, renowned surgeon, operated: gentle medical wizard had suffered spinal tumor; arm, paralyzed, swung in terrifying rotating shoulder brace, but hand precise as arrow. For private nurse, uncle snared noted Hopkins figure who had been head nurse for famed neurosurgeon Harvey Cushing in First World War. I tried to distract patient by sitting at bedside, relating how uncle had taken me, as young man, to Marlborough Apartments, on Eutaw Place, to view great collection of Dr. Claribel and Miss Etta Cone, still on private walls, prior to donation to Baltimore Museum of Art. Picasso, van Gogh, Cézanne. But Matisses the true treasures—single largest Matisse collection in United States. Said, "When you get well, we'll go to the museum and see them." "I'll get well," she said. And did.

Reverie broken. Conductor wanted ticket. "Anybody tell you about the curves?" he said. I said yes. "Anybody tell you we make a constant examination of these tracks before and after X2000 passes over them? Try our fancy john."

John super. Locks automatically when door closes. For soap, press white button over sink. For water, press red button. Back to seat. Attendant passing out elaborate questionnaires. Queasy feeling. Reminded of College Boards. Sample: "What day of the week is it? What percentage of your total leisure or non-business trips . . ." Abandoned questionnaire, observed soft Maryland countryside slipping past. Strikingly high bridge over Susquehanna: on left, whole vast interior of continent; on right, waterway to Chesapeake Bay and Old World. Never cross this bridge without thinking of Havre de Grace and immortal lines from "Guys and Dolls" that go something like:

COP: What's the name of that place in Maryland where people get married in a hurry?

GAMBLER: Pimlico.

Delaware whizzing past. Dozed for a blink, Delaware come and gone. Looked out window, reflected on sobering visit day before in Washington with veteran diplomat, retired foreign ambassador. "The struggle in Russia is philosophically between Solzhenitsyn and Sakharov, between Dostoyevski and Turgenev, between East and West," he said. "Russia is a wounded animal. Losing Ukraine was a humiliating loss. Some of those Harvard economists giving advice had better be careful—Russia is not a Third World country but a highly developed one that's tragically run down. And, remember, you can't suddenly tell a Socialist country that it must suffer unemployment of thirty million."

Philadelphia: 8:19. One hour twenty-nine minutes. Usual time, one hour thirty-six minutes. Told self progress is slow, can't expect miracles.

Philadelphia jumble of thoughts. Remember torrid, steaming night in 1948, Democratic Convention prepared to nominate Harry Truman. I'm high up in balcony. Truman kept waiting interminably on ramp outside stage entrance while Southern segregationists ranted, stormed out of hall. Rousing pro-Truman speech by firebrand mayor of Minneapolis, Hubert Humphrey. Truman finally nominated, delivered impassioned stem-winder, sawing air with familiar parallel gesture of both hands. Convention adjourned in wee hours. No cabs, long walk to station. Now passing sand-colored Philadelphia Museum of Art. Quirky reminder of American painter Edwin Dickinson. Knew him on Cape Cod, recalled seeing above his mantelpiece palette from his early classes at Pratt with William Merritt Chase. Remember dreamlike visit one morning to Philadelphia Museum: I turn corner, bump into Dickinson—perfect self-portrait, hanging on wall. Now, passing boathouses on Schuylkill, in mind's eye see Eakins' scullers on this river.

Cross Delaware at Trenton: 8:45. Been travelling one hour fifty-five minutes. Usual time, two hours twenty minutes. Sign on bridge reads, "Trenton Makes—The World Takes." From dreary scene whizzing past, find this doubtful. Heart of industrial East now: abandoned factories, broken windows, run-down infrastructure, crying for help. Suddenly, remember passing Red Lobster restaurant earlier on this trip. Night after night, on tube, watch vivid ads of crustaceans bubbling in butter, see platters of succulent shrimp, but never find Red Lobster on home turf. Hurry to front of car, insert credit card in phone, call home to wife:

ME: I've actually seen a Red Lobster!

SHE: Big news in a troubled world. Say hello for me.

Newark: 9:11. Usual time, two hours thirty-six minutes; this train, two hours twenty-one minutes. Spotted twin towers of World Trade Center, top of Empire State. Zoomed into tunnel under Hudson. Sudden recollection of Arthur Train's famous Mr. Tutt, consummate fictional lawyer, and story about big lawsuit involving train stuck in tunnel: New York jurisdiction or New Jersey jurisdiction?

Loudspeaker: "In approximately three minutes, we will be arriving at Pennsylvania Station, New York City. Thank you for riding Amtrak's X2000. And have a goo-ood day!"

Precisely on time: 9:25. Two hours thirty-five minutes, against two hours fifty-five minutes.

Small step for mankind. Big step for Amtrak.

Mrs. Roosevelt, Eight Feet Tall

Penelope Jencks, the sculptor, is a good friend of mine, and a Cape Cod summer neighbor. Eleanor Roosevelt is someone whose memory I—and millions of others—hold dear. So when I heard that Jencks was working in her studio, in Wellfleet, on a statue of Mrs. Roosevelt, to be placed at the southern tip of Riverside Park in Manhattan, I picked up the phone and called her. "I am deep in the project, and totally dedicated," she said. "I know where I'm going, but it takes time. Come on up, and we'll talk."

Wellfleet is a venerable town (incorporated 1763) jutting out into the Atlantic on one side and Cape Cod Bay on the other, near the hooked elbow of Cape Cod. Jencks lives in a gray-shingled Cape Cod–style house on the bay side in a part of Wellfleet known as Bound Brook Island, and works in a shingled studio a short distance away. In the early days of the Republic, Bound Brook actually was an island. Then, with the coming of the railroad and its dikes, the land was gradually filled in, and Bound Brook is an island no longer. Even today, though, driving over to Bound Brook (a matter of minutes) leaves one with a sense of having travelled to some dreamlike far-off place. You follow narrow, unmarked sand roads, framed by tall oaks and pines, up and down steep hills, and there are only a few spots where you can turn in and wait for an oncoming car to pass. Wellfleet residents take a certain fierce and obstinate pride in the signs that identify their houses. Metal nameplates would be considered scandalously infra dig. Residents merely find a small piece of wood, preferably of irregular shape, paint their name on it, and nail it to a convenient tree. Time and weather take their inevitable toll of the markers, and many of the signs have come perilously close to invisibility. Although these particular woods happen to be full of artists, poets, and professors, there is nothing remotely spurious, or falsely modest, about the simplicity of these nametags. Eleanor Roosevelt would feel completely at home on Bound Brook.

The Jencks house sits on a broad slope leading down to the bay. The vista is striking: at this point, the bay seems as wide as an ocean, and on windy days it kicks up high, proud waves. I never visit the Jencks place without imagining that I am at Dingle Bay, in County Kerry. Penelope Jencks was in her studio when I arrived. She is a tall, strikingly handsome woman in her fifties, and some of her features have an uncanny resemblance to Eleanor Roosevelt's—she has the same inquiring eyes and mobile mouth, and she moves in the same self-respecting and forceful manner. I looked around. County Kerry disappeared from my mind. I had entered a cluttered world dominated by the image and the personality of Eleanor Roosevelt. Scattered about were half a dozen bronze maquettes of the sculpture Jencks is working on. They show Mrs. R., her left hand under her chin. Hatless and wearing a long coat, she is leaning against a rock. Her feet are crossed. Everywhere I looked, I saw large bulletin boards displaying more than two hundred photocopies of Mrs. R., in myriad poses. "I've collected these from everywhere," Jencks said. "They are a tremendous help in my attempt to make the sculpture believable." In some pictures, Mrs. Roosevelt is smiling; in others she is not. In some she is standing, in others sitting. In some she wears a hat; in others she is hatless. The bulletin boards have been skillfully arranged. For example, one of the pictures shows her facing right. In another, she faces straight out; in still another she faces left. "I study them continually," Jencks said. "I like looking at them. I study them for the shape of the neck, the way the neck rises. I find her hair beautiful. I am fascinated that although the upper part of her face remains constant, the lower part constantly changes. I often wonder, am I looking at the same person?" In all the pictures, Mrs. R. is alone. There are no pictures of F.D.R. in the room.

Smack in the middle of the studio was an eight-foot-tall object, haphazardly wrapped in swirls of black and white plastic and leaning against a plaster rock. "Mrs. Roosevelt?" I asked.

"I hope so," Jencks said. "In clay. Once I am satisfied—and I am hard to satisfy—it will be cast in plaster, and, finally, in bronze." The figure stands eight feet tall—two feet taller than Mrs. R. herself, and two feet one inch taller than Jencks. "What you see here," Jencks said, waving her hand in a wide arc, "is work in progress. Everything is in flux, everything constantly changes. There are moments, as I'm working on the sculpture, when her body language becomes overly strong—so much more important than the face. While doing certain parts, I feel that I know exactly what she looked like at exactly that moment. The other day—for a moment—the head seemed too low. Those moments! And the meaning of those moments! One instant, Mrs. R. is there before me. The next instant, she is not. I suppose that I never stop thinking about what I am working on. Let's talk about rocks. I love rocks. In fact, I adore rocks. When I was younger and was living in Westport, Connecticut, I would swim out around the breakwater and admire the rocks—just because they were rocks. My sculpture of the great historian Samuel Eliot Morison—it stands on the corner of Commonwealth Avenue and Exeter Street in Boston—has Morison sitting on a rock. He has binoculars in one hand and the other resting on a stack of books, is wearing a yachting cap, and steadfastly looks out to sea. But that sculpture, in a sense, is dominated by the rock. For this work, the opposite must be true: Mrs. R. must dominate the rock. The rock, for me, is really a transition, an imaginary space. The rock is the pedestal—the viewer's space, the world of the normal-sized person in relation to the sculpture. Without the rock, you would have an oversized person. The rock brings the sculpture to you and separates you from it at the same time—a breathing space for the viewer."

I asked how Jencks had become involved in the project.

"I have always admired Mrs. Roosevelt," she said. "It's a mysterious symbiosis. I have always felt that I could identify with her as a woman. This is hard to explain: She was always, for me, a presence, even when I was younger. A *real* presence. For example, my mother was quite tall, and people often compared her, physically, to Mrs. Roosevelt. This did not please my mother one tiny bit. She was vain and didn't wish to be compared to anybody. For another thing, I have always been in sympathy with Mrs. Roosevelt's politics, her idealism. Also a certain awkwardness, what some people saw as plainness. I've read a great deal about her, and about her uncle Theodore Roosevelt. I've spent time at the Roosevelt Library, at Hyde Park. In reading about her in books by Joseph Lash, I felt a special, intimate empathy. I wondered how she had gone from a shy childhood to the dominant, outspoken public figure known around the world. All this intrigued me. So when I read in the late eighties that a man named Herbert Zohn—a New Yorker—was anxious to sponsor a statue of Mrs. Roosevelt, to be placed near where he lived, and was getting together a jury to pick a sculptor for the task, I became intensely interested. There were some four hundred entries— slides of previous works were submitted—and ten people were invited to make maquettes. Happily, I won. My proposal seems to have struck the right note." Jencks walked over to a nearby table, picked up some papers, and handed them to me. "My proposal," she said.

I jotted down some excerpts: "I would have her alone, solitary. When she felt troubled or in need of peace and quiet she would sometimes find time to spend in the woods. While in Washington, she wrote in her diary of visiting the Mrs. Henry Adams monument by Saint-Gaudens. She spoke of its setting in Rock Creek Cemetery." At this point, Jencks reminded me that Mrs. Adams had taken her own life. I went back to the proposal: "She felt that its quiet strength was not despair but the triumph of the spirit over sadness and grief. . . . I would like to think that she might have had a similar sort of response to this piece that I propose to do of her. . . . I am trying to capture a sense of peace and strength, a brooding, pensive woman leaning against a rock, not quite seated, her hand under her chin (as she often held it), gazing thoughtfully out into the park. In spite of her tremendous energy and activity, I believe that her true strength came from an inner searching, an almost overwhelming honesty, and a conviction that mankind has the ability (and desire) to 'do the right thing' if only that thing can be discovered."

Jencks has found that working on the statue has become a consuming passion. Since she displays all the characteristics of a true perfectionist, no step in the process comes easily. Although she usually spends winters with her husband, Sidney Hurwitz, who is a noted printmaker and teacher (he teaches art at Boston University), at their house in Newton, just outside Boston, this past winter she stayed on the Cape alone, her only companion being Sam, a newborn black poodle. "Great company," Penelope said, "especially when I was deep in work." The winter was a rigorous one, with frigid temperatures and heavy snowstorms. "There were days when I was truly isolated here," she said. "Immense snowdrifts, perniciously icy roads—weather that would have been a challenge to Mrs. Roosevelt. She was intrepid. I think she would have loved it. Often, I had to call in to town for help—someone to come and plow me out."

From the start of the enterprise, Jencks found herself getting deeper and deeper into the matter of the rock on which Mrs. Roosevelt leans. Manhattan schist, the type of rock found in Riverside Park, comes in layers and is flaky—unsuitable for a sculpture. So Jencks chose granite. But when it came to the shape of the rock, she found herself in an area of great indecision. Exactly what shape should it be? She would go off to a quarry in New Milford, near Danbury, and stay for weeks at a time. There she made rock portraits in clay—twenty of them. (Each model was scaled at an inch and a half to the foot of the plan for the statue itself.) The weather was so cold she had to work in fingerless gloves, and, because it was deer-hunting season, she wore a red hat and a pink jacket, and left the car radio on, turned up to ear-blasting decibels. To amuse herself, and also to ward off hunters, she would hum Bach's D Minor Double Concerto. She saw only two hunters, was never mistaken for any species of quadruped, and worked undisturbed.

Jencks now went into the next room, and returned with two cups of coffee. She began to talk about herself. She was born in 1936, in Baltimore. Her father, Gardner Jencks, was a concert pianist and composer. Her mother, Ruth, was the daughter of Raymond Pearl, a professor in the Department of Hygiene and Public Health at Johns Hopkins University. The family moved to Westport when she was six, and she was brought up there and on the Cape. She went off to school at High Mowing, in New Hampshire; later, she spent a year at a school in Geneva and then two years at Swarthmore, mostly studying French, and ended her formal education, having turned permanently to art, after receiving a B.F.A. in painting from Boston University. A major influence in that decision was her study of art with the painter Hans Hofmann, who conducted classes in Provincetown. "He was the most wonderful teacher," she said. "He made you feel that being an artist was the most important thing in the entire world. He gave me a sense of monumentality. He made me see objects in relation to one another, and to reality. There is no way in which I can express what the Hofmann experience meant. His presence is still with me."

One of the joys of working on the statue, Jencks told me, is the friendship that has developed between her and Franklin Roosevelt III, Mrs. Roosevelt's grandson, who is in his fifties and teaches economics at Sarah Lawrence, and his daughter, Phoebe Roosevelt, who is twenty-nine and is a graduate student in American history at Columbia. Jencks first met Roosevelt, who goes through life under the rubric Frank Roosevelt, in 1988, at a gathering that celebrated her selection as the sculptor. A crowd was milling around, and someone said to Jencks, "Are you part of the family? There's a resemblance." This gave her a small, surreal jolt, since all along she had felt a mysterious connection between herself and her subject. Some time later, while spending the night with Frank Roosevelt and his wife in New York, she remarked that although her models were tall she was having trouble with the proportions of the torso. "I don't really have a proper model," she said. "I like a human body I can relate to." Mr. Roosevelt's wife, Jinx, spoke up. "Our daughter doesn't look like us, but she bears a resemblance to Eleanor Roosevelt. Give her a call. Perhaps she'll be willing to do some modelling for you."

Working on the statue has also led to a visit, with Frank Roosevelt, to Hillary Rodham Clinton in the White House. "A memorable experience," said Jencks. "We met in the Red Room. I mostly remember a nice old fire, a portrait of Audubon, and how warm and friendly she was when she entered the room and gave Frank Roosevelt a kiss. We dipped into pastry delights—éclair-type stuff with strawberries on top. Someone told her that I was spending the winter alone on Cape Cod, working, and she said, 'I remember a book about a man who spent an entire year alone in a house far out on a Cape Cod beach.' 'That's Henry Beston's "The Outermost House," ' I said. The connection was instantaneous and important to me." Mrs. Clinton remarked that she felt close to Eleanor Roosevelt. Until she came to the White House herself, she said, she had not realized the degree of vilification suffered by Mrs. R. when she was First Lady. She felt that she would get through the thickets, and took courage by thinking of the example of Mrs. R. "I didn't say anything, but I suddenly remembered how Mrs. Clinton had said that throughout the campaign she had often kept up her spirits by having imaginary conversations with Mrs. R., and how this was distorted and uglified by some radio commentators into an absurd demonic matter of mystical 'voices'—horrid stuff." The poodle interrupted our talk. "Impossible to be lonely with Sam around," Jencks said.

In New York, I had a chat with Frank Roosevelt. A modest man, he is delighted to be associated with the Jencks project, for it brings back tender memories of his grandmother. "I had an apolitical upbringing," he said, "but I vividly recall my father telling me how his mother had taken him, during the Depression, to the edge of Riverside Park—prophetically, near where the sculpture is to be placed—to see the jerry-built, improvised shanties of the unemployed, at a spot known as Hooverville. My mother and father were divorced. My mother moved to Detroit, my father to a farm in Dutchess County. I'd spend winter holidays with Mother, summer vacation with Father. I didn't think too much about my grandmother until I was about halfway through Yale. In my junior year, I went to South Africa for three weeks with an Afrikaner classmate. I guess this was the point of awakening. I went to Alexandra. I went to the townships. I saw what that was all about. And when I came back to the States I connected what I had seen to my own country and to my grandmother. I woke up one day and realized that this woman was not just the lovely, friendly grandmother who would buy Christmas presents for her grandchildren all through the year and store them in a closet. I realized this was Eleanor Roosevelt, and her interests and mine were converging. I wrote her, and she responded, and we became friends. I'd come down from New Haven to New York or Val-Kill Cottage, at Hyde Park, occasionally to have lunch with her and some people she had invited who fascinated me, like Walter Reuther. We corresponded about the United Nations, about China. She was knocked down by a taxicab around this time, and I was upset. My concern touched her. I recall once writing a fourteen-page review of a book by William Buckley. I didn't like the major thrust of his ideas, but I was confused by his raising the question, at one point, of whether Social Security should be compulsory. This troubled me. I wrote my grandmother and she became my teacher. She explained the necessity of the Social Security system.

"I've had some exhilarating experiences in connection with Penelope's sculpture. Back in February, 1993, there was an event called 'First

Ladies of Song' at Alice Tully Hall. Kitty Carlisle Hart was there; also Lena Horne and Judy Collins. And Mrs. Clinton. Mrs. Clinton talked about Mrs. Roosevelt. She spotted a thirty-inch maquette of Penelope's sculpture on the stage, and instantly said, 'I would like to have one of those for my desk.' Penelope kindly agreed to make a smaller version of the maquette, fourteen inches tall, and make copies available for purchase to help raise money for the sculpture. I wrote Mrs. Clinton and said we would like to present her with the first one. No reply for some time. Then, one day last winter, the White House called and invited us down. Going there was ecstasy for me. I was struck by Mrs. Clinton's warmth. I talked with her briefly, thanking her for bringing back the memory of Mrs. Roosevelt, and I said that we had waited a long time for this. I was deeply moved at being brought back to the White House by Eleanor Roosevelt, some thirty years after my last visit there."

I also had a chat with Phoebe Roosevelt, the great-granddaughter of Eleanor Roosevelt. "I loved being in Wellfleet, and with Penny," she said. "I had never modelled before. Somehow, I felt that this had nothing to do with me. I was—and am—merely facilitating her vision of Eleanor Roosevelt, helping Penelope achieve what is in Penelope's head. I found that I wasn't the least bit shy. I felt that she looked a bit like my great-grandmother—someone I never knew, since I was born in 1965 and she died in 1962. I found that Penelope has the relentless energy that I have always associated with Eleanor Roosevelt. Also, she has a tremendous sense of precision—knows exactly what she is looking for. She spent a great deal of time going over my shoulders—felt they were closer to Eleanor Roosevelt's than any of her previous models'. She did a great deal of measuring of the torso, with calipers, in relation to the legs. She was concerned with the look of the statue, but also deeply concerned with exactitude. Penny talks a great deal while working. She would tell me not to be offended if she sometimes asked me the same questions she had asked a minute before. 'I get so absorbed in my work,' she would say. As for Eleanor Roosevelt, most of what I know I have reached through my reading, or by listening to my father and grandfather. I am taken with her boldness and her humanity. A teacher of mine in high school was deeply influenced by her and, in a strange way, wanted to express gratitude through me. This gives me an odd feeling."

The other day, I went back to Wellfleet and poked my head into Penelope's studio. The sun had just set, and the bay reflected a gentle sky of grays and blues. Sam, the poodle, greeted me at the door. He's a big boy now, and almost knocked me down. I walked into the studio, which was still dominated by the statue. Eleanor Roosevelt's presence is almost palpable. Jencks has built two high, sturdy wooden platforms onto which she can climb to work on the face. Those panels of hundreds of photocopies of Mrs. R. in all sizes and shapes and poses have now been placed on four high easels, which Penelope can look at while standing on the platforms. "I'm moving along," she said. "I have a long way to go. I'm still in the process. Not long ago, I got back basically to the skeleton. Then I put on a head, and realized, quite unexpectedly, that it looked a great deal like the head of a sister of my father's. I had incorporated my aunt into the sculpture. I think this was because my father always said I reminded him of his sister, and her name was also Eleanor. In a sense, I had gone on automatic pilot. One tends to do a self-portrait—one's own proportions seem to come through. I realized that I had to shake off all the intertwining personalities, and I said to myself, 'You must get back to the Eleanoid and the Rooseveltoid.' A strange dream has helped me immensely. I was working away in the studio, in the dream, kneeling and sculpting, when I heard someone say, somewhere, 'Oh, here comes Mrs. Roosevelt!' I instantly thought, What a relief—I will never have to search for a model again. She walked right in that door. She was twenty feet tall. My God, I thought, I will never be able to sculpt this heroic figure, but without saying a word she smiled at me with such a beneficent smile—not a touch of grandiosity—that my fears melted away. Then she disappeared, just melted away. But I am secure in the knowledge that I have found Eleanor Roosevelt in my dreams."

TELEVISION

After a year of music reviewing, I reminded Mr. Ross and Mr. Shawn of my intention to move on to something else. Mr. Ross, under the impression that television was here to stay, immediately suggested that I write a television column, the magazine's first venture into that cultural minefield.

Peeping Funt

A gentleman named Allen Funt, who presents a television program entitled "Candid Camera," has succeeded, I think, in reducing the art, the
purpose, and the ethics of the "documentary" idea to the level of the
obscene. Mr. Funt, who airs his program Monday evenings over C.B.S.
and who is sponsored by Philip Morris, employs a simple, deadly formula. Equipped with a hidden movie camera and microphone and a
crew of assistant snoopers, he roams the city in various poses, pretend-
ing to be, say, a banker, a bootblack, or a mattress salesman. He records
on film the words and actions of unsuspecting people, and, when he has
finished with them, tells them what he has done to them, asks permission to televise the pictures, and explains that they will be paid off in
cash and, I guess, in some dubious fame. For the purposes of his program, he then throws together a half hour of selected shots. Not long
ago, for example, a lady entered the mattress department of R. H. Macy
& Co. with nothing more in mind than the purchase of a mattress.
Approaching what she thought was a salesman, she asked him to show
her some mattresses. She naturally thought that the fellow was just
another salesman employed by R. H. Macy & Co., but—you're right—
he was Allen Funt, the Candid Camera Man, and he had been hanging
around the mattress department, evidently with the jovial connivance of
R. H. Macy & Co., ready to pounce on just such an innocent party.
Without the customer's knowledge, he switched on his equipment, and
from that moment forward almost everything possible was done to make
her look foolish. The salesman (Funt) wondered who was to use the

mattress. An old lady, said the customer. How does she sleep, asked the salesman. "Well," said the customer, "she generally sleeps on her back with her toes up." "With her toes up!" exclaimed the incredulous salesman (Funt). "We have no mattresses for sale here for people who sleep on their backs with their toes up." The customer was flabbergasted, but, being a lady and wanting to buy a mattress, she was patient with the salesman. He next wanted to know whether the old lady snored. "Sometimes," said the customer. "Try the mattress for comfort," said the salesman (Funt). "Bounce up and down on it." The customer bounced up and down on the mattress, right there in the mattress department of R. H. Macy & Co. What a gimmick! She thought she was just testing a mattress, see, but actually she was bouncing up and down, potentially, in the view of thousands of Peeping Toms watching her on television. Finally, Funt confessed to her that her every word and her every action had been recorded, and her embarrassment at this disclosure was likewise recorded.

For the same program, which was broadcast last week, Funt posed as a businessman and called up a messenger service and asked to have a boy sent around to his "office" to pick up a package he wanted delivered. When the messenger arrived, Funt handed him an unwrapped dead fish and ordered him to take it to a certain address. The messenger wondered, politely, whether he might wrap the fish. Nix, said the man (Funt), deliver it *as is*. "Holy cow!" said the messenger. "Down Fifth Avenue you want me to deliver this fish, walking down Fifth Avenue with fish—holy cow!" He was terribly, terribly embarrassed, and he wondered if he might call his office and find out whether he had to fulfill this dreadful mission. He called his office, and somebody at the other end of the line apparently told him to go ahead and deliver it. I shall not soon forget the essential nobility of this messenger. Mr. Funt had faced him with a painful situation. Obviously, his inclination was to tell the man (Funt) to go to hell, throw the fish in his face, and depart. But the messenger had a job, and, I gathered, needed the job, and at unknown risk to his self-respect he said, "O.K., I'll take the fish." Preparing to leave, humiliated, fish in hand, he remarked, quietly and expressively, "It would be different, you know, if I had caught this fish myself, somewhere out in the country."

Mr. Funt and C.B.S. and Philip Morris feel, I suppose, that Mr. Funt is giving the television audience portraits of "life in the raw," pictures of

ordinary human beings trapped by strange circumstances and react-
ing like "people." In reality, he is demonstrating something that spies
have known about since spies began to operate; namely, that most
people are fundamentally decent and trusting and, sad to tell, can
readily be deceived. Mr. Funt bases his program, purely and simply,
upon deceit. Persuading his subjects that he is something he is not, he
succeeds in making them look foolish, or in forcing them to struggle,
against unfair odds, for some vestige of human dignity. For my money,
"Candid Camera" is sadistic, poisonous, anti-human, and sneaky. The
men who control television have tremendous opportunities for recording our times; they can go into people's homes and offices and factories,
they can go through the great cities or take their cameras to remote parts
of the country, as Robert Flaherty did in "Louisiana Story," and show us
how people live and behave. The catch is that the true documentarian
must respect his fellow-man and feel that what he has to say is worth
hearing. For years, radio has been showing its basic contempt for the
dignity of man, and now television, with "Candid Camera" as a con-
spicuous example, is following suit.

Those Syracuse Boys Again

—————

About one-fourth of the way through the Kraft Television Theatre's presentation, last week, of William Shakespeare's "The Comedy of Errors," there was a pause for a commercial. Matters had already got pretty well out of hand. I, for one, had only the barest notion which fellow was Antipholus of Syracuse and which fellow was Antipholus of Ephesus, and when it came to distinguishing between Dromio (Ephesus) and Dromio (Syracuse)—well, both the Bard and the cheese people had me there. As for the sisters Luciana and Adriana (one was married to an Antipholus), for all I knew, one of them was Nurse Edith Cavell and the other was Gypsy Rose Lee, brother-in-law to Howdy Doody, a peasant. To add to the general misery, there were a goldsmith, trying to collect on a gold chain sold to an Antipholus (the goldsmith was having my trouble finding out which Antipholus was which), and two clowns who kicked up their heels and indulged in humor of the "Nay, then, thus!" and "Away, sirrah, away!" variety. Then came the commercial. I had never believed it possible that a commercial could quiet jangled nerves. This was a simple commercial, simply presented, and its simplicity has made me a lifelong chum of Philadelphia Cream Cheese. The announcer, who spoke while a picture of a bowl of mashed-up Philadelphia Cream Cheese was flashed on the screen, had the voice of an old family doctor, soothing, understanding, all-wise. He urged his listeners to put Philadelphia Cream Cheese in *their* bowls, add a bit of lemon juice and a dash of Worcestershire, and then toss in some minced clams. "Stir it up," he said as though he were prescribing a month in the Adirondacks for a very tired patient. "Stir it up well, and—oh, it's delicious!" I believed every word the man said. Then the audience was returned to the Antipholi and the Dromii. By this time, the situation had become hazardous. A host of ancient Greek types—a duke, a courtesan, policemen, and the like—put in an appearance on my tiny screen to express their bewilderment, and to mirror mine, at what was going on. Finally, after several welcome interruptions to reveal additional cheese surprises, "The Comedy of Errors" drew to a close, precisely one hour after it had begun.

Later, while admiring a Philadelphia Cream Cheese in the kitchen, I tried to figure out what had gone wrong, and concluded that time, the enemy of all things, had whipped this particular production to a pulp. "The Comedy of Errors" is difficult enough to grasp when presented, God forbid, full length. Try to squeeze it into one hour, to the minute, and you end up with something less than comedy and more than error. The actors did quite well, I guess, and I have no complaint to make about the Antipholi, the Dromii, Adriana, or Luciana. The goldsmith, Vaughn Taylor, was especially effective (for one thing, he was the only goldsmith), and the camerawork was stunning. There was an intimacy about the production that was appealing, and I kept regretting that so much effort and skill had gone into so utterly hopeless a case of mistaken identities.

A Letter

_____

DEAR AUNT PAULINE:

It sure is lucky I work nights. I've been meaning to write and thank you for sending the cookies, but I've been so glued to my video machine the past ten days that I've barely had time to shave, much less time to write and say thanks for the cookies. Aunt Pauline, the things I've seen right in my own room, and the *people*! That first Monday morning, when I switched on my video and witnessed an odd-type crime-and-courtroom program getting under way, seems a long, long time ago. I remember thinking, This is a funny program to be televising in the A.M., which they usually devote to telling the people how to boil an egg and where to buy a hat and other useful things, but I settled down before the machine. A group of serious-looking men were seated at a courtroom bench, and a witness was seated below them at a table, and they were questioning this gentleman, who wore pince-nez, about some people they referred to as "bookies" at his race track, out on Long Island, N.Y. I gathered that this man ran the race track and that he had paid a very important man called Mr. Frank Costello sixty thousand dollars to get the "bookies" off the track, and that he never had asked Mr. Costello how he performed this service, or whether he did a good job, or anything. He just paid him fifteen thousand dollars a year for four years, and the only reason he stopped paying it was because the federal income-tax people wouldn't let him deduct the expense on his income-tax blank. I figured to myself, Aunt Pauline would certainly enjoy watching this program, especially with Uncle Ned always whooping and hollering around the house about taxes, and how the big fellows get away with murder and the little fellows pay through the nose.

Well, when this program kept right on going, through the afternoon and the following day and the day after, I realized it was a serious, real-life drama, and no laughing matter. Fellow after fellow came before the cameras—a round-faced Mr. Erickson and a natty Mr. Adonis—and the serious men on the bench kept hinting that these fellows were shadowy figures of the "underworld," controlling big enterprises and activities, but none of the fellows seemed to have any brains at all; they couldn't remember a thing. I couldn't figure out how they could run such big businesses, they acted so stupid. The most important man was that Mr. Costello. He turned up time and again, and the men on the bench seemed awfully anxious to snoop into his affairs. A very intelligent-looking man on the bench, a Mr. Halley, asked most of the questions, and he left the impression that Mr. Costello had his fingers in almost *everything* in New York City—gambling and politics and night clubs—and was just about the most important man in the city, in a scary sort of way.

This Mr. Costello himself was one of the most interesting men who have ever been in my house—through video, I mean. He started right out by saying, by way of his lawyer, that he didn't want his face televised, because it would make a spectacle of him, and the cameras focussed on his hands. I thought this made him more of a spectacle than if they had shown his face, and I didn't think they had any right to photograph his hands. (As a matter of fact, Aunt Pauline, the more I watched this engrossing program, the more I wondered how fair it was to ask witnesses to appear on video, if you know what I mean.) Mr. Costello was quite shy and reticent. He had more ways of not answering a question than anybody I have ever listened to. He would say, "It's Greek to me," or "I'm retired," or "I don't remember," or "I don't answer no trick questions," or "I'd sooner *him* answer that question," or "Not to my knowledge, no," or "Anything's possible," or "That don't make me a liar," or "I might have—on and off," or "I don't remember that partickler conversation," or "I'm not trying to get away with nothing," or "You aren't going to put any words in my mouth," or "That's ridikulus," or "I been racking my brains," or "I couldn't give you no dates," or "I'm denying nothing but I'm admitting nothing," or "I can't remember *everything*," or "If you know, why ask me?"

Although he was very secretive about his enterprises, he did admit to some facts about his private life. He certainly gets around, and to the best places. He's been having his hair cut at the Waldorf-Astoria Hotel barbershop for twenty-five years! He eats at restaurants like Gallagher's and Moore's and Shor's and the Colony, and he has drinks, from time to time, at the Biltmore bar. All sorts of people come to his home for cocktails and meals, including numerous big politicians in Tammany Hall, but he said that he hates politics, and when these people start talking politics, he doesn't listen—politics is that distasteful to him. He is very, very loyal to his friends. He won't let a pal down. He'll even sign a note for hundreds of thousands of dollars for a pal and never worry what for. And he works hard. He gets up early every morning and makes all sorts of phone calls around the country, long distance, before 9 A.M. He has a strongbox at home with forty to forty-three thousand dollars in cash in it, and both he and his wife have the combination. He golfs frequently. He takes airplanes, but his wife won't fly—she takes the train places. He goes to New Orleans for the "carnival." (Huey Long once asked him to come to New Orleans to make a "survey.") Mr. Costello is the type of man other men have faith in. They ask his advice on all manner of things, including whether an act in a night club like the Beverly Club in New Orleans is good or not. If he says it's good, his pals believe it's good. And Mr. Costello apparently gets around to the bars a lot, and he'll suggest to bartenders and customers that a particular brand of whiskey is good and they should drink it, and they take his advice. He called this "spreading propaganda." It certainly was interesting to hear him talk. Also, he had a smart lawyer with him who wouldn't let him answer some of the questions at all, not even with an if-you-know-why-ask-me answer.

For a couple of days during this program, Aunt Pauline, the ex-Mayor of New York City, Mr. William O'Dwyer, was in the witness chair. He's now the United States Ambassador to Mexico, but Mr. Halley, who asked most of the questions, never asked him one about Mexico. Mr. Halley wanted to know about the time Mr. O'Dwyer was the Mayor of New York, and the time, before that, when he was in the Army, and the time, before *that*, when he was the District Attorney of Brooklyn. He wanted to know had Mr. O'Dwyer ever noticed a "link" between crime and politics, but Mr. O'Dwyer was another of those fellows who would never let a pal down. He talked a lot about "little" things—he kept referring to the "little" people and their "little" pockets, and he even talked about some "little" pickets. Once, he said that when he was in the Army, he had just been a "little" major. He talked about schools and hospitals and slum clearance and harbor pollution and the bad days of prohibition. He admitted that some of the people he had appointed to public office had apparently been friends of the "underworld" characters, but he was firm in defending them. And he stoutly defended Brooklyn as against Manhattan, and the Police Department as against the Fire Department. He seemed like a very loyal man, and also a very sad one. He seemed sad about life in general and his life in particular. He was awfully realistic about life in a big city. He didn't seem to think there was anything surprising about a man's being Mayor and knowing people who knew reputedly bad people, and he kept saying, "I did the best with a bad situation," or "If you're ever Mayor, you'll see what happens," or "Nothing that occurs in Manhattan ever surprises me." He didn't have a lawyer with him, but, like Mr. Costello, he had a number of ways of not answering questions. Right at the end of all the programs, an elderly, white-haired man on the bench shouted out, with great passion, "Public office is a public trust," and I was reminded that Uncle Ned has been saying the same thing for years.

Well, be good—or they'll get you. And thanks again for the cookies.

Your loving nephew.

Giants Walk the Earth

The Columbia Broadcasting System, in one of the boldest and most ambitious ventures since Professor Auguste Piccard's balloon ascension, has set out to capture a large segment of the audience that watches Milton Berle. The mere thought is staggering. Mr. Berle—or Uncle Miltie, as he is known to millions of fun-lovers, both young and old—holds forth on Tuesday evenings from eight to nine over N.B.C. Since television's earliest commercial days, this has been regarded as a sacred hour, and producers, account executives, and soapsuds manufacturers have been loath to trespass upon it. True, there have been a good many interesting presentations over rival networks at the same time, but they have generally been, in the quaint language of broadcasting, "frontal-lobe programs"—discussion groups, programs dealing with natural history, and other lobe massages—and hence of no consequence whatever in the two-fisted, realistic world of advertising. Well, sir, C.B.S. has now decided that the time has come to challenge Uncle Miltie's hold on Tuesday evenings from eight to nine, and the man they have chosen to perform this herculean task is Frank Sinatra. (I hesitate to think of the hundreds of man-hours that must have been spent pondering over who could do the trick, or of the hundreds of cigarette butts and empty coffee containers that must have been scattered about the offices of the men in charge of preparing the great challenge.)

One recent Tuesday evening, I turned to "The Frank Sinatra Show," and within four or five minutes it had become clear that Uncle Miltie—cavorting, even then, on N.B.C.—had nothing to fear but fear itself.

From the moment Mr. Sinatra—a slight, undernourished figure with padded shoulders, standing alone before a curtain—made his appearance, I felt that he had been ill-advised to take on the champion. He seemed entirely too defenseless and fragile to throw down the gauntlet to anyone. He wore on his face an expression of the utmost melancholy. Furthermore, he seemed to be in some sort of somnambulistic state, as though he had wandered onto the stage by accident and was mercifully unaware of his whereabouts. When he opened his mouth and began to croon, I became convinced that he either really *was* asleep or else was quite ill, and should be gently led away and put to bed. Immediately following Mr. Sinatra's vocal effort, Jackie Gleason, the comedian, came on the stage, and he and Mr. Sinatra enacted a sketch that had something or other to do with the two of them entraining for Las Vegas, where they confidently expected to break the bank. Mr. Gleason is a large man and he was very wide-awake. When he placed a hand around one of Mr. Sinatra's legs and remarked loudly, "Now, *there's* a calf that left its mother too soon," and Mr. Sinatra looked at him with his big, sad eyes, I could bear it no longer, and at 8:18 I turned to Milton Berle.

Uncle Miltie was engaged in some raucous high jinks with Edward Arnold, but the precise nature of the proceedings was obscured by Uncle Miltie's helpless and hysterical laughter at his own jokes. He said something to Mr. Arnold and promptly doubled over in a spasm of merriment. His laugh was infectious, and a moment later Mr. Arnold doubled over, too. Then the studio audience caught the fever, and burst into shrill cries of glee. Uncle Miltie, by now a figure of utter madness, fell on the floor and kicked his feet in the air. "G'wan and turn on your radios!" he shrieked insolently at the audience. He rose, wiped away the tears that were coursing down his cheeks, and threw his arms around Mr. Arnold, who was sobbing with delight. All in all, it was a remarkable exhibition of bold and brassy self-appreciation, and I was grateful that Mr. Sinatra was unable to observe it, for it would unquestionably have inflicted irreparable damage on his morale.

A Few Statistics

By and large, television writers are fascinated by death. They do not seem capable of keeping it out of their scripts, and week after week, program after program, death, in one form or another, assumes a major role. Death, in fact, is rapidly replacing Milton Berle as Mr. Television. Over the past year, I have assiduously kept a check list of the death toll on my tiny screen, and the results are, to say the least, appalling. Looking at my list, I find that 16,932 men, women, children, and animals have passed away on television programs since the night of November 1, 1950, most of them in a sudden and quite violent manner. Death by shooting has been far and away the most popular method employed by script-writers to rub out their characters, accounting for 9,652 deaths, or more than half of the fatalities. In television shootings, revolvers have led the field four to one, but since the Kefauver hearings, with their dark references to mobs and mobsters, the machine gun has been coming into its own. Not only do machine guns make more noise on television than revolvers but they get rid of more people, and quicker, too. Mobsters, using machine guns, have sent 894 men across the bar, 762 of them since March 14, 1951, the third day of the Kefauver telecasts in New York. These machine-gunnings usually take place in a gaudy night club or hot spot, and the man behind the gun is inevitably in the employ of Mr. Big, but sometimes they take place in alleys, also a favorite spot for the old-fashioned, or smoking-rod, type of death. My list shows, for example, seventeen deaths in alleys in July alone, five of them by machine guns. All the alleys were dark, and there wasn't a policeman in sight. As a matter of fact, there never *is* a policeman in sight until rigor mortis sets in, but private eyes tumble over one another to reach the scene of a crime. Private eyes, according to my calculations, turned up—late, as usual—in 391 cases of death in the period under scrutiny. Sixty per cent of all these private-eye deaths were attributable to gunfire of one type or another, fourteen per cent to fire (generally of an incendiary nature and mostly in warehouses), twenty per cent to poisoning, and six per cent to miscellaneous causes, including ingeniously contrived electrocutions at the hands of simple home appliances. Also under miscellaneous I found deaths from lye-and-cement jobs, and snakebites (three).

When the programs leave the turbulent urban centers of crime and head into the great, clean, wide-open spaces of the Far West, the crime statistics leap upward like a giant bird of prey. I find that no less than 7,358 persons and 249 horses bit the dust out West, either on the range or high in the hills outside town or in front of a saloon or just inside the corral gate. (I find a curious reference in my list to "Possum: Strangulation by Indian 5/13/51" but have no recollection of the incident, and have not included the figure in the over-all total.) Par for deaths on a cowboy program of thirty minutes' duration is forty-six. Cowboys habitually pass on in groups of from ten to fifteen at a time, the most common method of dispatching them wholesale being large boulders rolled over cliffs, customarily by Mexicans with dirty faces. I hasten to point out that cowboy-mortality figures are not completely reliable, for it often happens that a man who has been gagged and bound hand and foot and left in a blazing cabin, along with a dozen or more of his mates, will turn up fifteen minutes later to get it again in the canyon, in the boulder-and-Mexican routine. Strangely, par for deaths on a cowboy program of sixty minutes' duration is not double that of the half-hour program but only sixty-four. Commercials during the second half of an hour-long cowboy program tend to cut down the death rate materially, and it is further held in check by prolonged conversations between the ranch owner's daughter and her blind father. Most of the time, the father, who always wears a nightgown and nightcap and has not shaved since Teddy Roosevelt was a boy, dies of natural causes. He takes a long time going, too, and it is hardly worth the effort, since it adds only one figure to the list.

A few words about animals. I find 102 entries under the heading "Canine Casualties," eighty-five of the victims belonging to small boys. Small boys are always losing their dogs on television. (Small girls take better care of their pets.) Most of the dogs are accidentally run over by cars or trucks, unhappily on the boys' birthdays, but the figures reveal seven cases in which dogs intentionally stepped in front of trucks, heroically sacrificing their own lives to save their little masters. Collies predominate, five to two, when it comes to heroics. Scotties get run over more often than any other breed. They don't look where they're going, or something. Bird casualties are negligible. An occasional parrot drops for the final count, and in the winter months sparrows die from time to time, symbolically; eighteen died last year. One night in June, a fawn stumbled onto some railroad tracks and was cut down by a swiftly moving train, but this is the only instance of fawn death in my records. Train wrecks, incidentally, accounted for 114 human deaths, thirty-seven of them on one trestle alone. Iron Curtain deaths (lengthy interrogation followed by extensive bludgeoning) amounted to 153, outstripping deaths at the hands of Nazis (less interrogation, more bludgeoning), which numbered sixty-two. I have arbitrarily entered political machine-gunnings in a category separate from Iron Curtain deaths and mobster machine-gunnings. There were ninety-eight of them, all in Siberia.

During the Yule season, there is a noticeable drop in violent deaths (except in the Far West, where the killings continue, regardless) and a marked shift to a softer and gentler reference to the Grim Reaper. I have in my file 312 references under the heading "Holly Haunts." Holly Haunts are a distinct contribution of the television writer to the Christmas season. A Holly Haunt is usually a dead person who returns home, mostly on Christmas Eve, to mingle with his family, who either (a) hear him but cannot see him or (b) see him but cannot establish communication or (c) are so disturbed by the mysterious blowing of a window curtain or some other manifestation of a presence that they can't figure out what the hell is happening. Some Holly Haunts, though as dead as the others, are unaware of their condition until the close of the program, when a small man in a derby comes and takes them far, far away. In the approaching Yule season, there will be forty-three small men in derbies or my filing system breaks down.

Burn a Rag

I suppose it was inevitable, things being what they are in the demoniac world of television, that sooner or later a program would consist entirely of a gigolo-type man appearing on the screen to make love, in silky and seductive tones, to the female members of his audience. One can imagine the desperately serious conferences, attended by layer upon layer of account executives, script writers, network vice-presidents, and ambitious office boys, that would precede the launching of so ambitious a project. First, the conferees would have to determine the most desirable time for such a program, and it would be pretty well agreed, I should think, that if the gigolo type was to be in any way effective, he must make his pitch toward the end of the evening. Next, it would have to be decided what type of gigolo type to employ, and the vote here, without question, would go to a man with a foreign accent, on the theory that the ladies are bored with the hard, dry, unromantic Amurrican tones of their husbands, or, if they don't have husbands, dream wildly of someday meeting a tall dark man from a foreign land, with sideburns. "I know all about the French as lovers," I can hear a network veep telling his spellbound associates in a cork-lined conference room. "I spent a couple days in Paris myself last summer. But French is too *obvious*, if you know what I mean." The ensuing deadly silence is ultimately broken by one of the office boys, a Phi Bete from Monongahela, who, taking his courage in his hands, says, "If I may make a suggestion, how about an *Italian*? They are of Mediterranean stock and extremely romantic." The office boy is made a vice-president on the spot, and, amid cries of "Roger!,"

(313)

"Check!," "Good deal!," and "Sockeroo!," the conference happily breaks up.

I cannot guarantee that such a scene preceded the launching, on Tuesday and Thursday evenings from eleven-fifteen to eleven-thirty, over C.B.S., of "The Continental," but I would make book that it did. The Continental is a tall, dark Italian gentleman, approximately forty years of age, with high cheekbones, fierce, penetrating eyes, and a soft, gooey accent. The first time I saw him, a week or so ago, he appeared in white tie and tails, slipping into a real high-class, dimly lighted room that contained, among many manifestations of elegance, a pipe rack, an ashtray, champagne glasses, and a bookshelf. "Don't be afraid, darling," said the Continental quietly, shutting the door behind him and gazing directly at the camera, his eyes alight with passion. "It's only a man's apartment, and here's the man." Then he asked, "You have no objection to champagne?" and poured two glasses, thrusting one toward the camera. The camera presumably took its glass, for the glass disappeared, and the Continental held the other one aloft and toasted the camera, remarking that Buntz, his butler, had retired for the night, and, like it or not, he and the camera were alone. "You know something, darling?" he said, moving closer to the lens. "You look prettiest of all when you are in love. You are like a precious jewel." From somewhere I could hear throbbing organ music. The Continental paused for a moment, and his eyes gleamed like a pair of dime-store onyxes. "Was *I* ever in love?" he said, as though answering a question put to him by the camera. "Was *I* ever a silly man going around with a chip on my shoulder? With me, the world is still young." Then he had a sudden inspiration, and, turning to the bookshelf, he drew forth a volume of verse and began to read. The poem had something to do with "Lying in the hay, games we used to play, only yesterday." The Continental went on to extoll laughter, lights, glamour, beautiful girls ("some of them mine"), and the wonder of lying on one's back under the stars and gazing at apple trees. "Dun't you *see*, darling?" he cried, moving still closer to the camera. He offered the camera a rose, and protested that darling was avoiding his gaze. Finally, coming as close to darling as he could without getting caught in the machinery, he announced that he was going to embrace it, and he let his arms steal tenderly about it. "There I go," he said, stepping back several feet, "acting like an orangutan again." The Continental became aware of the time (almost eleven-thirty), and, smiling toothily, he said, "And so good night, darling. *A rivederci, carina.*" And he was gone.

I found it difficult to believe that any such performance would be repeated, and a few nights later, armed with a beer bottle, I lighted up the tiny screen at eleven-fifteen. There, by golly, was old Snakeyes again, this time wearing a business suit and a striped tie, and although his pitch was a shade less torrid, he still had his mind on the same topic. This time, he read the camera some excerpts from Elizabeth Browning, lifted his champagne glass, asked the camera why it was so pensive, and remarked, "I am not ashamed to admit that I have a line. A man without his line is like a Fuller Brush man without brushes." He seated himself at a piano and indulged in a few trills. He appeared tired as he told the camera a tale of magical love in a gondola passing under the Bridge of Sighs, and he seemed ready to fold as he drank a toast, inhaled deeply, said, "Keep dreaming, darling," and went away. He made it just in time. I was about to let fly with the beer bottle.

Back to Chicago

I am a reasonably old eye at this television game by now, I guess, but the coverage of the Democratic National Convention last week beat anything I had ever seen on land, at sea, or in the air. The tiny screen at our house was alight for days and nights on end, meals were eaten in front of the set, friends came and went—some for Stevenson, some for Harriman, and some for Barkley, including a voluble Southern lady who burst into tears during the Vice-President's speech and sang "My Old Kentucky Home" until silenced by the local chair. The only dissenter throughout the proceedings was a five-year-old boy who boards at our place and who, frustrated almost beyond endurance by his continuing inability to make contact with Howdy Doody, kept demanding; "When is this stinky program going to end?" Now that it *has* ended, I find myself wondering just what there was about it that kept me so entranced. Unquestionably, one factor—and this, of course, was true of the Republican proceedings as well—was the mechanical miracle of the thing. I felt this most strongly on Friday afternoon, during the early balloting. The Missouri delegation was being polled individually on the floor, and the cameras were focussed on the delegates. I happened to be watching an N.B.C. station when, without warning, the convention floor disappeared and I saw a long black limousine slide up beside a huge airplane. An announcer broke in to say that the President of the United States was at that moment about to fly from Washington to Chicago and that we were to witness his departure. Seconds later, I heard again the voices of the Missouri delegation answering the roll call and hollering the names of this candidate and that, but on the screen the President was stepping out of his car, waving genially to the crowd at the Washington airport, and mounting the ramp to his plane. As he turned for a last salute, I heard from Chicago the voice of his alternate, Mr. Gavin, announcing that his—and the President's—choice was Governor Stevenson, of Illinois. It was uncanny and it was wonderful.

Still, there was more to it than the mechanics of television, and as I think back on the whole business, I'm sure that—as in the case of the Republican meeting—the important thing was one's sense of participation in matters that concern one deeply. Television, covering affairs of this sort, makes the viewer a member of a community vastly larger than his own without demanding that he sacrifice any of his individuality. It does not require him to judge, nor does it judge him—a nightmare envisioned by George Orwell and mercifully not in prospect. It simply makes it possible for a person, if he so chooses, to be present at, listen to, and watch an event that in the ordinary course of things he would have to depend on others to explain and interpret for him. In a sense, television coverage of a national convention turns the entire nation into a huge town meeting, which one can attend, ponder over, and depart from with one's opinions still one's own.

The Democrats in charge of the proceedings at Chicago made it known, both in the press and over the air, that they had observed the Republican Convention on television and that they wished to avoid some of the errors they felt the Republicans had made on it. For one thing, they said the Republicans had been wrong in not permitting a camera to face the speakers on the platform head on, which meant that there could be only profile shots of them. So a huge platform was erected directly in front of the speakers' rostrum, enabling us to see the orators full face. I don't think it made one bit of difference. The Democratic high command also announced that it was going to avoid the distracting effect—or what it considered the distracting effect during the Republican do—of people moving about behind and to the sides of the speakers, and consequently it went to great lengths to keep the floaters out of range of the cameras. I don't think that this made one bit of difference, either. Once the convention got under way, the people on the floor and on the platform became so interested in what they were doing or saying—so passionate and involved and alive—that the viewer at home ignored everything else on the screen. This was especially true when Governor Stevenson made his acceptance speech early Saturday morning. I even felt that the often stupefying pollings of individual delegates, which many people seem to have resented on the grounds that they held up the proceedings but which were, in truth, the proceedings themselves, were irresistible, being a manifestation of the right of every delegate—and, by extension, every citizen—to take a direct part in the choosing of his President.

Well, things have quieted down around our place; the little boarder, twice displaced during the past month, has reëstablished his beachhead in front of the tiny screen and has renewed his friendship with Howdy Doody and all the other causes he feels so deeply about. I don't think I'll try to explain to him just yet that his loss has been the country's gain.

Rotation Blues

———————

"See It Now," the Edward R. Murrow–Fred Friendly half-hour show on Sunday afternoons (C.B.S.), stretched itself to a full hour a week ago Sunday and came up with a film of the war in Korea, "This Is Korea, Christmas, 1952," which I think we can safely put down as one of the most impressive presentations in television's short life. I was as much moved by "This Is Korea"—and in the same curiously disturbing way— as I was a year ago Christmas by the tender sweetness of Menotti's television opera "Amahl and the Night Visitors." "Amahl" gave us a legend of the past as seen through the eyes of a child, and did so with great piety and understanding. Mr. Murrow and his associates went over to Korea and pictured for us a tragic living legend of our own time, and did so with great piety and understanding. They captured the heartbreak of Korea by the seemingly simple method of concentrating on individual human beings—their faces, their problems, the terrible places so far from home they find themselves in—and by so doing they reduced the Korean horror to its essential meaning: the outpost fight for the right of individual human beings to survive as individuals. While Mr. Murrow's method looks easy, I venture to say that nothing is more difficult, and that it would have been far simpler to slip into the accepted commentator-with-maps routine, pointing at a great many obscure Korean places with a long stick, issuing stentorian, full-blown phrases about liberty and truth, and interviewing innumerable members of the high brass. Mr. Murrow avoided all this, and the results were triumphant.

There was no chronology, thank heaven, to "This Is Korea." Scene after scene of soldiers in the cold, of soldiers at the front, of soldiers in the ruined cities unfolded with unhurried casualness. Some scenes stand out in my memory as almost inexpressibly stirring. For example, at one point Larry LeSueur (Mr. Murrow was assisted by a battalion of C.B.S. newsmen, all bundled to the ears) was talking in the snow with a French lieutenant. For some reason, Mr. LeSueur spoke in French, and the French lieutenant in English. Mr. LeSueur wondered what the officer thought about the war—how would it end, what was it all about, anyway? The lieutenant was a thoughtful and sensitive man. He had a lean, perceptive face. He took his time answering. He said he had been with the French battalion since November, 1950. He thought the war was a dreadful but necessary thing. He deplored the stalemate but saw clearly both the danger of extending the war and the danger of withdrawing from it. He was philosophically resigned to the fate that had set him down in that place at that time and for that purpose. "It's a good joke for the Russians," he said, quite sadly.

Mr. Murrow and his associates kept asking the same question— "What do you think of this war?"—wherever they went, and they received a variety of answers. Indeed, the haphazard multiplicity of views was perhaps the most eloquent, democratic tribute to the enterprise. A number of G.I.s did not have quite the clarity of expression of the French officer. Some of them felt we should push ahead to the Yalu, others just wanted to get the hell home, others thought the whole affair "nonsense," and still others knew exactly what they were doing in Korea and why. A British colonel, sticking his head out of a dugout and pointing north to snow-clad mountains and frozen paddy fields, spoke crisply of his military problems. The colonel had no illusions. He was in a war, all right. "It's a queer war," he said, almost as though he were speaking of something already in the history books. "We sleep by day. The real war begins at night." Mr. Murrow and his troupe never once tried to prod anyone into giving an answer that might sound proper or official. Soldiers, white and black, put their faces before the cameras and spoke unashamedly—"Thanks for the presents," or "Hello, Mom," or "Tell Dad I'll be coming back soon to help on the farm," or "I'll be home in ninety days," or "I wish it was over a long time ago," or "The food is good, considering," or "I'm from Denver, Colorado, and when you say that you better smile." Mr. Murrow waved no flags about the United Nations (in fact, I have the impression that the term itself was never used), but there was no doubt by the end of the hour that the Korean war is a United Nations venture. We had seen the Frenchman, we had seen the Englishman, we had watched Ethiopian troops play a strange form of hockey, and we had seen the Koreans—men in the R.O.K. regiments, women flying over enemy lines dropping propaganda leaflets, and children playing with American soldiers. We had seen, too, helicopters landing the wounded on hospital ships (there was one interview with a wounded soldier that I felt perhaps overstepped the line, since the man seemed to be in great pain), barrages being laid down, patrols going out on their deadly business, soldiers celebrating Christmas, nurses discussing casualties, jets taking off, mail being picked up for our prisoners of war by mechanical-looking men from North Korea (Mr. Murrow wondered whether the mail is ever delivered), and, always, the hard ground, the frightful mountains, and the snow.

I guess the high point of "This Is Korea" was a brief interlude in which Mr. Murrow turned his camera upon a group of G.I.s who were singing a ballad called the "Rotation Blues." I feel sorry for anyone who didn't hear it. We saw and heard the men singing, and once in a while the camera would show us a foot tapping away to the music. The words said everything they were supposed to say, and the tune was mighty mournful:

> I'm a lonely soldier sitting here in Korea,
> I'm a lonely soldier sitting here in Korea.
> With the rotation comin', what have I got to fear?
> I've got the rotation blues.
>
> This rain in Korea sure is cold and wet,
> This rain in Korea sure is cold and wet.
> These rotation papers are hard to get;
> I've got the ro-rotation blues.

The Human Comedy

Perhaps one of television's greatest contributions to art is its creation of a type of program we shall call, for lack of a better term, the Half-Hour Domestic-Comedy-Situation-Farce-Husband-and-Wife Playlet-Plotlet. I have no doubt that in the years to come, when the historians of television get down to the heartbreaking task of classifying early television programs, the Half-Hour Domestic-Comedy-Situation-Farce-Husband-and-Wife Playlet-Plotlet will be known by another name. Meanwhile, for the purpose of getting along with the thesis, we will abbreviate the term to HHDCSFHAWPP, or, even better, FHAWPP.

There are a number of Fhawpps on television these days, and they have several things in common. They involve, as their name suggests, a husband and wife who are ensnarled in some domestic situation, around which a thirty-minute playlet with a gimmick has been written. This analysis encompasses, of course, only the bare framework of a Fhawpp. Examined more closely, these programs reveal that both the husband and the wife, although living in passably decorated homes with large living rooms, large bedrooms, and all-electric kitchens, have mental ages that hover between eight and twelve. For another thing, the husband and wife in a Fhawpp have stepped, historically, from the comic strips, rather than from the farce of either stage or screen. Thus, although television marks a great advance in the technique of electronics, it has gone back, at least in Fhawpps, to that earlier means of communication, the newspaper. Small episodes within the half-hour span of a Fhawpp come and go with the rapidity of daily installments in the funnies; minor climaxes are reached every five or six minutes, just as minor climaxes are reached in the comics in every third or fourth frame; and by the close of a Fhawpp the audience has watched the equivalent of a whole week of funnies. Television has improved upon the comics somewhat by abandoning, for underlining climaxes or sub-climaxes, the use of the words "Zowie!," "Whaam!," and "Kerplunk!" Instead, in Fhawpp climaxes or sub-climaxes a character slaps a hand to his mouth, pops his eyes, and shakes his head in utter bewilderment. Variations consist of rubbing the chin, popping the eyes, and shaking the head; pursing the lips, popping the eyes, and shaking the head; and placing a finger in one ear and working it up and down, popping the eyes, and shaking the head. Otherwise, there is less difference between a comic strip and a Fhawpp than between your butter knives and your grandmother's.

Let us inspect in somewhat closer detail a specific Fhawpp, "I Married Joan" (Wednesdays, 8–8:30 P.M., N.B.C.). The first person singular of the title is Judge Bradley Stevens (judges are setups for leading roles in Fhawpps; they lend an easily punctured dignity to the proceedings, and they can tidy things up at will by calling upon the forces of law and order), who is married to Joan Stevens, a blond of the type known as "dizzy." Since her husband is the judge of what I take to be a criminal court in a small town, her particular brand of dizziness is especially embarrassing to him, and he is forever fearful that one of her empty-headed notions will cause him serious trouble. On "I Married Joan" the other night, we first saw the Judge and his wife at breakfast. Mrs. Stevens, who was reading the morning paper, announced that the Blond Bandit, a local criminal, was still at large. "She's struck again," said Mrs. Stevens. "What for?" asked the Judge. "Better pay?" Once the tone of the Stevens household has been thus established, the Judge sets out for work, carrying with him a suitcase he wants to have repaired. Mrs. Stevens, eying the suitcase, wonders whether he is giving her the heave-ho, and, to show interest in his work, asks his permission to visit his court that morning. The paragon of justice grants his consent.

We next see the Judge questioning a man suspected of breaking into a safe. The man is on the witness stand, he looks like a thug, his name is Rocky Slattery, and he answers no questions, merely grunting, "I stand on de Fift' Amendment." The Judge's wife is seated in the rear of the courtroom, alongside a blond young lady who turns out to be Mrs. Slattery. Later, when she and Mrs. Stevens go outside for a cup of coffee, she convinces the Judge's wife that poor Rocky is innocent. Mrs. Stevens takes Mrs. Slattery home for supper that evening. The entrance of the Judge into his house, his astonishment at encountering the wife of a man on trial in his court, his attempt to explain the ethics of the situation to the two ladies, and his harassed cry of "Well, let's eat!"—here was Fhawppery at its best! A rapid-fire sequence of events followed. Mrs. Stevens is certain that her husband is about to convict Rocky on circumstantial evidence alone. To prove that circumstantial evidence is not enough, she pretends to be the celebrated Blond Bandit. The Judge becomes aware of her plot and turns the tables on her in a manner that I simply do not have the strength to relate. At the close of the Fhawpp, the Judge and his wife are about to go to sleep. Placidity and an air of quiet domesticity have returned to the Stevens' house. Mrs. Stevens thinks that her little adventure has made her husband ponder circumstantial evidence more carefully than in the past. No, not at all, says the Judge. He looks pretty arch. Mrs. Stevens might like to know, he goes on, that Rocky confessed that morning, and that the Blond Bandit is none other than Mrs. Slattery. Mrs. Stevens slaps a hand to her mouth, pops her eyes, and shakes her head in utter bewilderment—a perfect ending to a perfect Fhawpp.

"They Haven't Killed Me Yet"

Last week, I held a Video Crime Festival at my house. Night after night, wearing a false mustache and with my hat pulled down over my forehead, I sat before the tiny screen and looked in on the criminal world. Anybody can do the same thing, week in, week out—it's a positive college education! One learns so much about crimes and criminals, about the habits of crooks and the way they live, about the sly ruses with which they attempt to defeat the stuffy old representatives of law and order. Altogether, it's certainly one of the great contributions that the television industry has made to twentieth-century living. Now that I look back upon the Festival, I realize a good deal of it is a blur in my mind, but some of the many programs I watched stand out, firm and defiant.

There was one, for example, about tong wars in Chinatown, which, although it was performed for thirty minutes in almost total darkness, did leave the viewer with a very real sense of how sinister an Oriental criminal can become when he settles down to his work. This one was called "They Haven't Killed Me Yet," and it dealt with a Chinese-American representative of the United States Treasury Department who, for civic reasons, decided to break up a local tong singlehanded. The tong was engaged in wholesale extortion of local business firms, and if a laundryman along Pell Street, say, decided to resist the tong, the hatchetmen would turn up and give him velly-velly. As I say, "They Haven't Killed Me Yet" was played practically in the dark. Shadowy figures crossed the screen, walking in and out of dirty, badly lighted places, but there was sufficient illumination at one point for me to make out, by squinting hard, a hatchet in the hands of one of the hatchetmen. It was the only hatchet I saw all week, and when the Festival was over, I gave the program third prize in the Special Effects Division.

"They Haven't Killed Me Yet" also captured second prize in the Dialogue Division, hands down, for the astonishing manner in which the tong chief spoke to his evil pals when the Treasury man was about to close in on the tong headquarters. The headquarters, or as much of it as I could see, was filled with Buddhas, incense burners, altars, back-scratchers, and other authentic Ming pieces, and the tong chief was clothed in a black linen nightie; he also wore a pigtail. "He is not a fool!" cried the chief, speaking of the Treasury man, one Gon Sam Mue. "He is not coming here to prove that he is without fear. He has a reason! Hide!"

A drama called "Last Chance" received second prize in the Romance Division, a fairly large classification when it comes to television crime stories, since so many of the safe-crackers, con men, sex maniacs, and hopheads who populate the tiny screen are at heart sweet and cuddly, as soft inside as bags of chicken fat. Have one of them pull a big job—a pay-roll robbery, for example—and make off with fifty Gs, and have him hide out in a room in a run-down boarding house (I am betraying no secrets when I say that this is the "plot" of "Last Chance") until Joey, or Louie, or Slopsie finds him a boat to South America, and put him on the roof with the landlady's suicidal daughter, and he goes all squashy and senti-mental. There, under the stars, with every blackhearted dick in town hot on his trail, he talks of love and life, of bees and flowers, and finally, true-blue criminal that he is, he turns himself in to the cops. A clear second prize; hardly any competition.

I awarded the Grand Prix, all weights, all classes, to one of those televi-sion crime stories that depict life inside the big house, or big houses, and show us how those who are paying their debt to society for their misdeeds live. You can find an example of this sort of story at least a dozen times a week, and sometimes three or four times a night. I have the feeling that the same set is used in all of them—a row of cells on one side, a corridor down the center, a door on the other side leading to either the dispensary or freedom, and another door leading to the warden's office, where the warden, sharp-eyed, weary, aware of every trick in the criminals' repertoire, sits and thinks and sighs. On hand, too, is a sloppy-looking guard, who slouches up and down the corridors and looks as though he couldn't keep goldfish in a bowl, much less seasoned criminals in their cells. Throw all these things together, add a bit of ominous electric-guitar or electric-organ music, and you have the makings of a Grand Prix winner. The particular champion I have in mind was called "Cage a Killer," and it will suffice to say that the killer of the title was a long-term server who, about to be released from prison, suddenly found himself faced with a murder charge in another state, one that practiced capital punishment; it seems that he had chopped up his wife, Alma, there some years before and buried the pieces near a motel. Now, his clever brain teeming with ideas of how he could escape the death rap, he turned upon his cellmate, a mute with whom he had cheerily roomed for three years, and strangled him to death, since murder in the state where "Cage a Killer" took place carried no death penalty. The sheer poetry of the grunts and groans, the shrieks and screams, the animal noises and bestial attitudes of the murderer, combined with the setting and the incidental music, made "Cage a Killer" something more than a natural winner. Indeed, it was one of those programs I should think the television authorities would run soon again, perhaps some Saturday morning, at a Junior Crime Festival.

What Hath Ford Wrought?

"King Lear," a drama of deceit, disappointment, and insanity, is, even in the best of hands, an almost insurmountable theatrical assignment. In "Lear," Shakespeare really let himself go. He reached for, and attained, a frightening pitch of eloquent despair, and in so doing he rendered it practically impossible for all but the most talented actors, actresses, and directors to deal with "Lear" without making idiots of themselves. The role of Lear himself, it seems to me, would be assumed only by an actor who either possesses a self-confidence that passeth understanding or has actually taken leave of his senses. Since Lear goes absolutely cuckoo in a special way, the actor who portrays him is forced into an inescapable test of his abilities. He either rises to the terrible occasion and becomes a tragic, doomed, and noble figure, or he slips over the edge into that dreadful abyss of comedy (of the Martin and Lewis variety) in which the aberrations of the ailing are considered funny. Mr. Orson Welles, who has most certainly not taken leave of his senses, assumed the role of Lear a week ago Sunday in a Ford Foundation "Omnibus" presentation, and for the better part of an hour and a half he wrestled with it unsuccessfully.

Facially, Mr. Welles resembled a man who has been hauled off a park bench and hastily pressed into emergency service as a department-store Santa Claus. His beard never seemed to work quite right, and was especially uncertain when he talked; his mustache had a curiously temporary and flighty air about it; and his wig, wild and woolly, struck me as extremely comic. His costumes were of the sort that children round up on rainy afternoons for impromptu shows in the nursery—an old sheet here, a lampshade there, something from Mother's closet, and so on. As a result, just looking at Lear started a smile, and that is fatal. When Lear began to talk, matters got even more confusing. Part of Mr. Welles' difficulty with his diction unquestionably arose from the hairy encumbrances he was hidden behind; Jove himself could not thunder forth clearly were he so burdened. But Mr. Welles' difficulty also had another source—one entirely distinct from his grotesque makeup. He apparently has the notion that if he starts a sentence far enough down in his stomach and sends it rumbling up through his system in ever-increasing volume until it reaches his larynx and heads for the open road, it will take on an impressive, tragic ring. He employed this method for all his lines, and in consequence Lear's longest, loneliest, and deepest thoughts emerged with the same echoing timbre as his cry of "Dinner! Dinner! I want my dinner!" Some of the lines never reached freedom at all; they died somewhere in Mr. Welles' vast frame and were transformed into grunts and bellows—mournful half cries signifying nothing, or nothing much. Mr. Welles was clear as a giant carillon in many of his shorter phrases, such as "Sirrah!" and "Whoa, boy, whoa!," and in his plaintive cry of "Where's my Fool? I haven't seen my Fool in two days!"

Speaking of the Fool brings us to other members of the cast. There was a Fool in the "Omnibus" version, all right, such a Fool as even Beerbohm never dreamed of in his most cynical consideration of Shakespeare. He wore a Fool's suit and carried a Fool's foolish little stick with bells on the end, and he acted foolish—entirely too foolish. Most of the time he was completely unintelligible, and when he occasionally quieted down and took a grip on himself, the most I got from him were lines like "Give me an egg." On hand, too, was the usual assortment of Dukes (Cornwall, Burgundy, and Albany), and Earls (Kent and Gloucester), as well as another King (France), but they were engaged in a private charade. In fact, a good deal of this "King Lear" was intramural—a colloquy between an actor and his colleagues with little or no regard for the audience. The ladies of the cast fared better. Beatrice Straight, as Goneril (bad daughter); Margaret Phillips, as Regan (bad daughter); and Natasha Parry, as Cordelia (good daughter) were handsome, intelligent, and clear-spoken.

Mr. Peter Brook, whose reputation seems to be boundless in his native England, was especially imported to direct the proceedings.

Before the play started, Mr. Alistair Cooke, the permanent "Omnibus" interlocutor, informed us that Mr. Brook had also edited it and chucked out the subplots. Mr. Brook has some unusual ideas about directing a television drama. For one thing, he doesn't appear to believe in visual clarity, and he managed to obfuscate or distort the faces and figures of many of his characters. Quite a few of his scenes revealed one character in clear focus and a host of other characters standing around mumbling and completely out of focus. I have no doubt that all of Mr. Brook's groupings were designed with an eye to some higher art, but it is an art that escapes me. For another thing, Mr. Brook enjoys stirring up a lot of motion and noise in his scenes—people leaping over tables or scuttling under them with no special object in view. At one point, I felt certain that a bat had got loose on the set, sending the Dukes and Kings flying every which way, but it was just our friend Brook riling up the cast. Toward the end, he turned on a variety of wind and rain machines that almost drove poor Lear off the screen, whipping his facial gear into a shambles and making him look more miserable than Shakespeare could possibly have intended. At the very end, when the untidy affairs of all concerned were presumably being tidied up, the production got entirely out of hand and lapsed into gibberish.

"Omnibus" does not have "sponsors;" it has what it chooses to refer to as "subscribers." The subscribers consented to hold their peace during the show, delivering their pitches fore and aft. Mr. Cooke paid special tribute to their self-sacrifice.

Crisp! Crisp! Deep! Deep!

A young man going on seven who boards at my place telephoned me the other day at the office and invited me to come home that evening promptly at six to watch "Superman" with him. He said, in one of his rare moments of generosity, that he wanted to share the program with me. Normally, I can no more break into our television room between five-thirty and six-thirty than I can watch the Duke of Edinburgh shaving, and, touched and honored, I rushed home at the appointed hour. All was in readiness for the great event. A two-year-old, who also boards with us, had likewise received the nod from the big boy, and he was on hand, in a maroon dressing gown and holding a cup of cocoa. "This program is wonderful," said the big boy. "Superman flies into space every Monday. Wait till you see." He twirled the dials with a professional hand to adjust both sight and sound. "Quiet, please!" he called out. "Super-MAN!"

"Superman" opened with a shot of Superman himself, clad in a handsome pair of long drawers and a sweatshirt bearing a large "S." He was a lithe and muscular figure, the prototype of what all good little boys who eat their cereal and don't ruin their eyes watching "Superman" can look forward to being. "He has changed the course of mighty men," intoned an announcer. "He fights a never-ending battle for the truth. . . . Crisp, crisp, crisp, with a deep, deep flavor." We saw a picture of a boy munching breakfast food. "W. K. Kellogg himself thought up the flavor," said the announcer. "Crisp! Crisp! Deep! Deep! Kellogg—the greatest name in cereal!" The commercial behind us, at least for the moment, the title of the evening's episode was flashed onto the screen—"Panic in the Sky." We saw a group of citizens gazing with evident fear into the heavens. A butcher standing in front of Dick's Meat Market turned to a lady beside him and remarked, "It's just a meteor, that's all." There was a buzz among the citizens. Panic was in the air as well as in the sky. We next saw and heard the hard-bitten city editor of the *Planet*. He was telling one of his reporters, Clark Kent, about the phenomenon. (As every man, woman, and child must know by now, Kent's secret is that he is Superman; he gains his strength by removing his glasses, which he requires for his daily tasks on earth, such as typing and crossing streets.) "An asteroid is what the scientists are calling it," said the city editor. "It goes wild all over the solar system. It's five miles and a quarter in diameter."

The scene shifted to an observatory on top of a hill. A man who looked very much like Sigmund Freud was peering into a huge telescope. He seemed extremely agitated. "Superman!" he called out. "Right over here, Professor!" cried a voice. "I'm just looking at it." Sure enough, there was Kent-Superman, long drawers and all, standing on a parapet hard by the telescope, his eye cocked toward the asteroid. Superman calmly allowed that, given the chance, he could knock the asteroid off its course and save the world. "Watch him!" said the elder boarder. "Here he goes!" Off into space went Superman, zooming gracefully and with the greatest of ease—up, up, up, into outer space. "It may cost the world Superman," said Professor Freud dolefully, from below. "Oh, no!" said the big boy. The younger boarder spilled his cocoa. Straight into the asteroid went Superman. There was a mighty crash and a spray of sparks, and the asteroid was deflected from its path. "He did it!" cried Professor Freud.

A moment later, we saw Superman land on a desert somewhere on Earth. He ducked behind a rock and put street clothes on over his telltale longies, emerging a moment later wearing glasses—just another civilian in a desert. A young lady came along in a truck, stopped, and gave him a lift. "Hear the news?" she said. "Superman done it." "Did what?" asked Kent. "Fixed the asteroid," she said. "Superman done it." Kent returned to his home in a state of near collapse. All he wanted now was a little shut-eye, but an agent of the city editor turned up. He asked Kent to find Superman, who, alas, was missing. Kent fainted in the shower and fell through the shower glass, but, strangely, was not cut. A commercial followed.

When the scenario resumed, there was chaos in the offices of the *Planet.* The asteroid was acting up again and behaving like its old perverse self. Superman had done a fine job, but apparently only a temporary one. Word had come that North Africa was suffering the worst tidal wave in its history. Earth was in for heavy weather. Back in the *Planet* office, the city editor's agent reported that Kent was sick. The city editor said that he wanted Kent, sick or well, he being the only man who had ever been able to get in touch with Superman. At his home, Kent struggled to regain his strength, groped his way to his closet, and selected a fresh sweatshirt from the dozen or more hanging there, all marked "S." Suddenly, we saw Kent, back in his longies, flexing his muscles in front of a mirror. He removed his glasses, put a fist through a table, splitting it like kindling, and took a dive out the window, headed for the observatory. One can imagine how glad Professor Freud was to see him again. The Professor handed him a small box and told him to make for the asteroid, and fast. "Throw the first switch when you land," said Freud. "Five seconds later, throw the main switch. The atomic-energy people think the asteroid can destroy Earth." Off went Superman into space, one arm extended straight ahead, the other clutching the box. "Doesn't he have any pockets?" asked the big boy. Superman made the asteroid, pulled the switches, blew the damn thing up, headed for Earth, and landed safely. Seconds later, there was old four-eyes, in civvies, back home eating Sugar Smacks. His city editor burst into the room, interrupting his breakfast. "News can't wait, Kent," he said. "Not even for Sugar Smacks." Kent told him that he was all wrong—that, indeed, Sugar Smacks *were* the news. The lovable city editor promptly sat down and dug into the Sugar Smacks. The episode closed on this touching domestic scene.

Hedda Get Your Gun!

The first time I saw "Hedda Gabler," Nazimova played Hedda, and, believe me, it was a wonderful experience, especially for a growing boy with vine leaves in his hair. Nazimova *was* Hedda, every last, deep, devious, frustrated particle of her. There is now a short pause for the passage of years, in the course of which I went back from time to time to what, in these days, one is forced to call "the original," and read and reread the play. An extremely impressive drama, no matter how you look at it. Then, a week or so ago, Hedda reëntered my life, and presumably the lives of millions of other video owners, when Miss Tallulah Bankhead took the plunge and played the role on "The United States Steel Hour." Poor public, poor Tallulah, poor, poor Henrik Ibsen! "Hedda Gabler" is a four-act play of standard length, but the steel authorities apparently decided that, like steel ingots, it could be cut down to size. The size they favored was an hour, with several commercial interruptions to demonstrate the massive power of a large steel mill and the wonderment of pouring molten steel from one hideous bucket into another.

The adaptation of "Hedda Gabler" was the work of a man called Erik Barnouw, who had, I guess, dipped into Ibsen's play before attempting his own curious version but, as far as I could make out, had almost entirely missed its point. The version that unfolded before us the other evening was distinguished by a lack of integrity and by a persistent attempt to turn Ibsen's thoughts topsy-turvy. I daresay that when Ibsen drew Hedda he did not intend to portray a character who performed evil actions joyously and without cause, much as some mad killer might march down a street and murder the first stranger who happened to come along. There were reasons for everything Hedda did, and even if she was not aware of them, by God, Ibsen was. Not so Barnouw, or Bankhead. By the time Barnouw got through with Ibsen, there wasn't much for Miss Bankhead to play with, but she took the little bit left and managed to compound the felony. She seemed to have the idea that Hedda was the sort of girl the celebrated Miss Mae West once delighted in interpreting—all waving hips, bouncing framework, and ninety-proof larynx. Now and then, Miss Bankhead abandoned the Westian interpretation and noisily shifted gears, emerging as a pallid imitation of Miss Ethel Merman in the role of Annie Oakley. The Mermanesque moments were most evident when Hedda went over to the old pistol box left her by her daddy, General Gabler, toyed with the antique firearm, and engaged in target practice. All in all, it was a messy, shrill, and meaningless hour, and only Luther Adler, as the sinister Judge Brack, gave the impression of understanding his role.

One of America's folk heroes, Bing Crosby, turned up on the tiny screen the other night in a half-hour show of his own, called, of all things, "The Bing Crosby Show." Mr. Crosby, it seems, has been quite shy about television, and has been biding his time, studying the medium and selling frozen orange juice. His program was an absurdity from start to finish— stiff, formal, humorless, and badly lighted. The great crooner appeared to be ill at ease, and his attempts to seem nonchalant and devil-may-care made me, for one, embarrassed and apprehensive. In a sense, the Crosby program was a throwback to the early days of radio—and the later days, too—when an old familiar favorite would introduce his act with a few private, sneering references to other radio favorites, sing a few songs, bring on a guest celebrity, go off the air, and head for home. The guest celebrity the other evening was Jack Benny. He indulged in several slick, homogenized jokes, and, in turn, introduced a torrid young woman, Miss Sheree North, who did an uninhibited dance that was not designed, I should think, for teen-age viewers. Miss North was an intriguing bundle of bumps and grinds, but her incendiary performance was something of an incongruity, set down, as it was, between the studiously antiseptic songs of Mr. Crosby.

Man from Indiana

There isn't a great deal to be said for most of the news commentators who appear on television. As a matter of fact, it is hard to tell one from another. I have the feeling that they have attended some sort of secret academy, which turns them out, perfectly appointed and almost identical, like motorcars rolling from the assembly line. Around the walls of a classroom in this academy, as I picture it, are dozens of clocks—clocks showing what time it is in Paris, London, Tokyo, Moscow, Des Moines, Butte, Shanghai, the Virgin Islands, and so on. If a fledgling commentator at the school cannot tell his professor instantly, and with his eyes shut, what time it is in, say, Azerbaijan, he flunks the course. This classroom is also filled with full-length mirrors, and the candidate commentators spend a good part of their academic day standing in front of the mirrors and preening themselves. They are taught to shoot their cuffs in a convincingly authoritative manner. An inordinate amount of time, too, is consumed tying their four-in-hands, which, according to the unflinching standards of the academy, must have enormous bulbous knots. Voice study is compulsory, of course, and the professors tell the students again and again that they must pitch their voices at the level referred to in their circles as "cold hysteria." The words "Berlin conference," they are told, must be delivered with precisely the same sense of doom, the same pulsating sense of import, as the words "Butter is down." They are taught to look the camera in the eye—indeed, to stare it into insensibility. And, finally, a day or two before they receive their gold-embossed diplomas, they are told that if they should ever want some news to talk about, they can get it from machines called "tickers."

All of which brings us to Elmer Davis, who, praise the Lord, is appearing each Sunday over A.B.C. to present a commentary on the news of the week. Mr. Davis breaks all the rules of the academy, and his program is triumphant. For one thing, he wears a bow tie; for another, he never shoots his cuffs. He looks at the camera only when he feels like looking at the camera, and that isn't often. There is no hysteria in his voice, either hot or cold—just the steady tone of a steady man from Indiana. However, Mr. Davis's major heresy is the fact that he has something to say each week—something important—and says it courageously, analytically, and brilliantly. His scripts are masterpieces. I know of no one who can compress so much news and so much clear and reasoned opinion into fifteen fleeting minutes. Mr. Davis understands the relative value of the various pieces of news that come to him; thanks to a lifetime devoted to the spreading of honest information, he can separate the peaks from the valleys. His scripts are also distillations of a lifetime of experience that has given him the courage to speak out in favor of what he thinks is good and true, and against what he thinks is foul and dirty, in the America he loves so much. The number of topics touched upon by Mr. Davis can be somewhat staggering. A week ago, for instance, he paid a brief, moving tribute to his good friend Frederick Lewis Allen, who "did a great deal to help people understand what is going on and what has been going on for the past fifty years;" he discussed the current campaign of the yahoo branch of the Republican Party to brand as atheist, sadist, traitor, or second-story man everyone who votes, or has voted, other than Republican; he talked awhile about the twenty-two hundred "security risks" dismissed by the present administration; and he said a few words about the Berlin conference, Germany, Austria, the French National Assembly, Communist tactics of deceit all over the world, Indo-China, Syngman Rhee, and the Chinese Communists. He slipped from one topic to another almost before the listener was aware of it.

Mr. Davis does not just read out bulletins. He has thought, and thought again, about every bit of information he is passing along, and he couches his thoughts in a style that is lean and strong. Since there can be no substitute for the genuine article, here are a few samples from last week's broadcast.

On the matter of five hundred and thirty-four "security risks" in the State Department:

Scott McLeod, Security Officer of the State Department, the great cleaner-outer, admitted that of the five hundred and thirty-four, only eleven were classified as loyalty risks, and action against seven of these had been started in the Acheson days. So the story that this administration has cleaned out the subversives whom past administrations had let into the State Department turned out to be a little more than ninety-nine and four-fifths per cent wrong. To be sure, Mr. McLeod has since said that there were not five hundred and thirty-four; there were only three hundred. So his story is only ninety-eight and two-thirds per cent wrong, but that's still pretty wrong.

On Speaker Martin's belief that what happens in the elections this year will greatly affect the future of religion:

Under the Democrats, what [Mr. Martin] called evil disbelievers . . . achieved some of the most powerful positions in our government. The conclusion, of course, [is] that if you believe in God and believe in America you must vote Republican this fall.

On Indo-China:

It would . . . be a great tragedy . . . if the Communists got possession of Indo-China. Before long, they would have all southeast Asia, and it seems doubtful if even India could last long after that. I have no idea what is the right thing for the United States government to do in a situation like this. Indeed, it may be one of those not uncommon military and political situations, like that in China a few years ago, where there's no right thing to do. China went Communist, and most of the opposition party in the United States promptly declared that this was not because there was no right thing to do, it was not even because we made mistakes, it was because of treason. It can be devoutly hoped the Democrats, now that they are in opposition, will have more patriotism and more sense than that.

Incidentally, Mr. Davis's program is unsponsored.

Man from Wisconsin

After his interrogation by Senator Joseph R. McCarthy a few weeks ago, General Ralph Zwicker, the commandant of Camp Kilmer, turned to his aides, according to the papers, and remarked, "Boys, now you've had an education." I felt the same way the other night after watching Edward R. Murrow's half-hour report on the Senator, over his weekly "See It Now" program, sponsored by the Aluminum Company of America (C.B.S., 10:30–11 P.M. on Tuesdays). Mr. Murrow brought off an extraordinary feat of journalism by the simple expedient of compiling a pictorial history of the Senator, complete with sound track, that showed him as he has performed in a variety of places and under a variety of circumstances during the past few years. Mr. Murrow let the Senator do most, but not all, of the work. We saw McCarthy speaking in Milwaukee, we saw him speaking in Philadelphia, we watched him conduct an investigation of the Voice of America, we heard a tape recording of a speech he delivered in Charleston, West Virginia, and we watched some of his operations during the 1952 Presidential campaign. We also got a pretty good look at the fellow—the best that I, for one, have ever got. To begin with, he's a big man, with big hands and a large head. Most of the time, he has a petulant, droop-jaw expression, as though, at the very instant he was all set to challenge everybody in the place to step outside, he was convinced that everybody in the place was about to jump him. He has a soft, almost silky, droning voice, which he tries somewhat too obviously to control. His laugh is frightening. He uses his hands a great deal for emphasis. While interrogating a witness, he gives the impression that all light, all truth, and all honesty belong at the moment to him alone, but then destroys the impression by appearing, curiously and unexpectedly, to be uncertain of his next move.

Mr. Murrow's intent was to pick the Senator up in a series of contradictions. He quoted the Senator as having declared in Milwaukee seventeen months ago, "If this fight against Communism is made a fight between America's two great political parties, the American people know that one of those parties will be destroyed, and the Republic cannot endure very long as a one-party system." He then let us hear the remarks of the Senator in Charleston on February 4th of this year: "The issue between the Republicans and Democrats is clearly drawn. It has been deliberately drawn by those who have been in charge of twenty years of treason. The hard fact is that those who wear the label 'Democrat' wear it with the stain of a historic betrayal." We saw the Senator in many moods—arrogant, aroused, fierce, and humble. To depict this last mood, Murrow threw a shot on the screen of a political dinner somewhere. An elderly gentleman at the speaker's table who was introducing the Senator became almost overwhelmed with emotion. He said he could not express what was in his heart, and he reached across the table and plucked some flowers from a floral arrangement, remarking:

> "Ah, 'tis but a dainty flower I bring you,
> Yes, 'tis but a violet, glistening with dew,
> But still in its heart there lie beauties concealed.
> So in our heart our love for you lies unrevealed."

McCarthy arose, gulping, and said, "You know, I used to pride myself on the idea that I was a bit tough, especially over the past eighteen or nineteen months, when we have been kicked around and bullwhipped and damned. I didn't think that I could be touched very deeply. But tonight, frankly, my cup and my heart are so full I can't talk to you." And he turned away, almost in tears.

Throughout the program, Mr. Murrow quietly added comments of his own. He made no attempt to hide his strong feelings of distaste and shock at the methods and language of the Senator. Murrow is, of course, a master of pictorial presentation and rarely forgets that television is designed for the eye as well as the ear. His most effective use of pictorial technique, it seemed to me, came in his discussion of the Senator's charge that "extreme Left Wing elements of press and radio" were attacking his committee over the Zwicker affair. Mr. Murrow had before him two stacks of newspapers, and, pointing to one, he said, "Of the fifty large-circulation newspapers in the country, these are the Left Wing papers that criticized." Then, pointing to the other, he said, "These are the ones that supported him. The ratio is about three to one against the Senator. Now let us look at some of these Left Wing papers that criticized the Senator." Thereupon he read editorial excerpts from the Chicago *Tribune*, the New York *Times*, the Washington *Times-Herald*, the New York *Herald Tribune*, the Washington *Star*, the Milwaukee *Journal*, the *World-Telegram & Sun*, and others.

Just before the conclusion of his program, Mr. Murrow fixed the audience with an almost glassy stare and read, solemnly and deliberately, an editorial he had composed for the occasion. I thought that he was especially impressive when he remarked, "This is no time for men who oppose Senator McCarthy's methods to keep silent, or for those who approve. We can deny our heritage and our history, but we cannot escape responsibility for the result. There is no way for a citizen of a republic to abdicate his responsibilities. . . . The actions of the Junior Senator from Wisconsin have caused alarm and dismay amongst our allies abroad and given considerable comfort to our enemies, and whose fault is that? Not really his; he didn't create this situation of fear, he merely exploited it, and rather successfully. Cassius was right: 'The fault, dear Brutus, is not in our stars, but in ourselves. . . .' Good night, and good luck."

The Chromatic Family

A friend of mine who owns a color-television set went out of town for a couple of weeks recently and left me the key to his apartment. "Use the set any time you want, old man. There's plenty of beer in the icebox," he said, just before leaving. "You may have a bit of trouble with the Convergence dial, and some of the purples run to green, but if worst comes to worst, you can always switch to black-and-white." A week ago Wednesday night, just before ten, I went over to his place to try to catch the C.B.S. color production of George S. Kaufman's and Edna Ferber's "The Royal Family," starring Helen Hayes, Claudette Colbert, Charles Coburn, and Fredric March. I had no trouble finding my friend's set. It's *big* (I had the impression that it was several stories high), resembling an upended trailer. I opened the doors of the cabinet and faced a terrifying array of dials—Tuning, Contrast, Chroma, Color, Background, V Hold, H Hold, Convergence, and Focus. Promptly at ten, I turned on the set, twisted Color, and waited. In came the first act of "The Royal Family," in blue—a lovely, dark, rich, midnight blue. I could see a butler wearing a short dark-blue jacket, and a maid wearing a blue uniform. The maid was fussing over a vase, arranging some blue roses. Charles Coburn appeared, blue as the Mediterranean. I crouched on the floor (several of the dials are on the lower part of the set) and turned Convergence. Mr. Coburn became a bright magenta—so bright, in fact, that I was afraid he was suffering some sort of stroke. I turned Chroma, and Coburn turned green. The roses turned green, too. Claudette Colbert showed up, in purple. Helen Hayes, who was playing the role of Fanny

Cavendish (the Grand Old Lady of the American Stage), hobbled down a staircase. She was dead white, with blue around the edges, except for the tip of her nose, which was yellow. The roses were now yellow. I turned Background, and Coburn went white as a sheet, while Miss Hayes blossomed forth with a case of measles. Fredric March entered, wearing a stunning green raccoon coat. At last, by turning Contrast, Chroma, Convergence, Focus, and Background in furious succession, I began to perceive a semblance of rational color—roses were red, violets were blue, Kaufman was funny, and Ferber, too.

"The Royal Family" is still a wonderfully witty play, and the antics of the Cavendish family are still something wonderful to behold. There were moments during the hour-long show when I felt that the director, Paul Nickell, permitted his charges to get out of hand and race across the tiny screen with too much velocity. It is one thing to portray a mad family on a big, broad stage, and another thing for the family to run around a limited enclosure. By and large, though, the production was successful, and the splendid cast performed with spirit and talent. It seemed to me that Miss Colbert, as Julia Cavendish (a reigning queen of the stage, and daughter of Fanny, the Grand Old Lady), took the honors the other evening, but Mr. March and Mr. Coburn were close runners-up. Miss Hayes, I am afraid, is not entirely suited to the role of Fanny Cavendish, but I cannot be at all certain whether I was disturbed by the thinness of her acting or by the constantly varying tints in which she appeared on the screen. It seems a long time—in fact, it *is* a long time—since "The Royal Family" opened, during the Christmas season of 1927, but the humor of Mr. Kaufman and Miss Ferber has survived a depression, a big hot war, and a long cold one, and is still glistening and bright, and something to treasure.

Dr. Oppenheimer

Mr. Edward R. Murrow, who has a passion for doing fine things on television, came along on his "See It Now" program (C.B.S.) last week with one of his finest things. His idea was basically so simple that it made one wonder why other members of the broadcasting fraternity hadn't beat him to it. It was to permit Dr. J. Robert Oppenheimer, the Director of the Institute for Advanced Study, at Princeton, to speak his mind for half an hour on a variety of topics, with Mr. Murrow remaining unobtrusively in the background, and only occasionally steering him into a particular channel of thought. When it was all over, I must confess, I was overwhelmed by the beauty and candor of the program, by the beauty and candor of the principal speaker, and by the courage of Mr. Murrow in pushing ahead with his project and seeing it through. To get right down to it, Mr. Murrow seems to have more courage—or, to use the midtown term, guts—than many of his brethren, and that alone may be the explanation of why he interviewed Dr. Oppenheimer before anybody else did. In any event, the half hour was thoroughly engrossing—even hypnotic—and it will be a long time before I forget it. For one thing, there was the office of Dr. Oppenheimer—the crammed bookcases, the desk littered with stacked papers, manuscripts, and books, the blackboard scrawled with the mysterious beckoning symbols of higher physics. For another, there was Mr. Murrow—quiet, smiling, an intelligent observer, and possessed of an obvious pride in the man he was interviewing—and, I hope, in himself. And, of course, there was Dr. Oppenheimer, a true study, I should think, in genius—tense, dedicated, deeper than deep, somewhat haunted, uncertain, calm, confident, and full, full, full of knowledge, not only of particles and things but of men and motives, and the basic humanity that may be the only savior we have in this strange world he and his colleagues have discovered.

Dr. Oppenheimer is a thin man, with crew-cut gray hair. He sat at his desk and smoked his pipe ferociously. It kept going out, and he kept lighting it, with fierce, sharp movements. Once, he rose, as if on a sudden impulse, and, moving over to the hieroglyphic-covered blackboard, discoursed on something that was clearly of the utmost aesthetic and intellectual importance to him and meant absolutely nothing to me. In short, he was himself at all times, and he had a great many things to say that bear repeating. Mr. Murrow wondered about the Institute itself—what it is like, and so on. Dr. Oppenheimer was charmed by the query. It was plain that he loves the Institute and what it stands for. There are no phones ringing, he said, and the people on the staff don't go to committee meetings. This lack of interruption, he maintained, is a great handicap for many people—they count on being interrupted, "in order to live." "Failure is, of course, I guess, an inevitable condition of success," he went on. "So they're used to having to attend to other people's business. When they get here, there is nothing of that, and they can't run away." He said that the purpose of the Institute is "to help men who are creative and deep and active and struggling scholars and scientists to get the job done that it is their destiny to do," and added, "This is a big order, and we take a corner of it. We do the best we can. The kind of intimacy, the kind of understanding, the kind of comradeship that is possible in a place of this size is hard to maintain in a place ten times as big."

And what sort of men work at the Institute? Dr. Oppenheimer's eyes became even more alive and burning, and he seemed excited beyond measure at the thought of the people he was associated with. There were the pure mathematicians—Hassler Whitney, for instance, whose field is topology, a study of relationships that deals with shape and arrangement, rather than measurements and size. There was Jean Piaget, who investigates the way children learn to think and "how they learn notions of cause, notions of time, notions of number—all the things Kant thought you were born with. But you are not born with them." There was Marston Morse—"I hate to say it, he is almost a statesman of mathematics." And Deane Montgomery, "who solved a famous problem of Riemann—which I'm not going to define—and astonished us all a few years ago." And a Dutchman, Abraham Pais, and an Englishman, Freeman Dyson, who "in quite different ways are struggling with the problems that interest me." And many more— Einstein ("one of the most lovable of men"), Bohr ("we have with him an arrangement which we reserve for our best friends"), and Panofsky. Is there reluctance on the part of scientists to work for the government? "No. I don't think so." But work for the government implies applied science, Dr. Oppenheimer said, and if every scientist devoted himself to applied science, "it would be terrible for us." He felt that all people, including scientists, enjoyed being called upon for advice. "I suppose that when the government behaves badly in a field you are working close to, and when decisions that look cowardly or vindictive or shortsighted or mean are made very close to your area, then you get discouraged, and you may—may—recite George Herbert's poem 'I Will Abroad.' But I think that's human rather than scientific." The impediments placed in the way of travel and free exchange of information among scientists? "This is terrible. This is just terrible, and seems a wholly fantastic and grotesque way to meet the threat of espionage. Just an enormous apparatus, surely not well designed for that, and terrible for those of us who live with it." Have we discovered a method of destroying humanity? "I suppose that really has always been true. You could always beat everybody to death. You mean, to do it by inadvertence? Not quite, not quite. You can certainly destroy enough of humanity so that only the greatest act of faith can persuade you that what's left will be human." A few more remarks: "It isn't the layman that's ignorant. It's everybody that's ignorant. . . . The trouble with secrecy isn't that it inhibits science; it could, but in this country it's hardly been used that way. The trouble with secrecy is that it denies to the government itself the wisdom and the resources of the whole community, of the whole country. The only thing you can do is to let almost anyone say what he thinks, to try to give the best synopses, the best popularizations, and to let men deny what they think is false, argue [against] what they think is false, have a free and uncorrupted communication. . . . There aren't secrets about the world of nature. There are secrets about the thoughts and intentions of men."

And there were a great many other notable things said by Dr. Oppenheimer, who is, incidentally, a security risk.

GAZETTEERS

After six years of writing a television column every two weeks, I wearied of the task and proposed to Mr. Shawn that it was time to leave the house (and the set) and travel around the United States. From 1959 to 1965, I visited some fifty-eight cities, writing pieces which appeared periodically under the rubric Notes for a Gazetteer. They particularly caught the eye of Alfred A. Knopf, who suggested that I collect a number of them, which he published as *An American Notebook*. In the Author's Note to that book, I wrote: ". . . from one chapter to the next, the reader can crisscross this vast, elusive, funny country. I crisscrossed the country a good deal myself, casting a highly personal eye on towns, some small and some large, but mostly medium-sized. I wanted to see what this country looked like, to capture the essence of wherever I happened to be, and I had no preconceived notions. Sometimes I would close my eyes, jab a finger at a map, open my eyes, say 'That's the place for me,' and take off. Often, I went to places I had long looked forward to visiting. Many times, I didn't know why I went where I went. . . . I walked around many American towns, breathed the local air and talked with many people, and I found each place more foreign than the last, and no two places the same—never the same realities or the same dreams or the same yesterdays or the same todays. How could it be otherwise?"

Bismarck, N.D.

Alt., 1,670. Pop., 27,670. The people of Bismarck are fond of saying that when it doesn't rain out their way it doesn't rain harder than it doesn't any other place in the United States. "Son," a Bismarck resident recently told a visitor, "our dry spells can best be described as torrential." Nobody thinks there is anything remotely funny about the weather in North Dakota, but people manage to stick barely this side of despair by almost continuously joking about it. "The jokes help," a local farmer said not long ago, "but not much." During a summer drought, when the land appears to shrivel up, and when everything on it seems to be either dead or dying, it is standard practice to scan the skies, especially the northern ones, wet one's finger, and keep a weather eye out for rain. Ironically, rain seems daily to be on the way. During the late afternoons, giant sheets of thick, ugly black clouds, miles wide and miles high, fill the skies. Sometimes they turn into brief, section-line rains, but more often they don't. People will stop each other on the streets of Bismarck, point at the dark curtain of cloud, shake their heads, make a few quiet remarks, smile ruefully, and pass on. "I've stood in downtown Bismarck during many a drought, for many a year, and watched these good folk looking at those afternoon clouds," a Bismarck man has said. "Over the years, people have a tendency to say pretty much the same things. They'll say, 'Well, here comes the rain again, but by the time it gets here it won't be wet.' Or they'll say, 'Here comes the rain again. It'll be the biggest dry rain in history.' Or they'll say, 'Our rain is fifty per cent moisture,' or 'Maybe we'll get a two-inch rain. Two inches between drops.' "

One cannot talk about the weather all the time, even in Bismarck. Fortunately, Bismarck has a conversational ace in the hole: General George A. Custer. General Custer's connection with Bismarck is a tenuous one, but as a talking point he is a life raft. One can always fall back on Custer. The General was not born in Bismarck, and he did not die in Bismarck, but he started out, in May, 1876, for his ill-fated rendezvous with Sitting Bull from Fort Abraham Lincoln, in Mandan, which is a few miles west of Bismarck, across the Missouri River. Custer fell at the Battle of the Little Big Horn, some three hundred miles west of Bismarck, in what is now Montana. This is quite close enough for Bismarck's purposes. Custer talk leaves little about Custer untalked about. People like to chew the fat about Custer's personality, his long blond locks, the personality of his wife (known to everybody in and around Bismarck as Libby), his political ambitions, his military prowess, his stability, and his instability. The Battle of the Little Big Horn is fought again and again, over tablecloths, with knives, forks, spoons, saltcellars, and sugar bowls. Particular emphasis is given to determining exactly where Custer himself fell. Passions run high.

"I say that he was spunk in the middle of the river," a Bismarck Custerite will remark, rapidly laying two knives (the river) parallel to one another and putting a saltcellar (Custer) between them. "He had just started across the stream on his horse, and was spunk in the middle of it."

"Nonsense," another Custerite will say, putting the saltcellar (Custer) behind one of the knives (riverbank).

To the people of the Bismarck-Mandan area, Custer is not always merely a saltcellar. During the summer months, a pageant, called "Custerdrama," is presented five nights a week in the Custer Memorial Amphitheatre, outside Mandan, and on those nights Custer is represented by a live actor wearing a long, tangled wig. On hand, too, are about a hundred other actors and a lot of dogs and horses. The souvenir program of "Custerdrama" carries on its cover the legends "Out Where the West Begins" and "May Their Glory Never Fade." Played on several levels of an open stage, the pageant itself offers the knife-and-saltcellar set little guidance, since it concentrates on the events at Fort Abraham Lincoln prior to Custer's departure. At last, the men and horses of the 7th Cavalry set out through great wooden stockade doors, amid huge swirls of real dust. A moment or so later, in the distance, on what passes

for a hill behind the amphitheatre, patrons can distinguish Indians sur-
rounding and attacking Custer and his men, to the accompaniment of
bloodcurdling shrieks. The actors are so far away that they are hardly
more than tiny figures in a pageant, and one man's guess is as good as
another's as to whether Custer was in the middle of the river or on the
riverbank.

The North Dakota State Capitol, in Bismarck, is eighteen stories
high, and is known, of course, as the Skyscraper Capitol. It can be seen
for many miles around on both clear and cloudy days. There is nothing
to obstruct a view of it. "A good many Bismarck people would have you
believe that if it weren't for the Rockies a man could stand up in a boat
out in Puget Sound, look east, and catch a glimpse of their capitol," a
Bismarck man said recently. "This is obvious nonsense." The building
met with considerable local opposition when it first showed up above
the prairies, in 1933, and again when it was completed, in 1935. It looked
much more like the home office of a large insurance company than it
did like a capitol, and it gave people an uneasy feeling that their state
government had taken an erratic, commercial turn. Time mellowed their
outlook, and these days people in Bismarck—and throughout North
Dakota—feel that the building represents a worthwhile, lasting investment. "Unique in its simplicity, usability, and practicability," reads a
brochure available to visitors to the Capitol, adding that the usual ver-
dict following an hour's tour of the place is "It is the most capitol for the
money we have ever seen." Many visitors are also of the opinion that it is
the most wood for the money. The Capitol is chock-full of wood. There
is rosewood in the Legislative Hall (with light panels of curly maple);
American chestnut in the House of Representatives (with chairs and
rostrum of American walnut); English quartered oak on the walls of the
Senate; laurelwood on the walls of the Governor's reception room; teak-
wood on the walls and ceiling of the Governor's private office; primavera
on the walls of the Governor's private corridor; rosewood again in the
Supreme Court room; American walnut again in the Supreme Court
elevator lobby. And so it goes—wood, wood, wood. Rubber tiling covers all the floors in the building except the floor of the Governor's reception room. The Governor, it was felt, deserved wood on his floor, and he
got wood—American white oak. No one around the Capitol understands the significance of all the wood. "Somebody just liked wood,
that's all," an attendant recently remarked.

A segment of Bismarck's population became uneasy all over again when a new ranch house, for use as a Governor's mansion, was erected at the edge of the Capitol grounds in 1960. "Doesn't look like a Governor's mansion" was the opinion of a large group of Bismarck residents. They were the same people, or descendants of the same people, who had not felt that the Capitol looked like a capitol at the time the Capitol was built. "They have become reconciled to the Capitol, and eventually they will become reconciled to the Governor's mansion," a Bismarck resident said not long ago. "For one thing, the place is a Governor's mansion by virtue of the simple fact that a Governor lives there." Bismarck people who are shaken up by the architecture of the Governor's mansion can generally find spiritual solace by attending one of the several livestock auctions held in and around Bismarck. A man knows where he stands, or sits, at a livestock auction. Auctions are held in an indoor ring, and buyers and their wives and children sit on wooden benches. The wall above and behind the auction ring is covered with flamboyantly illustrated and highly tinted advertisements for Herefords, horses, ranches, Western shops, chiropractic clinics, and so on. In the advertisements, rivers flow through deep canyons, mountains glistening with snow come to needle-thin peaks surrounded by supernal blue hazes, and plump livestock gaze blissfully down upon the red-faced and blue-shirted buyers and sellers. The wall resembles a curtain in an old-fashioned variety hall. In an open booth facing the ring and the spectators sits the auctioneer. Two big wooden gates are on either side of him—one to let the animals into the ring, the other to let them out. The auctions run on all day. The entrance gate swings open and a large sow strolls into the ring, blinks at the spectators, blinks at the auctioneer, blinks at the animal pictures on the walls, as the auctioneer drones on ("...thirty...forty...fifty...sixty....Sold"), and the sow is shooed out through the exit gate as the entrance gate swings open and a huddled knot of sheep enter, preceded by a wiry lead goat with a Sinbad beard and a knowing, weary air. The lead goat performs only half duty; he brings the sheep in, but he does not stay for the sale. The auctioneer's voice keeps up its singsong, children fall asleep on their parents' shoulders, acres of popcorn are consumed, and sharp-faced men seated along the benches touch their ears, twitch their noses, tap their stomachs, shift slightly, and otherwise maintain the old and arcane ritual of bidding. "Men's habits change slowly out this way," a Bismarck man has said.

"Perhaps a bit more slowly than other places. I suspect it's the broad open spaces and the huge sky coming down on all sides. We look out over all the space and figure, hell, it's too big for us, it's too wide, there's too much of it, and we get gloomy. Your North Dakota man can get good and gloomy."

Often, when the people of Bismarck tire of talking about the weather, General Custer, and livestock sales, they switch to Reinhold Delzer. Mr. Delzer is a successful contractor. "Delzer is what you might call a new Bismarck man," an old Bismarck man said recently. Mr. Delzer does not trifle with ordinary construction—houses and such. He thinks big and he acts big, and his construction is of the big, heavy variety (bridges, filtration plants), and many of his contracts are with governments (federal and municipal). He reserves his biggest thoughts, however, for the continuing fulfillment of a childhood dream—the tender maintenance, in his home, of a large theatre organ. "I was just a lousy usher in a Bismarck theatre when I was a boy," Mr. Delzer said not long ago. "It was the Eltinge Theatre, and when the organ in that theatre played, I would get so excited that I would drop my flashlight. Day after day, I would hear the notes of that theatre organ, and they did something to me, way down deep inside. I vowed that someday I, Reinhold Delzer, would have a theatre organ in my own home." As Mr. Delzer began to climb the ladder of success in the filtration-plant and heavy-construction world, he bought the organ from the Eltinge Theatre itself and installed it in the living room of his house, a many-levelled structure on what passes for a hill in a modern residential section of Bismarck. The house is furnished in a style that might best be described as Bismarck Roxy, and the organ does not clash with any other object in the room. Soon, the construction business being what it is, Mr. Delzer had his eye on larger game, and when he heard that the forty-three-hundred-seat Radio City Theatre in Minneapolis was about to be razed and turned into a parking lot, he instantly thought of that theatre's organ—*a mighty Wurlitzer*! "I can't tell you how many times I had gone down there to hear Jesse Crawford at the giant console," Mr. Delzer said recently. "That organ was the dream of my life. I *had* to have it." He has it. It is now enshrined a level below its little sister from the Eltinge—in a specially constructed basement room half the size of a basketball court. Mr. Delzer's friends gather in the long room, at small cocktail tables, to listen to the organ. They face a tan-and-gold curtain, which opens silently, at the push of a button, to reveal the immense cream-and-gold console bathed in changing hues from hidden lights. The spectacle is overwhelming, and when Mr. Delzer sits down at the mighty Wurlitzer to play "The Stars and Stripes Forever," the locks on his doors, the pictures on his walls, the windowpanes, the house as a whole, and a number of the neighbors rattle from the mighty vibrato. Sometimes, at night, when the cattle auctions are over for the day, and the livestock is silently bedded down, Bismarck people like to stroll over to the Northern Pacific depot and watch the fliers screech into town. (Bismarck got its name because the Northern Pacific Railroad, back in 1873, wanted to entice German capital to invest in the completion of the railroad.) The fliers pause briefly and then start up again across the prairies toward the Bad Lands (West) or Minneapolis (East). Even as the long trains come in, their diesels honking, many people claim that they can hear Mr. Delzer, high over the city, at his mighty Wurlitzer, playing "I Wanna Be Loved by You."

Butte, Mont.

Alt., 5,767. Pop., 27,877. Butte draws its strength from The Hill. "You could go as far as to say, stranger," a Butte resident recently told a visitor, "that Butte is The Hill and The Hill is Butte. God made The Hill, but the Anaconda Company owns it, and it is known as The Richest Hill on Earth." The Richest Hill on Earth is a very nice name for a hill, especially in a mining town. It has a comfortable, reassuring sound, a ring of promise. Since Butte is in the middle of the Rockies, and the jagged massif of the Continental Divide lies only a few miles to the east, the casual eye has considerable difficulty distinguishing The Hill from the rest of the city, but the visitor soon learns that it has a character all its own. The Hill covers four square miles of an uphill portion of the city, and its streets are twisty and steep. Some people say that three billion dollars' worth of mineral wealth has been extracted from The Hill—mostly copper in its raw state. Others say that four billion dollars' worth of mineral wealth has been extracted from The Hill—mostly copper in its raw state. In any event, people have been chipping away at The Hill for more than ninety years. They dig holes in it, build tunnels in it (there are 2,630 miles of tunnels in The Hill), hammer, shovel, and blast, and in the past few years, using a process known as open-pit mining, have even begun to level it. Mining shifts change three times a day—at 7 A.M., 3 P.M., and 11 P.M.—and, each time, the mining population of Butte, which amounts to about three thousand men these days, turns over. Friday is payday at Anaconda. The paymaster's office is a pink building, and between it and a convenient local bank stands the Classic Bar. On

Fridays, the Classic Bar does a brisk business, "God Bless America!" rings out from the chimes on the Metals Bank, and all over town people munch on Bonanza Burgers, taking their change in silver dollars. Silver dollars are common currency in Butte.

The phrase "back in the good old days" has achieved the status of a litany in Butte. "Actually, the good old days were probably just as horrible as the bad new days," an old-time Butte resident said not long ago, "but they sound more romantic and we're stuck with them." In Butte, "the good old days" refers to any day except today or tomorrow. "Why, back in the good old days, five, six years ago, some six thousand men were working on The Hill," a Butte man will say. "Back in the good old days—and I'm talking about the years right after World War I—Butte had a population of ninety thousand," another Butte man will say. "In the good old days back in 1915," still another will say, "there were a hundred and fifty shafts working, with fifteen thousand four hundred men underground. One shift went off at 4:30 A.M., and another shift went on at 6 A.M., and The Hill looked like an anthill, what with the people trudging up and down." A good-old-1915-days man can make an anthill sound attractive. Any good-old-days man is filled with laments. "China-town was two blocks wide and four blocks deep," he will say. "Now there's one Chinese laundry left in town, and no tickee, no washee." In the good old days, fifteen hundred girls worked three shifts in the red-light district. Even funerals are said to have been more fun. "It's been years since there was a real, honest-to-goodness wake in a private home," a man said not long ago. "And in the good old days, on the way back from the cemetery, the old Irishmen would hire two white horses and a whip and head for the roadhouses that dotted the road into town. Last man in paid for the drinks." The old roadhouses are gone. Today, on the main roads leading from the cemeteries, mourners pass only new places—the Nite Owl, the Red Rooster, and the Skookum Motel. Houses are boarded up all over town, and the sight of them—many perched precariously on the steep inclines of The Hill, in the shadows of abandoned mine shafts—brings back strong memories.

Talk about the good old days is second in importance only to talk about the Company (Anaconda), and how many men will be working where, and when, and for how long. Some sixty-five or seventy per cent of Anaconda's copper now comes from Chile, and the uncertainties of the present easily give way to what now appear to have been the certainties of the past. "Today," an articulate Butte man said recently, "things are pretty well mechanized, and people talk in terms of numbers, figures, statistics. They'll tell you about a shovel that is so big that it can dig into the side of The Hill and pull out twenty-two and a half tons of earth at one time—I'm talking now about the massive open-pit job at the Berkeley Pit, that great big hole at the edge of town, with the huge trucks creeping up and down all day long, scooping out The Hill. Twenty-two and a half tons of earth at one time! Well, Mister, the figure staggers me, but it leaves me cold. I'm proud of that shovel, but I'm not what you would call satisfied. Someone will say, 'We're getting ten to twelve pounds of copper per ton of Hill down at the Berkeley Pit,' and I am fascinated by the figure, but it leaves me cold. I'm all for science. I guess we should be fascinated by the way they bore holes forty feet deep and nine inches wide into The Hill, down in the Pit, and take samplings, number all the holes, and list them on a big board in the superintendent's office. The samplings go off to the Assay Office, and the word comes back swiftly on the copper content of the earth they have extracted. Anything naught point five or above, they'll tell you, means ore, naught point two to naught point four means leach, and anything less means waste. They'll tell you that trucks go up a fifteen-degree incline in the Pit, and that when a truck lets out one long toot, that means the truck is loaded with earth and ready to start up the incline. They'll tell you about horsetail—ore with seams in it—and how they couldn't handle it in the old days but can today, and how men scratching around in the Pit come across veins that had been missed in the old days by just a few feet. As the scoops plunge deeper and deeper into The Hill, they come across ancient timbers from tunnels where the miners worked in the past. Maybe they'll take you down into the Kelley Mine—one of the places where they're still working underground—and you'll have your goggles on, and carry an alkaline-battery torch that is good for eight hours. Maybe you'll go down thirteen hundred feet, maybe more. They'll tell you that they plan to go down forty-six hundred feet one of these days, and connect with other old tunnels, and get greater tonnage. The signs down there read 'Don't Save Electricity'—in other words, keep your torch lighted—and you'll sidestep the little trains rolling along the tracks loaded with ore, and you'll hear occasional blasting down there in the earth, and hear the elevator bells signalling what level a car is to stop at. The Kelley world is a dark world, filled with men and machines; it's a mining world, and it runs like clockwork. After you come up, maybe they'll run you over to the town of Anaconda, some twenty-five miles away, where the big processing plants are located, and you can watch the whole pageant of turning the scooped-out earth into copper. They'll tell you that Butte sends a million tons of earth there in twenty-four days, and that nine hundred and sixty-five thousand tons of it will go into waste, piled high in a mountain all its own. They'll show you the tallest smokestack in the world—five hundred and eighty-five and a half feet tall—and you can walk down miles of aisles, past the flotation machines, with great gray bubbles of copper erupting on the surface, and you can see the Reverberating Department, with huge caldrons pouring molten metal, and a great clanging going on all around, and intense heat. And you'll be stunned—you'll be mighty impressed. Forty-five tons of copper can be made in from six to nine hours with one converter, they'll say. Copper, they'll say, is just two days from the earth when it goes through the plant at Anaconda. But afterward you'll want to stop by the bar at the old Montana Hotel, over in Anaconda, and see the head of Marcus Daly's favorite horse, Tammany, inlaid in the floor in more than a thousand squares of hardwood. And you'll be right back in the past!"

Most often, it is the evening hours that bring forth the reminiscences. Twilights are always nostalgic, but especially in the Rockies. Families will get together for a barbecue, and whenever they do, someone is bound to mention Marcus Daly, one of the founders of Anaconda. A statue of Daly may be seen near the Montana School of Mines, in Butte. It was moved there several years ago from a spot downtown. As Daly is portrayed in the statue, he is a small, powerful-looking man, carrying a bronze coat over one arm and a hat in the other hand. He gives the impression of being on his way either from or to a board meeting. When Butte boys pass Daly's statue, they don't tip their hat; they sing a ditty that begins, "There you stand in dirty bronze, Copper King . . ." Should pastry turnovers be served at the barbecue, the floodgates of memory open wide. In Butte, pastry turnovers are filled with meat—they are really meat pies—and are known as pasties. Pasties were once a way of life in Butte. Today, they tend to be somewhat on the bland side—delicious but well-mannered. In the old days, they were filled with all sorts of loin tips, plus generous supplies of potatoes and onions. Connoisseurs, though, claim that the quality of the crust determines the quality of the pasty. One bite, even of a latter-day pasty, and a Butte resident gets the faraway look that spells the good old days. "Harry Lauder once called Butte the Broadway of the West," someone will say. "He thought of Broadway when he saw all the lights twinkling on The Hill." "John McCormack came out here one time to sing," someone else will say, "and met a pal called Cummings, and didn't turn up for his concert for a week. But when he did, he sang like an angel." More pasty bites, more nostalgia.

The pasty brings up memories of nationalities, and in the good old days Butte was a complex of nationalities—all living somewhere on The Hill, all working in the mines. Pasties were a specialty of the Cornish, a large Butte group who lived on the east side of The Hill, and who were known as Cousin Jacks. Their wives were Cousin Jinnies. Cousin Jinnies are remembered for having turned out the most delectable pasties. A pasty was known as a "letter from 'ome"—a touch of the old country, a link with the land across the sea. Not only all Cornishmen but all Englishmen were known as Cousin Jacks, and they all ate pasties. If a man brought a stranger to a foreman and introduced him with the words "This is my Cousin Jack," it was a signal for the foreman to give the man a job. The Irish called themselves the Hot Water Plugs, and lived in Dublin Gulch, also on the east side of The Hill. They ordered Sean O'Farrells—a shot of whiskey and a schooner of beer. Today, their sons ask for a whiskey and a beer chaser. The Finns lived in Finntown—east on Broadway as far as Gaylord. Some of the Irish lived in Walkerville, a more than usually steep section of town, and in Centerville, and all sorts of people spilled into Butchertown and Seldom Seen, including those who worked in the mine called Never Sweat. Austrian and Slavonic people lived in McQueen. Meaderville was as distinctly Italian as McQueen was Central European. "In the good old days," a Butte man will say, helping himself to a slice of pasty, "the Italians took their winemaking seriously. Boxcars filled with grapes always stood on sidings in Meaderville." A considerable amount of wine was consumed in Meaderville. "Meaderville was tough," a Butte man said recently. "In fact, all those different parts of town were tough." The Cousin Jacks and the residents of Meaderville worked out a plan: the Cousin Jacks carried extra pasties to work in their lunchboxes, and kept them warm, and then swapped them for some of the wine that residents of Meaderville carried into the mines. A Cousin Jack's lunchbox couldn't very well accommodate both warm pasties and cold water, and anyway wine was more refreshing, especially drunk underground. On Saturday nights, people would pour out from Meaderville and Finntown, from McQueen and Dublin Gulch, and head for Columbia Gardens, the amusement park operated by the Company (Anaconda). Everybody didn't fight everybody else every Saturday night, but everybody thought about it a good deal. Columbia Gardens is still open, and is still operated by the Company. Its dance pavilion is newly painted, its formal gardens are lovingly tended, and the formal symbol of the Company—an arrowhead—is a blaze, in summer, of bright-colored flowers. Dances are sometimes still held on Saturday nights, but the fight seems to have gone out of them.

The ghosts of Butte are certainly some years away from taking over the town, but a good many local citizens view the boarded-up houses, the closed-down retail stores, and the decreasing population as ominous signs. The former palace of William Andrews Clark, another early copper magnate, is now a rooming house, where lone roomers cook their suppers over electric plates as the last of the light shines in through stained-glass windows. "Frankly, sir, there are too many ghost towns nearby for comfort, if you know what I mean," a Butte resident said not long ago. "Every once in a while, I drive my family up to Elkhorn, about fifty miles to the north, and I get the cold chills. It used to have ten thousand people and fourteen saloons. Today, nothing—except for a few summer folk from Boulder, thirty-six miles to the northeast." People who drive up to Elkhorn find their cars overheating as they turn and twist on dusty roads that climb dizzying heights. On all sides are the Rockies. Elkhorn itself stands silent: houses with their shutters flapping, an old schoolhouse with the floor boards gone, a rusted safe in a paymaster's office, tattered flowered wallpaper, floors covered with magazines and newspapers from the past, and the sound of cowbells tinkling far off somewhere, in the overgrown grass. Gold and silver once came from the hills around Elkhorn, but the mining became unprofitable, and the people moved on, leaving Elkhorn to the silence of the hills. Sourdough Gulch, Ninety Cent Gulch, Slaughter House Gulch—all today are silent. "Doesn't take much to make a ghost town," a Butte man said not long ago. "It all depends on the price of whatever metal is being taken from the earth. When the price drops, the people drop, and the town drops, and is gone."

Butte becomes quieter every year, except for the never-ending stream of trucks lugging earth up the steep inclines at the Berkeley Pit as

Anaconda inexorably lowers the level of The Hill. A man called Luigi, who presides over a narrow bar and dance floor called Luigi's, on The Hill, does his best to maintain the wild abandon of the good old days. He is a fierce-looking man, tall, with high cheekbones and fanatical eyes. The walls and ceiling of his place are covered, top to bottom, with thousands of mechanical figures, including wooden dolls and metal spiders. Patrons wait an hour or more for "the mood" to come on Luigi. They know it will come. Luigi, a one-man band, sits quietly on the bandstand, surrounded by assorted drums and other percussion instruments, which are also waiting. The dolls are silent, the spiders at rest. "Don't hurry me, don't hurry me!" cries Luigi. "I must warm up my bongo drums! I must do it in my own time!" Only Luigi knows when the time is ripe for "the mood," when the bongo drums have reached the proper degree of heat. Then, in a flash, pushing a button on the bandstand, he transforms his establishment into a nightmare of spasms and contortions. Every last inch of Luigi's bursts into action: crazy dolls dance crazily, animals leap and jump, spiders spin tiny mechanical webs across the ceiling, bells ring, drums beat themselves, the bar shakes, the seats tremble. Patrons, unable to sit still amid the general chaos, rise and engage in spasms and contortions of their own. Luigi's eyes blaze, and his mouth becomes set. He twists his body sidewise and forward. He looks like one of his dancing dolls. Everything in Luigi's seems about to be torn loose from everything else, and to come tumbling down. There, above the winding tunnels of The Hill, Luigi lets out loud cries of delight mingled with cries of despair as he pummels his bongo drums.

Gettysburg, Pa.

Alt., 520. Pop., 7,960. No more egregious error can be committed by the visitor to Gettysburg than to assume that the Battle of Gettysburg (July 1–3, 1863) is over. In fact, there is reason to believe that hostilities are only just beginning. Skirmishes take place all over town, and the most obscure details of the huge, sprawling battle are made available to strangers, in one form or another, every hour of the day. "I tell you, I was just an ordinary fellow, with an ordinary fellow's interest in the Civil War, until I spent two days at Gettysburg," an ordinary fellow who gave the impression of having been through a protracted siege said not long ago. "Now I think I could lecture at the War College. It all began when I took a room in a motel on the edge of the battlefield. This particular motel lay almost directly in the line of Pickett's Charge—athwart it, you might say. Pickett's Charge, of course, was the unsuccessful offensive mounted by the Confederate troops on the afternoon of July 3rd, when Pickett and his men marched out from the Confederate left flank on Seminary Ridge and crossed an open field to meet the Union troops head-on on Cemetery Ridge. I would place the start of the charge at approximately 3 P.M., Eastern Standard Time. I won't go so far as to say that Pickett's men would have come right *through* my bedroom, but they might well have bruised themselves on the television set against my southern wall. Actually, I feel certain that Pettigrew's men—he was stationed to the left of Pickett—and the men of Archer, Davis, Scales, and Lane would have come right across my bed, knocking over the telephone and the bed lamp. They ran into Meade's men—Hays, Webb,

Gibbon, and the rest—and at the Angle it was bloody beyond description, and the Confederates were turned back at the Copse of Trees, at what is known as the High Water Mark of the Confederacy. The Rebels were said to be incapable of ever again mounting an offensive. Pickett's Charge was all over by ten minutes to four, but I kept going in Gettysburg pretty much around the clock, taking bus rides with built-in sound effects describing every last inch of the battle, watching an electric map with hundreds of little lights blinking and winking to show the position of the troops, looking at a cyclorama of the battle, walking over the battlefield, taking a guided tour in my own car, with a hired guide, and buying toy cannons, old bullets, flags, literature of all sorts, and tons of picture postcards. Now, if I had been Pickett . . ."

A man can visit Gettysburg, not even stop at a motel, and garner a rich historical background—merely by buying postcards. Postcards abound. They outnumber the people in the town by approximately twenty to one. They have a tendency to jump off the racks and hop into one's pockets. There are pictures of everything and everybody—Devil's Den, General Warren on Little Round Top, Big Round Top, the Valley of Death, Spangler's Spring, General Lee, General Lee's horse, Culp's Hill, the Wheatfield, the Virginia State Monument, the North Carolina State Monument, the Peach Orchard, McPherson Ridge, Barlow Knoll, Oak Hill, the Copse of Trees, the Angle, General Meade, General Meade's horse, General Meade's headquarters, the Jennie Wade House, and so on. The sense of history that pervades the city often produces an anesthetic effect that can take days to shake off. This happens most often to people who hire an official guide to accompany them as they drive around the thirty-odd square miles that constitute the battlefield. Groups of these guides—elderly men, for the most part—sit and sun themselves in front of small stone houses that are scattered about the edge of the field. Many of the guides would make interesting picture postcards. They leave the impression that they are veterans of the battle. They are staggering repositories of information, much of it in the general area of blood and gore. They feel that, seated beside a person who has hired their services for an hour or an hour and a half while he drives along the quiet tree-lined and gun-lined roads, they have a duty to dwell upon the horrors of war. Actually, bodies no longer lie out on the gently rolling, alternately brown and green fields, but the guides are corpse-conscious just the same, and they cannot pass a gully, an open stretch, or a battery of guns without making vivid references to the toll of human life that was taken at Gettysburg. They savor casualty figures, and roll them over and over on their tongues, with special attention to the number of hours or days that "the dead lay out there in the hot sun." Nor is their arithmetical ardor confined to casualty figures. The cost of various monuments titillates them to a frenzy of statistics, and they cite to the penny the amount expended on every monument they pass. "When I got through with one of those guides," a visitor to Gettysburg remarked recently, "I had the feeling that I had been driving around with a man from Price Waterhouse who had come to the field, eagle-eyed, to examine the books." Most of the guides are brigadiers *manqués*, or at least colonels *manqués*, possessed of a mysterious, superior untapped skill in commanding vast armies of men over broad areas under optimum conditions of strategy and tactics. They find it difficult to concede that the generals who fought the battle knew what they were doing, and they make it clear that if *they* had been consulted, little of what did take place would have taken place. For the most part, they would have everywhere attacked sooner, or later, in a different spot, with different equipment and radically rearranged formations. "By the time I was through with my guided tour, I had no possible way of knowing which side, if any, won the battle," a man who had visited the battlefield said not long ago. "I decided to go home and read a book about it. The book said the North won."

Gettysburg strongly feels the presence of two former Presidents of the United States—one dead, one living. Lincoln is everywhere: in the National Cemetery, where he delivered the Gettysburg Address; in the tiny maroon-and-gray railroad station (now a tourist center), where he got off the train from Washington the afternoon before he delivered the address; in the Old Wills House, where he spent the night before he delivered the address; and on the old streets down which he rode on horseback on his way to the cemetery and the delivering of the address. The casual visitor poking through the souvenir shops is likely to feel that he is almost entirely surrounded by Lincoln—Lincoln staring at him from picture postcards, miniature busts of Lincoln in imitation bronze and silver, and copies of the address on postcards, silk scrolls, and wooden plaques. Gettysburg's living President is Dwight Eisenhower. Pictures of Eisenhower, and of his farm and his wife, are not in short supply, either. The people of Gettysburg may not catch sight of Eisenhower for weeks at a time—he drives from his farm to his office, on Carlisle Street, swiftly and with military precision and efficiency—but they derive comfort from the fact that he is around. "You can go into a lot of towns that call themselves historical—they are more like historical markers than towns, really—and they leave you with a sense of ancient matters settled long ago," a Gettysburg resident remarked the other day. "It's different here. We don't have much in the way of industry—just a shoe factory—and wages are generally low, and the tourists pour through, but we do have this indefinable sense of living history. These two strikingly different men, Lincoln and Eisenhower, have much to do with it. They elevate us and make us feel as though we were actors in some strange pageant that keeps unfolding and is something larger than ourselves."

A recent visitor to Gettysburg, having walked slowly down the main street, past the brooding photographs of Lincoln staring at him from shopwindows along the way, paid a call on General Eisenhower in his office, which occupies a modest three-story red brick building on the campus of Gettysburg College; formerly, the house was occupied by the president of Gettysburg College. The Venetian blinds are always drawn. Visitors encounter an elaborate but unobtrusive security system at the front door—an intercom mechanism through which the visitor announces himself. If he is expected, he is told in metallic tones to enter. Visitors may also be admitted through the back of the house. Several secretaries work there, in an enclosed porchlike extension, amid tall rows of metal filing cabinets with heavy locks. Inside, the house has a comfortable, easygoing air—warm draperies, many oil paintings, rooms lined with bookcases containing bound volumes of government reports. In a large room on the ground floor, the visitor found Colonel John Eisenhower, the President's son. Colonel Eisenhower has left the Army and is now working for a publishing house, helping his father put together his memoirs of the White House years; his desk was covered with galley proofs of the President's work. "He's deep in Volume Two," said Colonel Eisenhower. "Working like fury on it, too, writing all up and down and along the margins of yellow foolscap. He has many of the tools to aid his memory right here, on the back porch, in those files you just passed, and I am cleared to go through them when he needs a fact to refresh his recollection. There are other files out in Abilene, but not of the same importance. And there is a great mass of stuff down at the

Library of Congress, in Washington, where my father's assistant on this project, Dr. William Ewald, has stationed himself. When Father sits down with pen and paper and relaxes and lets his thoughts spontaneously flow forth, we get some pretty vivid, colorful recollections. These are then typed up and checked over, and then he goes at them again, rearranging and polishing. He's very fussy about his work." The Colonel, who is a tall, slim, engaging-looking man with a casual air, then said, "I have a single-engine Comanche that I keep out at the airport here, and every chance I get, I go up in her, and fly around the countryside, over the battlefield—everywhere. I just wheel around and get out of myself and get off the ground. I feel so free when I am in the air. I am out of myself. I love it."

The President works in a corner room on the second floor. He feels that if he worked downstairs, people would be trying to peer through the windows. Across the hall from his workroom, a retired brigadier general acting as an aide handles the large flow of correspondence and other matters that press into the life of an ex-President. Five stars, forming a circle, are etched in glass on the door leading to the President's workroom. He sits at a wide desk that is almost totally uncluttered, being embellished only by a few gadgets and a tiny silver bust of Lincoln. Behind him are the United States flag and the Presidential flag. The visitor found him relaxed and cheerful, possessed of a strangely old-fashioned and yet military courtesy, his voice soft but somewhat clipped, his words often tumbling out but giving the impression that at his own command they would instantly cease and he would turn his thoughts to other concerns. His cheeks had a healthy tint, and his eyes were clear blue and quietly scrutinizing. "I sit here and admire that watercolor by Andrew Wyeth," he said suddenly, pointing to a framed picture on the wall across from his desk. "I suppose I admire his work above all others. I have no idea how he does it. Just look at those sycamores! Wyeth did that watercolor on my farm, did it in about twenty minutes—faster than I can conceive of a man turning out such a superior piece of work. I hope you noticed my oil by Churchill on the way up the stairs—a favorite scene of mine, a wadi in North Africa. I love the mountain scenes—the Rockies, the Atlas Mountains. I can look at them for hours. I have most of what I need here to work with. It's great fun to test my memory, see what I can remember from the crowded years."

The President took off his glasses and toyed with them. "Twenty-

twenty hindsight is so easy, but I find myself trying to track down the minutiae, the considerations that lay behind a decision," he said. "When the war was over, I wanted time to reflect, to think back, but then SHAPE came along, and the Presidency, and all the years. I had wanted to declare myself a one-term President, and then take a long look, have a breathing spell." The President shifted slightly in his chair. "Now, when I look back, I realize that I was never one for bombast, you know. Persuasion was more in my line. And a great many people still look upon me as a rather unwelcome entry." The President smiled, and put on his glasses. He leaned forward intently. "The Gettysburg roots go deep," he said. "That picture over there on that wall, that's my West Point class of 1915, taken right here in Gettysburg on May 3, 1915. We visited here for three days, pored over every inch of the battlefield. There wasn't much about Gettysburg that we didn't study at the Point, and then we came down to the field itself and studied some more. During the First War, I was stationed here at Camp Colt. Tanks. I went from captain to lieutenant colonel, and I trained my men in discipline and all aspects of this new type of warfare, including machine guns, telegraphy, and the mechanics of tanks. The battlefield fascinated me. I suppose I must have read thirty, forty books on the subject—everything from the Comte de Paris to Haskell. I still read everything I can lay my hands on about the battle. In the old days, during the First War, I would climb into my old Dodge and tour the battlefield and explore every corner of the field and relive the battle. I am still impelled to do it, and from time to time, at dusk, I pack up and look around. Sometimes, I climb one-third of the way up one of those metal lookout towers that are scattered about the field. Don't go all the way up anymore. I had a heart attack, you know."

The President pulled a fresh sheet of paper toward him and swiftly, in a few pen strokes, drew the battle lines of Gettysburg, with the fishhook of the Union lines unmistakable. His eyes were brighter than ever now, and he seemed absorbed in the rapid sketch he had made. "Everybody will argue this battle—*everybody*," he said. "I think one would be safe in saying that Gettysburg was the high-water mark of the Confederacy, all right, even though you mustn't forget that Grant took Vicksburg the day after the battle ended here. Meade, of course, had his armies lined up and prepared to fall back to Pipe Creek, near Taneytown. Lee didn't have much here, really, and Meade had a great deal. Certainly Lee might have attacked Washington and Baltimore, thrown panic into the North, and appealed to much Northern sentiment to end the war. Let me tell you, the sense of history is here. With you all the time. Oh, you just get me started on the Battle of Gettysburg and there's no telling where we'll end up!"

The President pulled another sheet of paper toward him and began to jot down some notes. "Back to work," he said.

The Old Wills House, where Lincoln spent the night before the dedication of the National Cemetery, lies two blocks down from Eisenhower's office and across from the Hotel Gettysburg, on the town's main traffic circle. It is now a museum of sorts, open to the public for a small fee. A room on the second floor is papered in bluish gray with a rose design, and contains a huge four-poster bed and heavy red draperies. A stovepipe hat lies on the bed, an old morning coat beside it. On a wooden table near one window are a white china pitcher and a towel rack, on which a few starched towels hang. In a chair by the bed, with a table before it, is a six-foot-four, life-size wax image of Lincoln. He is a startling figure, seated at the table in his shirtsleeves, wearing glasses with thin metal frames, and holding a piece of paper. Visitors to the museum are asked to forget themselves for the moment, let reality slip away, and try to believe that the paper he holds is a rough draft of the Gettysburg Address. The six-foot-four image and the small, stuffy room produce a strange effect. When the lights dim, the men, women, and children huddled on chairs around the room fall into an uncomfortable silence. Recorded music is heard from somewhere, with the old strains of "The Battle Hymn of the Republic" becoming louder and louder. (Sane men keep telling themselves, "Hokum, hokum," but it is a losing fight, with the battlefield and the cemetery a scant half mile away in one direction and a living ex-President a scant two blocks away in another.) Suddenly a voice is heard. It is an actor, recorded, impersonating Wills. "There are fresh towels here, Mr. President, and paper on the desk," says the voice. "May the night bring you a pleasant sleep." Then the voice of an actor impersonating Lincoln is heard saying, in measured tones, "Thank you, Wills, thank you. You are most kind." The silence becomes almost unbearable, but then one can hear the scratching of a pen on paper and, once again, the voice of Lincoln, quietly reading the words of the Gettysburg Address. When the lights go up, the wax Lincoln is still there at the table, the paper in his hand, and the people file out with odd looks on their faces.

Gettysburg, Pa.

The lady in charge of the Wills House, who has collected fifty cents from every adult and twenty-five cents from every child to visit there, refers to the wax figure as "Mr. Lincoln." There appears to be no doubt in her mind that Mr. Lincoln lives in the house. She says she believes that on certain days one can see his shirt front rise and fall as he breathes. Many visitors, she says, swear that Mr. Lincoln stands up several times during the queer séance to move around the room, and that when they reach out to touch him, they feel flesh.

Hot Springs, Ark.

Alt., 608. Pop., 29,212. A large portion of the social life of Hot Springs takes place in the hot tubs and steamy massage rooms and tall-backed porch rockers of the brick-and-stucco bathhouses along Bath House Row, a quiet, tree-shaded stretch of street, dead in the center of town, that lies within the confines of Hot Springs National Park. The park is no Yellowstone or Zion—it consists of only one and a half square miles, in and around the city—but deep in its wooded confines lie forty-seven mysterious underground springs, which send forth a continuous flow of almost a million gallons of water a day with a temperature of approximately a hundred and forty-three degrees. The water flows into reservoirs and then, carefully controlled and cooled, into the tubs of seven bathhouses along Bath House Row and eleven registered bathhouses in other parts of town. Bathing in this water is said to be good for what ails a person, especially a person suffering from what is known in Hot Springs as "that rundown feeling" or from trouble in the joints, and thousands of people, attracted by the city's official slogan, "We Bathe the World," turn up there. Any city frequented by troubled joints has a tendency to start its day slowly, and during the early-morning hours—from seven to nine, say—Hot Springs presents a somnolent aspect. An early riser who recently spent a few days in Hot Springs reported that at seven o'clock one morning he stepped out of his hotel, a mammoth establishment directly across from the park, and walked through the park for quite some time in stark solitude. "There was not a living soul to be seen along its neatly tended paths," he said. "It was an odd experience—all alone in a national park." Forty-five of the forty-seven springs have been sealed off from public view, but near one that was bubbling forth from between some rocks—and giving off small puffs of steam—he spotted a button near an inconspicuous display board describing the park. He pressed the button, and was delighted to hear the sound of a human voice. It was a recorded message from a National Park Service man, speaking clearly and firmly. "Indians bathed their sick and injured here long before the explorers visited the area," said the voice. "In 1541, the Hernando de Soto expedition may have been led to the hot springs by Indian guides." The city not only has hot water, the visitor thought, but has *old* hot water. The visitor was just about to ask the voice what made the water hot when the voice asked, "Are you wondering what makes the water hot?" This so unnerved the visitor that a good deal of the explanation escaped him, but he felt later that he had got the gist of it: the area was once covered by a great ocean, and on its floor there accumulated thick layers of silt and mud, which turned into sedimentary rock that buckled and wrinkled as the earth moved, and then, as the earth pushed up and the ocean drained away, cracks and fault zones formed in the rock, through which hot water has since been rising from the center of the earth—itself a mass of molten rock—and becoming mixed with ground water in the right proportions to create hot springs. The voice, suddenly becoming stern and scholarly, intoned that the water contains blue-green algae of a kind to be found elsewhere only in Banff. "Because of the high temperature of the water, practically no animal life can survive," said the voice, "and therefore the thermal water is bacteriologically pure."

The visitor, reassured, walked out of the park. It was just a few steps to the street and Bath House Row. The bathhouses—each with a ramp leading from the sidewalk to the main door—were still closed. He passed the Buckstaff, the Ozark, the Hale, the Maurice, the Superior, the Lamar, and the Quapaw—imposing structures built along the general lines of seaside villas. Bath House Row lines one side of Central Avenue, a principal street, and at intersections "Walk" and "Don't Walk" signs were flashing on and off. At the end of the row, facing a corner of the park, the visitor noted a few signs of hesitantly emerging animal life. There was no vehicular traffic, but several people were dutifully waiting for the traffic signs to change to "Walk" before crossing the street to a drinking fountain outside the headquarters of the park superintendent. Water from the hot springs was gushing from the fountain. "It was a strange phenomenon," the visitor later told a friend. "They were the early-morning drinkers—water drinkers, you understand, who are the firsts to appear—but they were unlike any other early-morning drinkers I had ever seen. There were just a few at first, but gradually I noticed that men and women were converging on the fountain from all over town. Their advance had the air of a pilgrimage—a slow, unsteady pilgrimage. Some of them carried those little folding metal cups that Boy Scouts take on hikes. Others had gallon prune-juice or cider jugs, with the labels still on them. Others held buckets—old-fashioned tin buckets, with dippers. One man had an eyedropper. They all scrupulously waited for the 'Walk' signs, although I could see how eager they were to get to the water. When the people got to the fountain, they filled their cups and drank the water, or they filled their buckets and jugs and went back to the curb to wait for the 'Walk' sign to flash, and then slowly crossed the street and headed for their motels or rooming houses. The man with the eyedropper carefully dropped some of the water into both eyes, and then shook his head like a dog coming out of a pond. I had some of the water myself. Just leaned over and put my mouth to the jet. It seemed fine to me—warmish but not hot, and odorless. Tasted like water."

The early-morning-water-hole crowd is distinct from the people taking the baths. The water-hole devotees merely drink the water; they do not bathe in it. An aficionado of hot-spring bathing generally signs up for a whole series of baths, and the bathhouse becomes his home away from home while he is visiting Hot Springs. A certain amount of prestige goes with taking the baths, and the names of bathers, listed both by bathhouses and by points of origin, appear each week in the Hot Springs *Visitor's Bulletin*, which is available free all over town. The *Bulletin* is the *Who's Who* of tubbing. If Earl Caauwe, from Iowa, bathes at the Lamar Bath House, this is duly noted, and by glancing down the list of names in the *Bulletin* Mr. Caauwe can discover that George Lantz, also from Iowa, is bathing at the same bathhouse. The bathers come from all over: the Griffins from Tennessee (Hale Bath House); Mrs. Meisenheimer from Texas (Maurice Bath House); Mrs. F. Ritter from Nebraska (Lamar Bath House); Mr. and Mrs. J. Trost from Missouri

(Buckstaff Bath House). People have a chance to get together after their baths, sitting on the glassed-in porches of the bathhouses and waiting for their pores to close. "It is extremely important for people to wait a minimum of half an hour for their pores to close after their baths," a bathhouse official recently remarked. "It would never do for them to get their pores all opened up taking their baths and then walk out of the bathhouse and catch their death." Television is provided on the porches, along with writing desks, mail drops, and the rockers. People like to sit down after their baths and write postcards home describing the water and its temperature. There is also a good deal of chatter on the porches, largely about grandchildren, diet, and aches and pains. Most of the talk is about aches and pains. Talk about aches and pains has a never-ending quality, for it presents an infinite series of possible combinations; it can continue as long as it would take, say, all living Chinese to pass a given spot. The broad divisions of the pain-talk curriculum are location, frequency, duration, previous history, and prognosis. A chain reaction inevitably sets in upon the porches, with one man's backache sliding naturally into another man's Charley horse. "Of course, we do not discourage talk about ailments," a bathhouse proprietor said not long ago. "It does people a certain amount of good to talk about their aches and pains, and to compare notes. I always point out that we have a hundred-and-twelve-year-old man who comes in here, and when he talks about the stiffening in his joints he is a positive inspiration to the others, who see how dang far they have to go and the improvements that can set in. We close down during the lunch hour, and in the afternoon a whole new set arrives, with a whole new batch of places that hurt. We're ready for them. The water contains silica, potassium, magnesium, nitrates, and phosphates, plus gases. Single baths run from a dollar eighty-five to two twenty-five, depending on the bathhouse, while six baths cost from ten fifty-five to twelve ninety-five, twelve baths from twenty dollars and thirty cents to twenty-five dollars and ten cents, eighteen baths from twenty-nine sixty to thirty-six eighty, and twenty-four baths from thirty-seven forty to forty-seven dollars. We bathe the world!"

The most expensive and elegant baths are to be found, or taken, at the Arlington Hotel, a celebrated resort hotel with innumerable corridors, card rooms, gift shops, lobbies, coffee shops, and restaurants. Drinking fountains offering water from the hot springs are conveniently situated on each floor of the Arlington, near the elevators. There are paper-cup holders beside them, and most of the guests swig a cup or two while waiting to go up or down. Special elevators whisk the guests from their floors to bathing headquarters, on the third floor, and guests have the privilege of walking down the halls in their bathrobes and slippers on their way to the delights of the baths. The manager of the Arlington, a jovial, portly man named Edgar A. May, who has an encyclopedic knowledge of the baths and a dedication to their way of life, makes frequent trips to the bath floor during the day. The knowledge that deep in the recesses of his establishment people are tubbing or steaming or being pounded by masseurs gives him a special sense of security. "Invigorating, health-producing, life-giving thermal waters!" Mr. May recently exclaimed to a visitor while showing him around the men's bath section, and went on to explain, "During February, when the racing season is on, we give the majority of our baths in the morning. People are then refreshed to go out to the track. In April and May, when people start golfing, we bathe large numbers in the afternoons. Summers, we bathe entire families all the time. For anything except the standard bath, a physician who is registered with the National Park Service must prescribe the regime. We are very strict about this. All people who come in for a bath must sign a sheet called 'Application and Certificate for Baths.' Either they must sign under the section saying they have engaged a doctor or person publicly professing to heal or cure or they must sign under the section saying they have not engaged a doctor or person publicly professing to heal or cure. They must sign under one category or the other. They must also put down their home town, and how they arrived in Hot Springs—by bus or car, or however. We have to be strict. We're dealing with thermal waters. For example, for the standard bath the tub temperature must be from ninety-eight to a hundred degrees and the maximum time permitted in the tub is twenty minutes. If the bather wants the optional, dollar-extra whirlpool action—a mixer-type device is lowered into the clear water and agitates it—the maximum temperature is a hundred degrees and the maximum tubbing time is fifteen minutes. One or more cups of water, from a faucet alongside the tub, are permitted while tubbing. You don't just sit in the tub. Heavens, no! An attendant massages your body with a special bath mitt, which has a rough fibroid surface, and which is made right here in Hot Springs. I haven't even begun. There are the vapor baths. This is steam. People stand in a showerlike arrangement, either with their heads in or with their heads out—two minutes for the head in, five minutes for the head out—*under the constant supervision of an attendant.* We prescribe a regular shower for two minutes at ninety-eight degrees. And packs—a maximum of thirty minutes in the pack room, during which one is permitted to drink one or more glasses of water. And then the massage. And, finally, there is the cooling-off period, when you just lie down on a cot and cool off. The temperature in the cooling-off room is ninety-five degrees. Some doctors will prescribe a tub temperature of a hundred and one or a hundred and two. The maximum would certainly be a hundred and four—*very* hot, and *very* special. For *extremely* odd aches and pains." Mr. May and his visitor were now in the cooling-off room, where twenty or more men, almost all of them of great bulk, with huge jaws and blue chins, were sleeping like babies on the cots. Mr. May appeared overwhelmed by the sight. "They've never felt better in their lives," he said softly. "They are ready for anything."

One thing that Hot Springs bathers used to get ready for was gambling after dark, but this they can no longer indulge in. The gambling is over at Hot Springs, to the considerable dismay of many clients, who felt that the wear and tear of standing at the gaming tables required them to be watered down and pounded into shape if they were to test their luck again the next night at blackjack, roulette, or slot machines. "You just try pulling one of those bandits all night, chum, and see if your arm doesn't need limbering up," a former game-of-chance client recently remarked to a man standing in the next vapor bath, with his head out. "I needed the baths real bad before and after a night at the Vapors Club or the Southern Club. It was a positive health necessity." He added that he could not understand why the State of Arkansas had taken such a narrow attitude toward the gambling places as to close them down. "Sure it was illegal," he said, his face half hidden by steam, "but the city collected taxes on the illegal take and was making notable civic improvements, including the building of a handsome new municipal auditorium. It is truly a pity." This man, who still goes down to Hot Springs for the baths and for bingo, is convinced that gambling will inevitably resume. "This sort of thing happens," he said. "It's a cycle in human nature. Public officials have a tendency to get virtuous from time to time. I was standing right here in the vapor bath yesterday, and I closed my eyes and went down Memory Lane, and I saw the dense smoke at the

Vapors Club, around the corner from the Arlington, and I saw the floor show, with people eating immense steaks while Mickey Rooney told jokes up on the stage and imitated Jimmy Stewart. I could hear people gambling in the next room, and I could see in my mind's eye the big doors swinging open to the gaming room and to the muted but hysterical hum of voices and the click of the machines and the strange-looking women betting like fiends, with their crazy blond hair and purple hair and green hair. Then the attendant cried 'Steam time up!' and, believe me, when I snapped out of it I was ready for a rubdown and a nap."

MOVIES

I was never one of *The New Yorker*'s regular movie critics. I was asked to fill in during summers, when the critics were on vacation. The assignment was a pleasant one, since I suffer immoderately from hay fever, and the air-conditioned theatres gave blessed relief.

Ach, Du Lieber Weltschmerz!

The Germans are making movies again, and the first one to reach these shores since the war is "Murderers Among Us," in German, with English subtitles, produced on the old UFA lot, now in the Soviet zone of Berlin. It is a tortured, turgid, monotonous tale, set in the desolate wasteland of the bombed German capital. A young surgeon, back from the war, cannot erase from his memory the part he was forced to play in the liquidation of more than a hundred innocent Polish men, women, and children on Christmas Eve, 1942, in occupied Poland. He spends most of his time staggering through puddles and rubble in a drunken stupor, occasionally dropping in at one of those intense cabarets indigenous to prewar German films and replete with the symbolic tinkle of shattered glassware, the outsize prostitutes with black garters, and *Weltschmerz* that cuts like butter. Once in a while, he goes home to a shattered flat, which he shares with a *Fräulein* who has returned from a concentration camp to find that he has moved into her quarters. Because of the housing shortage, she lets him stay on. She tidies up the place, and, *Gott in Himmel*, they fall in love. Meanwhile, the surgeon's wartime commanding officer—the fellow who issued the liquidation order—is in Berlin, too, manufacturing saucepans from helmets, making scads of marks, and not worrying about the past.

The film stumbles to its climax when the surgeon, with intent to kill, tracks down the manufacturer on Christmas Eve, in 1945, and finds him standing under a Christmas tree at his factory, surrounded by his workers and oozing *gemütlich* Yule sentiment. Observing this touching scene, the surgeon recalls with hideous clarity the Polish episode and returns, in his mind's eye, to Poland. The camera being a magical instrument, we go to Poland, too. There is the captain standing under a Christmas tree, and there is the surgeon begging him to cancel the massacre. "Captain," he says, "how can you do this thing on *Christmas Eve?*" The captain sneers. "But must we kill the children? Why the *children?*" pleads the surgeon. The massacre comes off on schedule, and the camera returns us to the Berlin of 1945, where the surgeon is prevented from murdering the manufacturer by the breathless arrival of the *Fräulein*, a girl with a passion for cleanliness. There are some impressive closing shots of the manufacturer shrieking, for all the world to hear, "I am innocent!," but the film's entire message was invalidated for me by those Polish scenes, since the guilt preying on the doctor's mind—and, presumably, on the minds of Germans in general—would appear to be less a matter of feeling heartsick at the murder of innocent people than of having committed the indelicacy of snuffing out children on Christmas Eve. I gathered that there would have been no feeling of guilt, and hence no picture, had the adults alone been murdered and the execution of the kiddies postponed until some lazy non-holiday. You can't blame actors for a wretched script, and it should be noted that Ernst Borchert, as the hapless surgeon; Arno Paulsen, as the captain-manufacturer; and Hildegard Knef, as the sanitary heroine, all registered the required agony. I was thoroughly delighted when this picture ended.

The Return of Nanook

Robert J. Flaherty, a consummate artist, turned out "Nanook of the North" more than twenty-five years ago, in the silent time. It was a stoic tale of almost classic simplicity, an hour-long documentary of the daily life of a Hudson Bay Eskimo and his family, and it revealed a profound knowledge on Flaherty's part both of his subject matter and of the power of the camera. Now "Nanook of the North" is back, enriched by an intelligent spoken narrative (written by Ralph Schoolman), some judicious sound effects, and a peach of a score. Herbert Edwards, who produced this edition of the film, has subordinated the sound to the picture itself, and the real beauty of "Nanook" is still in the hands of Flaherty and his camera. Flaherty lived among the Eskimos on the eastern shores of Hudson Bay. He watched their ceaseless struggle to stay alive and their strange communion with, and antagonism to, nature, and he marvelled at their adaptability, season in and season out. Few people presumably remember that Nanook—The Bear—is the name of an Eskimo, whose earthly possessions, including his wife, two sons, and a sister-in-law, can all be stowed away, when he is travelling by water, inside a single kayak. Nanook is forever on the move. Spring brings him to the trading post, where he sells his skins of sable, seal, fox, and polar bear, and listens, for the first time, and with complete bewilderment, to a phonograph. During the short summer, he fishes and sets his traps. Fall and winter find him crossing the seemingly endless ice, seeking food for his family, building his igloo at the close of the day, bedding down family and dogs at night, and rising again another day to repeat the struggle. Through Flaherty, Nanook emerges as a truly great man. He is swift as a cat, genial, undefeated, a proud father who transmits his knowledge to his children, and just about the most capable fellow, I am sure, north of Boston. Nanook keeps alive through his mastery of his hunting knife; he never lets the weapon out of his hand. As pictured by Flaherty, Nanook's knife becomes the brush of an old master and the scalpel of a surgeon, now cutting through the ice, now ripping open a huge walrus, now fashioning a window for his igloo. Hollywood has debased the word "epic" by applying it to almost all of its dreary little products, but epic is the word for "Nanook," and a good word, too.

A curiously disturbing short, "Letter to a Rebel," has been produced by RKO-Pathé, in its widely advertised "This Is America" series. It calls for some comment, since I am afraid that the film is sadly symptomatic of the complacent poster propaganda and one-dimensional patriotism that we are in for these days. A young college editor writes to his father, an old-time country editor in an idyllic upstate New York town, and expresses some confusion over what he takes to be inequalities and strains in our economic system. Father sits right down at his trusty Underwood and bats out one of those bargain-basement-Whitman replies to Son. Now, I have no quarrel with Father's thesis that this is a wonderful country, but I do quarrel with his emphasis on what makes it fine. Father thinks it is fine mainly because of the big, shining super-markets, and the canned pineapple juice ("How much do you think that would cost in rubles, Son?" he asks, irrelevantly), and the corner gas station. Father makes a point of reminding Son that men are actually permitted to picket in this country, speaking as though the rights of labor could be controlled by spigots, to be turned on and off. I seem to remember a time when lip service, at least, was paid to America's greatness as a giant melting pot of rich strains and wild ideas, but Father merely reminds Son that his ancestors fought at Bunker Hill. There is an unmistakable odor of herring about this picture. No special color. Just herring.

Among the orthodox new films, "Escape," from the Galsworthy play, comes closest to being passable, but stress has been placed more on the routine aspects of a man hunt than on Galsworthy's serious concern with the inexorability of the law and its effect upon a sensitive Englishman. . . . "Pitfall" quite lives up to its name. Fair warning.

The Great Man

These are the dog days in the motion-picture-exhibiting field, all right. When I say "dog," I am not referring to small dogs—Pekes and Poms— but to great big, snarly, ill-tempered beasts. Up and down Broadway, the mastiffs are now on display, and the only conceivable reason people pay their money to attend is that they have an uncontrollable urge to climb into an icebox and stay there for a couple of hours.

In contrast to what is laughingly called "the current cinema"— so hot, so dry, so cruel on the mind—I should like to recommend an eight-year-old creation of W. C. Fields', "Never Give a Sucker an Even Break," mercifully resurrected at the Avenue Playhouse. I seriously doubt if you will find anything funnier in town. (I seriously doubt if you will find anything else in town that is funny at all.) At the risk of having to fight a duel with the earnest group that believes "The Bank Dick" is Fields' masterpiece, I hereby enter "Never Give a Sucker an Even Break" as my nomination for his funniest picture. In it, the boozy old Master has a wild and glorious fling. Largely responsible for the semblance of plot, he has cast himself as The Great Man, an avuncular fixture at a studio named Esoteric Pictures. The Great Man is peddling one of his own scenarios, a script of classic dimensions in which he has outlined for himself, naturally, the leading role. Most of "Never Give a Sucker an Even Break" consists of scenes from this imaginary film, perhaps the sharpest parody of Hollywood ever made. We see Fields high in the skies in a fabulous airliner with his beautiful niece, a child singer of the species *Durbina durbina*. This child bursts into song at the slightest provocation. Dawn breaks, and The Great Man, in his aerial upper berth, is suffering from the usual complaint. "Are you sick?" asks the hostess, peering through the curtains. "Somebody put two olives in my Martini," moans The Great Man. "Would you like a Bromo-Seltzer?" asks the hostess. "I couldn't stand the noise," says The Great Man. A moment later, and he is on the open observation platform of this mythical plane. He places a bottle on the window sill, and over it goes. Over, after it, goes The Great Man. He lands on a settee high on a mountaintop, in an idyllic garden, alongside one of the loveliest chicks imaginable. "Are you a man?" she asks. "I have never seen a man before in my whole life." The Great Man can barely restrain his delight. He teaches her a little game they play down below called Squidjum, in which people close their eyes and press their lips together. Just a game, he assures her, and she enjoys Squidjum like merry hell until her mother, a witch type, appears and wants to play, too. Over the side of the mountain goes The Great Man, and into a Russian village where the happy peasants are singing frantic songs dedicated to the beauties of the soil.

There is small point in pursuing further the logical line of this drama. Before The Great Man is through, he has encountered a huge gorilla, blown the foam off an ice-cream soda, and wildly driven an elderly lady to a maternity hospital, under the mistaken impression that she is about to have a baby. Believe me, there has never been anything like that automobile ride anywhere, not even in "The Bank Dick."

The Bad Old Days

Compared to the glimpses I caught of twelfth-century England in M-G-M's "Ivanhoe," the twentieth century, with its hydrogen bomb and cold war, is a lazily swinging hammock on a peaceful summer day. According to my count, "Ivanhoe" lasts a hundred and seven minutes, and of them approximately ninety-one and a half are devoted to outsize physical violence. There is not a king, a pretender, a knight, a squire, a manservant, a handmaiden, a fief, a fife, or a foof on the premises who does not carry at the very least a bow and arrow or some sort of murderous medieval billy, and even the Fool (who brought to mind Max Beerbohm's comment on Shakespearean fools, "Methinks the Fool is a fool") packs a heavy wallop between his bad jokes. Everybody fights everybody else twenty-four hours a day—sometimes hand-to-hand; sometimes with chairs and tables; sometimes with axes and heavy balls attached to chains; sometimes with grouse legs and shanks of mutton; sometimes by tossing vast quantities of rocks off the parapets of keeps; sometimes by raising and lowering drawbridges over moats and thereby plunging shouting, screaming, punching knots of Middle-Aged muscle men into the narrow drink beneath; sometimes by lunging at one another with long lances while on horseback, occasions for which the principals get both themselves and their mounts up in the best traditions of Macy parade couture. When matters temporarily quiet down, barbecue pits are made ready for human beings to be roasted over; stakes are erected for the purpose of burning beautiful young women; or all hands repair to the Great Hall, or cafeteria, where they savagely head into huge platters heaped with meat and bone, storing up energy for the next round. Two or three times during the hubbub, I was tempted to turn to the man in the next seat and sock him in the nose, just for the hell of it.

According to the scenario, this ceaseless ruckus has something to do with a difference of opinion between the Normans and the Saxons, the former having pledged their allegiance to a long-faced, sallow fellow travelling under the name of Prince John, the latter having done likewise to his brother, King Richard the Lion-Hearted. Beneath and around the bloodshed, M-G-M has made a solemn attempt to tell, with a good many variations, the story that Scott put down on paper, and before matters are brought to a rousing conclusion (King Richard, who has been held captive in Austria, rides up in a terrific cloud of dust, accompanied by a massive posse of henchmen), we have witnessed the devoted efforts Wilfred of Ivanhoe (Robert Taylor) makes in behalf of Richard (Norman Wooland); his romance with the beautiful Rowena (Joan Fontaine); his attentions to the Jewess Rebecca (Elizabeth Taylor), whose father, Isaac (Felix Aylmer), raises the ransom money to spring Richard from his Austrian captives; and his struggles with his gruff but lovable daddy, Sir Cedric (Finlay Currie). The adapters, when not intent on exterminating every Norman and Saxon, wrote several sensitive passages about the plight of Rebecca and her father in an England that considered them infidels and outcasts, but they neglected to say why, if Rebecca and Isaac are such outcasts, they always manage to have front-row seats at the big lance jousts. To be sure, they aren't in the Turf & Field Club, along with the Royal Family, but they nonetheless have choice locations.

Jean Cocteau, who is no longer an *enfant* but who might reasonably still be described as *terrible*, has come along with a tortured, violent study of diseased adolescence called "The Strange Ones." In this one, Sis loves Brud with such passion that she destroys a love letter he has written to his sweetheart, thinking thus to keep him for herself. He ends up by eating an exotic poison, *nature*, and she, exposed at last for the foul little creature she is, shoots herself with a forty-five. I guess I am not the man to tell you what M. Cocteau, who helped adapt the picture from one of his novels, had in mind. . . . Rita Hayworth is back, in a spy-chase thriller, "Affair in Trinidad," and you would hardly know she had been away.

Their Finest Hour

Once upon a time, on the Island of Celluloid, as the legend goes, seven writers—Franco Brusati, Mario Camerini, Ennio de Concini, Hugh Gray, Ben Hecht, Ivo Perilli, and Irwin Shaw—banded together, left their families and their homes, and went out in pursuit of an old man called Homer. Their motive will perhaps always be shrouded in mystery, but the fact remains that they caught up with him, and, to employ the hallowed Greek expression, they Let Him Have It. They Let Him Have It with a movie called "Ulysses." Indeed, what they seem to have resented most about the old man was a poem he had written, called "The Odyssey," the central figure of which was a hero named Ulysses, a resident of Ithaca, the husband of Penelope, and the conqueror of Troy. The seven writers, who were known collectively as the Furies, planned their campaign skillfully. They were well financed, and money was no object. They moved into the Mediterranean area with cameras and camera crews, built galleys, courts, palaces, and a Trojan Horse. They hired sirens, kings, princesses, and one-eyed giants. They took along a fellow named Kirk Douglas, to play the part of Ulysses, and a girl named Silvana Mangano, to play the part of Penelope. Douglas is a muscular, heroic-looking chap, but the Furies felt he needed that old Greek Touch, so they put a beard on him. Miss Mangano qualified perfectly as the lovelorn Greek Penelope, since she is Italian, and the Mediterranean laps the shores of both Greece and Italy. Furthermore, she is stately, speaks no English (her voice had to be dubbed in), and looks as though vitamins might restore her pep. (*Peperi* is a Greek word, meaning "pepper.")

When everything was ready—cameras, sets, and cast—the Furies decided the time had come to let go on old Homer. Did he think he had a story there, with his moth-eaten, rundown, cliché-ridden "Odyssey"? They would show *him* how to spin a tale, how to depict character, how to slow a story down to a standstill one minute and jazz it up with jet dialogue the next. They would make Ulysses what Ulysses was all long (except that Homer didn't have sense enough to know it)—a rip-roaring, block-busting, straight-shooting chap who could lick all the machines at Las Vegas and in his quieter moments run the General Motors agency for all southern Greece. When the Furies were through (the massacre lasted an hour and forty-five minutes), the carnage was horrible to contemplate, and the people on the Island of Celluloid ought to sing sad songs about it, but probably won't.

Low Noon

The moment this fellow rides into town on a mule wagon, you know darn well it's Jimmy Stewart. There's something about the slope of his shoulders and the quiet, easygoing, self-possessed way he handles the mule team that *makes* you know it's Jimmy Stewart. There's something else, too. You can tell by looking at the mules' ears. The mules know that no ordinary actor has hold of the reins. They know when a star has hold of the reins, and their ears go up. I've seen it happen a hundred times. Well, Jimmy Stewart has ridden all the way from Laramie, Wyoming, to the town of Coronado, New Mexico, and he has a solemn mission. Seems that his kid brother, an Army man, was ambushed and killed in Coronado by a bloodthirsty band of Apaches armed with automatic rifles. The question naturally arises: Who sold the Apaches the automatic rifles? It must have been someone in Coronado, and this is the someone that Jimmy Stewart is after. Jimmy takes a hundred and four minutes to discover the culprit. Part of the time (incidentally, the film is called "The Man from Laramie"), one would be entirely justified in believing that the villain is an Indian who works in a drygoods store. This Indian is a sneaky-looking chap, full of dark scowls and soft, patty-pat steps. Now you see him, now you don't. He never smiles. But he isn't the villain. One might think that good old Donald Crisp, who plays a rugged, individualistic rancher, is the villain. Not on your life. Old Donald Crisp is too smart a rancher to get mixed up with the Apaches in a wicked deal. Then there's the old rancher's niece, Cathy O'Donnell, who is fresh out of the Connecticut College for Women and is in love with the old rancher's No. 1 man. It's hard to tell about Cathy, because she's so demure and reserved and the producers always might just fool you and make the girl a villain. But no. The rancher has a hysterical, sadistic son, but it's clear to any practiced moviegoer that *he* can't be the villain. And at no point, it should be stated, is Jimmy Stewart suspect. He is pure as pure can be, and he is the victim of so much brutality—he is dragged around at the end of a rope attached to a horse, he is jumped on and beaten, he has his hand shot full of lead at close range—that you know perfectly well he will end up in Heaven. Aline MacMahon is in the neighborhood, too, but *nobody* would suspect her. She is a rugged ranch owner who lives in Coronado, and every move she makes, and every word she speaks, is a tribute to her talents as an actress. In the end, the villain is uncovered—polished off, in fact—and Jimmy rides back to Laramie, his shoulders sloping and nobility apparent in his every gesture. The film is in color, but not especially bright color; I gather it is quite dark and blue in New Mexico a good deal of the time.

Big, Bigger, Biggest

Leo Tolstoy's novel "War and Peace" has been turned into a motion picture that lasts three hours and twenty-eight minutes. And that's a long time to spend looking at a movie; the way things are going, in a couple of years a fellow will hop aboard his intercontinental ballistic at Hollywood and Vine in the morning and get to the Hilton-Khrushchev three hours and twenty-eight minutes later, in time for brunch. All sorts of persons, places, and animals have been folded into this version of Tolstoy's vision and achievement—an Italian producer, an American director, and actors from England, Ireland, Central Europe, the Dominions Beyond the Seas, and Kansas, not to mention Henry Fonda, Mel Ferrer, Audrey Hepburn, 18,796 horses, 9,359 carriages and wagons, and an indeterminate number of palaces, not to mention sleds, Russia being snowy in the winter. Moreover, 33,749 muskets are employed, and they fire, in the aggregate, 634,729 rounds of ammunition, roughly divided between the French and the Russians. No expense has been spared; clearly, everyone connected with the enterprise put on his thinking cap, and thought big.

What opinion Tolstoy, who was quite a big thinker himself, would have of all this expenditure of time, talent, and energy is debatable, but it seems likely that he would want to slope off by himself and die in a small wayside railroad station. As I need hardly say, Tolstoy loved people—perhaps adored them—and he was forever trying to figure them out, and trying to figure out, too, the reasons for the glorious uncertainty of life. Well, the boys who produced this film have practically knocked themselves senseless in reducing the characters to stereotypes (girl likes boy's face, boy lowers eyes, girl lowers eyes, they kiss, he dies in war, she sees another boy, boy likes girl, boy lowers eyes, they kiss) and reducing the uncertainty of life to that of a Lackawanna timetable (great big house is filled with servants, war comes, family departs, family returns, life goes on, tune in tomorrow).

The writers (six) of the current adaptation of "War and Peace" have concentrated on the Rostovs and the Bolkonskys. The head of the Rostov clan (Barry Jones) is a splendid, healthy Muscovite who gives the impression of having been born, if not in London itself, at least in one of its suburbs. The head of the Bolkonskys (Wilfred Lawson) is an eccentric do-it-yourself man who hails, I suspect, from Dutchess County. Rostov's daughter Natasha (Miss Hepburn) is a troubled adolescent whose love life is as cluttered and shallow as that of a subdeb and whose method of expressing deep feeling is to flutter her eyelids, gasp, and twitch the corners of her mouth ever so slightly. Mr. Ferrer, as Andrey Bolkonsky, one of the men in her life, is a paragon of woodenness. When he dies (twenty-two minutes), he does it the hard way, with grunts, groans, sobs, and always, of course, a stiff upper lip. Mr. Fonda, as Pierre—and a Bezuhov, by God—is the egghead of the production. He wears glasses, thinks solemn thoughts, and stumbles about a good deal, butting into battles, picking flowers, and trying to solve the riddle of life. Napoleon is played by Herbert Lom, who simplifies matters by portraying the Emperor as an elegantly tailored juvenile delinquent. Mr. Lom paces a good deal, and keeps one hand behind his back. Oscar Homolka is cast as General Kutuzov, and he miraculously manages, amid the wholesale carnage, to put a brilliant and genuine imprint of his own upon the film. When last heard from, the French (187,694 strong) were headed back toward Paris, and Napoleon was looking for a softer job.

Love

Ah, the French—or, at any rate, two films about the French, "La Parisi-enne" and "A Certain Smile"! *L'amour, toujours l'amour!* No colonial problem, no monetary difficulties, no splintered parliaments, no schem-ing Left, no sullen Right. Only *l'amour.* *L'amour* for breakfast, lunch, and supper. *L'amour* in the wee hours and in the not so wee hours; in jet planes, flashy motorcars, sidewalk cafés, dark *bistros*, halls of learning, and bathtubs; on public conveyances, motor bikes, and duck shoots; at beaches and airports; along riverbanks and in formal gardens. Puppy love, passionate love, bored love, crazy mixed-up love, love with young men, old men, upstairs, downstairs, all around the town. *L'amour, tou-jours l'amour!*

To get down to cases, let us take the simpler one first—"La Parisi-enne." Here is love scrupulously tailored to the talents of Mlle. Brigitte Bardot. Now, to some, Mlle. Bardot may be incontestable proof that there is a just and benevolent deity; to others, that, after millions of evo-lutionary years, the female form has finally been perfected; and to still others, perhaps more cynical than the rest, that a young, pretty woman with a highly developed comic sense is a pleasure to watch on the screen, regardless of the merits of the script. In any event, here is Mlle. Bardot at her beckoning, feline best, cast as the daughter of a French Prime Minister. She is recklessly nubile, and addicted to pert pouts, fast driving, and sloping around the house clad, or half clad, in a bath towel, or half towel. The object of her desire is none other than her father's *chef de cabinet*, a stunning young specimen of the French Civil Service, wildly ambitious and even more wildly interested in the opposite sex, but desperately anxious to avoid marriage ties. Mlle. Bardot pursues him with a commendable, if somewhat wearing, persistence—through the streets of Paris, in her father's outer office, and ultimately into his bedroom, where she is discovered by fully two-thirds of the French government in his bed (he's there, too, but was expecting someone else), smiling her fetching jungle smile. Her father's honor, career, and government must, of course, be preserved, and the *chef de cabinet's* own career must not be compromised, and so a stately church wedding is hastily arranged and performed. The young lady's husband, however, although properly hitched, retains his wandering eye, despite the fact that his wife employs every trick she knows, including that darn bath towel, to claim his sole attention. When all else fails, she seizes upon the royal visit to Paris of a charming, graying, elegant prince, an experienced man of the world, to make her husband jealous. I wouldn't think of divulging the details of her success; suffice it to say that someone throws a cold lobster at someone else, the dignified prince sneaks off incognito for an afternoon's swim on the Riviera with our heroine, both heroine and prince catch cold, and all ends happily. Mlle. Bardot is an accomplished comedienne, whose style and dash enable her, with the help of several other members of the cast—Henri Vidal, as her reluctant spouse; Charles Boyer, as the royal foil; Nadia Gray, as his princess; and André Luguet, as the harassed head of the French government (no wonder they fall)—to turn this preposterous romp into an hour of reasonable entertainment.

STANLEY

Stanley pieces appeared in Talk of the Town. Their origins are misty, but the generally accepted history is that Mr. Ross, who was tirelessly interested in everything, was curious about small, little-known islands in the East River and New York Harbor. Thinking of Stanley and Livingstone, he assigned an exploring reporter—Our Man Stanley—to visit the sites. Over the years, and without any formal assignment, I found myself writing many Our Man Stanley pieces, so many, in fact, that I decided to put them in a book, an enterprise Mr. Shawn heartily approved. In the Author's Note, I wrote: "I have been Stanley a great deal more often than any other person has been Stanley. As Stanley would say, in his curious, telegraphic style, 'This fact statistical.'. . . I am a writer not an actor, but I love to play Stanley. . . . Stanley's world—*my* man Stanley's world—is a joyous one, where people are still capable of laughter.' "

Below Zero

We put in a call for the Explorers Club last week and got our man Stanley out of the fireplace and on his way to the factory of the Sperry Gyroscope Company in Brooklyn, to investigate the all-weather laboratory we'd been told they have there. Stanley reports that this is unquestionably one of the wonders of the city. The Sperry people built it a year ago to test some of their products, such as gyros, gyro horizons, high-intensity searchlights, and the like, under the equivalent of various extreme weather conditions, ranging from polar blizzards to tropical heat waves. Sperry figured that there was little point in having the Army lug, say, an 800,000,000-candlepower searchlight all the way to Iceland and then discover that it wouldn't work in the cold.

Stanley went over to the Sperry plant on a mild Brooklyn day (max. temp., 65°F.; min. temp., 40°F.) and was greeted at the laboratory door by the engineer in charge, Robert W. Waring, who was swathed to the ears in a sheepskin coat. He offered Stanley a similar coat. "You'll need this," he said, remarking that the temperature inside the laboratory was ten degrees below zero, Fahrenheit. Stanley quickly got himself into the sheepskin and followed Waring into a stainless-steel room, ten feet high by eleven by eleven, equipped with a table and chair, numerous icy coils along the ceiling, and wooden floor planking covered with an early-morning frost. "Wonderfully crisp," said Mr. Waring, rubbing his hands. He told Stanley that he was currently testing the resistance to cold of twelve greases. These samples were encased in cylindrical metal containers lying on the table. Once an hour, Waring said, he would peek in and see how each of the greases was coming along. Stanley began to lose touch with his toes. "Some greases turn to paving stones in this temperature," said Mr. Waring.

With white clouds issuing from his mouth, Mr. Waring gave forth with a few facts about the room's construction. Sperry engineers experimented for two years before picking stainless steel, a substance relatively moisture- and corrosion-proof, and resistant to damage by ultraviolet rays, used occasionally to simulate torrid sunlight. Changes in temperature make the room expand or contract, and Sperry met this problem by suspending the room from the ceiling of the sixth floor. At no other point does it touch the building. "It's like a big can floating in a crate," explained Mr. Waring. Heat and cold are regulated from a control panel in an adjoining room. Waring has found dry ice to be the best medium for producing extreme cold. He never gets the room hotter than 150 degrees or colder than 50 below zero, which is not quite as frigid as the stratosphere but near enough for most test purposes. Men in the laboratory communicate with the outside world by signalling through a small window (six layers of glass) and talking into a two-way speaking device. If Mr. Waring wants a heavy fog in the room, he turns on some water sprays along the ceiling. Blizzards are a cinch, too, requiring only that the door be left open while the room is at a low temperature. Waring offered to whip up a blizzard for Stanley, but Stanley noticed that his hands had turned purple and asked to leave the room.

While Stanley thawed out, Waring told him that he and his associates wear bathing suits when working in tropical temperatures. In extreme Arctic or Newfoundland weather they put on heavy flying suits, leather helmets, and leggings. Nevertheless, it is not uncommon for a man to emerge from the room after bucking a North Atlantic gale with his chin frozen solid to his coat collar. When the laboratory first opened, a physician used to meet Waring and his men each time they returned from the Arctic, wrap them in heavy blankets, ply them with hot drinks, and make them sit around for a while with thermometers in their mouths. Nobody ever got sick and he gave up in amazement.

Summer Day

Our man Stanley, wearing a white linen suit and a Shredded Wheat hat with a maroon pugaree, dropped into the office on a recent warm afternoon and deposited the following dispatch:

"Have just spent delightful Sunday afternoon in New York. Summer resort, American plan. Bright, cloudless, toasty day, intermittently fanned by blessed breezes from two rivers and an ocean. Strolled through Grand Army Plaza, at Fifty-ninth Street, admiring statue of William Tecumseh Sherman, Pulitzer Memorial Fountain, pigeons, other Sunday strollers, and numerous horse cabs lined up between Fifth Avenue and Hotel Plaza. Some cabs open to sun and air, but most covered with summer canopies, fringed. Drivers uniformly antique, crusty-looking. Acted on impulse, hopped into rig drawn by piebald mare, driven by florid-faced man wearing battered black silk topper, spinach-green wool jacket, gray trousers, and high-button brown shoes. Asked him how much through Park. 'Four dollars,' he said, turning around and baring toothless grin. I stayed aboard. 'Tchk, tchk,' said driver to horse, and horse turned north and headed toward Park. Horse stopped alongside A.S.P.C.A. white water wagon on west side of Plaza. 'Free Water for Horses,' said sign on wagon. Driver hopped down, filled bucket with water, and placed it before horse. Horse thirsty. 'What's her name?' I asked driver. 'Nelly,' he called up. 'She's thirsty. I'm thirsty, too, but there's nothing the A.S.P.C.A. can do for me.' Driver hopped back onto rig. 'Tchk, tchk,' he said. Nelly, refreshed, started up.

"Clippity, clop, clop, clop. Clippity, clop, clop, clop. Into Park at

Sixtieth Street. Verdant paradise. 'Get out of here!' cried driver sharply. Pigeons. Pigeons scattered. Nelly picked up speed for a while, slowed down as we passed elephant house, on right, in Zoo. Throng watching big elephant. Elephant putting on Sunday act—waving trunk wildly, jigging. Elephant filled with summer delight. Clippity, clop, clop, clop. 'Where did you get the hat?' I asked driver. Driver let reins slacken, turned, and grinned again. (Horrible!) 'Hats are easy,' he said. 'We get the hats from gentlemen who leave the Hotel Plaza late at night. Many of these fine gentlemen desire to avail themselves of our services in the early hours of the morning. During the winter, mostly, when we drive the closed broughams. They obligingly leave the silk hats with us. They are often under the influence, if you know what I mean. We grab these hats whenever we can get them. They lend dignity to the ride. Get out of here!' Pigeons. 'Whenever I get a hat that doesn't fit,' said driver, 'I take it to my shoemaker, who stretches it to fit my head.' Driver handed his hat to me. 'Select Quality Silk Hat A,' said label. Tried hat on for size. No good. Returned hat to driver. Leaned back to enjoy sights. Passed three men asleep on grass, two of them barefooted. Passed sailors, with girls. Passed family eating picnic on the grass. Passed lovers on the grass. Clippity, clop, clop, clop. Driver entangled in traffic at junction of East Drive and Seventy-second Street road. Driver held out hand with air of authority. Cars behind screeched to halt. 'I'll show them,' said driver, turning left on Seventy-second Street road, and heading west. 'Thought you went all the way up through Park for four dollars,' I said. Driver turned around again. (Ghastly grin!) 'Can't do it any more,' he said. 'We have short rides these days. Liable to be hit by rocks further along in Park. Delinquent boys, you know. Would take two hours, anyway, and cost a fortune.'

"Sat back, relaxed. Passed boat lake. Wonderment of colored rowboats, shirtsleeved rowers. Boats all jammed together—Renoir stuff. Passed cyclists. Passed statue of Daniel Webster—'Liberty and Union, Now and Forever, One and Inseparable.' Daniel solemn, dressed for winter. Turned south on West Drive. Dachshund on leash ran in front of Nelly. Pulled back just in time by owner. 'Give her a little milk, lady,' said driver. Lady laughed. Passed family of four, all in beach chairs, on the grass. Passed six children, who waved at Nelly. Driver waved back. 'Nelly would wave if Nelly *could* wave,' said driver. Passed bust of Mazzini. Mazzini feeling the heat. Passed beautiful girl in pink jersey, riding horse. Nelly whinnied. I whinnied. Passed Tavern-on-the-Green. Plenty of parking space. Clippity, clop, clop, clop. 'Some nights,' driver said, 'the swells hop in and want me to take them to the Waldorf or the Stork. I oblige. The sky's the limit for those fellows. They'll pay anything for the feel of riding around town in a horse cab at night.' Out of Park at Sixth Avenue and Fifty-ninth Street. Clippity, clop, clop, clop. Passed the St. Moritz, passed the Hotel Plaza, went back to where we started from. 'Whoa,' said driver. Hopped out."

White Tie

Our man Stanley blew into the office the other day wearing a rented topper and the cool, detached expression of a man who has seen history in the making. "Jacqueline is yummy," he said cryptically, and deposited the following dispatch:

"Have been to Inaugural Ball, in Washington. 'Ben-Hur' intimate, cozy affair by comparison. Was house guest of friends in Georgetown, block or so from President's former home, mile or so from President's new home. Heart of things. Earlier, had spent several frigid, numbing hours on snow-swept Capitol Hill, watching swearing-in ceremonies. Moving, impressive beyond measure, but lost contact with seven toes. Returned to Georgetown, lay down under heavy blanket, concentrated on reëstablishing liaison with missing toes. When all ten toes present and accounted for, rose and dressed for small private dinner with host and hostess, several guests, and my companion, a rose-beige job with close-fitting bodice and velvet trim. Ran into snag with wing collar. Wing collar a little devil. At dinnertime, entered drawing room wearing tailcoat. Ladies in party glittering in sequins and satins, gloves drawn up to shoulder blades; men elegant, distinguished, filled with muted national gaiety. Small talk. 'Remarkable speech,' 'New national purpose,' 'Rededication,' 'Don't forget your tickets,' and so on. Gobbled dinner, donned overcoat and white silk scarf, patted topper into position, and climbed into limousine for long drive to National Guard Armory. Armory miles away, on other side of town, through glazed streets. Passed Lincoln Memorial, ablaze; Washington Monument, ablaze; White House whiter than white, ablaze; and bright dome of Capitol, ablaze. Snow piled everywhere. Skiddy, brilliant night.

"Armory ablaze, too, from huge spotlights. Long parallel lines of cars drawing up to green canopies stretching from Armory to street. Arrived as Russian Ambassador arrived in parallel lane. Stepped out of car as Russian Ambassador stepped out of his. Moment of peaceful coexistence. 'Slushy,' I said, 'but probably more like a spring night to you, with your long winters.' Ambassador noncommittal. Trained diplomat. Smiled, said nothing. Too soon to begin negotiations anyway. Handed ticket to man at door, walked onto vast Armory floor—stunning orange-and-tan drapes hanging from ceiling, floor sanded, great golden bandstand along one side, long box on other side embellished with royal-blue drapes and with seal of the President and the Vice-President. Handed ticket stub to Ruritanian general, who summoned West Point cadet—from long line of cadets and midshipmen—who graciously stepped forward, offered arm to my companion, escorted her to box. I walked alone. Box a sort of stall, containing camp chairs, tray with empty glasses, and empty ice container wrapped in silver foil. Shook off cadet and asked companion for a twirl. Still room to twirl. Meyer Davis orchestra playing. We twirled, exchanging discreet national gaieties. Presidential box still empty, except for Senator Dirksen, alone in rear seat, wearing ruminative smile. I headed, with companion, for frigid refreshment tent at east end of Armory. Refreshment tent offering domestic champagne in paper cups, various colas, orange pop, slices of fruitcake. Ate slice of fruitcake, hurried back to warmth of Armory. Armory now taking on aspect of mob scene. Meyer Davis, on revolving bandstand, revolved. Count Basie orchestra swung into view. Basie in *full* swing. Raised temperature in Armory fifteen degrees. Not much room to dance. Estimated fifteen thousand now in Armory. Passed block-long confectioner's display, surmounted by cake of White House. White House cake almost as big as White House, decorated along side of base with red sugar roses. 'Please don't nibble the cake!' short man standing alongside cake cried out. 'We want to keep it looking beautiful for when the President arrives.' Man said that Local 51 of Cake Bakers Union had baked cake and made twenty-five thousand slices in addition, for this and the four other Inaugural Balls that were going on simultaneously. Struggled over to post beneath Presidential box. Boxes on each side filling up—friends of the President, aides-de-camp, admirals, generals, politicians, cousins. Swish of taffeta almost drowned out Count Basie. Flurry of excitement in Presidential box. Mr. and Mrs. Joseph P. Kennedy arrived, headed for seats in front row center. Mrs. Kennedy in sequined white. 'Molyneux,' whispered my companion. Joseph Kennedy removed overcoat. Also inadvertently removed tailcoat. For few moments, President's father, high in box, in shirtsleeves. Instantly rescued by Mrs. Kennedy, other ladies, restored to paternal elegance. Several regiments of uniformed men cleared center aisle between bandstand and Presidential box, pushing throngs on each side behind white ropes. Count Basie disappeared, Meyer Davis reappeared.

"Crush overwhelming. Now impossible to twirl. Pretty lady in front of me fainted dead away, was carried off by two sailors. Future admirals, those chaps, friendly, quick to perform duty. Mounting excitement in Presidential box. Vice-President and Mrs. Johnson arrived with Linda Bird (in white), Lucy Baines (in blue). Lady Bird in pink. Greeted crowds warmly. Mrs. Johnson spotted friends, gave short, fluttering greetings, tugged at Vice-President's sleeve. Nice family. Suddenly, fanfare from band, intake of breath from crowd. Into box stepped First Lady, a vision, poised, regal, with melting, restrained smile. 'Sheath of peau d'ange,' whispered my companion. 'Overblouse of white chiffon. Silver-embroidered bodice. Long white gloves. Hair bouffant, but not *too* bouffant.' 'Golly Ned,' I said. Band played 'Hail to the Chief.' The Chief arrived, tanned, confident, controlled, swift-moving, happy. Bet he had no trouble with *his* collar! Box suddenly filled with Kennedys— sisters, brothers, brothers-in-law, sisters-in-law. Vigorous, athletic faces aglow. President and Mrs. Kennedy stared at packed mass below, packed mass below stared at the Kennedys. Inaugural Ball had now become Inaugural Viewing. Crowd cheered and cheered again, fluttered handkerchiefs. President and his wife smiled, waved. Dignified smiles, dignified waves. President on top of world, but his waves were Presidential waves, restrained, powerful. Great musical fanfare as Cabinet, led by Mr. and Mrs. Stanley Woodward (Mr. Woodward co-chairman of Ball), walked in brisk line down center aisle and passed in review under Presidential box and out into the night. Orchestra played new, specially written song entitled 'Jacqueline' ('Jacqueline, Jacqueline, Jacqueline, she is charming, she is sweet') and one entitled 'Lady Bird' ('I keep my eyes on the skies with my dreams about Lady Bird'). Jacqueline and Lady Bird smiled politely. President got up, moved around restlessly, and shook hands all over box. Mr. and Mrs. Joseph Kennedy sat down alongside Jacqueline and chatted with her. Medley of Texas songs brought Johnsons to their feet, waving; medley of Irish songs revealed gleaming teeth of Kennedy family. Couldn't take my eyes off Jacqueline. Couldn't move even if I had wanted to. She chatted with Johnsons, smiled her detached smile. She looked around once or twice at President, who was still in motion. I spied Hugh Gaitskell, Hubert Humphrey, man from Local 51. More flourishes, and Presidential party suddenly departed—heading for more balls, and White House, and the long big years. Hail to the Chief!"

Pageant

Our Special Inauguration Correspondent, back from several frigid days of pomp and circumstance in the nation's capital, and now thoroughly thawed, has filed the following dispatch:

Must have heard "The Battle Hymn of the Republic" at least forty-seven times. Deeply love the piece, and always get a lump in my throat (visions of Honest Abe), but wish it were played with somewhat more discretion. Arrived on Friday (two days before private swearing-in at the White House, three days before official swearing-in at the Capitol) and settled into hotel room overlooking White House and Lafayette Park. Stunning view of the grand old house, gleaming brightly in snowy grounds, with Washington Monument behind. Lafayette Park another matter: chockablock with huge motor vans containing television equipment and temporary offices for broadcasting people; a truck marked "PEPSI;" a truck marked "GOURMET PRODUCTIONS—THE ROLLING FEAST;" and signs reading "LIVE BY THE BOMB, DIE BY THE BOMB," "LOVE IS THE WAY TO WIN," and "WANTED: WISDOM AND HONESTY." Brief walk through eerily quiet streets. Gridlock worse than in New York. Impossible for anything to move in any direction. Heimlich maneuver obviously required. Stood for a moment at dusk outside Russian Embassy and watched stolid-looking man in dark suit sticking head out of first one Embassy window and then another, methodically closing metal shutters on windows. Embassy a huge mansion, but great metal gate in front gives one the feeling it's an impenetrable fortress. Strange sensation, heightened by fact that Polish Solidarity flag flies directly across from Embassy, in front of headquarters of International Union of Electronic, Electrical, Technical, Salaried and Machine Workers, A.F.L.-C.I.O.

Getting dark now, and much colder, and time to head for Ellipse and the first official Inauguration function—a Prelude Pageant set in the packed snow of icy park behind White House. Rigid security. Had to pass through airport-type detectors; nearby woman's handbag subjected to intense scrutiny—every item removed and examined. Bitter, biting winds as a hardy band of spectators faced a garish stage topped by an immense red-white-and-blue eagle that bore an unkind resemblance to a Thanksgiving turkey. Many police with dogs on leashes. Sudden stir behind stage as long, dark motor cavalcade, punctuated by red motorcycle lights, swept up, having silently wheeled around from the White House. Vice-President and Mrs. Bush appeared, waved briefly, and entered glass booth to one side of stage. A moment later, President and Mrs. Reagan walked out onto stage, he bundled up in long, dark greatcoat, with white scarf, she in vivid-red coat. He has a distinctive walk—a rolling lope of great vigor—and an easy wave of the hand. He entered glass booth and, I hope, was warm. I was cold, but I'm not President. Reagan and company listened to pageant narration delivered by Fess Parker (Daniel Boone and Davy Crockett of television), who left few notes in American history untouched, with heavy emphasis on Valley Forge, Bull Run, Gettysburg, settling of the West ("Trappers and traders. Much like the films we used to make, Mr. President"). Clichés danced in the bone-chilling night: "Storm clouds were gathering on the horizon" (this was the Civil War), "The country was looking for a man in shining armor" (this was the Depression, and the man, who has become an anomalous folk hero to the incumbent, was Franklin Delano Roosevelt). Songs and dancing by courageous young performers jumping up and down in red-white-and-blue costumes. Then fireworks, an immense display of sound and light, completely illuminating capital's sky, and the President and his party, silently, almost mysteriously, were gone. Brown clouds of acrid smoke settled over frozen Ellipse.

On Saturday, hotel took on air of almost imperial importance. Security people everywhere, presumably guarding unidentified prominent guests. I noticed outside several rooms along my corridor men's knee-length embroidered alligator boots, Texas-style, waiting to be shined. Buzz in lobby became noticeably higher. Many tall, well-turned-out, tanned men and tall, well-turned-out women waiting for stretch limousines to appear in hotel driveway. Many women garnished with wide variety of deceased animals, often floor length. Down to Capitol for vital credentials, past more of same intense security, and into cozy office of Roy L. McGhee, genial superintendent of Senate Periodical Press Gallery. Splendid credentials issued for prime seat facing Inaugural stand at west end of Capitol. Had afternoon to wander through beauties of horizontal Washington (low buildings, vast spaces, sense of history). The National Gallery an extraordinary spot: so many mothers wheeling children in strollers, atmosphere of accessibility so much stronger than in many museums I will not mention. Saw stunning portrait by Edward Savage of first First Family. The only one of Washington, Martha, and his stepgrandchildren painted from life, it also included, in the background, his hunting companion and Revolutionary War attendant, William (Billy) Lee, a black man. Washington is seated at a table examining a map of the city of Washington, and is elegant, composed, and utterly superior in appearance. Out again into cold, and followed my instinct to the Vietnam Veterans Memorial, not far from the Lincoln Memorial. My first experience of this, and a sobering, shattering one. Memorial is a triumph of abstract art, one polished black granite wall of vertical slabs sloping gently downward to form an angle with another wall, which slopes gently up again. The walls (designed by Maya Ying Lin, of Athens, Ohio, a Yale student) are inscribed with fifty-eight thousand and seven names of those killed in the war, and the cumulative effect of the tiny, neat etched names—each slab reflecting the living observers with mirrorlike clarity—becomes overwhelming. Hundreds of people here, extremely silent, many placing small floral arrangements or American flags in front of a name here, a name there. Quiet National Park Rangers and volunteers holding thick paperbound directories of the names, to facilitate locating particular persons. Many young people, bundled up against the cold, and many older people, most of them simply dressed, and always that strange silence of questing people, seeking comfort in the snow.

·   ·   ·

On Sunday, President and Vice-President sworn in at private ceremony in White House. Gave me a neighborly feeling to watch ceremony on a set in my room and, at the same time, look out upon White House itself. Distinctive feeling of reality intermingled with make-believe. President and Vice-President were to make a brief appearance outside, on North Portico (the one I was facing), a moment after the swearing-in, but a large white wall had been erected in front of portico, so there were the two men on the portico on the set, but no sight of them when I glanced out the window. Snow now swirling through streets in circular formations, temperature in low teens. Streets deserted. Down to National Air and Space Museum to hear Red Clay Ramblers in an Inaugural concert. Ramblers an Appalachian string band with banjo, guitar, harmonica, fiddle, bass, piano. Museum totally jammed (over ten million visit it each year), mostly with young people carrying packs, many of whom were curled in corners, their packs beside them. Outside, through huge windows, snow swirling madly across Mall. Almost every young person's jacket had a legend on the back: "Avengers," "Crusaders," "Percussion." To one side of Ramblers, stretching vertically into upper reaches of museum, rose grim reminders of past, Hitler's V-1 flying bomb and V-2 rocket; next to them were two space capsules joined nose to nose—the Apollo-Soyuz Test Project, common docking system of 1975 exchange in space between the two superpowers (quiet symbols of hope). "Oh, how I wish I was back in Peoria, Oh, how I miss the girls in Peoria," sang Ramblers.

Monday, day of official outdoor swearing-in. Early-morning temperature four degrees below zero, Fahrenheit. All outdoor tickets declared invalid. Disappointing. Went outside hotel to watch President Reagan arrive for prayer service at St. John's Church, across from Lafayette Park. *Most* elaborate security. Hand-held metal detector pressed against my coat and under my arms as I stood and watched Presidential party arrive: motorcycles, police cars, long black limousines, then limousine with Presidential seal, then open Secret Service car, then more motorcycles and police, and an ambulance. The President, hatless, strode into church. "I'm glad he's praying," said man next to me. Sudden word from friend McGhee that a ticket available for me in the Rotunda. Wild taxi ride to Capitol. Was stopped by police and Secret Service near foot of Capitol Hill, stopped by police and Secret Service at top of Capitol Hill, but tightly clutched tickets previously issued got me inside building, where I was escorted by kindly McGhee to Rotunda. Truly a sight. Rotunda is *enormous*—nearly a hundred feet across, more than a hundred and eighty feet high—with sandstone walls, sandstone floor, classic frieze circling entire room high up, and, higher still, at tip-top, an allegorical painting depicting General Washington (dim in the distance) seated between Liberty and Victory and in close proximity to Arts, Sciences, Commerce, and Agriculture. Sun streamed in through windows in huge dome. Floor of Rotunda solidly packed with members of Congress, diplomats, Supreme Court, Marine Band (blazing-red jackets), Cabinet members. A small platform had been erected near center of Rotunda, with a lectern for use of the President. At very center of Rotunda, over a white marble disc in the floor, twenty-six Americans have lain in state, including Abraham Lincoln, the Unknown Soldier, John F. Kennedy, and Hubert H. Humphrey. Didn't have much chance to think about past, although past was everywhere. Hand of Marine Band's leader was poised in midair, awaiting cue. Suddenly, his hand moved, and "Hail to the Chief" boomed through the hall. The acoustics were perfect, the moment solemn. The President entered with his usual brisk walk. Dressed in a dark-blue suit, the inevitable white handkerchief in his jacket pocket. The oath of office was quietly administered by a dark-robed and intensely white-maned Chief Justice Burger. The President, without a TelePrompTer, and in subdued, almost intimate tones, began his address. Behind him were his family and Cabinet, before him the representatives of the people. Facing him were huge murals of Washington resigning his commission, Cornwallis surrendering at Yorktown. The President seemed deeply affected by the unexpected indoor surroundings. He spoke conversationally, unpretentiously. He talked of "the American sound—hopeful, bighearted, idealistic, daring, decent, and fair." Prayers, "Hail to the Chief," and the President was gone—to lunch and four more years. I, too, said a small prayer—for daring, for decency, for fairness.

REMEMBERING

Mr. Shawn

This curious, complicated, fascinating man—unlike anyone else I have ever known—often gave the impression of being totally and mysteriously detached from the grit and dross of ordinary human beings. He worked so hard and seemed so durable that many of us fooled ourselves into thinking that he would live forever. Of course, this was nonsense, but nobody wanted to admit it. Beneath the soft voice and the elaborate manners, Shawn was a most passionate fellow, and his greatest passion was words. To Shawn, words meant thought, civilization, decency. Words were the linchpins of a just and orderly society. He approached words with caution and deep respect. Certain words appeared to make him almost physically ill and were instantly stamped out, but when someone handed him words strung together in graceful sentences that touched his mind and heart he experienced the joy that many feel when they hear a Bach sonata. Somehow, by encouraging his writers to feel free, to be bold and truthful, he brought them to the peak of their powers.

I worked with him from 1939 until 1987, often from the initial proposal of an idea (he grasped ideas with the speed of light) through the cherished phone call of acceptance and through galley and page proofs. These sessions were mostly brief and businesslike: a word here, a nuance there, a fact to be further clarified. But there is one evening in the late forties that is indelibly impressed on my mind. I had written a long report on a visit to the Argentina of Juan Perón. The narrative ended with Señor Perón unexpectedly introducing me, as he opened elegant

French doors in the Presidential palace in Buenos Aires, to Evita Perón. I wrote that I took her hand and found it "stone cold." Shawn and I were going over the proof. The time was around 10 P.M. He became agitated. " 'Stone cold,' " he said, "requires a hyphen."

I became agitated. "Put a hyphen there and you spoil the ending," I said. "That hyphen would be ruinous."

"Perhaps you had better sit outside my office and cool off," he said. "I'll go on with my other work."

I took a seat outside his office. From time to time, he would stick his head out and say, "Have you changed your mind?"

"No hyphen," I replied. "Absolutely no hyphen." I was quite worked up over the hyphen.

Sometime around two-thirty in the morning, Shawn said, wearily, "All right. No hyphen. But you are wrong."

We remained dear friends, hyphen or no hyphen, to the end.

Remembering Mary Bingham

Everything about Mary Caperton Bingham was upbeat. She was ninety years old, and dauntless. She was a good friend of mine and my wife's, and just a few weeks ago we spent a long and lovely weekend with her at her home, outside Louisville, Kentucky, having a hard time keeping up with her schedule as she shepherded us to eight plays in three days at the celebrated Humana Festival of the Actors Theatre of Louisville, one of the many special pleasures in her life. Mary was the widow of Barry Bingham, the legendary publisher of the liberal and influential Louis-ville *Courier-Journal*, and for many years she had been the literary edi-tor of the paper. Her invitations arrived like beneficent beams of sunlight, accompanied by cautionary reminders that the world is a seri-ous place. She would send a flurry of blue Post-its, containing, in her hand, such welcoming words as "joy," "embrace," "delight," and "can't wait," but printed at the bottom of the slips were such messages as "Annually, each American pays taxes of $1,137.28 for the military, $201.00 for education and 68 cents for the arts." And then, under those, in her own hand, "Love, Mary."

Shortly after our weekend, she attended a large testimonial dinner in her honor in Louisville. She rose, with a captivating smile, and said that she had been so touched by the evening that "the best thing would be for a big pink cloud to come down and take me away." She then plunged into her speech. More money was needed for the Louisville Free Public Library. Something was amiss with the press: it was neglecting its responsibilities in a democracy. She was halfway through, coming to a paragraph that contained the words "I think another and understandable reason for the public's growing distrust and dislike of the media—and not only of the talk-show rabble-rousers, and the primates on the far religious right, but of the formerly respected mainstream media—is the media's self-righteous pomposity and their sneering and contemptuous coverage of all public figures," when, suddenly, she toppled over, and within seconds her pulse stopped.

Mary lived in what was called the Little House, as distinct from the Big House, which is now occupied by her son, Barry, Jr., and his wife, Edith. The estate has a baronial quality, but Mary's house was both elegant and cozy: fireplaces; small, jewel-like libraries; intriguing nooks and crannies. How to recall our last wonderful, carefree weekend with her? Piles of books and magazines placed at our bedside (poems, *The Economist*, books on civil rights, on art, on Adlai Stevenson, on theatre). Watching, openmouthed, as Mary tripped lightly up and down a series of steps in the three-level Italianate house, while we grabbed at the bannisters. Mary showed intense interest in all the plays we saw. One of them, "July 7, 1994," by Donald Margulies, depicting a harrowing day in the life of a woman doctor in an inner-city clinic, so affected all three of us that at the end, like children, we burst into tears: a responsive bond I will never forget.

From time to time, back at the house, during infrequent rest periods, memos would arrive, such as "From Mary Bingham. 'I have always considered complaints of ill-usage contemptible, whether from a seduced disappointed girl, or a turned-out Prime Minister.' Lord Melbourne, Letters." There were visits with family, fine meals, and, to my special delight, copious strips of bacon served as canapés. At the crack of dawn, the Louisville *Courier-Journal* and the *Times* were delivered to the guest-room door.

During our last lunch together, Mary asked me, "What is your favorite passage in the Bible?" and, somewhat startled, I heard myself saying, "From Ecclesiastes: 'Man goeth to his long home, and the mourners go about the streets.'"

Joseph Mitchell

Joseph Mitchell and I were close friends for some six decades. When I heard that he was gone, I comforted myself by dipping into his work. There they are, the stray phrases lodged forever somewhere in the subconscious. From "Lady Olga," the bearded lady: "If the truth was known, we're all freaks together." From "Old Mr. Flood": "I love a hearty eater, but I do despise a goormy." Over the long years, there were hundreds of lunches and dinners, walks and talks, but what suddenly swims into mind is a long and lazy Saturday some thirty years ago when Joe asked me to join him in a visit to a man he deeply admired, Mr. George H. Hunter, the distinguished chairman of the board of trustees of the African Methodist church, who lived in a house with lightning rods on the south shore of Staten Island, and who had been immortalized by Joe in a story called "Mr. Hunter's Grave." Mr. Hunter must have been close to ninety, perhaps older. It was his birthday, and he had prepared a royal chicken fricassee and a memorable lemon meringue pie. We ate and talked and walked away the afternoon. We visited the Sandy Ground cemetery, where Mr. Hunter planned to be buried. Joe had a special kinship with cemeteries. Like waterfronts and wildflowers, they soothed his bouts of gloom. To capture the spirit of that afternoon, and of my friend, I must quote from Joe's story itself, describing a similar visit, with Mr. Hunter talking. "After dinner, we sit around the table and drink Postum and discuss the Bible, and that's something I do enjoy. We discuss the prophecies in the Bible, and the warnings, and the

(421)

promises—the promises of eternal life. And we discuss what I call the mysterious verses, the ones that if you could just understand them they might explain everything—why we're put here, why we're taken away— but they go down too deep; you study them over and over, and you go down as deep as you can, and you still don't touch bottom."

Citizen Gill

———

My first view of Brendan, in 1939, was angular. On my first day at *The New Yorker*, St. Clair McKelway, then the managing editor, escorted me to my office, a narrow chamber that would have been comfortable quarters for a good-natured mastiff. "A bit crowded here," mumbled McKelway (a truly great editor, but he mumbled). "Your roommates are David Lardner, youngest son of Ring, and Brendan Gill, a Yale man. They're out now, but Gill's desk is by the window, and Dave's is here by the door." Moments later, a gap-toothed man whose hair stood straight up burst into the room. "I'm Ross," he said. "Welcome and God bless." And he was gone. I am in a strange and wonderful world, I told myself as the door opened again and a tall, lithe, jet-black-haired young man vaulted over my desk with the grace of a gazelle and landed in a chair by the window. "Brendan Gill," he said, extending a hand. Thus began a close and treasured friendship that survived some six decades. Somewhere along the line we began calling each other Uncle Phil and Uncle Brendan. To me, he was always avuncular: almost careless in his sharing of time and help to those less gifted. That was a problem with Brendan: he was blessed with an overabundance of talent. He was a brilliant writer, critic, and social historian, but he was also a devoted parent to a vast and adoring family; a social being of charm and wit, who felt that missing a party was a mortal sin; and a citizen in the true sense of the word—a protector of the city he loved. Often, I had the ridiculous notion that Brendan—a Prospero in the lives of those who knew him—would beat the odds, and go on for two hundred, perhaps three hundred years. When I last talked to him, a week or so ago, he ended, as he so often did, with the words "Carry on."

A NOTE ABOUT THE AUTHOR

Philip Hamburger was born in Wheeling, West Virginia, in 1914. At an early age he caught a sleeper to New York City. Except for a wartime stint in Washington and overseas assignments, he has lived there ever since. He is a graduate of Johns Hopkins University and Columbia University. Since 1939 he has been a staff writer at *The New Yorker*. He is a recipient of the George Polk Career Award. A superstitious man, he spends a good deal of time knocking wood.

A NOTE ON THE TYPE

This book was set in a typeface called Bulmer. This distinguished letter is a replica of a type long famous in the history of English printing
which was designed and cut by William Martin about 1790 for
William Bulmer of the Shakespeare Press. In design, it is all but a
modern face, with vertical stress, sharp differentiation between the
thick and thin strokes, and nearly flat serifs. The decorative italic
shows the influence of Baskerville, as Martin was a pupil of John
Baskerville's.

Composed by Creative Graphics, Allentown, Pennsylvania
Printed and bound by Berryville Graphics, Berryville, Virginia
Designed by Robert C. Olsson